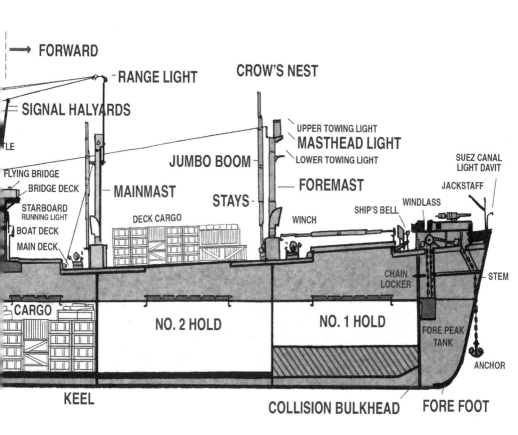

FORWARD

RANGE LIGHT

CROW'S NEST

SIGNAL HALYARDS

LE

FLYING BRIDGE

BRIDGE DECK

JUMBO BOOM

UPPER TOWING LIGHT

MASTHEAD LIGHT

LOWER TOWING LIGHT

SUEZ CANAL
LIGHT DAVIT

MAINMAST

STAYS

FOREMAST

JACKSTAFF

STARBOARD
RUNNING LIGHT

DECK CARGO

WINCH

SHIP'S BELL

WINDLASS

BOAT DECK

MAIN DECK

CHAIN
LOCKER

STEM

CARGO

NO. 2 HOLD

NO. 1 HOLD

FORE PEAK
TANK

ANCHOR

KEEL

COLLISION BULKHEAD

FORE FOOT

LAUNCHING LIBERTY

The Epic Race to Build the Ships
That Took America to War

DOUG MOST

SIMON & SCHUSTER
New York Amsterdam/Antwerp London Toronto
Sydney/Melbourne New Delhi

Simon & Schuster
1230 Avenue of the Americas
New York, NY 10020

For more than 100 years, Simon & Schuster has championed authors and the stories they create. By respecting the copyright of an author's intellectual property, you enable Simon & Schuster and the author to continue publishing exceptional books for years to come. We thank you for supporting the author's copyright by purchasing an authorized edition of this book.

First Simon & Schuster hardcover edition August 2025

SIMON & SCHUSTER and colophon are registered trademarks of Simon & Schuster, LLC

Simon & Schuster strongly believes in freedom of expression and stands against censorship in all its forms. For more information, visit BooksBelong.com.

For information about special discounts for bulk purchases, please contact Simon & Schuster Special Sales at 1-866-506-1949 or business@simonandschuster.com.

The Simon & Schuster Speakers Bureau can bring authors to your live event. For more information or to book an event, contact the Simon & Schuster Speakers Bureau at 1-866-248-3049 or visit our website at www.simonspeakers.com.

Interior design by Wendy Blum

Manufactured in the United States of America

10   9   8   7   6   5   4   3   2   1

Library of Congress Control Number: 2025007984

ISBN 978-1-6680-1778-4
ISBN 978-1-6680-1780-7 (ebook)

For Mimi, Julia, and Ben

Together we are shipbuilders. The fate of our own country is in our own hands, where it belongs.

—Henry Kaiser

We are in a war of transportation—a war of ships. It's no damn sense making guns and tanks to be left in the United States.

—Admiral Emory Scott Land, Chairman,
U.S. Maritime Commission

CONTENTS

CONTENTS

WONDERBOAT

Saturday, November 7, 1942

A FEW MINUTES BEFORE MIDNIGHT, CLAY BEDFORD STARED out from his perch in the main office building at Richmond Shipyard No. 2 on San Francisco Bay. He could not believe how many people he saw. His shipyard was overrun with a sea of random onlookers. Even some of his own late-night workers were abandoning their assigned posts, sneaking away like frisky teenagers and climbing fences and ascending scaffolding just so they could get a glimpse of what was about to unfold. Nervous about someone getting hurt, Bedford could only think about a terrifying accident at a nearby shipyard a few weeks earlier that by some miracle had not killed or maimed anyone. It served as a reminder of how one careless slipup could spell the end of a single worker or a hundred, a chance Bedford did not want to take. He took hold of a microphone that projected his voice across the yard, reminding the workers that only those with a red card identifying them as working the midnight shift should be there.

"I know you're interested," he boomed. "I know that you would love to see us win this little race. But for God's sake, get back on your own ships because if you don't have a red card, you can't help us. Only red cards are supposed to be on that ship, and we've got all the people we need. But thank you very much for your enthusiastic interest!"[1]

A radio address broadcast throughout the shipyard had just informed the nation that American and British troops had landed in French North Africa. Cheers erupted. Now, as the clocks inched toward twelve, the excitement was palpable. Bedford's plea for calm was ignored. Nobody was going anywhere.

FLOODLIGHTS BATHED THE grounds of the shipyard in a bright white light. The assigned workers scrambled to get into their positions, like football players lining up for a last-second play. On some of the scaffolding inside the shipyard, messages had appeared: FIVE-DAY BOAT NEXT! read one. BRING ON THE WONDERBOAT! read another. Twelve thousand volunteers—equivalent to an entire Army division—would work round the clock to build the record ship. And not even one of them could have known that the ship would one day soon slip in quietly near the shore of Normandy, France, to offload tanks and trucks and troops onto Omaha Beach in what would become a defining event in their nation's history.

As the seconds ticked down to midnight, they were focused on the present, and on the enormous cranes rolling into place. Piles of pipe lay everywhere, tied up tightly in different bundles, each one marked with a number. Plates of steel were piled high, with some so freshly cut they were still hot enough to grill a burger. Buckets of bolts littered the grounds. Portholes, giant anchor chains, mirrors, radiators, and washbasins were all laid out. Sitting by itself was a three-story-tall, hulking metal engine. The entire scene resembled a junkyard of random steel parts rather than the state-of-the-art shipbuilding operation that it was.

Signs marked every piece of equipment, every pile of steel, every bucket: "Hull No. 440." Other signs were more explicit. DON'T TOUCH. RED HOT.

The task at hand was going to require 250,000 individual parts and pieces to all come together with a robotic efficiency in a goal of roughly 170 hours, or seven days.[2] There would be no room for error. The shipyard superintendent, a friendly fellow named J. C. McFarland, told his workers in a memo three days earlier that speed during the construction was imperative, but only up to a point. "We want to impress on everybody that under no circumstances will we tolerate the sacrifice of safety for speed," he wrote. "Every precaution for the protection of every employee must be taken." He ended with an emphatic point. "REMEMBER, SAFETY PAYS!"

Their goal was to build a giant cargo ship—one hundred feet longer than a football field and taller than a ten-story building—and to build it faster than any ship had been built before. Faster than the thirty-five-day ship finished a few months earlier, faster than the twenty-six-day ship that followed, and even somehow faster than the unthinkable ten-day ship built only a few days ago. More than two hundred letters with suggestions from shipbuilders had been collected and sorted. They would be using the most advanced techniques, the best tools, the smartest inventions available—just so they could prove to themselves, and to a worried nation, what Americans were capable of in a moment of desperation. This was that moment.

For more than a year, Germany's chancellor, Adolf Hitler, had been openly mocking the United States shipbuilding industry. And nothing made him prouder than seeing his own fleet of U-boats, or *Unterseeboots*, for "undersea boats" in German, torpedoing one British or American vessel after another. "I can beat any other power in the world," Hitler boasted in a radio interview.

Hull No. 440 was the clearest message President Franklin Delano Roosevelt could fire back at Hitler. It was long overdue. While Germany was pushing out fifteen new submarines every month in the war's early days, the United States had been slow, disorganized, even apathetic about building ships, taking six, seven, eight months, even a year to build out a single vessel. German U-boats were sinking American and British cargo vessels faster than they could be built, a trend that Roosevelt knew was unsustainable. Those cargo ships were the lifeline to American troops around the world, the only way for them to be fully supplied. Hull No. 440 was going to show the Nazis that the greatest threat to their pursuit of world domination was not the American armed forces. It was the American shipbuilders.

The main deck of the ship, normally separated into twenty-three pieces, sat nearby in just seven large sections, advance building work that the shipbuilders hoped would save hundreds of man-hours when they were lifted into place. The hull of the ship, which normally took a week or longer to weld together, was almost entirely prefabricated into five enormous pieces, the largest one weighing 110 tons. Seventeen separate banks of welding machines were set up on each side of the empty shipway to maximize the volume of welding that could be done at the same time. Each crew that had been handpicked to work had their assigned job, their location, and their designated shifts all mapped out. A dozen women welders had threatened to quit unless they were included. And they were. Already 152,000 feet of weld had been completed on the assembly tables, leaving just 57,800 feet left to be done on the shipway. Yet nobody saw the advance work as cheating. They saw this project for what it was—an experiment in speed and efficiency, to push the boundaries of shipbuilding and set a record, once and for all, that other yards would see as unbeatable. The race had been building through the late summer and into the fall and elevated morale around the country with each new launching.

Normally the shipbuilders knew their assigned ship by its hull number rather than by its designated name, which was revealed on the shipway for the christening ceremony. But in the case of Hull No. 440, there was no interest in keeping it secret; there were too many other things to worry about. The name of the ship was painted onto a prefabricated piece, gray with big white letters, and left uncovered on the grounds at the shipyard a half mile away from where the ship was being built. It was waiting for its turn to be picked up and put in its place. When a group of workers wandered past and saw it lying there, "resting on the ground like a hedgehog," as one of them recalled later, the secret was out. They were building the SS *Robert E. Peary.*

"That's the payoff!" he shouted at the others as they stared at the ship's honored soul. "The name in place, but the keel not yet laid!"[3]

As midnight arrived, nobody was thinking about their next paycheck. They were only determined to beat their rival shipyards, to be the fastest at what they were hired to do, to win a competition that their own government had encouraged. Their boss, the man who formed an emergency shipbuilding partnership with the president of the United States, who found the land to build a shipyard, who created the jobs that they were hired to do, was nowhere to be seen; he was across the country in New York City already attending to his next priority. But his presence loomed all around, and he was in touch by phone every few hours. Hull No. 440, the work of a team he called his "Speed Kings," was to be his crowning achievement.

At 12:01 a.m. on November 8, 1942, the piercing whistle at Richmond Shipyard No. 2 shattered the still nighttime air. Clay Bedford's workers burst into action.

A SHIPBUILDING GLOSSARY

Aft: The direction toward the rear of a ship.

Amidships: In the vicinity of the middle portion of a vessel as distinguished from her ends. The term is used to convey the idea of general locality but not that of definite extent.

Boom: A term applied to a spar, or support, used in handling cargo.

Bow: The forward end of the ship.

Building slip: An inclined launching berth where the ship is built.

Bulkhead: A vertical partition wall that subdivides the interior of a ship into compartments.

Burners: Men who operate gas torches for burning plates and shapes to proper sizes for assembly into the structure.

Cargo hold: The empty, cavernous space below a ship's main deck for carrying large volumes of materials.

Deadweight cargo: The number of tons remaining after deducting from the deadweight the weight of fuel, water, stores, dunnage, and crew and their effects necessary for use on a voyage.

Deck house: A term applied to a large superstructure that is the largest part of the topside of the vessel and houses the bridge, navigational equipment, and the majority of the crew's berthing compartments.

Flange: Flanges are used to connect pipelines, cooling systems, and fuel systems; a flanger's role is to ensure the safe and effective integration of a ship's operating systems.

Forward: The opposite of aft, the direction toward the front of the ship.

Hull: A reference to the main body of a ship that forms its lower shape.

Keel: A centerline strength running along the bottom of a ship and often referred to as a ship's spine or backbone, connected to the hull by riveting or welding.

Outfitting: After a ship was launched, it would go to an outfitting dock for finishing touches such as wiring and plumbing and to be loaded up with cargo.

Prefabrication: Method of construction in which parts and components are built in sheds and buildings on land, away from the water, then brought to the ship finished, saving vast amounts of work hours.

Reciprocating engine: The type of engine used in Liberty ships; a vertical, three-cylinder engine that operated by having two oil-fired boilers feed steam to the engine, which produced up to 2,500 horsepower. (The engine of an average car today has about 200 horsepower.)

Rigger: A shipyard position or trade. A rigger erects, maintains, and dismantles various types of scaffolding and can also operate cranes, and is responsible for performing the lifts on and off a ship.

Riveting: When a metal pin is used for connecting two or more pieces of material by inserting it into holes punched or drilled in the pieces and upsetting one or both ends.

Shipfitter: A worker charged with building, maintaining, and repairing a boat or a ship.

Shipways (or Ways): A reference to the space in a shipyard directly on the water where ships are finished and launched from.

Stern: The rear of a vessel; the part farthest from the bow.

Tonnage, gross: The entire internal cubic capacity of a vessel expressed in "tons," taken at 100 cubic feet each.

Welding: The method of connecting two pieces of steel through heated welding torches; it was viewed as a stronger and safer bond than riveting.

AUTHOR'S NOTE

THIS IS A STORY ABOUT PROBLEM-SOLVING. OR MORE specifically, it's about one problem—and how America solved it during one of the most precarious periods in the nation's history. It's a story that begins with a young man clutching a worn, brown leather briefcase full of secret blueprints. Stocky and strong from his college years playing rugby, he boarded a passenger ship just outside London in the fall of 1940, leaving his family behind to sail through ocean waters that were swarming with enemy submarines. We'll get back to him shortly.

It's easy to forget that long before the Japanese attacked Pearl Harbor on December 7, 1941, the United States was already at war. German U-boats had fired torpedoes on half a dozen American ships, sinking two of them and killing American sailors, prompting President Franklin Delano Roosevelt to issue a "shoot on sight" order for Navy ships that confronted German subs.

Roosevelt knew it was only a matter of time before America was drawn into the battle raging between Germany and Great Britain. He also understood when that day arrived, the fighting would not take place on American soil—in the streets of New York City or along the California coast. The war would be fought thousands of miles away, across the biggest oceans in the world. That meant that all of the guns, tanks, jeeps, torpedoes, airplanes, canteens, bombs, and bullets that America was furiously building would be useless without a reliable way to deliver that arsenal—on a massive scale, at urgent speed—to the faraway battlefields and armies. Roosevelt had been there during World War I when the United States had been caught unprepared for overseas fighting and American troops were forced to use mostly French and British equipment and artillery. That would not happen on his watch.

Cargo planes like the Douglas C-54 Skymaster could zip a few hundred troops or a couple of tanks across an ocean in a matter of hours. But if hundreds of thousands of troops, along with enough supplies to feed, protect, transport, and shelter them for months or years, were needed, there had to be a bigger and better way to move that much cargo. This was the problem America needed to solve.

There was a limited supply of American and British cargo ships in the decade after the Great Depression. The ones still floating from the previous war were obsolete, and the new cargo ships being built took up to a year to finish. Far too long.

German U-boats and attack boats sank more than 215 mostly British merchant ships in a short span in 1939, sending a breathtaking 748,000 tons of shipping to the bottom of the Atlantic.[1] A desperate Prime Minister Winston Churchill sent a letter to Roosevelt, explaining that German subs were sinking Allied ships faster than new ones could be built. "The U-boat menace," the British prime minister wrote, had become the most important issue facing Great Britain, and it was only a matter of time before no ocean passage will be safe. He said he stayed awake at night haunted by a single image: "The spectacle of all these splendid ships being built, sent to sea crammed with priceless food and munitions, and being sunk—three or four a day—torments me day and night." The only solution, in his view, was to build so many ships as to overwhelm Germany, and to build them faster and faster, so that the enemy could not keep pace. "A ship not sunk in 1943 is worth two for 1944," Churchill wrote.[2]

Roosevelt knew that if America was going to help, a new strategy was needed—not to mention new shipyards and tens of thousands of new shipbuilders. And it needed to build them with the same efficiency and speed that Henry Ford perfected to roll 500,000 new automobiles off his Detroit assembly lines in a single year. But how? Building fifteen-foot-long automobiles fast was one thing. Building steel cargo ships longer than a football field fast was another.

THE SOLUTION THAT emerged in the early days of the war is what led me down a gravelly, dead-end road just outside downtown Baltimore on a bright and steamy summer morning. At precisely nine o'clock, I got out of my car and walked to the end of the quiet pier looking out on the Patapsco River and Chesapeake Bay, where I could almost reach out and touch the light gray hull of the SS *John W. Brown*. Her enormous anchor was pulled up tight and she was tied to the dock by a few heavy white ropes. Small white numbers painted on her side told me how deep she was sitting in the water. The water came up to the number 11, meaning eleven feet of her steel hull sat below the surface. A few minutes later I learned that the weight of the cargo she carried during World War II—more than ten thousand tons—sank her hull so deep that the number 30, the highest number on her hull, disappeared.

Between 1941 and 1945, inspired by a ship-loving president and led by a dynamic builder of highways, dams, and bridges, but who had never built a ship in his life, the nation's workforce came together in the greatest emergency shipbuilding program the world had ever seen. Driven by their partnership, the United States spent $18 billion on ships for the Navy and $13 billion on ships for the Merchant Marine,[3] most of which were cargo vessels. More than 13,000 ships were built and launched. Of those ships, one-quarter of them, 2,710 in total, were of the exact same shape, design, and weight—precisely 441 feet, 6 inches long, 57 feet wide, and 7,463 tons when empty. But when they were packed full of cargo, these ships could hold the equivalent of what 300 railroad boxcars could carry. One ship could hold 2,840 jeeps, or 440 tanks, or 430,000 cases of rations, enough to feed more than three million men for one day. At first these ships came to be called "Ugly Ducklings," a nickname that ignored the historic role they played in the war's outcome. The government eventually called them Liberty ships and the SS *John W. Brown* was one of the first to be built. It remains one of the last ones still floating today, along with the SS *Jeremiah O'Brien* in San Francisco.

AS I CLIMBED the rickety catwalk up to her deck, I stopped and stared for a long moment at a single, enormous bolt on the side, about the size of an orange slice. That bolt was one of 250,000 pieces that had to come together to build a single Liberty ship. And the *John W. Brown* came together in fifty-four days. One ship—start to finish—in less than two months. As fast as that seemed, other Liberty ships that followed were built faster.

Throughout history, our ability to solve big problems has been the hallmark of a great nation's progress. When horses and sailboats were too slow, motors and engines propelled us faster and farther. When overcrowded cities needed relief, we moved trolleys underground and we built taller buildings with elevators to lift us into the sky. When lamps powered by oil burned out too easily and left us in the dark, we harnessed the power of electricity to light up our cities and streets. When mailing letters took too long to reach their recipients, we used needles, wires, and batteries to make a phone call. And when plaques clogged the arteries that pump our blood, we invented tiny balloons to inflate inside our bodies to keep our oxygen flowing. Problem-solving drives a society forward, and the Liberty ships were one more solution to a problem.

As I reached the top step to board the SS *John W. Brown*, I was met by Dick Sterne, a friendly, retired firefighter from Washington, D.C., who knows every bolt, ladder, beam, and button that went into building the ship. Standing on the deck, I looked out toward the heavy tarps covering the ship's five enormous cargo holds. I glanced back at the elevated platforms holding the machine guns. And I looked straight up at the tiny windows in the deckhouse.

He led me into the deckhouse first. This was where a crew of young Merchant

Marines made their home for months at a time during the war. Next Sterne showed me their rooms fitted with bunk beds, and the mess hall, the chart room, and the radio room. The solid red oak furniture glistened. We walked past a room full of the tall metal lockers sailors used to store their belongings. In the deckhouse, I stood behind the wooden helm and looked out at the bay through the narrow windows, imagining the tension that must have filled the room during a wartime voyage. Sterne showed me how square boards could quickly be lowered to cover the windows and prevent enemy spotters from seeing inside and shooting their targets.

After visiting the engine room, Sterne led me through a short hallway and down a series of steep metal staircases. I could hear clanging and hissing below us that grew louder with each step. As we moved deeper into the dark and greasy bowels of the ship, there were men on their knees painting over a rusted deck, and a few tourists wandering inside a gift shop. Down on the floor, we walked toward the ship's bow, stepping inside one of its five cargo holds. The ceiling looked so high. The tallest ladder I'd ever seen leaned against a wall in a corner. I looked up and envisioned how a crane would slowly lower tanks and jeeps and boxed-up airplanes and crates filled with machine guns, rifles, and ammunition into the space, piled all the way to the top.

THAT'S WHEN IT hit me—this is where the war was won. Nothing could ever diminish what happened out on the battlefields and in the war at sea. But it was these enormous cargo holds that delivered Roosevelt's Arsenal of Democracy to American and British troops around the world when they needed it the most. From the earliest days after Pearl Harbor, in 1942, to the Battle of Stalingrad in the early days of 1943, when the war's momentum began to turn, to the invasion in the summer of 1944 at the beaches of Normandy, loaded-down Liberty ships were there to ensure that American troops were armed, nourished, and protected.

As Sterne and I stood in silence inside that echoing, cavernous cargo hold, it felt like I had stepped back into history. Back to a time when people from all parts of the country and all corners of society—poor housewives, farmers, plumbers and PhDs, inventors and patriotic handymen, brilliant engineers, hard-driving politicians, and billionaire businessmen—all came together to solve this one problem: to build giant steel cargo ships faster than the Germans could sink them.

But first, they needed a blueprint. They needed a simple design to build the perfect ship, one that could be replicated over and over, faster and faster, at any shipyard around the country. On a late September day in 1940, that blueprint, the solution to America's problem, was tucked safely inside the young man's leather satchel, crossing the Atlantic Ocean on its way to New York Harbor, with German planes buzzing overhead and Nazi subs lurking below.

PART I

The Plan

CHAPTER ONE

Zigzagging the Atlantic

HOUSEWIVES AND CIVIL SERVANTS, STUDENTS AND ENGI-
neers, merchants, authors, and government officials, they came from the city
and the countryside, from every corner of Great Britain. They arrived on a gray
autumn Saturday, September 21, 1940, with all the anxiousness expected before
a long journey. A stream of passengers, 806 of them to be precise, lined up at
the Customs Shed at the Port of Liverpool, tickets and paperwork in hand, to
board the Cunard White Star luxury ocean liner RMS *Scythia*.

She was loaded up with everything from engine grease to asparagus, dish-
rags to lightbulbs, noodles to pillowcases. An army of polishers, painters,
cleaners, plumbers, upholsterers, and even a piano tuner finished preparing
her for the trip, and the crew got ready as well. Chefs who had to provide their
own kitchen knives sharpened each one for meal prep, and the women officers
made sure their evening dresses were ironed and hanging.[1]

Transatlantic crossings were routine journeys for steamships like the *Scythia*,
a 600-foot, black-hulled vessel that featured an elegant dining hall and a movie
theater, and could cross from England to New York City in less than two weeks.
In the days after her maiden voyage in 1921, she was described as "the ship of the
future" with her size, speed, and the capacity to carry more than 2,300 passengers.[2]

As the passengers continued boarding—third-class passengers first and first-class last—the ship's crew checked each person's papers to confirm their age, occupation, native language, permanent residence, and marks of identification like scars or birthmarks. If their ship was attacked, that's how bodies could later be identified.

Blending in among the passengers were two sharply dressed men, one of them taller, stockier, and older, the other more athletic-looking and toting a brown briefcase.[3] They were not wearing uniforms or badges, any hint that they were traveling on behalf of the British Admiralty. The older one seemed more serious, business-minded, while his companion tended to smile and laugh more easily. The briefcase was the only hint that they were traveling on a work matter rather than for pleasure.

As the ship continued to fill, something different about the passenger manifest became apparent. There were so many children boarding. From toddlers to teenagers, there were 260 of them on the list, almost one-third of the total number of passengers. The majority of them were traveling as a group of refugees organized by United States first lady Eleanor Roosevelt.

Just before boarding, many of the children had been filled up with ice cream to help distract them from what lay ahead. It seemed to work. They ran up the ramp onto the deck of the ship and flashed a thumbs-up sign to people back onshore before scrambling off to play. Keeping their spirits up on the journey would fall to their escorts or parents, and to a ship orchestra that was prepared to lead them in song. It would not be easy. Cunard's ships displayed evidence all over of the danger that lay ahead.

Posters alerted passengers on what they should do in the event of an attack. One urged them to keep flashlights and life preservers on their body at all times, to sleep in their clothes for the first two days after leaving England, and to be sure to attend dinner on time so that the watertight doors separating the dining room and kitchen could be kept closed. A second poster was more grave. "If an enemy attack is anticipated, the following signals will be used: Four blasts on the ship's whistle and four rings on the electric gongs. At this signal, passengers must take cover below C Deck in the nearest dining room and remain under cover until the attack is over or the signal is made for the boat stations." For the unaware, that terror-filled signal would be six short blasts followed by one long one.[4]

Only a few days earlier, German submarines had torpedoed the SS *City of Benares* as it carried British families to Canada, killing seventy-seven children. Now, for the passengers boarding the *Scythia*, the question seemed to be, where would they be safest: At home in England, where a German invasion seemed imminent, where bombs were raining down and the London Underground was being used as an air raid shelter? Or out on the ocean, sailing on a ship crossing the Atlantic, where German U-boats lay in wait, torpedoes at the ready?

A YEAR HAD passed since Germany invaded Poland on September 1, 1939. Britain declared war on Germany two days later, launching a second world war a little more than twenty years after the first one ended. Using precision aircraft assaults and relentless submarine attacks, Germany swiftly seized control of the European coast, from the northernmost region of Finland south through Sweden and Denmark, down past Paris, and all the way to the Pyrenées Mountains, a stretch covering 2,500 miles. German chancellor Adolf Hitler had France, Denmark, and Sweden all in his hands. But he recognized he would never control Europe until he had seized its largest country, and he had fixed Great Britain in his crosshairs.

In a recent speech to the House of Commons, Prime Minister Winston Churchill had used words like "slaughter," "ruins," and "casualties" in describing the state of the war. He asked his fellow countrymen and women to remember those fighting to protect them. "Never was so much owed by so many to so few," he said.

For a leader just three months into his term, Churchill exuded confidence in his address. He said forcefully that Britain would defeat Germany. "Our geographical position, the command of the sea, and the friendship of the United States enable us to draw resources from the whole world and to manufacture weapons of war of every kind," he stated.[5] In the days following his speech, Britain's situation grew more bleak.

On Sunday, August 31, two Royal Navy destroyers were sunk off the Dutch coast, German planes continued their assault on British airfields, and Nazi fighters dropped bombs across England, marking the beginning of the London Blitz. The toll just for the Royal Air Force over the month was staggering—344 aircraft downed and 139 pilots and crew members killed—and it was about to get worse. German U-boats sank 47 British merchant ships in 1939, vessels that carried precious food, raw materials, weapons, and supplies to troops. Britain was on its way to losing another 395 cargo ships in 1940, not including the hundreds more that sustained so much damage they were out of service for months.

As Germany's attacks across Europe intensified, the U.S. president, Franklin Delano Roosevelt, faced the most challenging crisis of his eight years in office. Roosevelt was a distant cousin of Theodore Roosevelt, the nation's twenty-sixth president, whose two terms in the first decade of the 1900s were marked by prosperity and excitement of the new century. The America that Franklin Roosevelt inherited in 1932 looked nothing like that. President Herbert Hoover's words at his 1929 inauguration, "In no nation are the fruits of accomplishment more secure," proved tragically inaccurate. Ten months later, Americans saw their savings vanish almost overnight and the arrival of the Great Depression. The Dow Jones Industrial Average, after peaking at 381 points in September 1929, plunged to 41.22 in the summer of 1932, its lowest mark of the century. It would not surpass its pre-crash high until 1954, an entire generation of anguish.

By 1940, FDR, now fifty-eight, had steered the economy mostly straight after eight years of New Deal programs. But now he faced an entirely differ-ent kind of crisis that challenged his unrivaled intellect and blue-blooded background—from boarding school in Groton, Massachusetts, to Harvard College to Columbia Law School. He spoke German and French. He was the son of wealthy, sixth-generation Americans, a former governor of New York, assistant secretary of the Navy during World War I, and a survivor of polio. And he'd come to despise all that fighting stood for.

"I have seen war on land and sea," he once said of his experiences. "I have seen blood running from the wounded. I have seen men coughing out their gassed lungs. I have seen the dead in the mud. I have seen cities destroyed . . . I hate war."[6]

Now war seemed inevitable. America's closest ally was teetering on the precipice of collapse to a maniacal leader, which would give the Nazis control of Europe. But Roosevelt's hands were tied. He could not fire first, even if he wanted to. The Neutrality Act of 1939 forbade American ships from entering a combat area and firing on any vessels if it was not at war with their country.

But it did not forbid Roosevelt from readying America for war with a new maritime strategy. He told Admiral Emory Scott Land, the director of the United States Maritime Commission, to begin drawing up a plan for an unprecedented expansion of the nation's moribund shipbuilding industry. Roosevelt's motivation came from the intelligence he was hearing about what was happening across the Atlantic, where Germany was ramping up its own production of hundreds of U-boats. If Hitler was going to build more submarines, Roosevelt believed America needed to race to build more ships. The two countries were not yet at war with each other. But that day was coming.

WHILE THE NEUTRALITY Act restricted Roosevelt's military might, forcing him to wait and watch as the war in Europe escalated, his wife faced no such moral dilemma. Nor did she have the patience to sit idly by as innocent families were torn apart. In the war's earliest days, Eleanor Roosevelt personally tried to sponsor a single refugee out of Europe. As the situation worsened, she broadened her efforts. The first lady saw the threat Nazis posed to British families, and so over the summer of 1940, she, along with a group of child refugee advocates, formed the United States Committee for the Care of European Children, with the mission of admitting orphaned and unaccompanied children. In its first few months the group successfully relocated hundreds of children, both Jewish and non-Jewish, and it would eventually rescue more than 1,300.

One passenger boarding the *Scythia* seemed unworried by the direction of the war in Europe. The British citizen, journalist, and author H. G. Wells, whose science fiction novels *The Time Machine* and *War of the Worlds* had made him something of a national treasure, was traveling abroad on his seventy-fourth birthday. As he prepared to embark on a ten-week lecture tour in the United States and Canada, Wells expressed confidence that Germany's momentum would stall and Britain would prevail. He told reporters America should stay out of the war. "Your party politics would swamp anything like a reasonable settlement," he told the newspapers.[7]

If Wells had only possessed the same knowledge of how the war was going as those two sharp dressed businessmen on board the *Scythia*, he might not have been so brash in his thinking.

A young British shipbuilder named Robert Cyril Thompson—Cyril or RC, he was called—carried the briefcase. Inside were architectural drawings for a new type of cargo ship his company had built, bigger than any cargo ship Britain had ever seen, and with a strangely shaped hull that looked nothing like an ordinary merchant vessel. He was accompanied by an older, experienced marine engineer named Harry Hunter. The blueprints with them had been seen by only a handful of senior officials inside the British Admiralty who believed this ship represented precisely the type that Britain needed.

With all 806 passengers on board and her dock ramp safely pulled away, the *Scythia* set sail, easing into the Atlantic under the light of the moon, a silhouette in the middle of an air raid. Searchlights beamed into the orange and black nighttime sky while two crew members stood on deck, watching as British antiaircraft guns fired away at German fighters buzzing past like a swarm of bees. Ahead, 3,140 miles of treacherous waters awaited.

CHAPTER TWO

"Secret: Merchant Shipbuilding Mission to USA"

NINETEEN DAYS EARLIER, CYRIL THOMPSON HAD ARRIVED in London for a high-powered meeting. He'd been summoned to the city by the Admiralty, the department that oversees the Royal Navy. Thompson had traveled two hundred miles from his home near Sunderland, on the northwest coast of England. His wife, Doreen, worried for his safety, jotted a short entry in her diary that night about the wailing sirens that filled her with fear for their two young children.

"Cyril up to London to see about this America idea. Two (London) raids," she wrote.[1]

J. L. Thompson & Sons had anchored a spot in Sunderland for more than a century. Britain had the largest fleet of merchant ships in the world, and the most powerful Navy, and Sunderland was one of the busiest shipbuilding ports in the world, with eight large companies all sitting on the River Wear at the mouth to the North Sea, churning out ships of all shapes, sizes, and specifications.

Thompson was just thirty-three years old when the Admiralty called. Recently married, and with two young children at home, he rarely went anywhere without a gold watch on his wrist, his gold pocket watch hanging on his belt, and his gold cigarette case at his fingertips.[2] Standing six foot three, with his round, boyish face, strong chin, muscular build from his rugby-playing days, and slicked hair parted neatly in the middle, he looked like he belonged back in the classrooms at Pembroke College. He had no military experience to boast of, but he had made several business trips abroad to the United States. And he understood how perilous a moment this was for Britain. He would not take this meeting with the Admiralty lightly.

J. L. Thompson & Sons had recently begun producing standard merchant steamships for the British government. But it was their latest project, a prototype for a cargo ship unlike anything they had previously built, that caught the attention of Sir James Lithgow. The controller of merchant shipbuilding and repairs, Lithgow believed this prototype ship just might be the key to Great Britain's future, which at the moment was facing grave peril.

Churchill had vowed to "manufacture weapons of war of every kind," hoping to reassure his people that no resource would be spared, no expense too great.[3] But the truth of the moment was different. "Weapons of war" were not Britain's greatest need in its battle against the Nazis. Great big cargo ships were. If Britain was unable to bring weapons, food, supplies, tanks, jeeps, and other necessities of war to its soldiers, it would be overwhelmed by Germany in a matter of months, maybe even weeks. In the summer of 1940, Nazi U-boats sank British ships at a rate equivalent to five million tons a year. Meanwhile, Britain's shipyards could only build two million tons.

Over in the United States, Roosevelt found himself pulled in two directions. He had seen the poll numbers. He knew that Americans wanted no part of a war in Europe. But he also knew the dangers of doing nothing. A memo that landed on his desk outlined for him how German U-boats were able to find British ships so easily in the ocean and destroy them with such frequency and accuracy. The manner in which merchant ships traveled was proving to be a huge concern. Because they are not speedy, merchant ships traveled in convoys and along a zigzagging course. But their convoy could only go as fast as their slowest ship, making them easy targets for torpedoes.

"The present German submarine menace takes on two phases—one, a question of speed, the other, a question of aircraft," the memorandum to Roosevelt said. "Recent German submarine successes are due in part to German aircraft advising German submarines by radio the location course and speed of British convoys, permitting submarines to locate themselves in advance of a probable convoy location at a given time where the submerged submarine attacks in or near the center of a convoy, thereby doing the greatest damage."[4]

The cigar-shaped U-boats had other advantages besides their ability to avoid detection. Their hulls were designed to swim deep, five hundred feet or lower, to avoid return fire from enemy ships. The biggest flaw with the U-boat was that its batteries ran out of power quickly when submerged. A U-boat had to surface at least once a day for up to two hours to crank up its two 1,160-horsepower diesel engines and recharge its batteries. Without that recharge, crews on board could not survive underwater.

The torpedo was the U-boat's greatest advantage. At 23.5 feet long and 21 inches in diameter, with fins and a tail, a torpedo launched with compressed air through horizontal tubes, shooting out at speeds approaching 50 miles per hour. In order for a torpedo to have maximum effectiveness it needed to strike its target straight on, or else risk thudding into a ship without detonating. The memo to Roosevelt explained that cargo ships, chugging along at 10 miles per hour, were too slow to outrun torpedoes, and they only managed to escape when the submarines had to reload. It was becoming an unsustainable toll for Great Britain.

"Besides decreasing the death rate we must increase the birth rate," Britain's minister of shipping, Robert Hudson, said.[5]

There was one problem. Every one of Britain's shipyards was already at or beyond capacity to tackle new construction; none of them had the space or the manpower or the resources to take on the emergency construction of massive merchant cargo ships.

THE ROOTS OF Cyril Thompson's company dated back to his great-grandfather, Robert Thompson, who was born in 1797.[6] As a young boy, and the son of a master mariner, he would lie on his mother's kitchen floor and sketch ships. By the time he was twenty-two, he had worked as an apprentice shipbuilder, become an expert draftsman, and even constructed several small boats. The Thompson men who followed him kept shipbuilding alive in their family throughout the nineteenth century and into the twentieth by building oil tankers made of wood and later of iron, as well as massive merchant ships that could carry enormous quantities of supplies.

Yet their company's mission never strayed from where it began. In Sunderland, near the entrance to the North Sea, they built big cargo ships—seventeen of them during World War I. During the Great Depression years, from 1930 to 1934, the Thompson shipyard failed to launch a single ship. But there was an upswing in 1936, and by 1939, thanks to rearmament, every British shipyard was busy, building naval ships or merchant ships, or, at the bigger yards, both.

The German strategy to overrun Britain focused on destroying its shipping with a nonstop barrage of torpedoes from more than one thousand U-boats patrolling the Atlantic Ocean like sharks, or as Hitler preferred calling them, sea wolves or the wolfpack. By the end of 1939, German subs had sunk more than 200 British merchant ships, an average of almost three per day.

Hitler also knew that Britain's closest ally, the United States, was powerless to help militarily. As long as the United States remained an observer to the war, the Neutrality Act forbade American ships from assisting Britain's. Hitler believed that as long as America remained on the sidelines, Britain was vulnerable, especially at sea. He even expressed his arrogance in a speech: "What is America," he taunted, "but beauty queens, millionaires, stupid records, and Hollywood?"[7]

Roosevelt forged clever workarounds to the Neutrality Act aimed directly at slowing the Führer's momentum. In May 1940, the United States leased fifty tankers to the British. Then as Germany's U-boats intensified their attacks on British warships, the United States took another step, agreeing to send fifty World War I–era destroyers to the Royal Navy in exchange for the United States receiving permission to build naval bases in eight British colonies in the Atlantic. It was an unusual deal that allowed both Churchill and Roosevelt to claim it as beneficial to their country, and that was how the American press saw it. Two of the bases, Newfoundland and Bermuda, were classified as gifts in recognition of Britain's "friendly and sympathetic interests in the national security of the United States," while the remaining bases were in lieu of cash payments.

"We haven't had a better bargain since the Indians sold Manhattan Island for $24 in wampum and a demi john of hard liquor," the Louisville *Courier-Journal* wrote of the arrangement.

Even with the American ships in hand, Churchill continued to press Roosevelt for more assistance. His messages began taking an increasingly ominous tone, going so far as to say if Britain were to be conquered, the blood would be on the American president's hands.

"In no conceivable circumstance will we consent to surrender," Churchill wrote to Roosevelt over the summer. But in the same breath, he acknowledged the British government could fall and be replaced with a pro-Nazi regime, and if that were to happen there was no telling what Hitler would do. "If this country was left by the United States to its fate no one would have the right to blame those responsible if they made the best possible terms they could for the surviving inhabitants. Excuse me, Mr. President, putting this nightmare bluntly."[8]

The problem for Churchill was that he didn't know whether Roosevelt would still be president in a few months. Americans were increasingly desiring isolationism, and when a poll came out in September showing 51 percent of voters favoring Roosevelt and 49 leaning to his Republican opponent, a little-known midwestern businessman named Wendell Willkie, it struck dread in Churchill.

Germany toppling Britain was Roosevelt's deepest fear. He needed the American people to share his fear. On a summer's day in 1940, Roosevelt traveled to Charlottesville to deliver the University of Virginia's commencement speech. His son, Franklin Jr., was graduating from law school. Eleanor recognized the awkwardness of the moment, a celebration at a time of peril for her husband. "The times were fraught with promise of evil," she recalled later. "Franklin's address was not just a commencement address. It was a speech to the nation on an event that had brought us one step nearer to total war."[9]

With rain falling outside, the president gripped the podium firmly in the school gymnasium, wearing a crimson academic hood and a tasseled, black mortarboard. He said it was time for America to "pursue two obvious and simultaneous courses."

"On this tenth day of June, 1940, the hand that held the dagger has struck it into the back of its neighbor," Roosevelt declared. "On this tenth day of June, 1940, in this University founded by the first great American teacher of democracy, we send forth our prayers and our hopes to those beyond the seas who are maintaining with magnificent valor their battle for freedom." Roosevelt said the United States would provide an unrelenting supply of weapons and resources to Britain, while arming itself simultaneously.

"All roads leading to the accomplishment of these objectives must be kept clear of obstructions," he said. "We will not slow down or detour. Signs and signals call for speed—full speed ahead."[10]

They were his most forceful words to date on the war, and the audience interrupted and cheered. Roosevelt left feeling encouraged by the response. Yet each step the United States took to help its ally only seemed to antagonize Hitler further. In an address to the Reichstag, Nazi Germany's national parliament, weeks after Roosevelt's address, Hitler issued a forceful response, insisting it was only a matter of time before Great Britain succumbed to the Nazis just as France, Denmark, and Sweden had.

"Ten months of war has served only to strengthen our zeal," Hitler said. "It is a misfortune that world opinion is not formed by men who see things as they are, but only by men who wish to see them as they wish. British statesmen are always somewhat slow in grasping facts, but they will learn to see this in time. For millions of other persons, great suffering will begin. Mr. Churchill, or perhaps others, for once believe me when I predict a great empire will be destroyed, an empire that it was never my intention to destroy or even to harm."[11]

Empires do not topple easily. The Battle of Britain raged through the month of August and showed how well prepared the Royal Air Force's sophisticated air defense system was for Germany's air force, the Luftwaffe. Germany's first defeat of World War II slowed Hitler's momentum. But the war was only a year old. Both Churchill and Roosevelt, their relationship growing closer by the day, wisely grasped that Hitler would not rest. They also recognized that this war would ultimately be won not in the skies or on the battlefields—it would be won in the oceans.

DURING THAT POST-DEPRESSION down period in the early 1930s when J. L. Thompson & Sons did not push out any new vessels, its reduced workforce stayed busy by remodeling its yard layout and by turning its attention to developing and testing new designs. Shipbuilders all realized that in order to survive, their industry had to find ways to build ships cheaper and faster, and to make them more efficient on the water by burning less coal.

Cyril Thompson focused on redesigning the ship's hull, the outer body of a vessel that gives a boat its shape and sits below the water's surface. The hull of a ship is by far its largest and most important component. It determines how fast it can travel, how stable it is on the choppiest ocean waters, and the tonnage of cargo it can hold belowdecks without sinking too deeply into the water and slowing it down.

In 1935, the workers at Thompson's shipyard began building and testing models of ships with different-shaped keels, the structural beam that runs the length of a ship from its bow to its stern. They used the testing tanks at the National Physical Laboratory to float models of their works in progress. The boldest change they tried was to reverse the traditional hull design. Instead of a sharp-edged bow, or front, and a fuller, rounded stern, they played with a rounded bow and a V-shaped stern.[12] This switch allowed for the ship's rudders, part of the steering apparatus, to be moved forward on the hull, rather than positioned at the very rear, thereby causing less drag when the ship was moving. This alteration from a U-designed stern to a V-design, along with an improved, more fuel-efficient engine, came together in a prototype ship. Importantly, Thompson believed that the new design, without sacrificing any speed on the water, could be built for under 100,000 pounds, meeting their financial goal.

The result was the SS *Embassage*. When she slid into the water on July 31,

1935, all 409 feet of her, loaded down with coal, the *Embassage* was powered by two steamship boiler engines. The engines mustered 1,500 horsepower and the ship reached a cruising speed of 10 knots, or about 11.5 miles per hour. Her efficiency was also impressive, consuming a low 16 to 17 tons of coal in a day, compared with the average of the day around 25 tons. Her deadweight, the amount of cargo, fuel, food, water, passengers, and crew members, maxed out around 10,000 tons.

But before widespread production of the *Embassage* got underway, Thompson tinkered a bit more with the shape of her bow and stern until he had produced a new and slightly larger vessel by the fall of 1938. The keel for this new version was laid on September 8, and six months later, on March 7, 1939, the SS *Dorington Court* was launched. She stretched 10 feet longer and about 18 inches wider than the *Embassage,* making her 100 feet longer than London's Big Ben tower lying on its side. Importantly, the modifications, which included a 2,500-horsepower engine, helped nudge her top speed up to 11 knots, or more than 12.5 miles per hour.

The *Dorington Court* was nothing pretty to look at when she made her maiden voyage on May 4, 1939. But she was huge. She had a raised upper deck, or forecastle, to accommodate sleeping quarters and a ship's store. The boiler room at the very rear also served as the sleeping quarters for the engine crew, since engineering crews and deck officers were not supposed to mix on ship. In the belly of her hull, she had five separate holds for cargo. Two giant derricks covered each hold, to lower heavy cargo items down into it safely. The five holds, in addition to the surface space, made the *Dorington Court* large enough to carry nearly 3,000 jeeps, or more than 400 light tanks, or enough rations to feed 16 million soldiers for a day. All on a single ship.

The *Dorington Court*'s design caught the attention of the British government and prompted Lithgow to invite Cyril Thompson in for a meeting. Thompson had been described to Lithgow as a go-getter, a job doer, a finisher. His shipbuilding expertise spoke for itself. But beyond that, Lithgow heard that Thompson's experience, knowledge, determination, and business acumen were the exact combination the Admiralty needed to lead a group across the Atlantic. On September 2,[13] Lithgow and Admiralty officials outlined for Thompson how critical their country's shipping situation had become and, because of how long it takes to build these cargo ships, they needed a partner to help them, or else Britain might not survive another year of Germany's attacks.

Thompson knew the situation was dire. He had read the stories of ship sinkings and Germany's U-boat strategy. But he could not have known his country's future hung on the shipbuilding industry's help. He headed back home that evening after his meeting and climbed into bed with his wife after two in the morning. A few days later, the details for his trip arrived, laid out in a letter he received under the heading: "SECRET: MERCHANT SHIPBUILD-ING MISSION TO USA."

The letter got straight to its point.

Sir, I am commanded by My Lords Commissioners of the Admiralty to inform you that they understand you are willing to accept an invitation to be the leader of a Technical Merchant Shipbuilding Mission to Proceed immediately to the United States of America to carry out the objects indicated in the attached memorandum.[14]

HE WOULD TRAVEL by ship, his costs covered by the British Purchasing Commission in New York City, and receive a stipend for food and expenses of $12.50 per day. Because he would be traveling across the ocean where German subs were lurking, the letter acknowledged that the trip would be dangerous for a man about to leave behind his wife and two children.

"Apart from the payment of your expenses," it read, "the question of the financial terms of your appointment, in particular that of insurance against risks, is under consideration and will form the subject of a further letter."

The attached memorandum outlined what his primary goal would be upon arriving: to obtain as quickly as possible a contract to build sixty merchant ships, or tramp steamers as they were called, that could carry up to 10,000 tons of cargo and were capable of about 10.5 knots when fully loaded. (They were called tramp ships because they were like vagrants on the waves, ships without established itineraries or home ports.) He was authorized to spend £10 million, or approximately $6 billion in today's dollars. If there was any question about whether Thompson was merely traveling to engage in talks with the Americans on behalf of the Admiralty, or whether he had permission to make critical wartime moves, one line in the memorandum put that to rest.[15]

"The Merchant Shipbuilding Mission," he wrote, "shall have full authority to make all decisions and take actions concerning all technical aspects, within the limit of expenditure of £10,000,000."

But for all its specifics, the Admiralty's memorandum did not say with any certainty who would build the ships, or where they would be built, or how the costs would be covered. Or even whether the United States had the capacity or the interest in helping Britain obtain these ships. That's because the British didn't know those answers. Thompson's marching orders were simple: *Go get us sixty Dorington Courts, or something similar. And hurry.*

THOMPSON'S PARTNER IN this mission, Harry Hunter, had been responsible for designing the engines for both the *Dorington Court* and the *Embassage*. Thompson knew his own limits—he was an expert draftsman. But when it came to the engineering specs of cargo ships, he left that to others, men like Hunter, who worked for North-Eastern Marine Engineering. Hunter was sixteen years older than Thompson and he had an air of confidence that allowed him to explain engineering intricacies to non-engineer types without appearing condescending, a skill Thompson knew would come in handy for delicate meetings with high-powered Americans and politicians who did not like being lectured.

The drawings Thompson had with him were not of the *Dorington Court*, the ship that caught the attention of the Admiralty.[16] Thompson had already moved on from that vessel, designing something better that was quietly under construction back at his yard in Sunderland. The *Empire Wave* was a few feet shorter than previous versions, but wider, enabling her to carry even more tonnage.

THE RMS *SCYTHIA'S* 3,000-mile journey was stressful for both its passengers and its crew. She zigged and zagged at her top speed of 16 knots to try to avoid German U-boats. A few days into the crossing, the passengers heard depth charges exploding some distance away, and on another day they spotted the wreckage of a vessel and an oil slick in the water, a chilling sight. There were rumors one day of a submarine periscope being seen, but nothing came of it, and on another day the crew of a friendly Lockheed Hudson aircraft flew overhead and waved.[17]

The children on board seemed oblivious to the tension. They played on deck throughout the day and gathered in groups for their meals. The ship's orchestra leader, Bert Binks, used his violin bow as a baton to lead them in songs written by a crew member.

"We are the sea-vacuees!" the children belted out. "Waiting for the message, 'All clear,' come home please!"[18]

One boy, twelve-year-old Nigel Fletcher, was traveling with his two younger sisters from London. One afternoon, the boy told listeners nearby that his father just wanted to find safety for them, and so he took out a map of the United States, closed his eyes, and plopped his finger down. It landed on Hutchinson, Kansas. And that's where he and his sisters were headed. Nigel said their father wrote to the mayor of Hutchinson and asked if he could find a home for his three children. The mayor wrote back that he had a lawyer in town with a cattle farm and a laundry plant, and the children were welcome to stay there as long as necessary.

"We are going to him," Nigel said with not a hint of fear. "I will work on the farm and continue my schooling. I intend to enter law."[19]

Other children said they were going to live with relatives, and those who did not have families or guardians waiting for them were told they were going to be sheltered in churches. None of the children seemed worried about their future. With a British destroyer often nearby as an escort, and other friendly liners carrying more refugees within sight, there was some measure of security for those on board the *Scythia* that they would reach America safely. On October 3, 1940, they did.

FOR THE 806 passengers stepping off the *Scythia* into New York City, it was a moment to relax and smile. They had left behind a country at war for a country that was not. American Red Cross volunteers walked up the ramp and greeted the hungry children with hot chocolate, biscuits, and jam, while representatives from the U.S. Committee for the Care of European Children waited to greet them and make sure none were left alone. Children who were chilly were wrapped up in sweaters, mufflers, and caps.

A reporter waiting for the passengers to disembark stopped fourteen-year-old Kathleen Davis to ask her what life had been like back in England before she left. She told him that it was frustrating at home because the air raids always interrupted her family's meals. And she said all signs have been removed from roads and railway stations, causing a lot of confusion.

"You have to count the stations to know where you are," she said.[20]

Two girls, both of them eleven years old, were asked if the war scared them back home.

"Oh no, we are quite used to hearing the bombs explode, and see the streets full of houses blown up," one of them said matter-of-factly. Some of the children smiled for pictures, while others hugged their relatives hello, or hugged each other goodbye.

Cyril Thompson and Harry Hunter had no interest in warm hugs or idle chitchat or tea and biscuits. They hustled off the *Scythia* and headed straight into lower Manhattan.

CHAPTER THREE

The Legend of Jerry Land

FIFTEEN BROAD STREET, A GRAY, L-SHAPED, FORTY-THREE-story tower in lower Manhattan, was one of the largest office buildings in the world in 1940. In addition to housing the headquarters of J. P. Morgan & Company, it was also the American base for the British Purchasing Commission, the office responsible for making sure everything was set for Thompson's and Hunter's whirlwind trip. If they were to make it home before the end of the year, they had less than three months to solve Great Britain's shipbuilding crisis. And this was more than a friendly, fact-finding visit. They needed signatures on papers and a deal in place in order to return home. Anything less would be a failure.

"The work of the Mission was to be considered as completed at the stage at which orders were placed," Thompson recalled later.[1]

Unfortunately for them, there could not have been a more distracting time to arrive in America for official government business than the autumn of 1940. A presidential election loomed. After insisting for months that he would not seek an unprecedented third term in the White House, Roosevelt reversed himself, enraging opponents who suggested he resembled a dictator more than a president. His decision was driven in part by public opinion, as well as by the war. Roosevelt believed no one else was positioned to keep the country united in the face of the Nazi threat. In June and July, he had received more than eleven thousand messages urging him to run. He was nominated by Democrats at their convention after they adopted a pledge that would make Roosevelt's job even more challenging if he won: "We will not participate in foreign wars and we will not send our Army, Navy, or Air Force to fight in foreign lands outside of the Americas, except in case of attack."

It sent a clear message to Americans. And it presented a contrast to Willkie, who favored stronger American involvement in the war. The most influential newspaper columnist in America, Walter Lippmann, seemed to side with Willkie, writing that Roosevelt's passivity was risking America's safety and that he ought to declare a state of national emergency. "Mobilize the entire manpower, machine power and money power of this country," Lippmann wrote. Everything else should be "second place."[2]

AT THE BROAD Street headquarters, Sir Walter Layton briefed Thompson and Hunter on the full schedule of meetings awaiting them. He also laid out two clear objectives for them to achieve. First, they had to persuade the American government to assist Britain in building sixty merchant ships. That was not a guarantee because of how deep American resistance was to getting too involved in the war. Assuming somehow that they won that assurance, they then had to identify the partner, or partners, who would help them build those ships. Layton told them that if their trip were to have any success at all, it would start with their first meeting the following day in Washington, at the office of the United States Maritime Commission. That's where a broad-shouldered, notoriously profane Navy man would be waiting for them.

Rear Admiral Emory Land was a onetime college football star and an old friend of Roosevelt. He often joked about being "the only man in the world who was ever twice called a damn fool in writing by the President of the United

States."[3] One of those times came in 1937 when he put in a request to retire from the Navy at the age of fifty-six. "What does the damn fool want to retire for at his age," FDR wrote on the paper.

The legend of Emory Land, or Jerry as he was known, began at the turn of the century with a touchdown he scored as a slim, 135-pound halfback, on a trick play to help Navy beat Army, 11–7, in their annual rivalry game, in 1900 in Philadelphia. Being carried off the field that day stuck with him through his life. Despite all his accomplishments, he wrote in a memoir, he recalled that game "as a high spot in my life."[4]

His football days left him a few scars—two broken ribs, a dislocated collarbone, a misshapen busted nose. He had grown up poor but happy, riding horses in a Colorado mining town called Canon City. He studied at the University of Wyoming and then the United States Naval Academy in Annapolis, Maryland, and rose through the Navy ranks to become a naval attaché in London. A pilot, a duck hunter, a tennis player, Land was a man of many stripes, but more than anything he was a man of details.

Meticulous to a fault, he once said that instead of Scott, his middle name should have been "Safety," because of how much he emphasized it throughout his career in aviation and later in ships. "The idea probably focused around my nine years in Naval aviation, where I had to review reports on Naval aviation crashes, not only once, but sometimes two or three times," Land said of his insistence on safety.[5]

Jerry Land was one of Roosevelt's staunchest supporters during his first run for the presidency in 1932, and that loyalty would be rewarded. When the Merchant Marine Act was passed in 1936 as part of Roosevelt's New Deal to breathe life into the American merchant fleet, Roosevelt put Joseph P. Kennedy, the father of the future president, in charge of it. But Kennedy faltered in the role. Roosevelt moved him to be ambassador to the United Kingdom. With nearly every U.S. merchant ship at least twenty years old or older, the president sought a firm hand to lead the Merchant Marine upgrade. Roosevelt, an old Navy man himself, turned to his loyal Navy friend to head up the U.S.

Maritime Commission, an independent agency in charge of America's long-range shipbuilding efforts.

With a quick wit and a tendency to take jokes one line too far and offend colleagues, along with a brusque, decisive manner, Land had learned how to get jobs done. When *Fortune* magazine wrote of him in 1942, it said he possessed a "seaman's picturesque language and a banker's sense of the value of a dollar."

Land described his own sensibilities a little differently. "If you want fast ships, fast shipbuilding, fast women or fast horses, you pay through the nose for them," he once said. In a speech to New York bankers about his frustrations with unions, he nearly started a riot when he said that "organizers" during wartime should be "shot at sunrise."[6]

He cursed so much, and with such little regard for where or when he let his vulgarity rip, that he told his longtime secretary, Eleanor Van Valey, whom the shipping men simply called Miss Van, why he valued her so much. "Part of your job," he told her early in their working relationship, "is to let me blow off steam." And she did, without ever flinching. In fact, she once told him that he "swore pretty," a compliment he wasn't quite sure how to take, but that only encouraged him to keep on swearing.[7]

He often said in speeches, "I have a mean S.O.B. of a job."[8] But he relished it. And when Land left his trademark *L* on any report or paper that crossed his desk, others knew that the pitfalls of bureaucracy were not going to stand in his way.

"I got my start in life by working from sunrise to sunset, with my hands, for $10.00 a month and keep," Land once said. He considered himself a friend of the shipbuilding community, and proof of that came when he was named president of the Society of Naval Architects and Marine Engineers. During his speech to accept the post, Land's blunt words reflected the personality that drew Roosevelt to him. "You know, I don't believe in the commission form of government; I think you ought to have a one-man show and shoot him at sunrise if he doesn't run it right."

Yet for all his contempt for bureaucracy and blunt talk, Land seemed content to work within its structure—as long as he reported to his friend, the president, and to no one else.

"My job," he said plainly, "is ships. Building them. Operating them."[9]

If Jerry Land did not like what he heard from Cyril Thompson and Harry Hunter, the British Merchant Shipbuilding Mission would be dead on arrival.

THE NEWS OF the British mission quickly spread among Washington insiders, and reactions were mixed as the purpose of the visit became clear. Roosevelt wanted to help any way he could, which is why he instructed Land and Admiral Howard Vickery, the soft-spoken vice chairman of the Maritime Commission, to meet with the British group and see if an arrangement could be worked out.

In political circles, Land and Vickery came as a package, working hand in hand, leaving all emotions out of contract talks. Vickery, the son of a Cleveland judge, excelled at negotiations. He was a brilliant mathematician at the Naval Academy, and he was one of the few people to go inside the German naval yard at Danzig,[10] where he witnessed firsthand Germany's ships being built in the early 1930s. When Roosevelt put Land in charge of the Maritime Commission, Vickery was one of Land's first hires, and their friendship blossomed even as they needled each other incessantly. But it was through their combined strengths that they were able to charm, coax, and bully America's shipbuilders to reach speed and production records they never would have imagined.

"Land whittles us down," one shipbuilder once complained, "and then Vickery tears us apart. Either one of them is bad enough. Together they're sheer murder."[11]

Between Land's broad knowledge of the state of shipbuilding in the country, and Vickery's encyclopedic intelligence of American ships and shipyards, including inside information on Germany's shipbuilding, Roosevelt was confident the two men would find the common ground necessary to strike a deal with the British.

America's shipbuilders were skeptical. They had heard that Britain wanted to build steel-hulled ships with sharp points and enormous cargo space that could only travel at 10 or 11 knots. They struggled to see the appeal or value in such a plan. At that size, and with that sort of speed, American shipbuilders believed the British-designed ships would be sitting ducks for German torpedoes whistling through ocean waters at 40 knots or more.

IN A LETTER sent directly to Roosevelt, the Foreign Trade Association of Southern California wrote that its members had passed a resolution opposing the construction of "outmoded" vessels. It begged the president to consider ships that moved at least as fast as 14 knots, because anything slower would handicap their ability to move goods speedily across oceans.

But it was not just the design that American shipbuilders hated. Word carried that Thompson was coming with his own drawings and blueprints that called for riveting ships together. That was a problem. After years of riveting parts, because the technique was fast and a team of riveters could easily connect two types of metal, like aluminum to steel, American shipbuilders had decided that it was not as strong as welding, and they had begun welding ships together instead.

Only a few months earlier, in Pascagoula, Mississippi, Ingalls Shipbuilding had proven that the old way of building a ship, starting with the keel and building up, needed to go. Instead they set up timbers and used enormous cranes to hoist different sections of the ship into place, from stern assemblies to pieces of the bow. Each section was welded together, not riveted. When welders worked through the night, it looked like fireworks were shooting out from the shell of the ship, as sparks would fly from the welding torch in all directions and ricochet off the welder's helmet. When the *Exchequer* slid into the water for a trial run and floated, a new future was born for America's shipbuilding industry, one that no longer required more than a million individual rivets to build a single ship.[12]

Welding did have drawbacks. It took longer, and it required considerable training and skill, along with specialized safety equipment like goggles and gloves. And there was some concern whether welded ships carrying huge loads of cargo would hold up on the rough seas. But welding assured a permanent bond between two surfaces, whereas rivets could be prone to separating or loosening.

There was another concern among the shipbuilding community that went beyond any technical issues. Their greatest worry was where these ships would be constructed. American shipyards faced the same capacity problem that forced the British Admiralty to look overseas for help. Like those in Great Britain, U.S. shipyards were already handling an overflow of Navy contracts to produce warships and merchant ships, and they were struggling to keep pace with demands to build them faster.

In recent months, the government had approved contracts to build 948 Navy vessels, among them twelve 35,000-ton aircraft carriers, 292 combat ships, and more than 200 destroyers. On any given day, America's shipbuilders were working around the clock, welding destroyers, cruisers, aircraft carriers, battleships, submarines, and small crafts to help seamen get to shore quickly. And that did not even take into account a smattering of smaller contracts with smaller shipbuilders for tankers and lesser cargo ships that were all valuable either to the U.S. Navy or as assistance to Britain. While the public might have felt reassured knowing so much shipbuilding was taking place, the shipbuilders themselves knew the real story—that building additional ships would mean building new shipyards, new shipways, new welding machines, new cranes for loading the ships, and it would mean training hundreds of thousands of new workers.

And now the president was welcoming the British to build even more ships on American soil. Just who did he expect to build them? And, more importantly, where?

ON FRIDAY, OCTOBER 4, barely twenty-four hours after arriving in New York, Thompson and Hunter flew to Washington, D.C.[13] Their first stop was the British Embassy, where they met up with the other three mission members for dinner and to work out their talking points for their meeting with Land. The other three members of the mission were already in the United States. They were Williams Bennett, a surveyor with Lloyd's Register of Shipping for the United States and Canada; J. S. Heck, an engineering surveyor with Lloyd's; and Sir Richard Powell, who had been appointed as the assistant secretary for the Admiralty and the secretary for the mission. No doubt a topic of conversation among the five men was the news from the day before that Neville Chamberlain, Churchill's predecessor as prime minister of the United Kingdom from 1937 to 1940, had stepped down from Parliament due to his failing health. He would be dead in five weeks.

The following day, a Saturday, the mission members sat down and explained to Jerry Land their country's needs, precisely as the Admiralty had laid out in its letter to Thompson. When Land heard the number of ships Great Britain was seeking, he was incredulous.

"Sixty ships! There are no existing shipyards where you'll get that number of vessels," he told them.[14]

"You haven't the facilities?" Thompson replied.

"No. You will have to see about building your own shipyards over here."

Land said Thompson could meet with and negotiate with any shipbuilder, as long as he understood that any agreement was subject to his approval and that American ship orders would always come first, before British ones.

Britain's hope that the Americans would happily absorb the cost of building or opening new shipyards seemed to be dashed. The Admiralty leaders had believed U.S. officials would see new shipyards as part of its defense spending and an economic boost. But Land made it clear that was not the case.

"If capital expenditure [to build new shipyards] is required to carry out the British Mission's shipbuilding programme, the British Government would probably have to meet it," Land explained.[15]

Land was not rejecting the British plan, he was proposing a compromise. He was suggesting that the British ships could be built in the United States, and he was confident that shipyards could be found, just not the Maritime Commission's existing, active shipyards. Instead, new or dormant shipyards would get the work, paid for by the British, to churn out British vessels built by American workers. Because the shipyards would be on American soil and owned by American businessmen, if at any time during the war the Maritime Commission needed to switch the workers over to build American ships rather than British ones, it could be done with the swipe of a pen.

It all sounded simple enough, until Thompson fully understood what this meant. The 10 million pounds he'd been authorized to spend would not be nearly enough. That amount was seen as covering the cost of building ships. It did not include building shipyards or hiring shipbuilders. In his notes encapsulating the meeting, Powell shared the tenor and the tone of the conversation.

Admiral Land said the Maritime Commission was anxious to be as helpful as possible. There was still shipbuilding capacity, unused, and he thought that the mission would be able to obtain reciprocating engines and Scotch boilers without interfering with the U.S. programme of merchant ship construction.[16]

There was one other important point that needed explaining. Powell made sure to tell the Admiralty that if the British ships had to be riveted, any deal was off the table. Thompson had done some rough calculating and determined that welded ships had both pros and cons. The labor required more manpower. But the ships required less steel. By their rough calculations, a ship the size of what they were seeking required 200 tons less steel if it was welded, a sum that could save significant money. It didn't matter whether it worked financially for the British. The Americans were done riveting ships together.

"I presume you have no objection to all-welded ships," Powell wrote, "as this appears essential to reasonable delivery."[17]

A message from the Admiralty came back promptly: "If you are satisfied, proceed. There is no other way."

ADMIRAL VICKERY PROVED more cautious than Land when Thompson met with him. Vickery explained the toll the Depression had taken on American shipbuilding, and that like Britain, its shipyards were at full capacity. American shipyards were in the midst of building 500 merchant ships, called C-type for cargo ships, or oil tankers, which were called T-types, in addition to handling warship orders from the U.S. Navy. He also echoed what Land said. If Britain wanted America's assistance, it would have to pay to reopen dormant shipyards somewhere in the country or find a business partner willing to construct new shipyards from nothing. Powell, as the designated secretary for the group, crafted letters covering their first few meetings, and wrote to the Admiralty in London to keep them abreast.

"I am enclosing notes of the proceedings of the Merchant Shipbuilding Mission so far as they have gone," he began in his letter a few days after arriving in New York. "You will see that we have not been idle—in fact I don't think that I have ever had three busier days in my life. Mr. Thompson and Mr. Hunter are certainly eager to get something done and to get it done quickly!"[18]

BUT RIGHT BEFORE Thompson was set to leave Washington to visit shipyards, Land and Vickery arranged one last meeting for him. They had a group in mind that they believed might have all the resources necessary to solve Britain's shipbuilding crisis. They were known for doing work on the other side of the country, most notably the Boulder and Bonneville dams. And the piers that had to be plunged deep into San Francisco Bay to help build the eight-mile San Francisco–Oakland Bay Bridge was another achievement of theirs.

A year earlier, in the fall of 1939, just weeks after Germany's invasion of Poland, the Maritime Commission had put out a call for bids to build five C-1 cargo ships, the largest type of such U.S. ships. Among the bidders was this hastily formed group that had never built a steel-hulled ship before. In World War I, a few people within the company had been involved in building concrete ships or wooden ships, but that was the extent of their expertise. Any other experience was limited to repairing ships rather than building them from scratch. And their operation was based on the West Coast at a time when almost all the major shipbuilding firms were on the East Coast, from Maine down to Pennsylvania, Maryland, and Virginia. All of those factors normally would have disqualified the group from even being considered for an American shipbuilding contract. But these were no ordinary times.

The West Coast group had a certain self-confidence bordering on arrogance that Land appreciated as the Maritime Commission reviewed bids for its C-1 ships. They seemed to recognize the expanded role shipbuilding was about to play for the United States. Shipbuilding, one member of the group wrote, "was about ripe to become big volume business and therefore it was a real possibility for our kind of operations."[19] They hoped that landing a small project would help them better understand what shipbuilding entailed before embarking on a larger investment. While they had never built ships before, they were hardly new to construction. Various members of the group had built hundreds of miles of highways and narrow country roads, enormous bridges, and massive dams, even earning the recognition of President Roosevelt. With such high praise in their pocket, the group believed their vast experience warranted giving them serious consideration for the C-1 ships.

The group was actually two businesses merged into one for the purposes of their bid—Todd Shipyards out of Tacoma, Washington, and a loosely formed conglomerate of multiple construction businesses operating under one umbrella called Six Companies.[20] Together they formed the Seattle-Tacoma Shipbuilding Corporation on a fifty-fifty basis, and their $9 million bid for the C-1 cargo ships was awarded the job. Their plan called for Six Companies to build the shipyard and to watch and learn as Todd Shipyards built the ships. Yet as soon as they got to work on the ships, they quickly recognized they were more than ready to take on additional capacity. They told Land to keep them at the top of his list should other shipbuilding needs arise, and that they were capable of taking on "not fewer than 20 nor more than 50 ships" in a contract.[21]

Land appreciated the offer. And he did not forget it. Knowing how smoothly that C-1 contract process had gone, he hoped that the same operation might be interested in the much larger British shipbuilding job, even though the numbers Thompson was seeking exceeded what the West Coast group had suggested they could handle. He urged Thompson to meet with the West Coast group, and he arranged for a meeting in Washington.

For John D. Reilly, the new president of Todd Shipyards, this was an enormous business opportunity. He was no hard-nosed corporate type. Tall and heavyset, with sandy-colored hair, he had no background in ironwork or engineering. A native of Yonkers, New York, he had a round boyish face that made him look more like a clerk than a company boss. But he understood government contracts. He was a decisive businessman who would not hesitate to tell a friend to "cut out the buccaneering."[22] And he understood that while building five government ships was nice, building sixty would transform his business. The group showed Thompson a handsome, colored drawing of a British tramp steamer, and, as Thompson recalled later, they "offered to build ships for us, providing they had reciprocating engines and water-tube boilers." They also made one other demand of the British mission, and they said it was nonnegotiable. "Your whole order or nothing," they told him.

FOR THOMPSON, IT all seemed almost too good to be true. Here was an American businessman, highly recommended to him by the head of the U.S. Maritime Commission, proposing to build ships for the British. It was as if some higher power had heard his plea and served up the solution on an engraved silver platter with his initials, RCT, carved right into the center.

"No large existing yards can undertake work for us," he wrote to the Admiralty. "[But] Todd Shipyard Corporation has been practically allocated to us by Maritime Commission—provided we act quickly."[23]

When Powell wrote his own, more detailed summary of the meetings, he got right to the good news.

"We have been very impressed the most, I think, by the scheme put forward by Mr. Reilly of Todd Shipyard Corporation. They operate on a very large scale as you will see and talked of an output of up to 150 ships per year." He said

Jerry Land assured them the business "will do what they say they can do, and cheaper than most."[24]

But Powell then made sure the Admiralty understood that more money was still needed. "If my arithmetic is correct," Powell wrote, Britain could possibly get ten ships at 10,000 tons deadweight with its current budget. "If what you want costs more than what we have been allowed so far, you will do your best to get more money made available."

With the Land and Vickery meetings behind him, and a tempting opportunity on the table, Thompson still wanted to explore all avenues available. Reilly had laid out a convincing argument. But Thompson was leery. The ink on the 1939 C-1 contract the group had landed was barely dry and that was their first genuine shipbuilding deal. Even though the work seemed solid, he could not see himself cabling back to the Admiralty that he had struck a business pact with a partner who was expert in repairing ships yet had almost no experience building them. This was too important a decision to rush. Reilly's offer could wait. There were dozens of more experienced shipbuilders out there, on both coasts, and Thompson knew that he had not come all this way just to meet with one group in an office in Washington, D.C., and declare his mission complete. He chartered a twin-engine Douglas Dakota and mapped out a barnstorming trip across North America.[25]

CHAPTER FOUR

17,000 Miles, Three Weeks

ON OCTOBER 8, 1940, THE THREE MOST IMPORTANT MEM-
bers of the British entourage, Thompson, Hunter, and Powell, took off in a
chartered DC-3 from Washington. Thompson would handle any negotiations.
Hunter was needed when conversation turned to the engineering specs of
shipbuilding. Powell would serve as the scribe, the communications liaison
with London to keep the Admiralty abreast of the progress they were making.
They not only mapped out the route of their trip, but they also worked out a
strategy for the stops. On each day they would use every moment wisely and
spend every dollar conservatively, fueling up their plane only as frequently as
necessary.

"Our method was to work away by day, interviewing shipbuilders and engineers and surveying sites in one particular area," Thompson recalled. "Then
we would fly by night to the next stop, sleeping on the journey. We never lost
any odd hours that way."[1]

It was not to be a glamorous adventure. Thompson wrote of seeing "innumerable mud-fields and stretches of coast where shipyards might be built."

Their first stop was brief, a visit to the Canadian capital of Ottawa, to see
whether Canada's shipyards and engine makers could assist them. Though

Canadian officials told Thompson they were happy to help, the Canadian shipyards were so far north, the icy winter climate made it challenging to reach
them, and Thompson made the decision to focus his efforts on the United States.

Their itinerary covered 17,000 miles, with scheduled stops at thirty-five
shipyards. Among their planned list of stops were visits to Mobile, Alabama;
Pascagoula, Mississippi; Portland, Maine; New Orleans; Los Angeles; San
Francisco; Portland, Oregon; Seattle and Tacoma, Washington; San Francisco;
and Vancouver and Victoria, British Columbia, because of their proximity to
the ocean. The goal was to be back in New York by November 1.

It took Thompson only a few days into their trip to realize that the mission's goals would be harder to achieve than he anticipated. The state of the
war in Europe was proving to be an obstacle. British citizens were living in
fear of being bombed every day, running for home-built shelters, basements,
or government-constructed community shelters at the first blast of an air raid
siren. When a siren wailed on one mid-October night, the rush for cover began,
with as many as six hundred packing into the Balham Underground Station
in South London thinking they'd be safe there. Two hours later, a 1,400-kilo-
gram armor-piercing bomb smashed through the ground above the station,
blowing an enormous crater in the road, swallowing up a double-decker bus,
and leveling adjacent buildings. With debris raining down, more than sixty
people died in the station and hundreds were injured.

Images from the blast were plastered on front pages around the world.
American businessmen, who were avid newspaper readers and regular radio
listeners, greeted the British visitors with trepidation. A dejected Thompson
wrote to the Admiralty that Americans viewed Britain like the horse projected
to finish in last place—not worth a bet of a single buck. "The general opinion
in the States among all classes, even among very high officials and officers,"
Thompson wrote, "was that Britain was on her last legs."[2]

With one grim story after another reaching the United States, Thompson
sensed that while American politicians saw Britain's desperate state as a reason to help their ally, American businessmen were putting their wallets first,
leaving Thompson little leverage when it came time to negotiate. "We got the

impression that they thought they were being invited to back a losing cause," Thompson wrote back home.[3]

EVEN THOUGH SOME of the shipyards that the mission did visit were building and launching impressive vessels, they found that new ships generally took more than a year to build. That was simply too long. The shipyards also clearly lacked the manpower or acreage to suddenly take on the construction of an additional huge order like sixty cargo ships. It became more and more obvious to Thompson that the best business deal he was going to find was the deal he had left behind in Washington.

This became even more clear in late October when the shipbuilding mission visited the Seattle-Tacoma Shipyard. They were immediately impressed with the operation. Two of the five C-1 cargo ships had already been built there since the contract was signed. When Thompson and Hunter inquired if the Maritime Commission was satisfied with the quality of workmanship, they were told yes, the ships were well built. And more important, the entire yard and the two ships all came together in less than a year. That kind of speed reassured Thompson, knowing how efficient an operation it was, and that if Seattle-Tacoma was awarded the much larger British ship order, it seemed capable of acting quickly.

During their travels, there was something else, or rather someone else, who left an impression on Thompson while they were on the West Coast. While visiting a shipyard in Portland, Oregon, he was introduced to a bald, heavyset man in his late fifties who took him on a tour of the buildings and grounds and various construction sites. Thompson could not quite tell where this man's expertise lay, if it was in shipbuilding or contracts or general construction. But when they met him again in Oakland, they began to see that he was more than a figurehead. He was clearly someone to be reckoned with. On a bright, sunny day, this plump, self-assured, well-dressed businessman took Thompson and Powell into his large, dark office where the tiniest bit of light shined on an oversize white blotter on his desk.[4] There was no reason for the poor lighting, which Powell could tell immediately. "He didn't have an eye complaint," he recalled later. "It was all done for effect. Pure theatre." But this was no show. Henry Kaiser wanted this job more than anything.[5]

"Give me the backing," Kaiser told Thompson, "and I'll build you 200 ships during 1942."[6]

Was this just bluster? Thompson was not entirely sure who Henry Kaiser was, or how exactly he was connected to John Reilly or the Seattle-Tacoma Shipyard or to Six Companies or to Todd Shipyard, or whether he even knew the first thing about shipbuilding. He didn't talk like a shipbuilder. And Thompson wondered just why, if Kaiser was so important to this operation, he was only meeting him now, and why had he not been present for their introductory meeting back in Washington that Land had arranged. It was all rather confusing to the Brit. But Thompson could not ignore how this slightly odd, roly-poly businessman exuded an obvious swagger. Kaiser assured his visitors that he could build the British two hundred ships, even though they were only seeking sixty, and it didn't seem like an outrageous boast. To Thompson it felt like a promise. As he stood there in that curiously pitch-black office, while it was broad daylight outside, his gut told him this was a businessman who would not make a promise he did not intend to keep.

BACK IN WASHINGTON, preliminary numbers were drawn up. The contract required the British to pay $96 million (or £24 million at the 1940 exchange rate),[7] a sum total that included the sixty ships at $1.6 million each. The British were promised their first ships would be completed and delivered within twelve months, or by the end of 1941, and the full sixty would be done within twenty to twenty-four months, or by the end of 1942.

Thompson and Powell knew that the dollar figures were laughable compared to the 10 million pounds they had been allocated to spend by the Admiralty. Powell needed approval as fast as possible and wrote up a cable for London. Germany had become expert at intercepting radio calls, so Powell sent his message on December 1, 1940, through a Typex, a cipher machine able to send encrypted messages. He explained that the U.S. government had approved the construction of sixty ships and he outlined the per-ship price. He ended by emphasizing the urgency of a reply.

"Thompson leaves for England in the middle of the month," he wrote.[8]

But Thompson decided he couldn't wait. He worried Powell's cable would not be well received back home. Yes, he had achieved his goal by closing a provisional deal. But there were so many questions still to be answered. The cost was more than double what the British had wanted to pay, and details about where exactly the ships would be built, what the precise ship design would be, and who the key players were still had to be finalized. Thompson did not want to wait around for answers. On December 6 he packed up his briefcase with draft contracts and the necessary background material on Britain's new potential business partners, and he booked a trip home on the passenger cargo liner *Western Prince*, a smaller ship than the *Scythia* known for its speed crossing the Atlantic.

Waiting for him back home was a homeland under siege. On a cold evening a few days before he left, air raid sirens blared for hours as German bombs rained down north of London. A land mine attached to a parachute struck a small college in Edge Hill. A building collapsed on top of a shelter, burying more than one hundred and sixty men, women, and children alive.

CHAPTER FIVE

Torpedoed

IN THE DARK OF THE MORNING, JUST BEFORE SIX O'CLOCK on December 14, the torpedo came whistling out of nowhere, an underwater missile slicing just below the whitecaps and leaving no time to get out of its path. A week into her trip, the *Western Prince* was 250 miles south of Iceland, zigzagging toward Liverpool. Chief Officer L. P. Ellis heard it first, an explosion forward of the bridge on the ship's port side. It sounded like a bomb, but he couldn't see any fire. All he saw was an enormous spout of water shoot up and nearly flood the deckhouse. The ship lurched violently and immediately started to sink.[1]

Thompson, like the rest of the sixty-one passengers, was asleep when he felt the explosion. He dressed quickly, grabbed his briefcase with the documents and contracts, and rushed up to the deck, where passengers were already being led calmly into lifeboats by the crew. Even though the ship seemed to be dangerously low, the captain was still waiting to see if she was going down, and so he ordered his crew members to swing the lifeboats out and lower them to the deck level until he gave the order to abandon ship.

"The captain called me to clear the ship and to wait for him, but he was now of the opinion she would not sink," Ellis recalled later. "I did not agree with him."[2]

Sure enough, the *Prince* kept going down and soon the lifeboats were resting on the water. Before he knew it, Thompson was being safely lowered, an oar was placed in his hands, and he laid his briefcase by his feet. He described the scene later as "a waste of sea that was dark grey and menacing."[3] An arctic wind blew the lifeboat around like a toy, while spray from the waves splashed on board and froze droplets on the faces of the terrified passengers.

James Bone, the London editor of the *Manchester Guardian*, was sitting in another lifeboat drifting away, watching the ship disappear as her captain, John Reed, remained on board. In her final act, she let loose two blasts on her whistle.

"That's the old man's last words,"[4] a sailor next to Bone said. "Goodbye to you."

Sixty feet away, the *Prince*'s passengers spotted a German U-boat surfacing. It made no attempt to contact the ship, though some passengers did notice flash photographs being taken of her as she sank. Less than an hour after the first explosion came a second one, followed by a wall of flames. Thirty seconds later the *Western Prince* was gone, taking sixteen lives, including a pair of newlyweds who had rushed to rescue some of their wedding presents, only to never make it back in time. Ten crew members went down with the ship, including Captain Reed.

Those on the lifeboats started rowing. "I pulled an oar with the other passengers for nine hours before we were rescued, with the precious dispatch case at my feet," Thompson recounted.[5]

Just when they feared they would have to spend the night drifting at sea, they were spotted by a British freighter, the *Baron Kinnaird*, which happened to be in the vicinity and spotted a flare that went up. The rescue effort, however, did not go smoothly. The ocean's heavy swell caused one of the rescue boats to be tossed around, throwing all the passengers to one side and then into the freezing water as their boat capsized. One woman disappeared in the blackness, and the *Kinnaird*'s carpenter, while trying to lift a passenger on board, felt his arm crushed between the rescue boat and steamer. As the lifeboats pulled up alongside the freighter, women, children, and older men were hoisted up in baskets first, including three babies, followed by the strongest of the passengers, men like Thompson and Bone. As one of the women set foot on the *Kinnaird*, she rewarded her rescuers each with a gentle kiss on the cheek. Admiralty officials, upon hearing the news of the *Western Prince*, feared the worst—not only the loss of life, but also the loss of valuable signed documents that were vital to their ongoing war with Germany.

Doreen Thompson had been listening to her radio at home in England, tuned to a station full of Nazi propaganda, when she heard a news flash announcing the sinking of a British ship bound for England from America. She knew that her husband was traveling back home by ship, and she wondered if he was gone.[6]

When Cyril Thompson finally reached shore and was able to open his briefcase, the papers inside were soaked. Some of them were only partly readable. He had to have them retyped so he could deliver them properly to the Admiralty. When he finally met with Sir James Lithgow, Thompson apologized, not only for returning two days later than anticipated, but also for having to hand over retyped copies of the documents he brought home rather than the originals.[7]

He regaled Admiralty officials with the story of the British Merchant Shipbuilding Mission's 17,000-mile journey across America, from the twin-engine Douglas Dakota they chartered, to the shipyards they toured, to the offers they received, to the politicians they lobbied. He could only hope that once Admiralty officials had absorbed his entire tale, they would be so engrossed by the characters and his descriptions of the shipyards and the operations that impressed him the most—not to mention his near-death experience at sea—that they would overlook the fact that they now owed some complicated conglomerate of inexperienced shipbuilders and slightly odd businessmen nearly $100 million if they wanted to hire the Americans to build their cargo ships.

PART II

Partners

CHAPTER SIX

Henry the Builder

STANDING ON THE SOUTHERN PACIFIC'S SHASTA LIMITED in front of an open door, Henry Kaiser looked out at the blur of Northern California trees as they sped by at about thirty miles per hour. And he knew there was only one thing to do. Jump.[1]

If life is a series of moments, interactions, and decisions that shape a person's journey, that fall day in 1921 was about to become one of those for Kaiser. Already bald and shaped like a bowling ball, the thirty-nine-year-old was no daredevil. But his young construction business was struggling, his finances were a shambles, and he was on the road so much that in order for his family to see him, they had to sleep with him in his car. He wasn't quite a failure, but nothing about Kaiser foreshadowed a dynamic industrialist who would play an instrumental role in lifting America to victory in a second world war and be the face of the Pacific Northwest's transformation—building winding roads and major highways, digging trenches to carry oil and natural gas pipelines, carving tunnels through mountain passes to speed cross country travel, and constructing enormous dams that controlled flooding and powered hundreds of thousands of homes.

Instead, as the wind whistled past while he looked out the door of the Shasta

Limited, Kaiser had to be wondering if it might be time for a fresh start. Kaiser was bound for San Francisco with Alonzo B. Ordway, his very first hire a decade earlier and now his leading construction supervisor. Ordway had been vacationing in San Francisco with his wife—his first vacation in a decade—when he'd overheard two men talking about a $500,000 paving contract up for grabs near Redding, California, up near the Oregon border. Ordway called Kaiser and the two men agreed they had to pursue it. Until that point, their biggest jobs were around $100,000, but now with California expanding they sensed that bigger projects were becoming available.

They caught a train together in the direction of Redding, except they misread the schedule. Their train would not be stopping in Redding. Kaiser's business needed this job badly, and he was not going to let their careless mistake stand in the way of winning a project of half a million dollars.

"I didn't want to jump," Ordway recalled later of that moment. "The train was going at a pretty good clip."[2]

When a brakeman told Kaiser they couldn't stop in Redding, he simply moved to another part of the train and opened a vestibule on his own. No matter that they were dressed in suits, and lugging heavy suitcases. Kaiser and Ordway both knew the train would slow down just enough at the small station in Cottonwood for the engineer to reach out and grab a bag full of orders off a pole. That would be their chance. When they felt the train easing up, they jumped, the roly-poly Kaiser leaping first with the younger Ordway right behind him.

"I had to jump off to see if he had broken his neck," Ordway said.

Kaiser bounced into a pile of railroad ties. Ordway ended up in some brush. Though both men scraped their knees and hands pretty good and tore up their clothes, they stood up relieved and unharmed.

"I've ruined my brand-new suit," Ordway snapped at Kaiser, who chuckled back at him.

The Cottonwood stationmaster saw the commotion outside and came running.

"You damn fools!" he yelled.

He wasn't wrong. But those fools hustled their way over to nearby Redding

to visit the construction site, took a night train back to San Francisco to final-
ize their bid for the job, and submitted it the next day. Their low bid won the
$527,000 project, making their risky jump worth the effort in Kaiser's mind.
There was a reason his employees would nickname him "Hurry Up Henry."
He wasn't very good at waiting.

FOR HENRY KAISER, with the right person by your side and a strong team
at the ready, any job could be accomplished. It was a lesson that struck him as
a young boy growing up in a modest farmhouse in upstate New York. Kaiser's
parents, Frank and Mary, were German immigrants whose families settled in
New York. Frank, who had been a shoemaker back in Steinheim, Germany,
near Frankfurt, opened a cobbler business that never managed to make much
money. But it was enough for them to live in the tiny town of Sprout Brook,
and after marrying in 1873, three daughters arrived in succession before Henry
John Kaiser was born on May 9, 1882.

Henry was a handful at home, gregarious, playful, and smart. One day, when
his mother asked what he wanted for Christmas, young Henry responded, "A
little sister."

"Sorry, son," she answered him, "little sisters take a lot longer than a few
weeks to make."

"But Mom," the boy said back, "I know you can do it. Pop says if you put
enough men on the job, anything is possible."

He quit school at thirteen, an odd decision since his studies were going
well. But he decided on his own that no teacher could help him more than he
could help himself.

"I thought I was ready to lick the world single-handed, so I dropped out,"
Kaiser explained many years later of his decision.[3]

His self-confidence came straight from Mary.

"I am certain that as a boy, I was less than average—to everyone except my
mother," Kaiser reflected in writing many years later. "No matter what opinions

others may have held of me, she thought she saw in me, as do other mothers when looking at their young sons, the makings of a man who could be of service to his fellow men." The values that she taught him—to love people and serve them, to love your work and pour yourself into it, and to always rely on your Christian principles—drove Kaiser in everything he pursued.[4]

That determination showed up in his pursuit of a bride in his early twenties. Kaiser was running a successful photography business in Lake Placid, New York, selling film to vacationers and then developing their pictures at night and smartly leaving the prints in their hotel room mailboxes by morning so they could enjoy them over their breakfast.

One day a shy and pretty young woman[5] with dark hair and a round face walked into his shop to purchase some film. Something about nineteen-year-old Bess Fosburgh caught the twenty-three-year-old Kaiser's eye. She was polite and well dressed, the result of her recent graduation from Dana Hall, a fashionable finishing school a few miles west of Boston, but also on vacation with her father. Kaiser had become something of a favorite son in town because of his popular business. But Bess seemed to be in another league than he. He used the one skill that he had to find a way to talk to her: he offered to take her picture in a formal portrait shoot.

In his pursuit of Bess, he used relaxing canoe rides on Lake Placid to romance her and small powerboats to excite her. He also used his own ingenuity, rigging up a one-horsepower engine with a simple ignition switch, installing it on the back of an Adirondack lake skiff and taking it out for short trips, barely reaching speeds of six or eight miles per hour.

When the impatient Kaiser wanted to marry this girl, her father stepped in. He was a lumberman who saw photography as more of a hobby, not a career, and certainly not worthy of his daughter's hand. He told Kaiser that if he wanted to marry her, he needed to go west for a year, save up $1,000, and earn at least $125 per month. To Kaiser, this was just another challenge. He vowed to be back for his fiancée.

Kaiser moved out to Spokane, Washington, and stumbled into a business that seemed to be the pulse of downtown—McGowan Brothers Hardware.

Kaiser noticed that every day it seemed as if men and women of all ages wandered in with a problem and left with a solution. He was intrigued. The owner, James C. McGowan, liked Kaiser, but he was distracted, reeling from a fire that had swept through the store and caused thousands of dollars in damage.[6]

"Don't you see, I'm almost ruined," McGowan told Kaiser. "How am I going to hire anyone new?"

Kaiser offered to help anyway. He brought in a group of local women to polish the products that were damaged in the blaze, so when they went back on the shelves they looked brand-new. McGowan was impressed with Kaiser's gumption. He hired him and made him his city sales manager. Soon Kaiser was earning enough to purchase a small house at 418 Fourth Avenue, and he set off back east to finish what he had started.

If Bess Fosburgh's father was shocked to see Kaiser return so quickly, he didn't know who he was dealing with. After their wedding in downtown Boston, the newlyweds headed west to Spokane, and a few days later Kaiser was back at the store, handing out cigars and candy, ready to get to work again. That's when Bess Kaiser first began to understand that her husband was a workaholic. The two sons she would deliver for them, Edgar, who was born in 1908, and Henry Jr., who arrived almost a decade later in 1917, would not change him.

As an important employee of a small business, Kaiser looked at problems not as obstacles to overcome, but as opportunities to learn. When he saw how wheelbarrows struggled to haul materials on construction job sites across mushy ground, because the iron wheels sank too deep, he devised a better contraption. His two-wheel, two-person wheelbarrow came with rubber tires, rather than iron, and a more shallow steel holding container for supplies that was set in a frame and easily dumped out of the sloped front end. His device rode more easily atop the marshy ground and ensured construction projects could stay on schedule.

One engineer who saw the dramatic improvement said Kaiser's invention was nothing short of revolutionary. "The rubber tire for the wheelbarrow is a lot of glory for any one man," he said.[7]

The leap from the hardware business into construction came easily for Kaiser thanks to the contacts he'd made. When one of Spokane's largest road and paving contractors offered him a job, he leapt at it. That relationship ended badly in a power struggle, but another door opened when a Canadian construction company went bankrupt. Needing capital to take over the business, he walked into the Canadian Bank of Commerce. He had no assets to speak of, no collateral to offer.

"You mean to sit there and inform me, young man, you want me to loan you $25,000, and you don't even have a company, you don't even have any equipment, you don't have any men?" Sir William McKenzie, a bank director, is said to have asked Kaiser.[8]

"Yes. That's what I'm here for."

Maybe it was the confidence Kaiser showed. Or the banker's soft heart. But he reached for a piece of paper, scribbled a note, and pointed Kaiser toward the cashiers. The note said: "Honor Henry J. Kaiser's signature for $25,000."[9]

Kaiser Paving spent the next decade digging, scraping, and paving its way through the Pacific Northwest. Each step he took, Alonzo Ordway stayed with him. With each job, Kaiser walked away with a new tool, a new gimmick, a new idea, or a new contact that made the next job easier. When he watched a strong horse pull one scraper along a road to smooth out the pavement, he experimented with a Caterpillar tractor pulling five scrapers. It saved time and it kept his workers fresh. When he landed a $20 million subcontract to build two hundred miles of roads in Cuba, a complicated project Ordway described as "the turning point in our history,"[10] they managed to finish a year ahead of schedule. Yet building roads was never going to be enough for Kaiser. A road was utilitarian, a means to get from point A to point B. There was no rush of satisfaction that came from finishing a road project.

The sound of a roaring, untamed river, however, was different. There was danger in a river. When the federal government announced it wanted to harness the power of the Colorado River, winding 1,450 miles through the heart of the Southwest, a river that had been the subject of heated debate for nearly thirty years, Kaiser knew this was it. This was the job that could transform him from regional road builder to American industrialist. But first, he needed to come up with $5 million.

CHAPTER SEVEN

Hoover

IN EARLY FEBRUARY 1931, A GROUP OF WEST COAST BUSI-
nessmen met up at the Engineers Club in San Francisco. They came from
various backgrounds—law, engineering, finance, railroads, sewers and tunnels,
and sand, gravel, and paving. There was an urgency to their talks, because bids
for a project that could change all their lives were scheduled to be opened in a
month. As they sat around a table, three separate bids were offered up for the job
within the group, and to everyone's shock, the three numbers were extremely
close, with only $700,000 separating the high and low figure.[1] When everyone
else left to grab sandwiches, one man stayed behind to work through lunch and
crunch the numbers. When the group returned, Henry Kaiser said they would
bid $40 million to do the work, with an additional 25 percent added in for profit.

Kaiser's road project in Cuba had earned him the respect he sought. He
became friendly with the biggest names in the construction industry, including
brothers Edmund and William Wattis, who ran a company in Utah; Harry
W. Morrison, who gained his notoriety in Chicago; Charles A. Shea from
Southern California; and Warren A. Bechtel, the most powerful West Coast
contractor, and the most politically connected. When he learned about the
Boulder Dam project, Kaiser nearly decided to pursue it by himself, hungry to

show his competitors he was just as much of a construction kingpin as any of them. But he knew better. This was too big for any one company, especially his.

Despite all his achievements, he remained unknown to most Americans in the early 1930s. Kaiser was nearing fifty. He found the thrill of competing for projects exhilarating, knowing that when he won, he'd earned it. That's what drove his relentless push to innovate. He had spent the last two decades building his reputation as a contractor who'd never met a project too big. He'd constructed roads and highways in Washington, California, British Columbia, and Cuba, battling hundred-degree days, drenching floods, paralyzing mudslides, ice and cold, dust, and drought. His business began with horses and mules and hard physical labor by hand, and it now included some of the heaviest, most sophisticated paving machinery in the world, along with honest crews and managers who took pride in their work. At a time when the automobile was flourishing, he was instrumental in opening up the West, earning a fortune in the process, even as he struggled to get his name into the right circles in Washington, D.C., so that he was no longer viewed as a Pacific Northwest contractor.

After he teamed up with the better-known Bechtel on some smaller, regional projects, the two men agreed to form Bechtel-Kaiser and to pursue the dam project together, along with other partners they would enlist. The final group was a hodgepodge of friendly competitors, each of them taking a 10 or 20 percent stake in the operation, except for Kaiser and Bechtel, who took 30 percent. Bechtel, ten years older than Kaiser, was more than happy to cede the administrative and bookkeeping responsibilities to his junior partner, and Kaiser embraced the opportunity to lead.

Lacking much time to come up with a creative name for their group, they called it Six Companies (technically they were eight companies, and the number would fluctuate over the years). On the late winter day bids for the Boulder Dam were to be opened in Denver, they set up headquarters in a room at the old Cosmopolitan Hotel. As word circulated among contractors that bids would be sought for one of the greatest engineering feats America had ever built, more than a hundred construction firms were expected to bid. It was one year into the Great Depression. This was the sort of job that could resuscitate and sustain a business for years, even decades, through the nation's economic turmoil. And it could rally Americans behind a project that would remind them of the greatness their country was once capable of, even in times of economic morass.

ON MARCH 4, 1931, a gray and cold morning greeted the contractors as they assembled inside 1437 Welton Street, a vacant store in downtown Denver that the Bureau of Reclamation had rented out to accommodate several hundred people. An American flag hung on the wall behind the officials' table, and reporters and photographers crowded the back of the room, along with insurance agents and contractors. The Six Companies bid of $48,890,990, in a sealed envelope, was placed in the pile on the table, and a few minutes after ten, Ray Walter, the chief engineer of the bureau and head of its Denver office, began unsealing the bids.[2]

The first bid he opened was $53.9 million, low enough to make the Six Companies' men sweat. Another bid unsealed said simply it would "do the job for $80,000 less than the offer of the low bidder," not exactly a serious offer to be considered. Comically, that bid also erred by describing the project as being in New Mexico, not Nevada. A $59 million bid was opened next, and for the Six Companies' representatives, they knew the job was theirs. When their figure was announced, it was more than $5 million lower than the next-lowest bid. The room filled with whistles and hearty congratulations.

A few days later, a group of the Six Companies men took their wives on a sightseeing trip into the canyon of the Colorado River. They admired the swift-moving water and soaked up the freezing spray that splashed up into their small boat. But it was the dramatic steep, sheer walls of the canyon, rising hundreds of feet on both sides of them, that left the group in awe of what they were about to build.

One of the men, Felix Kahn, shouted above the roar of the river: "Think of it, we're going 150 feet this way [he pointed into the river] and 750 feet that way [he pointed straight up]."

His wife clung to his side and looked over at him.

"Felix," she said, "I don't know whether to call you courageous, or crazy."

Six Companies had 2,565 days to finish the dam. For every day they were late, the government would issue a fine of $3,000. Kaiser was the least experienced of the bunch but the Six Companies members selected him to work with the leaders in Washington finalizing the contract. Their trust in him stemmed from how hard he worked. For weeks leading up to the bids being unsealed, Kaiser had driven back and forth through the night from Oakland to the dam site any chance he could get. He would work a full day at his office, drive his yellow Marmon speedster 70 miles an hour until he could barely keep his eyes open, then pull over and rest, before continuing. When he got there, he studied the canyon walls, the desert grounds, the dirt roads leading in and out, as if he were the job superintendent rather than the financial overseer in charge of the books and deadlines. This was to be the most visible project of his career. He was not leaving anything to chance. They had seven years to finish it—by the summer of 1938.

ON THE FIRST day of April 1931, work began. For unskilled laborers, the rate of $4 a day was heaven-sent money, and workers of all shapes and sizes and ages (but only men) flocked to the area from around the country. Most came from Nevada and California, but every state was represented (except for Vermont and North Dakota). Their average age was thirty-four. Any excitement they had about landing the work probably disappeared the moment they set foot on the job site. Conditions in Black Canyon were horrendous and dangerous. Temperatures reached triple digits on many summer days, sometimes soaring to 140 degrees in the scorching sun, but then dipping to 20 degrees during the short winter, when winds could whip up fiercely. The canyon was also remote, nowhere close to a big city, meaning heavy machinery, small supplies, food, water, flush toilets all had to be brought in from great distances, a time-consuming and costly exercise. Boxes of dynamite were often stored right in the open, under a blistering sun, next to cans of gasoline, creating the possibility of combustion and explosion that workers lived with daily.

But it was also a mesmerizing project to watch unfold, even for the workers. As the giant wall of concrete slowly rose in the western flatlands, exhausted workers who had spent a long day in scorching heat would often sit on the ledge at the end of their long days and watch the sun set as they admired the achievement they were building. In the first year of work, during a one-month stretch from late June to late July, fourteen workers died from heat prostration. The conditions tested Kaiser's business mettle. When a thousand workers walked off the job in protest of a wage cut, and demanded purer water and more flush toilets on-site, Kaiser said the position of Six Companies remained speed, speed, speed. They could not afford to fall behind schedule and risk heavy government fines.

Kaiser spent more time in Washington, living at the Shoreham Hotel for almost three months straight in 1932, than at the newly erected Boulder City, the makeshift grounds set up to house the workers for the duration of the project. He absorbed criticism for spending too much time on the reputation and bottom line of Six Companies while ignoring "how your labor feels and thinks, and what it needs and wants."[3] And when Congress threatened to withhold the money to finish the Boulder Dam, Kaiser's negotiating skills were put to the test. The dam was the crown jewel in the portfolio of Six Companies, and he protected it as if it were his own child, appealing to every contact he'd made in Washington and flooding the offices of politicians with flyers and articles and science-and-engineering newsletters that highlighted the work being done. It helped that he had shrewdly hired his own newspaper "reporter" to ensure that "the facts are truthfully presented to both magazines and newspapers," and that prominent visitors were invited to the job site to see for themselves the progress being made.[4]

His election as national president of the Associated General Contractors in 1932 firmly established his arrival. It also opened the door for him to be introduced to President Roosevelt, who in November soundly defeated the incumbent Republican, campaigning on the promise of a "New Deal" for

Americans that would reverse the failures of the Hoover administration that led to the Depression.

LESS THAN FIVE years after the dam's work began, on the morning of September 30, 1935, a motorcade whisked Roosevelt from Boulder City straight to the top of a steel and concrete dam in the middle of the Arizona desert.[5] Stepping out of his limousine, he went to the specially constructed observation deck, wearing his white brimmed hat and a gray double-breasted suit buttoned up snugly over his broad chest. Roosevelt, his sharp blue-gray eyes behind his round spectacles, looked down at the man-made lake beneath him, a warm but pleasant sun beating down and glistening off the water below. He stepped toward the microphone set up to broadcast his remarks across radio networks throughout the country.

Only a few years earlier, this had been miles and miles of nothing but dirt and cactus. Now it was perhaps the most astonishing structure built by hand anywhere in the world. At 700 feet tall and 660 feet wide at its base, the dam stood taller than the Washington Monument and almost equal to the length of two football fields. The reservoir at the bottom disappeared into the distance, stretching 110 miles long. More than a hundred men died during its four years of construction. And yet, as with everything that Henry Kaiser seemed to touch, it was finished two years ahead of schedule and $4 million under budget. By the time of the president's arrival, along with the governors of six states, senators and representatives, officials from Six Companies, and some twelve thousand people from throughout the region, the dam was all but complete.

"This morning, I came, I saw and I was conquered, as everyone would be who sees for the first time this great feat of mankind," Roosevelt began.

Ten years ago, the place where we are gathered was an unpeopled, forbidding desert. In the bottom of a gloomy canyon, whose precipitous walls rose to a height of more than a thousand feet, flowed a turbulent, dangerous river. The mountains on either side of the canyon were difficult of access with neither road nor trail, and their rocks were protected by neither trees nor grass from the blazing heat of the sun. The site of Boulder City was a cactus-covered waste. The transformation wrought here in these years is a twentieth-century marvel.[6]

Kaiser had just orchestrated a magnificent, backbreaking construction achievement worthy of a presidential visit and the highest praise. Flowing through seven states—Wyoming, Colorado, Utah, New Mexico, Arizona, Nevada, and California—the Colorado River served as the largest source of surface water for the Southwest. The river had to be physically turned so its waters could be diverted into tunnels and the riverbed then exposed to build the foundation of the dam.

"This is an engineering victory of the first order, another great achievement of American resourcefulness, skill, and determination," the president said. "I have the right once more to congratulate you who have created Boulder Dam and on behalf of the nation to say to you, 'Well done.'"

Kaiser was nowhere to be seen as the president praised the work of Six Companies and its men. Feeling under the weather, he was back in Oakland at his office, pursuing a new dam project in Bonneville, Oregon. A few days after the Boulder Dam dedication, he received a letter from the White House. In a personally signed note, Roosevelt acknowledged Kaiser's regret at having to miss the celebration, and he offered his "best wishes for your speedy recovery."[7]

The New Deal had frightened many American businessmen. Not only did they question its long-term possibilities and usefulness to lift the economy out of the lingering Depression, but they also were deeply skeptical of Roosevelt's chances to win reelection and see it through. Kaiser was not among the cynics. Even though the dam had been started during the Hoover administration and was initially called Hoover Dam, Roosevelt's secretary of the interior, Harold Ickes, did not want the president christening something named for his predecessor, so he quietly changed the name in the requisite paperwork and speeches to Boulder Dam. (Congress later changed it back.)

Kaiser had expended enormous energy and time and money building close ties in Washington to get the job done faster and cheaper than anybody thought possible. It was not perfect. Six Companies was forced to settle forty-eight carbon monoxide lawsuits after some workers died of respiratory ailments that they were told by doctors was pneumonia. Ickes fined Six Companies $350,000 for committing 70,000 violations of the country's eight-hour workday law. In order to ensure the maximum number of workers were hired for the Boulder Dam project, the contract banned any overtime for workers except for emergencies. Six Companies, on the other hand, was solely focused on speed and more speed: more workers and more shift changes only slowed work down. To pressure Ickes on the fine, Kaiser produced a slick booklet of all the crises they had overcome, titled *So Boulder Dam Was Built*. He shared thousands of copies throughout the halls of Congress, and with high-powered reporters, and he took to the radio to tell the story of Boulder Dam's construction. He bombarded Ickes and even President Roosevelt with telegrams, insisting the fine was egregious and angering Ickes no end.

"Frankly, he is doing himself and his company no good by his lack of composure," Ickes confided to a senator who was close with Kaiser. The senator shared back that Kaiser had the "jitters" about the fine. In the end, Kaiser negotiated the fine down to $100,000.[8]

WHETHER IT WAS through a misstep or an achievement, Kaiser learned that the key to earning the respect of the White House was through flattery, and keeping the right people informed of the progress being made and the obstacles encountered. Senators, congressman, and certainly the president did not like surprises. When the first poll from a company called Gallup in 1935 found that 6 in 10 Americans believed the government was spending too much money, it was the kind of news that did not help Roosevelt's popularity as he was ramping up for his reelection. But after everything the president had done for him, Kaiser was not about to turn his back on Roosevelt. The New Deal had expanded the government in ways that helped industrialists just like

Kaiser. If anything, he hoped he had earned the White House's trust so that opportunities even bigger than the Boulder Dam would come his way.

Throughout the remainder of the late 1930s, Kaiser continued to position Six Companies to pursue more federal dam projects, including the Grand Coulee and Bonneville dams. The conglomerate balked at some jobs, and jumped at others, with some of the members splintering off and then reuniting when the right opportunity arose. With each new contract he landed, Kaiser discovered new tactics and techniques that he would carry on to the next project. When the Columbia River dam turned into a far more complicated project than he'd envisioned, with dangerous flooding, he split up the work into two teams, one led by his son Edgar and the other by his most trusted supervisor, Clay Bedford, a strategy he would carry forward again and again.

The bigger his operation grew, the more Kaiser hated relying on others for his critical supplies like sand and steel and concrete and magnesium, and when his engineers discovered that Permanente Creek in Santa Clara County, California, was flourishing with limestone deposits, he pounced. On Christmas Day in 1939, the newly employed men at Permanente Cement handed their boss a heavy bag from what would become the largest cement plant in the world.[9] But even as he was celebrating, Kaiser was looking ahead.

Ever since Roosevelt had witnessed in person what Kaiser and Six Companies had accomplished at the Boulder Dam, the two men began to grow closer, each realizing just how much they could help one another. Kaiser wanted to amplify his enterprise through government contracts, and his business interests were now more varied than ever. In a series of rapid moves in the latter half of the 1930s, Kaiser entered the cement, magnesium, and sand-and-gravel industries. Nothing that Kaiser did was random. There was always a plan. All the industries he chose produced products he knew would be essential, if not today, then tomorrow. And all the industries he was investing in also required two constants: new jobs and government contracts. With war becoming increasingly imminent as the decade neared its end, Roosevelt recognized that Kaiser was a valuable businessman to keep close at hand.

When Nazi Germany invaded Poland on September 1, 1939, two men who had both been born in 1882, only a hundred miles apart in upstate New York, were each positioned to play a vital role in protecting the interests of the United States. They were on opposite coasts. One was a household name, a politician recognized around the world, the other a businessman still unknown to most Americans. But they were about to learn how much they would need each other to achieve their respective goals.

If the United States got drawn into the fighting, FDR would be forced to create an entirely new wartime economy and to build a wartime workforce from scratch. Henry Kaiser, with all the resources that he controlled, all the experience and contacts he had accumulated, and all the men he employed, was poised to become one of the president's most important allies.

CHAPTER EIGHT

A History Lesson

ROOSEVELT WAS DETERMINED TO NOT REPEAT HISTORY, especially a history he had personally witnessed. World War I caught America off guard and unprepared for overseas fighting—its fleet of 430 cargo and passenger ships was minuscule. It was only when the United States officially entered the war in the spring of 1917 that the nation moved forward with a program called Bridge of Ships. Under the U.S. Shipping Board Emergency Fleet Corporation, American shipyards built 2,316 ships at record speed to carry supplies to troops in Europe. Hog Island, just south of Philadelphia on the Delaware River, became the nub of that emergency effort to build standardized ships as fast as possible. It was the world's largest, most advanced shipyard, with more than 250 buildings, 80 miles of railroad tracks, 50 shipbuilding ways, and 28 berths for outfitting ships. "Hoggies" laid the shipyard's first keel on February 12, 1918.

Six months later, the morning of August 5, President Woodrow Wilson and his new wife, Edith, rode a train to Philadelphia. The day was too steamy for speeches, so a brisk ceremony concluded with the first lady christening Hog Island's inaugural ship in front of sixty thousand onlookers, splashing champagne across the front of her lavender dress. As tens of thousands of shipyard employees looked on, the SS *Quistconck*—named for the Lenape name for the site—slid down its shipway and splashed into the river. A buoyant President Wilson waved his hat in the air along with the crowd's cheers, believing this was the start of something momentous.[1] And for a moment, it was.

At its peak, Hog Island with its 35,000 workers resembled a small city. The shipbuilders laid a new keel every five and a half days, and on May 30, 1919, in celebration of Memorial Day, five ships splashed into the Delaware in forty-eight minutes. Hog Island boosted the nation's morale as it set new standards for innovative shipbuilding, for using creative, assembly line techniques, and for giving new life to America's woeful fleet of Merchant Marine vessels. But any surge of excitement from its early days was short-lived. World War I ended on November 11, 1918, only a few months after Hog Island's work began, rendering the ships that came in the following months and years meaningless in terms of wartime needs. By 1922, Hog Island was closed and dismantled, and its ships were soon obsolete.

Fifteen years later, as Roosevelt began to see storm clouds on the horizon, he grew determined to not make the same mistake as Wilson by waiting until war visited the United States to begin building ships—and tanks, planes, guns, and other military needs. When America entered World War I in 1917, the U.S. Army had just 121,797 enlisted men and 5,791 officers. And they were spread around in places like Cuba, Panama, and Puerto Rico. The Army had only a few hundred planes, and no tanks to speak of, and while the Navy had 300 ships and 60,000 sailors, it was dwarfed by Britain's powerful Royal Navy, which had more than 200,000 sailors and a fleet of the most advanced submarines and warships. The awkwardness of American pilots and soldiers having to fly French and British planes, shoot French and British guns, and drive French and British tanks in the Great War had stuck with Roosevelt. He knew Americans were in no mood to join another war, given how fragile the psyche of his nation was after enduring years of standing in mile-long lines for bread and soup and sleeping in sidewalk shanties. But he desperately wanted to give his people a reason to trust their government again. The best way to do that was to remind them of the kind of miracles America's workers were capable of and what American ingenuity and military might stood for.

On March 4, 1935, he transmitted a speech to Congress with an appeal. The president had grown up collecting beautiful wooden models of ships, and listening to stories of the whaling trade from his family. He went on to serve as assistant secretary of the Navy during World War I. He prided himself as a man of the sea and told Congress it was time America got back into the boatbuilding game.

"The American people want to use American ships," his message said. "Their government owes it to them to make certain that such ships are in keeping with our national pride and national needs."[2]

He listed three reasons to support a strong U.S. Merchant Marine. The first two were pragmatic. Other nations could undercut prices on foreign goods during peacetime, reducing the need for American shippers. And when war erupted elsewhere, while America remained neutral, commerce would be crippled without an adequate Merchant Marine to move goods. Roosevelt's third reason reflected his awareness that peacetime would not last forever. "In the event of a war in which the United States itself might be engaged," he said in a message to Congress, "American flag ships are obviously needed not only for naval auxiliaries, but also for the maintenance of reasonable and necessary commercial intercourse with other nations."[3]

After listening to Roosevelt's plea for a modernized Merchant Marine, Congress had taken his words to heart and passed the Merchant Marine Act of 1936, the first step toward replacing the vintage Hog Island vessels from the early 1920s with five hundred modern merchant cargo ships. If Roosevelt's worst fears were ever to be realized, his nation would at least be better prepared than it was for the last war. His challenge now was to deliver America another miracle, another Boulder Dam—and not another Hog Island.

CHAPTER NINE

Henry the Shipbuilder

ONCE HE HAD FINISHED BUILDING THE BOULDER DAM, Henry Kaiser went in search of an escape from his big-city office headquarters. He wanted a vacation property on the water that was a drivable distance from Oakland. He'd grown up near the Erie Canal and he learned how to boat as a teenager while spending time on small rivers near Utica, New York, later working the tourist boats in Florida to boost his photography business. The more comfortable he got on the water, the more he appreciated the romance of it. He wooed Bess Fosburgh by rowing her in a canoe out into the middle of small lakes and ponds. Later, as a young father, he and his sons tinkered with the engines on their small powerboats to keep them running. So when he searched for a retreat, one of the first places to catch his eye was Lake Tahoe.[1] Peaceful and private, and only two hundred miles from Oakland, everything about it reminded him of his rural East Coast upbringing. He discovered a fifteen-acre tract of lakefront property with a stream running through it, and even though neighbors saw it as an undevelopable parcel, Kaiser knew better.

"Kaiser bought the land on Saturday, had power shovels, dump trucks, and bulldozers at work on Sunday, was draining the land and dredging a speedboat harbor by Monday, had an architect down from Portland, Oregon, on Tuesday, began building a lodge, boathouse, and four stone cottages by Wednesday, with a crew of 100 men at work," the *Saturday Evening Post* reported later. His neighbors tried to stop him, because the noise was so loud at night, but before their injunction went anywhere, he was done—in twenty-eight days. He named his estate Fleur du Lac, "Flower of the Lake" in French.

As fascinated as Kaiser was throughout his life with boats and with the water, the idea of getting into the business of building ships was not in his plans in the early 1930s. His growing company was focused on dams and roads and bridges. When he was asked years later about his initial interest in the shipbuilding business, he admitted, "I had never seen a ship launched."[2] The war in Europe changed his thinking.

Toward the end of 1939, Kaiser's Permanente Cement plant was so productive that he had an excess of cement that he wanted to sell on the open market. Meanwhile, the Navy, leery that it was only a matter of time before America was drawn into the war in Europe, moved to strengthen its West Coast and Pacific island defense operations with new naval bases and more modern warships. Cement was an essential ingredient for that expansion. With a new government contract in hand, Kaiser needed to bring his materials to Navy stations in the Pacific, particularly to Honolulu, which the Navy worried could be vulnerable to attack from the Japanese. He bought two old ships, the *Anton* and the *Cristobal*, to move cement in bulk amounts by using compressed air to blow it into and out of the ship, something never done before. But in order for the ships to be retrofitted for the work, they were brought up to Seattle's Puget Sound, where a repair yard for a New York–based operation called Todd Shipyards, under its new president, John Reilly, could help.[3]

Kaiser's cement business was becoming one of his defining achievements, not only because it turned a handsome profit before taxes of more than $1 million a year, but because his timing could not have been better. "The importance of the cement plant to the Six Companies goes far beyond its being merely a profitable addition to their portfolios," *Fortune* magazine wrote in 1943 in retelling Kaiser's story.[4] The magazine quoted one western railroad man and friend of Kaiser, who said, "If Kaiser's life can be said to have a turning point, it was then. He licked a tough bunch. From that time on, he wasn't afraid to tackle anything."[5]

The marriage between Kaiser's cement business and Reilly's ship repair operation set in motion a series of introductions, meetings, relationships, and partnerships that pushed open the door for Kaiser to enter a world he knew nothing about—shipbuilding.

TODD SHIPYARDS HAD been around since 1916, and after building ships during World War I, it turned its focus to repair work and refitting old ships throughout the 1920s and 1930s to stay in business during the economic downturn. Toward the end of the 1930s, Reilly began thinking about bringing his business back into shipbuilding. He was introduced to Kaiser, a man who not only shared his interest in exploring new industries but also brought with him a bounty of resources and workers and government connections. The two men were hardly an ideal match—Kaiser was a loyal, married husband and father who preferred a quiet, conservative lifestyle; Reilly enjoyed flaunting his success, traveling by private railroad coach and often with a young mistress in tow. But in business, they found common ground.[6]

They started small by forming the Seattle-Tacoma Shipbuilding Corporation. Kaiser and Six Companies would supply the cement, gravel, sand, and workers to build their shipyards; Reilly and Todd Shipbuilding would handle the rest. With Kaiser more of an invisible partner, they quickly landed a $9 million contract to build five C-1 cargo ships for Jerry Land's Maritime Commission.

IN THE FALL of 1940, Alden Roach, the president of one of America's biggest steel corporations, was in Washington, D.C., meeting with Admiral Vickery. Roosevelt had been demanding his country increase its shipbuilding capacity, prompting Vickery, in an off-handed moment, to ask his visitor from

Consolidated Steel Corporation if he knew of any West Coast operations that might be interested in building ships. East Coast shipbuilders were at capacity and Vickery wondered if he should be looking across the country. As luck would have it, Roach had bumped into one of the Six Companies partners the night before at the Shoreham Hotel, and he told Vickery he might know just the right company for the work. The following day, Roach played matchmaker, introducing Vickery to several of the Six Companies partners in town. "Next thing I knew," Roach recalled, "they were right in the middle of the shipbuilding business."[7] Up to that point, Vickery had never heard of Six Companies. He also didn't know Kaiser, despite being in business with him on the C-1 ships, because Reilly, as the shipbuilder, had handled all of the contract details. But the more Vickery learned how Todd was intertwined with the much larger Six Companies conglomerate, and the more he shared with his boss, Jerry Land, the two men realized that this Six Companies gang might solve all of their problems. At the center of it all was Kaiser—a partner with Todd Shipyards and a partner in Six Companies.

WHEN THE BRITISH Merchant Shipbuilding Mission finally met with Kaiser and his Six Companies partners in the fall of 1940 about building sixty cargo ships, it seemed like a poor match. The British were interested in the Seattle-Tacoma Shipyard building their ships, but the shipyard wasn't big enough and it was already falling behind on its C-1 ship order, so there was no way it could take on the additional work. When Cyril Thompson learned that news, the two sides pivoted to a new approach, realizing it was too much work to ask of a single shipyard. Rather than commit to building all sixty ships at one shipyard on the West Coast, a compromise was needed. Thirty ships would be built on the West Coast, and the other thirty ships on the East Coast, with a partner that Reilly would find. This was an important approach to Thompson, and it was just as important to Jerry Land, who held final approval over any agreement between the two countries.

Because so much of the American shipbuilding effort was based on the East Coast, Land wanted to avoid too much competition for labor, steel, and coal-fired steam engines with the existing shipyards by ensuring that some of the British ships would be built far away, on the opposite coast. At the same time, he worried about antagonizing the long-standing East Coast shipbuilders if he didn't give them some of the British business and sent it all out west. Splitting the work up solved his dilemma.

The arrangement suited Kaiser just fine as well, except for one problem. If the West Coast ships weren't going to be built at Seattle-Tacoma, where he and Reilly had all their operations and shipbuilding resources established, where would they be built? Kaiser went searching for land, and when he found eighty acres near his office in Oakland, a barren mudflat on the waterfront at the Port of Richmond, California, across the bay from San Francisco, he snatched them up.

ON NOVEMBER 5, 1940, hours before polls would open on Election Day, the Admiralty petitioned Great Britain's War Cabinet for more money to deliver to the British Merchant Shipbuilding Mission, stating that every day without a deal for new ships was a day closer to Britain's demise. "In view of the abnormally heavy losses our shipping has recently suffered, all 60 vessels should be ordered at the earliest possible date," Admiralty officials said in their petition.[8] The War Cabinet approved the additional funds two days later, and when Thompson got the word back in Washington, he wasted no time firing up the DC-3 propellers. The group took back to the air for one more visit out west.

On the day they landed, a cold, wet wind was blowing across the barren mudflats of Richmond, California. There wasn't much of anything to see. Kaiser, who had already displayed his flair for theatrics in his dark office weeks earlier in Seattle, brought Thompson and the rest of the mission here for one more show. He had promised them ships. Right now, all he could offer them was his word.

"But where are your shipyards?"[9] Thompson asked Kaiser as they looked out at the land. Surely, he thought, they had not flown all this way just to see acres and acres of a windswept mudflat. There had to be more. As they stood there shivering, the British men wondered if this was all a giant mistake.

"There are our shipyards," Kaiser said, waving his hand out at the mudflats. "It's true you see nothing but mud now, but within months this vast space will have a shipyard on it with thousands of men and women building the ships for you. This is an ideal place."

Henry Kaiser had never built a ship before. He didn't own a single shipyard. And now he was waving a magic wand. Thompson panicked. He had come to America to find a shipbuilder, and the money he had been allocated to spend was for ships. It had not occurred to him, or to the Admiralty for that matter, that they might also have to pay for new shipyards to be built first before any shipbuilding got underway. But Thompson's time was running out. And so were his options.

For the West Coast shipbuilding, the two sides agreed on the Todd-California Shipbuilding Corporation, which would start immediately on constructing a seven-way shipyard on San Francisco Bay, in the small city of Richmond, where Kaiser had asked Thompson to trust him. None of his Six Companies partners objected when Kaiser said he would run the Richmond shipyard. His reasoning was sound. The Grand Coulee dam project was nearly done, meaning 6,000 of his workers who were experienced in using heavy machinery and loading heavy materials were about to be looking for their next assignment.

Just as the deal was being finalized, Cyril Thompson received an alarming cable from the Admiralty, instructing him to change the size of all the ships being considered for construction, with most of the alterations calling for slightly shorter and wider hulls.

"Oh, hell!" Thompson thought.[10]

It wasn't serious enough to endanger his efforts. But he had to spend the next few days modifying the drawings and specifications, even though he had no idea why. Fortunately, the changes were easy and did not impact the timetable. There was one last step—finding a partner to handle the East Coast shipbuilding.

CHAPTER TEN

A Clambake Seals the Deal

WITH THE BRITISH MISSION'S CONTRACT SO CLOSE TO BEING finalized, a group of more than two hundred officials headed north from Washington to New England. Representatives from the State Department, the Navy, the Maritime Commission, Todd Shipbuilding, and the British Merchant Shipbuilding Mission landed in Portland, Maine, and made their way to the state's rocky coastline. William S. Newell, or "Mr. Pete"[1] to anybody who knew him, owned Bath Iron Works. He was legend in the industry, and John Reilly knew that if he ever had a chance to work with Newell, he would grab it.

Newell, a salty seaman with a knack for salesmanship, was born in Albany, New York, and graduated from the Massachusetts Institute of Technology. He grew up around ships, working in the engine rooms of passenger ships and becoming a yard manager in Bath, Maine, during the shipbuilding boom of World War I. When Bath became a ghost town after the war, described by one historian as "defunct, stripped, and decaying,"[2] he moved south to stay in shipbuilding, but he hankered to get back to Maine even though the old Bath Iron Works had been knocked down. He took his chance when he noticed how many millionaires in the late 1920s were demanding to have their own private yachts to compete in the America's Cup races off the coast of Newport, Rhode Island.

Pulling some strings back home in Bath, he secured a bank loan of $100,000, threw in a few bucks of his own, and bought four shipways and some cranes.[3] It didn't take much convincing from Newell, a local son, to lure some of Maine's best shipfitters, caulkers, and riveters away from their lobster pots and hot dog stands to go back into shipbuilding. And before long, Bath Iron Works was back in the boat business, with plenty of contracts for 150-foot private yachts from Brookline, Massachusetts, and Glen Cove, Long Island. That work led to a Navy contract to build destroyers, and soon Newell had accumulated enough shipways to build eleven ships at once, and its reputation as a productive, quality shipbuilding city was restored. Bath Iron Works' payroll rocketed from 800 in 1932 to more than 4,000 by 1940. Bath, Maine, was all the way back thanks to Pete Newell.

One of the secrets to his company's survival was the loyalty of his employees. Newell used his nearly photographic memory to recall every worker's name, family story, and any troubles they were struggling with. Despite his wealth and position, he managed to come across as caring rather than condescending or paternalistic. He organized an annual picnic for employees and their families, and everybody had a ball trying their hand at skeet shooting and three-legged races while chowing down on lavish boxed dinners of fried chicken, lobster, pickles, boiled eggs, chips, and coffee. Newell took pride in creating a family-first company and listened closely when gripes surfaced. When a hundred welders on the overnight shift walked off their job to protest the demotions of three colleagues and the suspension of a fourth for repeated absenteeism, management agreed that their punishments were overly harsh and the walkout was over in a matter of hours.

When it came to shipbuilding, though, Newell was all business. As the tensions in Europe were heating up, he sensed an opportunity was looming for him. "I'll build anything," he was prone to saying. One day in 1938, he had wandered into the New York City offices of Gibbs & Cox, a prominent ship design firm responsible for a number of the Navy destroyers that Bath had built. Newell didn't have an agenda when he walked in, but he spotted a large easel with a drawing covered by a veil and his curiosity got the best of him. He was told it was a secret.[4]

"Look here," he snapped, "I own a chunk of this place. Let's see it."

The cloth came down and Newell let out a lengthy whistle as he eyed a drawing of an 80,000-ton monster warship, the largest he had ever seen. She was a centaur of a vessel—part aircraft carrier, part battleship, armed to the teeth, and designed to ward off the heaviest aerial bombardment. Except it wasn't built for American defense. The Soviet government had requested it. Newell's first reaction was wonder. His second reaction was interest.

"Why, there's not a yard in the country can handle that order," he said. "You couldn't find a spot to build her in."[5]

But he teased the designers by saying he knew of the perfect place a ship of that size could come together. He called for an office boy and fetched him to run down to a marine supply store and get him a map of Portland Harbor. When the boy returned, Newell pointed to the South Portland coast, about fifty miles south of his Bath shipyard. He noted there was no shipyard there. The undeveloped shoreline was ideal for this type of work.

Even though he had not secured a contract, Newell was so infatuated with his own idea, he went back to Maine, managed to secure an option on the stretch of coastland for $500, and set to work on surveying the area and drilling down into the rock. To his surprise and pleasure, he found that twenty feet down was a solid foundation on which to build.

"I didn't tell anybody what I was doing," Newell said later. "Not even my wife. If she'd known I was spending all that money she'd have been after me."[6]

The Russian ship never happened. But Newell knew it was only a matter of time. Back in Maine, he spent his days sitting at his rolltop desk, a hat always covering his bald head, because he knew that one day that land would come in handy for him.

THAT MOMENT CAME in late 1940, when a sharp-dressed group of men from the State Department, the Navy, the U.S. Maritime Commission, Todd Shipyards, and some British gents showed up on his doorstep. Reilly thought

Newell could be the ideal partner on the East Coast and when he had first reached out to him about taking on a cargo ship contract for the British, Newell, even though he was buried in Navy destroyer construction, didn't blink. He got hold of an aerial photograph of Cushing Point in the waters just off South Portland and sketched out a layout for a shipyard and sent it to Jerry Land at the Maritime Commission.[7] Apparently it was a good sketch, because the next thing he knew he was hosting a group of dignitaries. He took his visitors to the spot he had chosen for a shipyard, and Newell spared no hyperbole: "God made this place for a shipyard ten million years ago," he said, "but he didn't tell anybody about it."[8]

For all of its beauty, the Maine location was nothing like the Richmond site. Richmond's ground was softer; a shipyard could easily be erected there on piles drilled into the ground in no time. Portland's site was a rock foundation, and Thompson and Newell agreed it would require much more civil engineering to get it ready than Kaiser's land in Richmond. They decided the Maine shipyard would have to be a series of shallow drydocks or basins so ships could be built at or below sea level, and then launched safely into the Kennebec River, which fed into the Atlantic.

Newell's enthusiasm as he led the group along thirty miles of Maine coast was impossible to resist, and completely opposite of the way Kaiser chased after the British. Kaiser went straight for the jugular—a mysterious office meeting, braggadocio, a huge offer, take it or leave it. Newell preferred a charm offensive, starting with a beautiful tour before taking his visitors back to his house in the evening for a New England clambake. It sealed the deal for Thompson.

"A super salesman as he is a super shipbuilder, Pete, with nothing more to show than a map, and a mudflat, and an idea, had secured himself a $50,000,000 contract!" a Maine historian and artist, Herbert G. Jones, wrote in describing Newell's effort. "Plus, the gastronomic joys of a real old-fashioned Down East clambake!"[9]

The bicoastal deal allowed the Maritime Commission and Jerry Land to revitalize two historic shipbuilding districts on opposite coasts, one on San Francisco Bay that was far away from likely attacks by the Germans, and the other in Maine, from which ships could quickly be launched straight into the Atlantic where they were needed the most. Each new shipyard would have seven bays for building and launching ships. It was a safe compromise in the event of an attack, ensuring that if one shipyard was lost, the other could continue on with the work.

LAND OUTLINED THE plan in a memorandum to President Roosevelt that he called "Proposed British Shipbuilding in the United States."[10] He told the president about the British Merchant Shipbuilding Mission, which had arrived in America two months earlier with about 10 million pounds to spend on a contract for British ships to be built in the United States. Land explained that he met with the British members and suggested they survey shipbuilders across the country for interest. He told Roosevelt the ships would have 2,500 horsepower and be capable of at least 10 knots on the ocean. The first ship would be delivered in eleven months, and the project called for one hundred ships per year after that.

"Type A ship is what I could call an emergency production type with a five-year life," Land wrote.[11]

He explained that the British started out with four preferred locations: Portland, Oregon, and Richmond, California, on the West Coast; Portland, Maine, on the East Coast; and Mobile, Alabama, on the Gulf Coast. Mobile, Land wrote to the president, was dismissed immediately as an option because it was too critical to the Navy for repair and new construction work being done. Last, he told Roosevelt that the project "was doomed to very unsatisfactory results" unless it had the backing of "American shipbuilding brains and some American capital." This was, he wrote, largely a shipbuilding assembly effort between American businesses and the British government.

Following a three-hour meeting on December 19, 1940, with his cabinet in Washington, President Roosevelt approved the arrangement. For a president hell-bent on creating jobs, the deal that Land brought to him would become a point of pride, as it resurrected two great American shipbuilding spots—San

Francisco Bay and Portland, Maine. The next day, at the 1 Broadway office of Todd Shipyards Corporation, John Reilly signed the shipbuilding contract, along with Powell and Hunter from the British commission.

Work on their respective shipyards was to begin immediately, and the contract estimated at least 5,000 new shipyard workers would be hired. The contract stated each ship would cost $1,600,000 to build, be 416 feet long, 57 feet in the beam, and capable of carrying 10,000 deadweight tons.

With a few pen strokes, two new companies were formed—Todd Bath Iron Shipbuilding Corporation, headed by Newell, to build and manage the shipyard in Portland, Maine, and the Todd-California Shipbuilding Corporation, under John Reilly, to do the same in Richmond, California.[12]

"It was said to be the largest ship order ever placed here when this country was not at war and marked the first time since the World War that ships for the British government had been ordered built in the United States," the *New York Times* reported. "An important feature of the contract is the fact that it will in no way interfere with other shipbuilding in the United States."[13]

Reilly and Newell would oversee their respective operations in California and Maine; they were happily expanding their businesses. But Henry Kaiser, nearing sixty years old, sensed this was just the beginning of his next chapter. From roads and bridges and dams, he had gone into the concrete business. And concrete paved a path for him to get into shipbuilding. He saw what was happening in Europe in late 1940. War was coming to America—that seemed inevitable—and Kaiser believed that when it did, the only thing that would decide if the U.S. remained standing was how quickly America's builders turned out ships, planes, tanks, and bullets. His multipronged operation of steel, sand, concrete, and magnesium, along with his thousands of employees, his land in Richmond, and his connections to private industry and now the Maritime Commission, were going to leave him in a position that any contractor would envy in the event of war.

"There is no such thing as work," Kaiser liked to say, through his bright brown eyes. "There are only occupations. There are two kinds of occupations—depressing occupations and stimulating occupations."[14]

It did not matter to Kaiser that he knew so little about ships and shipbuilding. It didn't matter that even as he was about to take on the most serious work of his career, he was juggling so many side projects it was hard to imagine how he could possibly handle construction of wartime merchant ships. Shipbuilding, he once said, was "just another branch of the construction business."

Kaiser had never built a ship in his life. Or an airplane. Or a car. And he wasn't an inventor or an entrepreneur. He wasn't Henry Ford. He admitted that himself when he said, "Call me a builder." He relied on government contracts for his work. Self-rigging engines onto ten-foot skiffs, which he did as a young man, was not going to help him build steel cargo ships, which is why *Fortune* magazine, having taken notice of Kaiser and begun covering his increased role in the reshaping of American roads and rivers and now ships, struck a note of worry in its profile of him.

"Whether Kaiser and his coterie of dam builders have bitten off more than they can chew remains to be seen," the magazine wrote.[15]

Kaiser ignored the noise. He and his partners had built the Boulder Dam to tame the mighty Colorado River, the largest dam built at the time. And then the Bonneville and Grand Coulee dams along the Columbia River proved to be even harder challenges that required enormous crews to work in remote regions and design innovative solutions to never-before-seen obstacles. To Kaiser, building thirty ships in a populated area with abundant resources all around him and design plans handed to him seemed like a breeze. To sneers, he called the bow of a ship "the front end" not because he didn't know the terminology, but to reinforce his core belief that you don't have to be an expert in something in order to do a job properly. You need to hire the right people, give them the right tools, and deliver them the proper training. Then it becomes just another construction job, no different from building a road, a dam, or a bridge.

THE CONTRACT HAD barely been signed when Kaiser picked up the telephone and dialed Corpus Christi, Texas. His head of construction, Clay

Bedford, was busy building a naval air station there. Over six months, Bedford had accumulated a team of 8,000 workers and completed $80 million of work. It wasn't finished, but for Kaiser it was close enough that he felt confident in handing it off to another supervisor. Bedford had joined Kaiser's company in 1925, just a year out of college. His father was an engineer who worked for the state of California inspecting projects. Bedford grew up riding around with his father and visiting big jobs, which is how he first learned about which employers to avoid and which ones to pursue.

"My father was the one who told me, 'If you want to be a contractor, I only know one honest one, and that's Henry Kaiser.'"[16]

And so Bedford followed his father's path. After graduating from Rensselaer Polytechnic Institute in 1924, he landed a junior role with Kaiser. Bedford was only twenty-five years old when he went to Cuba as a young field engineer to build two hundred miles of complicated road there under dire conditions, but he never showed a hint of fear or doubt and instead he grew into becoming the project's general manager and saw it through to the end. By the time 1940 rolled around, Bedford had more than fifteen years of experience under Kaiser, which is why he was not the least bit surprised to get the call from his boss while he was working in Corpus Christi, Texas. Clay Bedford had been there for Kaiser, always.

Fifteen years after he first interviewed for a job with Kaiser, Bedford now was a seasoned thirty-seven years old. He knew Kaiser well enough to tell when he was joking, and when he was being serious. When he got Kaiser's call in late December 1940, there was no doubt in his mind about the gravity of the message. Bedford, who was born in northern Texas, also knew nothing about ships. Kaiser didn't care. Bedford had vast experience in driving piles into the ground, in moving mountain-sized piles of dirt, and keeping a labor force on task and on budget until a job was done.

"Clay? This is Henry," Kaiser said. "We've got thirty ships to build at Richmond for the British. You'd better get up there and do it."[17]

CHAPTER ELEVEN

Arsenal of Democracy

ON OCTOBER 29, 1940, WHILE THE BRITISH MERCHANT SHIP-building Mission was quietly flying around the country in search of shipyards, Secretary of War Henry Stimson stood surrounded by a phalanx of powerful men, including President Roosevelt, at the War Department's auditorium. Sixteen million men had been registered for the draft as required by an act of Congress. And now a glass fishbowl held their fate.[1] It sat on the table in front of Stimson, and a roomful of grim faces stared back at him from the chairs filling the room.

Election Day was less than a week away and Roosevelt feared not for his own future as much as for the nation's. Hitler was threatening to invade Britain every day. British shipbuilders couldn't keep up with their losses at sea, while American shipbuilders were busy focusing on ramping up their own production. With his race against Wendell Willkie tightening, Roosevelt viewed the events of this day, America's first peacetime draft, as a necessary step for the country, even as he knew it could spell the end of his presidency.

At the start of the war in Europe, Americans were divided because there was growing uncertainty about whether Britain could keep the Nazis at bay.

Those who preferred generosity called themselves "all outers" and supported doing whatever was necessary to support Britain, win or lose against Germany. Those who leaned toward selfishness were the "not-quite outers," more resistant to transforming the American economy to support Britain.

But then over the summer of 1940, a slow shift began in the country from favoring isolationism to favoring a fight. From July into August, polls increasingly showed seven in ten Americans favoring a draft. For those in the minority, they did whatever they could to try to scare certain politicians to support an isolationist position. An organization calling itself the Congress of American Mothers visited Washington. Its members stood outside the offices of politicians dressed in black and veils as symbols of sons, brothers, and husbands lost to war.[2] They kneeled and they cried and they even chased congressmen down hallways, yelling and spitting at them. When Florida senator Claude Pepper learned a mannequin of him had been lynched from an oak tree near the capitol, he shrugged it off as a demonstration "of what we are all trying to preserve—freedom of speech and freedom of action."[3]

Their efforts failed. On September 16, Congress approved the Selective Service Act, immediately registering men between the ages of twenty-one and thirty-five. And six weeks after that, Stimson, in a crisp black suit, allowed a yellow blindfold to be wrapped around his head before he reached inside the bowl with his left hand to begin the draft process. The bowl was filled with tiny blue capsules, each one having a slip of paper inside. The papers had a number that was attached to a name on a list. He pulled out the first number and handed it to Roosevelt, standing by his side. More than 6,000 men who had been assigned the number that Roosevelt held in his hand would become the first men to serve. Roosevelt had no idea if he would be the president to send these boys off to war, or if it would fall to Willkie, but his duty was to simply read the number aloud and so, after a tense moment of silence, he did.

"The first number is one fifty-eight," Roosevelt said into a cluster of microphones that carried his voice on to radio networks and into living rooms around the country.[4]

A gasp erupted in the room. A dark-eyed, dark-haired woman, with tears forming, identified herself as Mrs. Henry S. Bell. She stepped forward and said her son, Harry Robert Bell, was one of the holders of No. 158.

"I could hardly believe it at first," Mrs. Bell said to the reporters who engulfed her. "I'm very proud."

By the time they finished, Stimson and Roosevelt had pulled out enough blue capsules to ensure that more than one million men would enlist.

ONE WEEK LATER, Roosevelt was reelected easily to an unprecedented third term, winning 38 of 48 states. The celebration was brief. German submarines continued to torpedo and sink British naval and merchant vessels, and they seized control of the shipping lanes in the Atlantic Ocean, choking off the flow of resources from the United States to Europe. On the same day that Americans voted to return him to the White House, the radio waves and the front pages of their newspapers were filled with all-too familiar stories.

"2 Liner-Cruisers Sunk by a U-boat," the New York Times reported. In fact, three British ships were sunk by a single German submarine, and five other ships, including a British destroyer and a 19,000-ton merchantman cargo ship, were badly damaged by German fighter bombers.

But those were British ships and British seamen, making those headlines easy for Americans to gloss over. News film footage from overseas had shown French and British troops being evacuated from the beaches of Dunkirk, bombs falling across London, and German soldiers on motorcycles riding down the middle of an empty Champs-Elysées, and slowly it became clearer that direct involvement was a very real possibility. Even still, the events in Europe were easy to ignore, and ordinary traditions that provided security and comfort in everyday life carried on as if the possibility of war for the United States remained a remote possibility, at best.

ON THE SATURDAY after Thanksgiving in 1940, a brisk, windy afternoon, Franklin Field in Philadelphia filled with 100,000 people who'd come to take in the annual Army-Navy Game, a tradition that began fifty years earlier. Millions more huddled around radios in their living rooms to listen to the game, even if they had never attended Annapolis or West Point. Though Americans were reluctant to admit it, there was a nervous energy to the game knowing that war was on the horizon and that if it came to pass, the players on the field, and even some of their coaches, would be called off to fight. And some of the fans in the stadium would be called to lead.

General George C. Marshall was there, sitting with the Army fans.[5] A combat veteran of World War I, he was Army chief of staff. Chester W. Nimitz was there, with the Navy fans, not knowing that in less than a year he'd be fighting the Japanese in the Philippines and directing the naval war as Admiral of the Pacific Fleet. Jerry Land was there too. He'd never missed a game in forty years as a fan, after his own heroics playing in the 1900 matchup. Navy celebrated the fiftieth anniversary of the first game by beating Army 14–0. But the excitement from the game was short-lived.

THREE WEEKS LATER, on Saturday, December 21, an unarmed tanker carrying an American crew of forty-two merchant seamen and owned by the Panama Transport Company, a subsidiary of Standard Oil Company of New Jersey, went down in the Atlantic off the coast of West Africa after leaving Aruba with five million gallons of oil. Even though two previous ships of the Panama company had been sunk by German torpedoes, the SS *Charles Pratt* was the first one carrying an American crew, and the first to report that two American crew members had been lost. The *Pratt* had been one of seventeen Standard Oil vessels transferred to Panama by President Roosevelt to allow it to maneuver in war-zone waters without fear of attack by U-boats.[6]

But even flying the neutral Panama flag and painting the Panamanian flag on both sides of her hull proved useless for the American crew. The German sub,

U-68, fired one torpedo into the *Pratt*'s starboard in broad daylight, showering oil and debris clear up to its mast and over the boat, lighting the ship on fire and forcing a cry of "abandon ship" from the captain.

The war in Europe had been raging for more than a year, and the Neutrality Act gave Americans some measure of comfort from the battles overseas, but slowly they were beginning to accept that it was only a matter of time before a German torpedo took aim on one of their ships, flying the Stars and Stripes. And what then? The sinking of the *Charles Pratt* made that question impossible to ignore any longer. America was not at war. But Arthur Duffy of Bayonne, New Jersey, and Patrick Dougherty of Philadelphia were both dead, blown overboard and drowned when a Nazi torpedo tore a hole in their ship. Americans were forced to wonder—if that wasn't an act of war against America, what was?

SHORTLY BEFORE NINE o'clock in the evening on December 29, wearing a gray wool suit, the president wheeled himself through the labyrinth of hallways on the first floor of the White House until he reached the Diplomatic Reception Room, from where he would deliver his sixteenth fireside chat. His closest staff was there, along with his mother and a few notable celebrities, including the actors Clark Gable and Carole Lombard.[7]

Roosevelt carried a grim face into the room with him. His mood matched the nation's. Americans were mourning the death a few days earlier of F. Scott Fitzgerald, the novelist whose writings, in particular *The Great Gatsby*, stood as symbols of the Roaring Twenties and the Jazz Age. On the same day of his death came the attack on the *Pratt*, which had left the president fuming. Hitler's planes were raining bombs on London with ferocity on the same evening as Roosevelt's speech—it would be the worst night of the war since the Battle of Britain had begun.

He had heard the questions from politicians and the press. How much longer could the United States stand by and watch as its closest ally suffered so many losses? He was already helping Britain build cargo ships, but was that enough?

Was it time to send Churchill American-made military bombers, tanks, and guns to defeat Germany? Was neutrality feasible any longer?

"My friends," he began, "this is not a fireside chat on war. It is a talk on national security; because the nub of the whole purpose of your President is to keep you, now, and your children later, and your grandchildren much later, out of a last-ditch war for the preservation of American independence and all the things that American independence means to you and to me and to ours."[8]

He was frustrated with Americans' ongoing apathy. One telegram he had received spoke to that. It begged him to not worry citizens with more talk about how easy it would be for American cities to be bombed and taken over by a hostile power. The message Roosevelt took away from the telegram was "Please, Mr. President, don't frighten us by telling us the truth." He did not see any other way.

"Frankly and definitely there is danger ahead—danger against which we must prepare," he said. "But we well know that we cannot escape danger, or the fear of danger, by crawling into bed and pulling the covers over our heads."

He explained the specific steps he was taking to increase the production of munitions through a coordinated defense effort and he referenced the ship-building contract that had been signed just nine days earlier.

"Guns, planes, ships, and many other things have to be built in the factories and the arsenals of America. They have to be produced by workers and managers and engineers with the aid of machines which in turn have to be built by hundreds of thousands of workers throughout the land. . . . But all our present efforts are not enough. We must have more ships, more guns, more planes—more of everything. And this can be accomplished only if we discard the notion of business as usual."

Nodding to history, he said not since Jamestown and Plymouth Rock had American civilization been in such grave danger. America's allies in Great Britain, he assured his citizens, were not looking for handouts, or for America to fight their war for them, but merely to help arm their troops for battle. More than a thousand British and American merchant ships had been sunk in the first year of the war. "They ask us for the implements of war, the planes, the tanks, the guns, the freighters, which will enable them to fight for their liberty and for our security." And Americans had stepped up, he said with pride. Those who manufactured sewing machines and lawn mowers were now building shells, tanks, and fuses. But it wasn't enough.[9]

"We must be the great arsenal of democracy," the president said, sending the phrase that would define his wartime presidency into approximately 17 million living rooms around the country.

Around the country at that moment, clothing for an army of 1.4 million men was already being stitched. Meanwhile, 17,000 heavy guns, 9,200 tanks, 130,000 engines, 380 Navy ships, and 50,000 planes were either under contract or under construction. The creation of his arsenal was well underway. But building it was only half the battle.[10]

If that rapidly growing armament ever needed to be carried from America's shores across oceans in a time of war, how would it be moved? Planes were fast, but not big enough. Trains were useless. And even four years after the Merchant Marine Act of 1936, the nation's fleet of cargo ships was still a dilapidated mess, nowhere near up to the task of war. And embarrassingly, some ships were diverted to Europe, where they were needed to bring home stubborn Americans who had ignored the State Department's advice to leave while it was still safe to go. All of this left Jerry Land's Maritime Commission with an empty cupboard at the worst possible moment. There was only one solution—America was going to need a flotilla of new cargo ships. Fast.

Two days after Roosevelt's radio address, as 1940 gave way to 1941, Hitler delivered a message of his own, no doubt determined to drown out the strong words of the American president who had insisted to the world that "the Axis powers are not going to win this war." Not only was Germany going to win the war that it started in 1939, Hitler said, it was going to win it in the coming months. "The year 1941," Hitler said in his New Year's proclamation, "will bring consummation of the greatest victory of our history."[11]

The dueling messages from the two leaders left no doubt that, one way or the other, the new year was going to reshape the course of world history. "For us this is an emergency as serious as war itself," Roosevelt had told his people.

A few days after the president's fireside chat, Jerry Land arrived at the White House to visit his boss. He did not come empty-handed. The director of the Maritime Commission spread out a series of blueprints across the president's desk.

PART III

Designs and Decisions

CHAPTER TWELVE

"Ugly Ducklings"

JERRY LAND RARELY DISAGREED WITH ROOSEVELT. HE ONCE said his duty was "to obey my commander-in-chief or get the hell out. I don't make policies. I take orders."[1]

But Land, a career naval officer with a notoriously profane mouth, also had a hard time staying quiet. The drawings he laid out for the president were for a slightly modified version of the same cargo ship that the British intended to build at the American shipyards. Roosevelt was ready to rush into an emergency shipbuilding program, and Land believed it was premature. Just because the British were about to build a fleet of hulking, slow, old-fashioned cargo ships powered by sluggish reciprocating engines did not mean the United States had to do the same. One of those countries was fighting for its survival, the other was still on the sidelines. And Land did not want to build cheap ships that might last barely half a decade before crumbling into the sea. He wanted fast ships, with modern turbine engines, that would survive a generation and make America's merchant ship fleet the envy of the world.

"We were still not in the war," Land recalled.[2]

In his eyes, the U.S. Merchant Marine was in an embryonic stage. His Maritime Commission was devoting its energies to building more traditional cargo ships that would have a life of twenty years or longer. Construction of those ships, however, was being delayed by other Navy priorities, mainly the position that combat ships like destroyers, aircraft carriers, and battleships had to come before unarmed merchant cargo vessels. It infuriated Land so much that, in a rare moment of defiance, he took a tone with Roosevelt few men would have been comfortable taking.

"Mr. President, your Navy and my Navy is trying to rape and ruin our Merchant Marine," Land wrote to the president.[3]

Land believed that if the government's priorities could be adjusted, his Maritime Commission could get on with its business of building sturdier cargo ships that would give Roosevelt what he wanted—the world's best Merchant Marine with a fleet of ships that would last for decades. He saw no reason to settle for a subpar vessel that might not survive the 1940s. At the bottom of a second typewritten memo to the president, Land, with the mistake of Hog Island on his mind, took the time to write a personal note in shorthand to be sure that his point could not be missed.

"The last thing I want to do," Land wrote, "is to repeat the mistakes of the last war and have a lot of obsolete vessels on our hands, unless the emergency is so great as to make this an absolute necessity."[4]

As the two men looked down at the blueprints Land had laid out, in Roosevelt's mind, this was just such an "absolute necessity." He convinced his reluctant admiral that there was a time and place for building the sturdiest and prettiest ships, just as there was a time and place for building ships fast and efficiently with no regard for appearances or aesthetics. Land knew that as much as this decision pained himself, it must have been even harder for his sea-loving president. After staring at the blueprints for a new type of cargo ship, Roosevelt came to a profile sheet of the vessel and stared at it. He backed away from the table and offered his opinion.

"Admiral, I think this ship will do us very well," Roosevelt said. "She'll carry a good load. She isn't much to look at, though, is she? A real ugly duckling."[5]

It was hardly a ringing endorsement from the commander in chief. But he was satisfied. And while it was unintentional, his lighthearted description of the ship to Land gave the press something to run with—and run they would. A few days later *Time* magazine wrote, "These ugly ducklings would help solve the shipping shortage at war's end, said the President. What he did not say was that they could also be of great help to Britain in replacing ships lost to Nazi submarines."[6]

Most of the early drawings for the British ships were being drafted in Great Britain and then flown to the United States, a time-consuming and burdensome process because of how rough the early sketches were and because the British simply produced far fewer detailed drawings than the Americans were used to. "Design details, often left out in Britain, where they were taken for granted, had to be incorporated in the blueprints in the U.S.," Thompson recalled later.[7]

If the president wanted his own version of the British ship for his emergency shipbuilding program, there was no time to start from nothing and design an American cargo ship. That would take months. Roosevelt and Land both knew their only option was to take the rough British drawings, make whatever important modifications were necessary to satisfy their own wishes and needs, and get going. If the design was good enough for Churchill, Roosevelt assumed it could be good enough for him.

THE PROFILE DRAWING of the ship that Land showed him was so basic and lacking in detail it looked like it could have been sketched by a child armed with a pencil and a ruler. Bow to stern, it stretched 441 feet and 5 inches, and at its widest point across it spanned 59 feet 10 1/2 inches. Starting from the bottom, it showed a simple, straight-lined hull designed to ride low in the water so that could it knife gracefully through the choppiest waves. From there moving up, five enormous cargo holds of varying sizes were drawn. Toward the middle of the ship was the ship's boiler room, right next to the engine room, and a watertight tunnel there allowed access to the No. 3 cargo hold. That hold could also be used to store backup fuel. Above the cargo holds but below the ship's main deck lay the tween deck compartments, five more valuable storage spaces set aside for goods or the coal to feed the engine. A small cabin store was also built into the tween deck toward the bow, sitting right below a saloon that sat right below the captain's bridge and the wheelhouse. Four lifeboats were visible in the drawing, as well as five hatch covers laid on top of the cargo holds. A curved profile at the stern wrapped around the top of the propeller. Two separate housing units were set aside on the main deck for sleeping accommodations that could hold officers and crew of up to sixty-five. One unit, for the captain and deck officers, sat midship between the third and fourth cargo hold and above the engine room, and the second smaller deckhouse was for the crew, at the rear deck. There were separate messrooms for deck officers, engineers, and crew. Five-ton steel derricks powered by steam winches towered above the ship's main deck, the means to reach over the sides of the ship and hoist cargo on board and lower it into the holds.[8]

Everything about the blueprint gave the president exactly what he had in mind—a huge, simple, boxlike ship that looked as if it could hold massive volumes of cargo and be built over and over with ease and efficiency.

AT 11:38 A.M. on Friday, January 3, 1941, President Roosevelt positioned his wheelchair behind a desk in the Executive Room at the White House for what would be his 706th press conference with the media. He was exhausted. The day before, his schedule had been packed with meetings, and he didn't retire to bed until after one in the morning. More than thirty reporters sat before him as he greeted them with a hearty "Good morning!"

Throughout the winter of 1940 and into early 1941, Hitler had been determined to overwhelm Britain with the same speed and strength he had used to conquer France only a few months earlier. The urgency of the situation weighed on the president as he looked out at the assembled media before him. He had decided only in the last few days that he would send his close friend and confidant Harry Hopkins over to London. Hopkins would not have any authority, or power, or even a title. He was merely going as a sign from one leader to another, from Roosevelt to Churchill, that America would be there.

After answering a few perfunctory questions about his senior staff and their whereabouts, Roosevelt launched into a prepared statement. Barely two weeks earlier, the United States had signed off on a contract that allowed its closest ally, Great Britain, to work with American shipbuilders to build giant cargo ships to help win its war with Germany. With Jerry Land's blessing, the British Merchant Shipbuilding Mission had spent a month crisscrossing the country exploring America's shipbuilding possibilities. And in the end they had found partners, they had identified shipyards—or future shipyards—and they were preparing to launch an aggressive shipbuilding program on American soil. The British Admiralty had done the United States a great service by discovering the possibility for expanding America's shipbuilding capacity. Now it was time for America to begin building new ships of its own.

"SO MUCH TONNAGE in the way of ships has been going to the bottom for a year and a half," the president said, a reference to the German U-boat attacks on British and American cargo vessels. "Probably at the end of the war, sooner or later, there will be a shortage—a world shortage—of tonnage, and therefore we have begun taking the first steps toward a program of building about two hundred merchant ships."[9]

He was not clear about who those two hundred ships would be built for. And it initially caused confusion. Were they for the British? Were they American ships? Roosevelt didn't say. By referring to the war on tonnage, the president was using a term unfamiliar to most Americans. It was maritime lingo, a way to express that every ship that went down required a new ship to replace it. If war was a game, tonnage would be the objective to win the game: whoever was able to sink more ships, more tonnage, and do so faster than the other side could build replacement tonnage would win. The Nazi U-boat chief commander Karl Dönitz was not playing a game when he coined the idea: "The shipping of the enemy powers is one great whole," he said.[10] "It is therefore in this connection immaterial where a ship is sunk—it must still in the final analysis be replaced by a new ship." That war on tonnage is also why Churchill, in a moment of reflection, said, "The only thing that ever really frightened me during the war was the U-boat peril."

As he addressed the media on that January morning, Roosevelt was in his element as he spoke about the challenges and intricacies of building seagoing vessels. "I love to be on the water," Roosevelt once said.[11]

Growing up, his father taught him how to sail in the family boat named *Half-Moon*, and they took frequent trips up and down the Hudson River near their summer home. When Roosevelt was sixteen, he got his own 21-footer, and on almost any warm summer day he could be found either sailing in his boat he called *New Moon*, or canoeing in a family birch bark canoe. Perhaps boats held a special place for him later in life, from the Navy to the White House, because on the same day he first began suffering the symptoms of poliomyelitis, August 10, 1921, he was out sailing with his family near Campobello Island, their summer retreat. Even with polio, he continued to find salvation on the water, from a houseboat in Florida to a sailboat on the Hudson. Roosevelt appreciated the beauty of a perfect boat's curves and lines, and how the shape of its keel determined its speed on the water.

He told the reporters that American shipbuilding efforts had already been ramped up considerably. But in the same breath he said it was simply not enough. He estimated that somewhere between $300 million to $350 million was needed to speed up production to his liking and fulfill the emergency shipbuilding program he demanded.

"The time seems to have come when it is advisable to create some new plants," he told the gathering. He said he had allocated $36 million to get started.

"Is that $300,000,000 to be for constructing new yards, or actual construction of ships?" a reporter asked.

"Actual construction," Roosevelt answered.

Questions continued to be hurled at the president about the cost and the details, and he handled each one calmly and in impressive detail. He reflected on his own experience building a shipyard near Quincy, Massachusetts, during World War I when he was a Navy leader. He explained the shipyard had cost very little to build, as it basically entailed driving piles into the shoreline, putting in a tin shed over the shipways, and erecting some light construction shops. He hoped this effort would be similar. He emphasized that the goal of the emergency shipbuilding program was not to create the best ships, or the handsomest ships, or the strongest ships or the fastest ships. No, Roosevelt explained, the emphasis must be on quantity over quality, a reflection of the desperate times.

When a reporter shouted, "What design of ships?" Roosevelt was ready, the blueprints he'd reviewed with Land still fresh in his head.

"Anyone of you that knows a ship and loves a ship, would hate them, as I do," he said. "In other words, they are the type of ship that is built by the yard or the foot. Nobody that loves ships can be proud of them; but it gets them out. And the difference, roughly speaking, in the time between building a ship like a square, oblong tank, and a ship that is really a ship, is six or eight months."

He paused, before finishing with the words that the media would instantly seize upon. "In other words, by building this dreadful looking object, you save six or eight months."

"Why not give them to the British?" one reporter asked, erupting the room into laughter.

By unhesitatingly calling the design of the ship a "dreadful looking object," Roosevelt seemed to give permission to the cooperative news media, and even to his own staff, to openly accept that these new vessels would be floating steel boxes, functional eyesores at best. They would be built fast. They would have massive holding capacity. And they would float. That's all the president was looking for right now.

As the press conference wound down, one more question was hurled at Roosevelt that he had hoped to avoid facing. "Where will the majority of the new yards be?" a reporter asked.

This was sensitive. And the president knew it. He did not want to start a bidding war among states and politicians for any new shipyards. There was no time for political infighting and wrangling and congressional hearings to decide where to build new shipyards or to add more shipways, just to give one state an economic boost over another.

"I thought I would not bring that subject up," Roosevelt deflected, "because if I were to say now one were to go to the State of X and another to the State of Y, they would at once try to get them away." He wasn't wrong. Letters from representatives and senators urging that their states and regions be considered were already flooding the White House.

Southern states argued that they deserved shipyards because they had large numbers of unskilled workers ready for training, plus the Gulf Coast saw itself as desirable because of its warm climate and it was protected from any large-scale attack, away from both the Atlantic and Pacific. The problem with the South, as Land recognized, was it lacked an abundance of skilled architects, engineers, and experienced foremen and managers. Northeastern states pushed their proximity to the Atlantic Ocean and Europe and better facilities for training as reasons why they were obvious candidates for shipyards. The western states were already busy with naval contracts and aircraft construction, so they had the facilities and skilled workforce, not to mention proximity to the Pacific Ocean. The West Coast also had other advantages for hosting wartime shipyards. Much of its coastline was still undeveloped land, ripe for new construction. Sitting directly on the Pacific made it easy to build ships and launch them from the same spot. And the Bay Area was tightly connected to America's growing rail network, making the delivery of raw steel or partially assembled steel parts simple and speedy. It would not be an easy choice.

WHERE TO BUILD the ships was only one of the questions that needed to be resolved before any shipbuilding could get underway. There were so many others that needed to be answered in the earliest days of 1941, so many decisions that had to be made. What kind of engine would power the ships and where would it come from? What about the labor force necessary to build a fleet of cargo ships—they would have to be hired, trained, and assigned to different roles. Also, the Maritime Commission needed to lay out the production schedule. What was the shipbuilding goal for 1941, for 1942, and beyond?

———

THE OFFICIAL PRESS release the Maritime Commission issued five days later announcing the emergency shipbuilding program offered some answers. It reiterated Roosevelt's pledge for $36 million and said the ships and shipyards would be owned by the government, but the land would be privately owned and the yards privately operated. The release also made no attempt to put a shine on the ships. "Tentative designs call for a single type cargo vessel of about 7,500 gross tons, 10 to 11 knots speed, oil burning, with water tube boilers and an overall length of about 425 feet," it read. "Simplicity and ease of construction will be paramount in order to meet the requirements of time. While simple and plain, the vessels will be commodious, efficient cargo carriers. They will not have the fine technical equipment, speed or sleek lines of the passenger and combination vessels of the Maritime Commission's long-range program."[12]

Details in the release about the ships were sparse. For good reason. There weren't any to be shared. Despite the president's unabashed optimism for his emergency shipbuilding program, the actual ship that he wanted to see built was little more than a sketch on the back of a napkin. The ship he described to the press during his January 3 press conference, that "square, oblong tank," the "dreadful looking object," had never been built before. It was modeled after Cyril Thompson's British tramp steamers, but nobody had any idea what it was supposed to look like on the water.

Donald Nelson, the president's director of the Division of Purchasing, described the ship as "the Model T . . . of the seaways."[13] The similarities were all there—both were no-frills, designed for function over form, and ideally suited for fast, mass production. But there were no detailed, three-dimensional blueprints yet for these ships. No models that could be built to scale, no specifications on the deckhouses, or the cargo holds, or the shape of the hull. Any new shipyards under construction would be irrelevant if there weren't step-by-step instructions on how to build the ships that Thompson had brought over from England and that Land and Roosevelt were now proposing to build.

Then there was the added complication that Cyril Thompson's original plans were intended for British ships with British specifications designed to be built in Britain's shipyards by British shipbuilders. They would have to be adapted for American shipyards and American shipbuilders using American tools and American measurements. Somebody needed to design Roosevelt's "ugly ducklings," right down to their last weld and screw.

CHAPTER THIRTEEN

A Boy's Dreams

ON NOVEMBER 12, 1894, A BLUSTERY, LATE FALL MORNING
in Philadelphia, a throng of 25,000 people rushed through the gates at Cramp
Shipyard to get a good, close-up look at the largest ocean liner ever built in
the United States, the SS *St. Louis*. President Grover Cleveland, serving the
second of his historic nonconsecutive terms, was there with his pretty and
much younger first lady, Frances Cleveland. So was the shipyard president,
Charles Cramp, his trademark silvery beard neatly groomed. And so were
two little boys, squeezed among the masses, eight-year-old William Francis
Gibbs and his six-year-old brother, Frederic. Standing alongside their father,
they watched with excitement as the music faded and the first lady smacked a
bottle of champagne across the hull of the 550-foot ship, nudging her to slide
down into the Delaware River with an enormous splash.[1]

The *St. Louis* was almost as long as two football fields, built of steel, decorated from bow to stern with colorful flags from around the world, and powered
by a pair of reciprocating engines that could propel her forward at a speedy
twenty knots. There was hope that she would one day be the ship to break the
transatlantic speed record held by the British Cunard liners.

"We may well be proud because we have launched the largest and most powerful steamship in the Western Hemisphere, built on American plans, by American mechanics, and of American materials," President Cleveland told the crowd.[2]

The imagery of that day stuck with little Willy Gibbs. Ever since he'd been a tyke of three years old, drawing ships in his home and burying his face in the technical engineering sketches on the pages of *Cassier's Magazine,* ships had fascinated William Gibbs. From their summer home on the New Jersey shore, he could spend hours watching for funnels of black smoke to appear on the horizon as ocean liners headed into or out of New York Harbor. But on that day in 1894, as he stood in the shadow of one of those mammoth vessels, it struck him in a profound way.

"This was my first view of a great ship," Gibbs would recall decades later. "And from that day forward I dedicated my life to ships. I have never regretted it."[3]

As he grew up, whenever the opportunity arose to experience maritime history, he jumped at it. Along with his brother, he boarded the luxury Cunard liner *Lusitania* in 1907 for a journey across the Atlantic soon after she had set the transatlantic record of 4 days, 19 hours, and 52 minutes, and eight years before a German torpedo would sink her, killing 1,195 men, women, and children. And the brothers made the maiden voyage back from Liverpool to New York on the *Mauretania,* which later broke the *Lusitania*'s records and held them for nearly twenty years.

After graduating from Harvard College and Columbia Law School, Gibbs halfheartedly pursued a career in law while pouring his side energy into his concept of building a high-speed, 1,000-foot ocean liner that could run at 30 knots. That was a good 5 knots faster than the *Mauretania.* By the time Gibbs was thirty, he had given up his law work to pursue his dreams of ship design. His rise was swift. In 1919, a *New York Times* sketch showcased an eight-column picture that lauded the ship William Francis Gibbs would be building. The caption announced:

DESIGN FOR THE TWO HUGE AMERICAN LINERS TO BE BUILT BY THE UNITED STATES SHIPPING BOARD FOR THE TRANSATLANTIC SERVICE.[4]

But success would have to wait. The postwar malaise led to a decline in the hunger for 1,000-foot luxury ships, and the Great Depression nearly sank Gibbs's dream. His business shrank to twelve men, and they were paid according to their marital status, the wedded ones taking home $50 per week, the unwed $25.

GIBBS WAS PARTICULARLY fascinated when ships sank. The *Titanic's* sinking in 1912, followed two years later by the tragedy of the *Empress of Ireland*, which sank near the mouth of the Saint Lawrence River in Canada after colliding with a Norwegian ship, left him with so many questions about why they went down at all. In his mind, those 2,529 victims who perished in the two sinkings should never have died. His experience of the *Lusitania* only bolstered his belief that ships should be designed to float, even when water floods their hulls.[5]

When he was given a chance in 1924 to design the largest and fastest luxury passenger liner ever built in the United States for the famed Matson Navigation Company, he used the opportunity to test out a theory. He subdivided the hull of the liner called the SS *Malolo* into individual watertight compartments, each one equipped with a hydraulically operated sliding steel door. Gibbs believed that as long as some of the compartments did not flood during a crash or from an explosion, the ship should remain afloat long enough for passengers to be rescued and for the ship to even be patched up and put back on the water. He did not expect his design to be tested so quickly, however.

On May 25, 1927, during a trial run with Gibbs on board, the *Malolo* was twenty-six miles off the island of Nantucket, Massachusetts, when a Norwegian freighter, the *Jacob Christensen*, appeared out of a dense fog and rammed into it midships.[6] The impact was as strong as the crash that doomed the *Titanic* and it tore a gash in the *Malolo's* hull. Gibbs rushed to the pilothouse and pushed a series of buttons he had designed to close the bulkhead doors below to contain the flooding only to the damaged compartment. The doors worked. And the *Malolo*, even with 7,000 tons of seawater in her hull, was able to float away safely until rescue boats arrived to tow her back to New York Harbor. There were no deaths or injuries.[7]

Marine engineer experts were unanimous in their praise of Gibbs's safety standards and design; they said any other ship would have surely sunk from such a crushing blow. A few months later, Rear Admiral William Benson noted that any ship that could withstand such a devastating gash would be invaluable in a war fought with submarines and torpedoes. "Money spent on vessels of this class would not be idle during peace, and the ships would be valuable in time of war," Benson said.[8]

From that moment on, anytime there was an important American ship to be designed, William Gibbs got the call.

GIBBS, WHO PARTNERED with a prominent yacht designer named Daniel Cox in 1929 to form Gibbs & Cox, hung around through the early years of the Depression. The 1932 presidential election provided their opportunity to take off. The newly elected, ship-loving president embarked on an ambitious Navy rebuilding program and even though naval vessels were unfamiliar territory for Gibbs or Cox, they were not about to let massive government contracts slip by. They landed a deal to build sixteen destroyers.[9] To assuage any doubt about his technical expertise to build Navy ships instead of ocean liners, Gibbs took a train to Washington so he could show what his lifelong obsession with ships had taught him. His audience included the head of Roosevelt's Bureau of Construction, one Jerry Land, who listened raptly for five hours as Gibbs went on about the complicated propulsion system he would design to create more space in the engine room, improve fuel consumption, and increase how far the ships could travel.

With the successful completion of the *Mahan*-class destroyers, more work followed. Navy contracts had Gibbs & Cox working with Federal Shipyards in New Jersey and a prominent shipbuilder up north, Pete Newell and his Bath Iron Works in Maine. Business blossomed. With a growing list of powerful contacts in the government, like Jerry Land, and in the shipbuilding world, like Newell, Gibbs was positioned perfectly for the next event that would elevate his profile higher than he ever imagined back when he was a young boy dreaming of building giant ships: war.

GIBBS NEVER LIKED the British. He was not a physically imposing man. He was tall and lanky and one magazine writer described him as a man "who looks as though he had just stepped out of a coffin." However, his eccentric, sometimes abusive behavior and his temper were famous and he often pretended to have the social graces of a child just to keep his business partners off balance. Not only was he the son of a millionaire, but his wife was the daughter of Paul Cravath, the founding partner of New York's most prestigious law firm.

Gibbs's blunt and arrogant business style clashed with what he believed was the condescending politeness of Brits. When he was given a brief opportunity to meet with Cyril Thompson and members of the visiting British Merchant Shipbuilding Mission in the fall of 1940, they were desperate for help in finalizing the template design for their new cargo vessels. Yet Thompson did not want the meeting in the first place.

Back in Britain, the shipyards held the responsibility not only of shipbuilding, but also of ship design, leaving them solely accountable for any flaws in the design or hitches in the construction. But Thompson was on foreign soil now. He had to play by the Americans' rules. That meant partnering with an outside ship designer and a separate construction operation. Thompson did not have the time, nor the leverage, to argue.

The war in Europe was a year old, and every day that passed when Hitler did not invade Britain seemed like a victory. The shipbuilding mission was a sign of how desperate Britain had become, and the Americans knew it. Jerry Land arranged the commission's secret meeting with Gibbs, and it was nearly a disaster. Gibbs, who at fifty-four years old felt no need to coddle anyone he disagreed with, did not greet them cheerily. And when they told him at first that they only needed to build twenty ships, it nearly made Gibbs walk out of the meeting.

"You don't need them," Gibbs barked at the British diplomats.[10]

They were stunned.

"If England is within twenty ships of winning the war, she has won the war already," he told them. Of course, he knew that England was nowhere close to winning the war. His point was that twenty ships was not a game-changing number.

"How many would you suggest?" one of the delegates answered him.

"Sixty would be a start," Gibbs said after a long pause.

Relieved that he hadn't simply walked away from their proposal, they quickly handed over their design for a basic steamship. They asked if it was something he could work with and modify into a design that American ship-yards could use. Gibbs was taken aback by how few details the British had in their designs. But he set aside his disdain and vowed to solve their problem.

Later, in his diary, Thompson detailed the role of Gibbs through his frus-trated eyes. "Their function was to produce a new set of plans based upon those provided by us, but modified as regards to the substitution of welding for riveting, and to suit American practice."[11]

GIBBS'S FIRST ACT was to take the British drawings and create a proto-type that could be easily assembled and replicated, over and over. That's what the British needed, and that was what Roosevelt had demanded for America's own shipbuilding program. Bringing nationwide standardization to American shipbuilding was essential to the success of the president's vision.

To do that, Gibbs decided he had to sacrifice some of the crew's comfort. This was not one of his thousand-foot luxury liners. This was a basic, crude cargo ship. The interiors would not be wood; they would be steel. Bathrooms would not be tiled; they'd be concrete. The crew quarters would have no electricity or running water and lamps would be lit with oil. Hatch covers, normally a heavy steel, would be made of wood, a safety step because in the event the ship was attacked, the hatches could float and help crew members survive in the water.

With standardization, it did not matter where a ship was being assembled and constructed or how well trained the workers were. If the shipyards had the drawings and specifications, and the workers had sufficient training, the proper tools and the right components, the precise same ship should come out of a California shipyard that came out of a Maine shipyard or an Alabama shipyard or a Baltimore shipyard. And once shipyards became efficient in building the ships, the process should only get faster and faster as they learned. Standardization had another advantage. It allowed the government to know exactly what parts and components were needed where, creating a nationwide assembly line of sorts, reducing wasteful spending.

PERHAPS NOBODY WAS happier with Gibbs than Henry Kaiser and his Richmond manager, Clay Bedford. The more that the shipbuilding process was standardized, the easier it was for him to keep track of where things stood. Parts and components for the vessels would all be ordered through one central clearinghouse, then mailed to the shipyard in need. Kaiser already stood to make a substantial profit on the operation. The British would not only be reimbursing the shipyard operators for the costs of building both the shipyards and the ships, but also there would be a $160,000 fee per ship.[12] So the quicker those ships got built, the quicker the money started to flow.

Gibbs, Kaiser, and Bedford all agreed the best way to build the ships was through a subassembly process. This involved fabricating and building enormous subsections of a ship at one location, then moving them a short distance to assemble them together with other large sections. They didn't know if it was feasible, but they were sure that if they could find a way, it would speed up the shipbuilding. Bedford and Gibbs worked together on the layout of the shipyard in such a way that subsections could be assembled and moved easily over short distances.

Gibbs was ideally suited for this job. Even though he struggled with math concepts and lacked any formal education in naval ship design or architecture, he was maniacal about details. Not satisfied with drawings of the ships, he created a three-dimensional model that showed where every piece and part went, so that shipbuilders could take it apart and understand the construction. Gibbs was both a fierce negotiator and a skilled administrator. He had a special telephone system installed at his office, through three hundred wires spliced beneath his desk, that allowed him to hold a conference call with half a dozen staff members at the same time.[13] His company had perfected the art of ship design so well that one shipbuilding executive described it this way: "We used Gibbs because his plans are so clearly worked out and his procurement of materials so perfect that the building of a ship is like putting together a set of child's construction toys."

His operation encompassed thirteen floors in lower Manhattan, and no detail was spared in the work. Draftsmen spent hours hunched over row upon row of drafting tables, and their drawings made their way to the one floor where brass scale models were built, to resemble a replica of the ship, right down to the scaled-down thickness of the metal plates. The models were so precise and detailed they even included engine and boiler rooms, piping and wiring, so that there was no question the working plans were accurate.

Gibbs would pace the floors, like a maestro waving a baton, knowing that the tiniest mistake in a drawing that was then used in a model and that possibly made its way to an actual ship's construction would destroy everything he had built in a heartbeat.

AS THE WAR in Europe intensified, Gibbs smartly expanded his company for an anticipated surge in business. By the end of 1940, when the British contract was signed, Gibbs & Cox had a thousand people on staff who were churning out more than 8,000 blueprints a day, representing what one reporter described as "26 acres of blueprints a month."[14]

On January 4, 1941, one day after Roosevelt had outlined to the media his plan for an emergency shipbuilding program, the president's team of technical advisers got together. They were scheduled to meet with Gibbs on January 8. But first they wanted to settle on some of the most basic specifications for this new ship.

Like the sixty ships for the British, the American model, they agreed, should be of similar size, 441 feet; it should be able to carry cargo of at least 10,000 tons; and, importantly, it should be able to travel at least 11 knots. Those figures were nonnegotiable. But they also agreed on one important variation from the British ships: the engines would fire oil instead of coal, which was cheaper and allowed a ship to be refueled at sea. This change also made sense because oil was more easily obtained, an important point since on the water the ship would guzzle down nearly 200 barrels of oil per day. It meant that fuel tanks had to replace coal bunkers in the design and the ships had to be equipped with safety tools to smother fires. Knowing that Gibbs had a reputation for being difficult, the Americans nervously hoped that he would not mind working with two sets of design plans: one for the British ships he was modifying for American shipyards, and a second just for the American ships.

One quirky aspect of the British ship design kept distracting the American engineers as their meeting with Gibbs loomed: the unique shape of the hull designed by Cyril Thompson, with its rounded bow and V-shaped stern. It might have been a smart design if one was building only a handful of ships. But Roosevelt expected fast, mass production, and a hull with multiple curves and bends and edges was not going to be easy to replicate in a speedy manner hundreds of times over. The steel plates necessary for that kind of hull would have to be heated in a massive furnace so they could be bent and shaped according to specs. Those were valuable hours and minutes they did not have. In the days and hours leading up to their meeting with Gibbs, the Maritime Commission engineers worked around the clock to try to design a hull that featured straight lines but that did not sacrifice any necessary speed in a ship that was already considered dangerously slow.

ON JANUARY 8, Admiral Vickery opened the meeting in Washington with Gibbs, which was also attended by representatives from the shipbuilding industry so they could share their technical input on the building process. Vickery explained that his Maritime Commission team had prepared an alternate design to the British ship, with the hope that it could travel just as fast, and carry just as much cargo, yet be constructed much quicker and more cheaply. Both sets of drawings were shown side by side, and the contrast between the one with the straight-lined hull and the curved hull was striking to Gibbs.[15]

However, his first reaction was that the straight-lined hull, the Maritime Commission's preferred design, would actually take more time, not less, to build than the British design. Vickery was surprised, but he trusted Gibbs's expertise. There was no time to build models or test designs or spend weeks tweaking. A decision had to be made. Vickery consulted with Land, who was close friends with Gibbs. Land was the one who first introduced Gibbs to naval shipbuilding, and he had heard the rumblings about him.

"While Gibbs and I were the best of personal friends, I found him a headache any time he did not get his way," Land reflected later. "He proved to be more than a headache with his interference in the Maritime Commission program, about which he knew little."[16]

Land stuck with the British design. He hoped Gibbs would be pleased and that it might even make him easier to work with. It would not.

THE DECISION BY Land essentially anointed Gibbs as the government's point person and chief marine architect for all the emergency shipyards nationwide. A new unit was created, the Division of Emergency Ship Construction, with the sole mission of getting ships built fast and bypassing any bureaucratic red tape standing in its way. The Maritime Commission even took the unusual step of setting up an office at 21 West Street in downtown New York, the same building as Gibbs & Cox. That meant fewer phone calls to be made and memos to be written, and fewer chances for miscommunications. As the drawings got underway for the ships, each specification had to be approved by the Maritime Commission's team. This became jokingly referred to as "bedside approval."[17]

However, any hope that drafting the plans would be straightforward quickly vanished. The British plans were not only vague, they were also in first-angle projection, meaning they lacked the depth and perception of three-dimensional drawings. Even with his enormous staff, Gibbs grew frustrated and he frequently ignored the commission's requests or communications.

Yet despite the constant bickering and micromanaging by the Maritime Commission's team, Gibbs never wavered. He received the requests for changes but rarely bothered to reply, simply following through on the requests. Land was able to let the tension pass only because he knew the work would get done and it would be of the highest quality. Eventually, the issue that would drive a wedge between the two old friends, money, was no surprise to anyone.

Gibbs continued to accept the commission's modifications to the British design. He didn't always agree with them but understood this was not his ship and these were not his plans. This shipbuilding program was not starting from scratch. It was starting with the drawings mostly of Cyril Thompson and his Sunderland shipbuilding operation. Gibbs was the caretaker of someone else's design, and his role was to merely update, revise, modify, do whatever was necessary so those plans made sense to American shipbuilders.

Under the original contract for the Maritime Commission to help the British build their sixty ships, the price for designing the entire lot was about $600,000. When the commission said that it wanted 312 ships for the United States under Roosevelt's plan, and it needed Gibbs to modify the design plans for the British in order to build them, the agreement called for Gibbs to be paid $1.1 million, a sum Gibbs found insulting.[18]

"We have no precedents for low compensation," Gibbs told Land.

But he was no quitter either. He told his staff to finish the work and that when they were done, he would cut off all work for the Maritime Commission and focus only on Navy projects. For Land, it was a relief knowing his days working with Gibbs were numbered.

"We felt that we paid plenty for it and they felt that we did not pay enough," Land testified later before Congress. "So we just split business with them and said, 'Good bye, boys.'"[19]

ONE OF THE major changes made during the design process involved the deckhouse. In the British model, there were two deckhouses on the ship, toward the front and the rear. But the Americans preferred one central deckhouse because it meant less piping for heating and plumbing.[20] Other alterations seemed trivial but were all made with the crew's well-being in mind. Nonslip deck coverings were added. So were ladders for crew members to easily get into and out of the upper and lower cargo holds without removing hatches, which was a dangerous practice on choppy ocean waters where the weather could turn in an instant. Twelve-inch searchlights were included, along with more storage space for refrigeration to hold perishable foods, and running water was added to the staterooms of officers.

Most changes to the British design passed without discussion. But a few did not. Doors sparked debate. The early drafts included a vertical sliding door that separated the engine room from the shaft alley. But it was decided that that type of door could jam easily and be left open. That made a ship more vulnerable to sinking quickly in an attack because the engine room could be flooded without a door to protect it. The British had eliminated that door in their design, and the Americans at first also left it off. But the issue was reconsidered after hearing from seamen, and a simple, hinged door was put back into the plans.

Two changes were made out of necessity rather than choice. During times of peace, the standard length of an anchor chain on a large vessel was 300 fathoms, the equivalent of about 600 yards. But with the possibility of war on the horizon, every foot, fathom, or yard of steel took on increased importance. It was agreed that the length of the anchor chain would be reduced to 240 fathoms (it would later be shortened even more, to 210 fathoms).[21] It was also standard for ships to carry two anchors, in the event of a glitch or a broken chain rendering one of them useless. But one anchor was instead included in the design of the ship.

Some changes were made, more than thirty of them, that strayed from the Maritime Commission's own safety protocols and were included in the plans purely as cost-cutting measures or to save time. They put the crew at greater risk in the event of an onboard emergency or attack and reduced the comfort level in some basic amenities.

Ceilings, linings, bulkheads, and furniture were made of inexpensive, more combustible material, meaning a fire could turn the ship into a roaring blaze in minutes. Mechanical ventilation was left out of cargo holds, boiler rooms, and crews' quarters, and mechanical gear was eliminated for opening skylights. Lockers and sleep rooms were shrunk. The fire detection system was omitted from the design. Even navigation aids, like a gyrocompass and radio direction finder, were omitted (though at the last minute, the direction finders were added back in). No radios or searchlights were included for the lifeboats.[22]

While steel was saved in the anchor design, extra steel was added back in for the booms on board. Large booms were deemed essential to hoist cargo from the shore, lift it onto the deck, and lower it into the cargo holds.[23] The British plans had suggested using booms that could lift up to five tons of weight. But the Maritime Commission anticipated those booms would not be nearly strong enough to lift much heavier items. For these ships to achieve their purpose, they had to be able carry hundreds, not dozens, of the heaviest wartime machinery, including aircraft that were boxed up to be reassembled on Europe's shores. A single Sherman tank could weigh thirty tons or more. Much larger booms that were capable of lifting fifteen, thirty, and sometimes fifty tons were going to be needed on these ships. Their cargo load would demand it.

BY THE MIDDLE of February 1941, the Maritime Commission engineers and the Gibbs & Cox staff moved into the final stages of redrafting the British plans for American shipyards. Their changes ran from the significant, like the single deckhouse, to the most mundane alterations, like switching to American-standard nuts and bolts and improving the hatch covers on the five cargo holds. But each change required details and time, and the aim was to have Gibbs & Cox begin to transmit building plans to the shipyards by late spring or early summer at the latest.

The ship design allowed for a crew of about eighty men, and all of their quarters were placed in the deckhouse. They would bunk four to a room most of the time and spend their days in their cabins or in a mess lounge that was outfitted with leather-upholstered chairs, magazines and books, and small tables to play cards. Shower rooms and the infirmary were tiled, and the captain's stateroom was given a light touch of luxury without feeling opulent.

As the designs of the British prototypes and the American ships progressed, they matured like twin sisters, sharing many of the same traits and characteristics that were both visible and invisible. There was another critical aspect to the design. Because it was so simple, and so easily replicated, virtually any part on the ship, from the engine to the steering mechanism to the winches and booms, could be easily repaired in any port around the world.

NO FEATURE OF the designs was more important than the size, strength, and shape of the cargo holds. The entire purpose of the shipbuilding programs, by both countries, was to move massive amounts of goods, weapons, and wartime essentials to their troops stationed around the world. Even though cargo ships were inherently slower than the aircraft of the day, the value of enormous ships was in their ability to carry huge volumes of goods. A World War II plane like the Curtiss-Wright C-46 Commando, a twin-engine military commercial transport, had a maximum cargo capacity of 15,000 pounds, or almost 8 tons. Just one of the ships under design by Gibbs could safely carry 10,419 deadweight tons.[24]

The ships would have five cargo holds, each one a different size and shape because of the contours of the hull. Hold No. 1, in the ship's bow, was the smallest, with a capacity of 76,077 cubic feet. Hold No. 2 was the largest, almost twice as big as No. 1, because it was the deepest, extending down to the ship's floor. Its capacity was 134,638 cubic feet. Hold No. 3 was more narrow because of the engine, but it was also deep, with a size of 83,697 cubic feet. Cargo holds No. 4 and No. 5 each had a capacity of about 82,000 cubic feet. Between these five holds, a ship's capacity was more than 500,000 cubic feet, or 7,800 tons, equal to a mile and a half of railroad boxcars.[25]

On paper, it was, in essence, a floating warehouse. The ships were designed to carry the heaviest and largest loads possible. That meant a single ship would be capable of carrying 2,840 boxed-up jeeps. Or 525 armored M8 cars or the same number of ambulances. Or 390 half-track, massive, M3 personnel carriers. Or 440 light tanks. Or, on the smaller side, one ship could be loaded up with 156,000 boxes of .30-caliber ammunition, or 217,000 crates of 75-millimeter gun shells. Or, if food was what the troops needed, one Liberty ship could be jammed full of 430,000 cases of C-rations, enough wet canned food to feed 3.4 million men for one day.[26]

And there was more space on top of the cargo holds. Up on the ship's main deck was additional storage capacity. Boxes could be piled on top of boxes on the deck, or vehicles could be lined up, side by side, to blanket the entire surface of a ship so that no inch was wasted. Smaller craft like patrol boats could be strapped down on the deck. A catwalk was designed to allow crew members to walk over any cargo on the main deck, to save even more space. And special storage space was carved out for highly sensitive cargo, like deadly mustard gas, or the most dangerous cargo of all—bombs.

CHAPTER FOURTEEN

Engines and Guns

IN 1941, CHARLIE MOORE WAS NEARING FIFTY YEARS OLD.[1] Standing a burly six feet six, he towered over his friends and coworkers. He quit school in eighth grade in Los Angeles and became a machinist on his own, working for the Sante Fe Railroad during World War I. He eventually found a sales job after the war. But when his boss told him he lacked the polish and education to succeed, he left and went out on his own and made enough money to buy the business. And to rename it: the Moore Machinery Company.

By the time the war in Europe broke out in 1939, Moore Machinery was manufacturing top-notch machine tools and was often the first call made by contractors across Southern California when they landed a big job. Almost always his tools worked to perfection. But it was one that did not that led to Moore's biggest break. A contraption he built for a California company that had been thriving since the Gold Rush days, Joshua Hendy Iron Works, didn't meet its expectations. When Hendy's business started to dry up, it went after Moore Machinery to help it recoup some of its losses suffered from the defective equipment. Hendy was preparing to sue if it didn't get help, and that's what led Charlie Moore to drive north to Sunnyvale one day in the fall of 1940.[2]

He hoped to persuade the managers at Hendy to simply drop their lawsuit, but as he walked through their tired plant that seemed to be filled with first-class, used equipment, Moore changed tactics. Founded in 1856 to make tools for gold miners, Hendy's equipment looked like it could have real value on the open market, maybe as much as $500,000. Moore no longer wanted to negotiate with Hendy. He wanted to buy it. The sale would make the lawsuit disappear, and it might bring him some additional income if the equipment could be sold for as much as he believed.

To find the cash he needed to buy Hendy, Moore called an old friend, the contractor Felix Kahn, who happened to be one of the partners in a conglomerate called Six Companies. He convinced Kahn to go in with him to buy Joshua Hendy Iron Works for $350,000, almost guaranteeing themselves a handsome profit if the Hendy tools sold.

Not only did the tools sell, but the deal looked even more shrewd a few weeks after it was finalized when the Navy approached Hendy to build torpedo mounts for ships and submarines. A contract worth $10 million was reached. Orders began pouring in after that and the company cleared more than thirty acres of trees in a pear forest in Sunnyvale to build 300,000 square feet of new buildings. As the Hendy plant was modernized and its workforce grew, Kahn convinced his Six Companies partners to invest in the business. One of the first to sign up was Henry Kaiser. He knew a good deal when he saw it, and he imagined tremendous value in owning a piece of a major machine tool and iron works business when his country was on the eve of war.

IDENTIFYING, PURCHASING, AND obtaining all the materials and equipment and parts to put a single cargo ship together was time-consuming and complex, and made more complicated by shortages in steel and government red tape that slowed up every transaction. No challenge was more difficult, yet more important, than finding the engines that would power the ships. With so much weight on board, the hulls of the ships were going to sink twenty or thirty feet into the ocean. They would need an especially powerful engine to propel them forward, and it had to be an engine that could be built quickly and easily shipped to yards around the country.

The engine Howard Vickery and William Gibbs chose was a dark gray steel, three-cylinder beast weighing 135 tons, or 270,000 pounds, and standing 21 feet tall, about two stories high. It was not designed for speed or durability or acceleration, any of the qualities that define a desirable engine. It was chosen because it could be manufactured quickly in mass quantities around the country; it was powered by oil; and, with 2,500 horsepower, it had just enough power to move the cargo ships at the barely acceptable speed of almost 12 knots, or about 14 miles per hour.[3]

When Vickery approached Kaiser about finding a source for these engines, Kaiser immediately thought of Moore, that likable, towering salesman he had just partnered with in Southern California. Kaiser knew that Hendy had made giant reciprocating engines during World War I. It didn't take long for Vickery to secure a deal with Hendy to become the country's primary manufacturer of the engines that would power the ships. Later, when the Maritime Commission demanded more engines, Hendy Iron Works was able to increase its production from ten a month to thirty, setting it on pace to produce more than one hundred for 1941, and eventually three hundred in 1942. It was an improbable story for eighth-grade dropout Charlie Moore.

FROM THE DAY American shipbuilders first learned about the intention to build these plodding steel cargo ships, first for the British and then for their home country, they were never able to hide their skepticism. In the middle of the vast Atlantic Ocean, the ships, they argued, would be so slow that enemy torpedoes would pick them off like ducks on a pond. Every knot mattered, good shipbuilders knew. Twelve knots was slow, but maybe just safe enough in a convoy to avoid enemy fire. But 13 knots, or 14 knots, lowered their risk dramatically of being sunk.[4] Navy battleships could cruise at almost 30 knots, or 35 miles per hour. Speed was the biggest reason why elegant and enormous passenger ships like the *Queen Elizabeth* and *Queen Mary* were used to carry thousands of troops during the war, unescorted across the Atlantic—they could reach 30 knots, fast enough to outrun almost any enemy vessel. These cargo ships would not even reach half that speed. And if they were confronted, what were the crew members going to do? Throw cans of beans at the Nazis?

Cargo ships were merchant vessels first; they were not instruments of war. They were, essentially, built to run errands for their countries. They posed no threat on the open seas to other ships or subs, and there was even an international maritime law written to protect them called the Protocol of 1936. Britain, Germany, the United States, and Japan were among the thirty-five nations that had agreed to it. The regulation allowed merchant vessels and merchant marines to be minimally armed, and to report to their navy when they detected nearby submarines, but the point was to protect them from blatant, unprovoked attacks from heavily armed subs or warships since they were largely defenseless and had no torpedoes or heavy artillery. The United States had gone even further with its Neutrality Act of 1939. Section 6 of the act prohibited the arming of American flagships engaged in foreign commerce.

So what was a nation to do when German U-boats ignored any restrictions and drew no distinction between the vessels they encountered, whether they were military or merchant? Roosevelt made his intentions clear.

"It is an imperative need now to equip American merchant vessels with arms," he told Congress. "We are faced not with the old type of pirates but with the modern pirates of the sea who travel beneath the surface or on the surface or in the air destroying defenseless ships without warning and without provision for the safety of the passengers and crews."[5]

He said it was cruel and unfair to send American sailors on missions connected with defending their country defenseless and unarmed.

"Although the arming of merchant vessels does not guarantee their safety, it most certainly adds to their safety," Roosevelt said. "In the event of an attack by a raider they have a chance to keep the enemy at a distance until help comes. In the case of an attack by air, they have at least a chance to shoot down the enemy or keep the enemy at such height that it cannot make a sure hit. If it is a submarine, the armed merchant ship compels the submarine to use a torpedo while submerged—and many torpedoes thus fired miss their mark. The submarine can no longer rise to the surface within a few hundred yards and sink the merchant ship by gunfire at its leisure."

The ships would be armed, for defense purposes only. Roosevelt got his wish. They were given one modification from previous versions of cargo ships. In the past, any guns on board could only fire from the rear of a ship, but given Germany's aggressive tactics, weapons were also positioned to fire ahead. Some designs called for 4-inch or 3-inch guns, or 20-millimeter cannons along with machine guns. Larger guns typically went at the stern, sometimes machine guns along with smaller guns. In sum, a single ship was given four guns of various size and caliber, at the stern, the bow, and along the sides. Hoses that stretched fifty feet were positioned around the ship to help extinguish fires, along with steam-smothering devices and handheld fire extinguishers. No one expected the ships to be able to defeat a U-boat or German warship. But the hope was they could hold off an attack long enough for crew members to be rescued.

"It is time for this country to stop playing into Hitler's hands," Roosevelt said, "and to unshackle our own."

But war is relentless, and there was no time for the president to celebrate a political win. He had a new problem to solve—a math problem.

CHAPTER FIFTEEN

Selecting Sites

HOW MANY SHIPYARDS AND HOW MANY SHIPWAYS WERE needed to build two hundred new American cargo ships, on top of the sixty ships that the British needed built? Roosevelt tapped three men to find him an answer: Jerry Land, Howard Vickery, and Roosevelt's wartime chairman of production management, William Knudsen, or "Big Bill" to his friends. Hours after the president's January 3 speech, they were put in charge of the calculations and got right to work. The president had given them one number to work off: 100. He wanted 100 shipways to build his 200 ships.

They thought at first that a handful of shipyards with 28 individual shipways to build ships felt right, but then they quickly pivoted, realizing that was too few yards for too much work. If one yard slipped behind pace or encountered labor problems, the burden would be too great on the others. Shipyards with 14 ways felt better, and even some that had fewer ways, from 4 to 6, could be added to reach their target. With the numbers mostly settled, their attention turned to the far more challenging question—locations.

A list was drawn up of fourteen yards.[1] Among the sites on the first list were Bristol, Pennsylvania; Groton, Connecticut; and Newburgh, New York, all of which had built ships during World War I and seemed worth reconsidering. But they were all dismissed because their machinery was either outdated or, worse, rotted. The first two shipyards that were immediately confirmed for the American work were obvious—Richmond, California, and Portland, Maine. Thanks to the British, both had already gone through a vetting process that Land had approved, and their leadership was firmly in place. Because they had to build ships for the British first, they would soon get contracts to add additional shipways to handle American ship orders. Shipyards in Los Angeles, Houston, and Portland, Oregon, were added next, as Land and Knudsen were determined to spread the work around the country, from the Pacific Northwest to the Gulf Coast. But both men knew the East Coast could not be ignored, because of its long history dominating America's shipbuilding prowess, and so Baltimore, with its proximity to Washington, D.C., and Chesapeake Bay, was a natural fit. They were almost done, but they were struggling with how to handle Newport News Shipbuilding in Virginia.

It was one of the oldest and most productive shipyards in the country, but because it already had an overflow of Navy contracts it had no capacity to build merchant ships. Land was insistent they be included. He called Captain Roger Williams at Newport News personally and, as he later recalled, he told him this "was a job with their capacity they could afford to do."[2] A compromise was reached—Newport News would build Roosevelt's emergency ships, but at a new shipyard farther south in North Carolina. Land, Vickery, and Knudsen were satisfied with their list; it covered nearly every corner of the country.

Just three days after his press conference, on January 7, 1941, the president got word that the House of Representatives had unanimously passed a bill authorizing the construction of his cargo ships. It would soon be on his desk to sign. He couldn't resist a quip when a reporter asked for his reaction.

"Fine speed," he said, "in spite of the fact that the ships are slow ships."

"Ugly ducklings!" the reporter shouted back at him.

———

THE NEXT DAY, the White House issued its press release announcing that nine sites for building two hundred ships had been selected.

- South Portland, Maine: Todd-Bath Iron Shipbuilding Corporation
- Richmond, California: Todd-California Shipbuilding
- Wilmington, North Carolina: North Carolina Shipbuilding
- Baltimore, Maryland: Bethlehem-Fairfield Shipyard
- Houston, Texas: Todd-Houston Shipbuilding Corporation
- Los Angeles, California, Terminal Island: California Shipbuilding Corporation
- Portland, Oregon: Oregon Shipbuilding Corporation
- New Orleans, Louisiana: Delta Shipbuilding Company
- Mobile, Alabama: Alabama Drydock & Shipbuilding

Of the nine shipyards awarded a share of Roosevelt's emergency shipbuilding program, two, Newport News and Bethlehem, had been in the shipbuilding business for generations, satisfying the old-timers in the industry. Newport News had also built the North Carolina Shipbuilding yard in Wilmington. Two other yards chosen represented the Deep South, a region not as well known for its shipbuilding experience but valuable because it was seen as safe from possible attack during a war.

The remaining five shipyards all had two names in common—the loose alliance of Todd and Kaiser, now known as Todd-Cal. The Maritime Commission was so confident in their work building the C-1 cargo ships, and in their handling of the British contract, it authorized them to get started building new yards in Los Angeles; Portland, Oregon; and Houston to join their existing yard in Richmond, California, and the South Portland, Maine, shipyard that came about from Reilly's relationship with Newell.

Henry Kaiser was still a newcomer to shipbuilding. His only experience was at Todd Shipyard's Seattle-Tacoma Shipyard, where his crews had basically moved tons of dirt and poured mountains of concrete and watched as the government's C-1 ships were built. That was all about to change. He put

Clay Bedford in charge of the yet-to-be-built Richmond yard, he assigned his associates from Six Companies to run CalShip in Los Angeles, and he had special plans for the yard in Portland, Oregon, which came to be known as Oregonship. His son Edgar, thirty-two, was finishing up the Grand Coulee Dam. He called him up to come build a shipyard on the Columbia River in Oregon, the same order that he had given to Bedford in Richmond.

And just like that, between John Reilly, the head of Todd Shipyards, and Kaiser, the unofficial leader of the Six Companies group, the two men and their intertwined business operation now controlled the majority of the White House's $350 million emergency shipbuilding program. Sixty of those ships were bound for Britain. But the other 200 would fly the American flag. And it was already obvious this was only the beginning. Talks back in Washington about expanding Roosevelt's shipbuilding program were heating up.

EVEN AS LAND, Vickery, and Knudsen solved one math problem, however, a new one surfaced. How many of their president's ships could be physically built and launched in 1941? After all, it was only January. They took stock of everything that needed to be done, factoring in the amount of time likely needed to build the new shipyards, to expand existing shipyards, to order the essential materials, to manage the crisis of an ongoing steel shortage, to hire and train tens of thousands of shipbuilders, and to finalize the actual design of the ships. It was a long list, and it seemed like an awful lot to get done fast.

But war was looming. To those in the know, it was inevitable. Roosevelt was demanding his ships in a hurry, and they did not want to disappoint him. Their original production schedule would have to be accelerated. Because right now, the number of emergency cargo ships they had projected to be completed in 1941 was exactly one.[3]

CHAPTER SIXTEEN

Liberty

AS THE DESIGNS AND DECISIONS FOR THE NEW SHIPS PRO-
gressed, one question emerged that on the surface seemed trivial but carried
real significance as the fighting in Europe grew more intense. What should
the new ships be called? After all, this was a program announced by the president, undertaken by the Maritime Commission, intended to bolster America's
naval defense, and aiming to rally skeptical Americans behind the increasing
likelihood of their country being pulled into war. The name mattered. The
government needed a marketing campaign. As one prominent California shipbuilder argued, "The ships are too handsome for the term 'Ugly Duckling' to
be used." It wasn't long before the ships took on other nicknames like "Kaiser
Coffins," an unsubtle hint of their questionable seaworthiness.

There was no denying that the ships were ugly and boring, plain and workmanlike. As one American newspaper wrote in a headline describing Roosevelt's program, "Sea Scows with Blunt Bows Will Carry the Tools to Britain."
Meanwhile, the "ugly duckling" reference popularized in a *Time* magazine
headline continued to be catchy and playful to reporters. But it was a label that
Roosevelt, Land, Vickery, and all government officials were eager to shed, as
it hardly inspired confidence or excitement. Officials were also eager for the

public to forget the president's unfortunate passing reference to "dreadful looking objects."

The Maritime Commission first had to come up with a technical name or designation for the ships, purely for paperwork purposes. It proposed an inelegant solution. The ship was dubbed an EC2. The E stood for emergency, the C for cargo, and the 2 for a midsize ship measuring between 400 and 450 feet. But building an emergency fleet of "EC2s" was hardly going to help lift a worried nation on the cusp of war.

A solution remained elusive until Land received several letters from members of Congress, urging him to settle on a name. The ships deserved something better, they wrote. He scribbled a note on the bottom of one letter he received.

"I agree. We can do our bit by calling them 'Emergency Ships,'"[1] he wrote, signing off with his trademark cursive *L*. But Land's idea seemed more like a description of the program than an inspiring slogan.

It was a press release that went out from the Maritime Commission in early spring 1941 that revealed a new label. Under the heading "Immediate Release," the May 2 memo read: "Official designation of the 312 emergency program ships, being built for the Maritime Commission as part of the National Defense and Aid-to-Britain effort, as the EC-2 type, was announced by the Commission today. Those which are to be operated under the American flag will be known, the Commission stated, as the 'Liberty Fleet.'"[2]

Liberty.

That was a word Americans could get behind. It was a word that had, throughout history, accumulated both dignity and gravity. It was also in the pocket of every American, right there on the wheat penny, the word *Liberty* sitting just above the raised profile of Abraham Lincoln. It was shouted inside a Richmond, Virginia, church by a young delegate named Patrick Henry, on March 23, 1775, urging his people to support what would become the Revolutionary War. "Give me liberty or give me death," Henry declared. It appeared prominently soon after that utterance in the Declaration of Independence, coined by Thomas Jefferson in the sentence, "We hold these truths to be self-evident, that all men are created equal, that they are endowed by their Creator with certain unalienable Rights, that among these are Life, Liberty and the pursuit of Happiness." And it was a word fresh in the minds of Americans. On January 6, 1941, as they huddled around their radios for the president's annual State of the Union speech, they heard Roosevelt feature the word prominently.

He opened his eighth address, which came to be known as "The Four Freedoms," with fiery words that were meant to shock and alarm his citizens.

"I address you, the Members of this new Congress, at a moment unprecedented in the history of the Union," Roosevelt began. "I use the word 'unprecedented,' because at no previous time has American security been as seriously threatened from without as it is today."[3]

He referenced the Neutrality Act by explaining that even as powerful as America had become, it could not hold off the entire world with "one hand tied behind its back."

No realistic American can expect from a dictator's peace, international generosity, or return of true independence, or world disarmament, or freedom of expression, or freedom of religion—or even good business. Such a peace would bring no security for us or for our neighbors. Those, who would give up essential liberty to purchase a little temporary safety, deserve neither liberty nor safety.

If this was to be the Maritime Commission's Liberty fleet, then that made the individual vessels the Liberty ships. It was the right word for the moment. The *New York Times* even wrote about the designation the following day—on page 54. If Roosevelt and Land were hoping to inspire a nation, it seemed they would need more than a clever name for their big ships.

PART IV

Ships and Shipyards

CHAPTER SEVENTEEN

Upside-Down Forests

O. H. MCCOON PLANTED HIMSELF ON THE EASTERN SHORE of San Francisco Bay so that he had a clear view of the mudflat in the town of Richmond.[1] McCoon was one of Henry Kaiser's most trusted project foremen. This was the spot that Kaiser had picked out, promising the British that it was perfect to build an American shipyard capable of pumping out cargo ships in record time. On a dreary, rainy morning in January 1941, McCoon wanted to see what Kaiser envisioned.

McCoon had earned the trust of Kaiser building dams. Within days of the contract for the British ships being signed, Kaiser had told McCoon to get himself north to Washington State to learn about shipyard construction from the yards there in Seattle and Tacoma. McCoon's visit was brief. He was eager to have some equipment explore the mudflat and maybe even start clearing a service road so that more heavy equipment could be brought in. But when he sent a tractor into the marshy area, he watched dumbfounded as it sank into the mud and almost vanished entirely from his view. In that moment, he recognized that before they could even think about shipbuilding, they had a far more rudimentary task to accomplish: They needed to create solid ground to build a shipyard so that no more tractors were swallowed up by the mud.

The next day, McCoon hired two carpenters and a day laborer, ordered a pile of lumber, and set the men to work building a temporary office. It should have been a quick job. Instead it rained so heavily for almost six straight weeks that the fiberboard panels used to support the office ceiling sagged as they became more waterlogged each day.[2] The warehouse and tool shed appeared first. The crews drained and filled the swamp, dredging the channel and starting work on the seven ways where ships would be constructed. It all happened even as workers were skidding, sliding, and sinking into the mud. An army of twenty trucks hauled in landfill, arriving on newly built roadways built to make the shipyard accessible. A routine project that should have taken a week or two dragged out more than a month.

"I remember going into the office and having to duck my head walking down the hall," Bedford recalled.[3]

Even as the rain kept falling, and Cutting Boulevard, the new road slicing through the shipyard, overflowed with water six inches deep, the main office was finished in thirty-four days. It was a miserable experience. The more dirt Ray Goodman and his crew dumped to widen and strengthen the road to withstand heavy shipments, "it only made the goo gooier," one of the workers recalled. When Goodman instructed one of his pavers to drag a shack down to the end of a questionable road and leave it off to the side, the paver followed his orders, pulled the shack into the muck, and then watched as it sank out of sight. But there would be no complaining. Some early news reports predicted that it would take six months just to get the ground ready for construction. Kaiser laid out his own deadline.

"That first keel has to be laid by March 7," Kaiser told Clay Bedford. That was six weeks away, not six months.[4]

BEFORE THE TURN of the century, Contra Costa County, on the eastern side of San Francisco Bay, had dual personalities. Looking eastward, it was mostly vast swaths of wide open, undeveloped land as far as the eye could see, some of it agricultural, full of grapes, oranges, wheat, and barley, but most of it desolate and unused. It was a different landscape looking westward. The choppy blue-gray waters of the bay separated Contra Costa County from the bustle of the big city on the western side. In 1900, San Francisco was America's tenth-largest city, with all of the others sitting east of Chicago, and California was the twenty-first largest state, trailing Iowa, Kentucky, even tiny Massachusetts. Along the eastern shoreline were several small landing spots that farmers could use to ship their produce over to San Francisco. The Golden Gate Bridge was still decades away, so moving goods across the bay was time-consuming and costly.

In 1905, about a century after Mexico won independence from Spain, a 17,000-acre area known as Rancho San Pablo was incorporated as Richmond, California, with 2,100 residents. Its proximity to San Francisco, as well as its thirty-two miles of shoreline, would make it an attractive site for developers.

In 1940, it was still a blue-collar enclave of 23,642 residents.[5] Most of the adults worked at a handful of small businesses along the shore, or at the nearby Standard Oil Refinery, or at the Ford Motor Company assembly plant that was built in 1930 and was the largest such plant on the West Coast. Macdonald Avenue, slicing through the heart of Richmond, was sandwiched mostly between small bungalows and tree-lined neighborhoods. What few in Richmond knew in the early days of 1941 was that their small town's fate had already been sealed. Thanks to the arrangement reached between Henry Kaiser, Cyril Thompson, and the Maritime Commission in the last days of 1940, Richmond was poised to become a rousing, round-the-clock, wartime production operation with people flooding its streets, shops, and hotels.

ACROSS THE COUNTRY, Pete Newell was applying his own pressure to start building his thirty ships for the British. The workers in Maine bore little resemblance to their fellow shipbuilders in California, their faces more ashen than golden under their visored caps pulled low over their foreheads. Their thick clothes and heavy sweaters were clumped at the waist under wool trousers or denim coveralls and their lumberjack boots looked ready to withstand anything. Some wore red-checked or green-checked plaid shirts and a few preferred red deer hunters' caps as their proof of north-woods heritage. A writer for *Harper's Magazine* who visited the Maine shipyard was struck by how many women he saw working on the ships. "Middle-aged women. Young girls. They wear the same clothes, their faces are bleared under the same grime. It's hard to tell them from the men and boys," essayist and novelist John Dos Passos wrote.[6]

By the middle of January, on the shore of the South Portland waterfront, the whine and hum and vibrations from an army of bulldozers, seventy-ton steam shovels, and buzz saws echoed through the frigid winter air. After snowfalls, dump trucks came in to remove snow and allow the work to continue. With icy blasts off the ocean plunging temperatures to 30 or 40 below zero on some days, workers bundled up in leather or sheepskin-lined jackets to keep their cores warm.

Maine's rocky coastline proved troublesome for building a shipyard; thousands of cubic yards of solid ledge had to be removed and more than 3,000 piles, most of them two-hundred-year old trunks of Maine virgin pines, were driven in to be used as foundations on which to rest the steel-sheet piling. Giant steel plates and bars of structural iron were shaped a few miles away at a plateyard and stored in racks with painted markings until they could be installed. The markings were critical to ensure that when a ship was placed in a shipway it rested precisely in the right position.

"Buildings were springing up overnight, new roads were pushing ahead, and huge, 70-ton steam-shovel-derricks were moving into place," the *Portland Evening Express* reported.

There was no resting. So that the work could continue around the clock, temporary lighting went up and floodlights bathed the workers in a white glow against the black Atlantic Ocean. In designing the Maine shipyard, natural sunlight was also deemed essential, since the weather in the Pine Tree State could be so unpredictable. It was decided that the biggest buildings in the shipyard would have entire walls of glass, to maximize the flow of bright sunlight that shined into the buildings to help the workers.

Day and night, heavy trucks rumbled across the land, hauling out loads of excavated dirt at rapid speed to construct a 1,500-foot steel and dirt enclosed basin where the water could be kept out while the work on cargo ships could begin. Dredging was a huge undertaking. Newell wanted an area 1,200 feet long and 400 feet wide, dug to a depth of 15 feet below the surface. Drillings were taken daily to measure the depth necessary to support adequate foundations for the concrete piers. In addition to the access roads, railroad tracks were also laid to connect the shipyard to a nearby fabrication plant. At the plant, racks were installed to hold the steel plates that would shape the hull of the ships.

"A ship, believe it or not, is built of rolled plates," Clay Bedford said. "You'd think a ship is curved in three dimensions, but it isn't. We can roll all those plates on a roll, and we did it. We had to heat and shrink, heat and shrink, to get the plates to conform to the slopes."[7]

The steel plates were simply too large to load onto trucks, and so flatbed rail cars were going to be essential. More than a thousand tons of steel plates began to fill the racks and to be fabricated into shape so that they were ready when it came time to lay the first keels. Once a plate was ready, painted markings were applied in precise spots so that the shipbuilders knew exactly where to place it.

In something of a miracle, the cofferdam—a temporary enclosure built within the water along the shoreline that could easily be pumped out or filled with water as needed—was finished in about four weeks from the day the first pile was driven in Maine. That cleared the way for excavation of the ship basins to speed up. The cofferdam was an engineering miracle in its own right, with portable trestles and gates that could be removed by cranes after a basin was flooded, allowing ships to float out to a pier for their final outfitting. The gates would then be put back into place so that pumps could drain the water and allow construction on the next ships to begin. The first buildings to be completed were to house machine shops, welders, and administrative staff, and as soon as they were done, the shipyard was almost ready for the real work to begin.

———

INTO THE EARLY spring of 1941, three thousand miles apart, the mudflat along the Northern California coastline and the rocky Maine peninsula both continued to transform at a backbreaking pace. Though both tracts were sitting on coastal bays, they could not have been more different for the workers tasked with erecting their respective shipyards. Casco Bay in Maine had swift tide changes thanks to how the Atlantic seeped into the rocky outlets along the coast. San Francisco Bay resembled more of a calm estuary with mostly stable tides.

The most important machinery to arrive at the sites were steam-powered pile drivers anchored to the ground by steel cables. They hammered wood pilings into the ground, first to forty feet, then to seventy-five feet, and finally until a hundred feet of the trees disappeared below the earth's surface, leaving enough of them exposed so that they could support buildings, shipways, cranes, railroad tracks. The pile driver struck each piece of wood with the force of 15,000 pounds, coming down at more than a hundred blows per minute and echoing for miles. When a piling needed to be driven far below the surface, up to 250 feet, a round piece of pipe was placed on top of the first one, so that a second one could be smashed on top of it, splicing the two together.

In a matter of a few weeks, the shipyards in Richmond and South Portland began to resemble upside-down forests, with pilings sticking out of the ground every few feet. The shipways measured about 630 feet long, leaving plenty of cushion on both sides for workers to complete the 441-foot-long Liberty ships.

Every day mattered. American and Allied merchant ships, as well as British vessels of all types, were under siege in the Atlantic Ocean. Their attempts to ferry innocent passengers or to bring supplies to British troops were being cut short by German torpedoes every day. American merchant ships were being sunk at a rate of 500,000 cargo tons each month. And on consecutive days in mid-January, two British ships, the passenger liner *Oropesa* and the refrigerated cargo ship *Alameda Star*, both went to the bottom of the North Atlantic, sunk by the same German sub, *U-96*. If there was any lingering doubt among Americans about the need for President Roosevelt's emergency shipbuilding program, that doubt was disappearing as fast as American and British ships.

In early February, Churchill, in a worldwide broadcast, pleaded with the

United States to show its support by sending arms to the British: "Give us the tools, and we will finish the job," he said.[8]

IN LATE FEBRUARY 1941, a new building opened on the South Portland shipyard that signaled the next phase of what was to come: thousands of welding jobs were about to open up in Maine, and a free school began to welcome young men to come and learn to use electric welding equipment. Within weeks the school was full of eager applicants and operating around the clock in four-hour shifts.

When Pete Newell convinced Cyril Thompson and his cohort of Brits about the appeal of a Maine shipyard, one of his primary selling points was an abundance of skilled and unskilled workers. What he couldn't offer was a workforce of experienced shipbuilders. Mainers who worked in the boatbuilding industry were used to constructing customized small crafts, from 16-foot sailboats to 60-foot private yachts. The Maine coast was lined with small, custom-sized slips and boatyards that built personal sailboats and fishing boats and the occasional 50-foot craft. Newell was happy to have their seagoing experience, but he needed more. Following Kaiser's belief that anybody could be trained to do a job, Newell started recruiting teachers, lawyers, fishermen, students, mechanics, butchers, car salesmen, artists—anyone he believed was either good with their hands or good at following instructions.[9] He figured if they could read and take orders and follow straightforward plans, he could easily turn them into welders, shipfitters, painters, electricians, burners, and any other role he needed to fill.

Not everyone agreed, as plenty of old-time Mainers warned him: "You can't build ships that way—that's goin' to be trouble."

But Newell wasn't done changing his ways. For the first time, he welcomed women to join the men in the shipyards, eventually hiring more than 3,700 women shipbuilders. Newell saw no other choice. He put his personnel supervisor, Phyllis St. Clair Fraser, in charge and she oversaw the hiring of more than three hundred women for Portland's new yard, assigning them jobs as stenographers and filing clerks, as well as welders, burners, pipe coverers, and electricians. She looked for certain traits, preferring women between the ages of twenty and forty-five, who were married and physically fit, and she had no problem finding them. She heard early gripes from some of the men, who worried they would be distracted by pretty, young women working alongside them. Then the women showed up for work.

"One look at the girls in their overalls, work shirts, and welders helmets, and all worries about glamour disappeared," Fraser said with a chuckle when she was asked how the genders were blending and getting on with the job.[10]

WHEN EIGHTEEN-YEAR-OLD ARTHUR Babineau heard about the new shipyard, he pounced. Living in Howland, Maine, two hours south of the Canadian border, his family didn't have a lot of money, and such a job opportunity was too good to pass up. He hopped on a bus for Portland to check it out, even though he had no experience around ships.[11]

"I applied for a job and I got the job on the same day," he said. "I got a room on Pleasant Street in Portland and I had room and board there. They told me the salary was $35 a week. That was very good money back then."

He was trained to work as a lead inspector who would check the welds on the steel plates that pieced together the hull. His responsibility was to make sure the ships didn't take on water and start to sink when they floated out into Casco Bay. If welding was the most important job in building Liberty ships, then this skinny teenager from rural Maine, only a few weeks out of high school, was suddenly holding the second-most-important job—inspecting those welds for cracks or leaks. Seven days a week, he would hop off his bus, walk into the shipyard, punch the clock, and round up his team of men, which ranged from ten to nineteen depending on the day. He would assign them to different parts of the ship, and then get to work himself. Most of the welds he inspected were solid, but Babineau found himself surprised at how many sloppy, inconsistent, dangerously poor welds he also came across.

"You had to check it for cracks and crawl into the bottom of the ship," he said. "I remember one ship had a particular problem. It was ready for launch in the harbor. I was checking the outside keel and I found two or three cracks, from three inches to nine inches long, but I didn't know how deep they were." So he kept checking, even climbing inside the hull to try and determine if the cracks went all the way through. "I found one crack that had passed inspection, and I told the foreman of the basin what I had found. At the time they didn't think it was too serious. But they ended up having to open up the whole front of the ship, from the inside out. Had that ship ever been launched to sea, and loaded with supplies, who knows what might have happened."

THE RICHMOND YARD was still coming together when Kaiser received a one-paragraph memo from Vickery at the Maritime Commission authorizing additional shipways, including three more at Portland, Oregon, six at Los Angeles, six at Richmond, three at Houston, and four at Portland, Maine. Each new shipway, starting from scratch, cost roughly $1 million to build. With so much construction to manage, Kaiser turned to the two men he trusted the most to lead his shipyards.[12]

The first was his oldest son. Edgar Kaiser was born in Seattle in 1908, and he was now thirty-three. As a young boy he spent time on his father's jobs, often hoisted onto the shoulders of workers in good fun. After starting out as a waterboy and timekeeper during his teenage years for his father, he had earned greater trust from his father helping oversee successful projects during the 1930s, in particular the Boulder Dam, Bonneville Dam, and Grand Coulee Dam. On each job Edgar had proven himself an increasingly capable and strong leader who had learned from his father the value of hiring the right people for the right tasks and staying on budget and on time. Do those things, his father taught him, and the work will keep coming your way. The dams all finished on schedule and were extraordinarily lucrative, helping to raise the profile of Henry Kaiser's construction enterprise.

He had the scars to prove he wasn't afraid of hard work. While he was running carelessly on one job, he slipped in the mud and a dump truck ran over his foot and crushed it.[13] Later a bucket of ore landed on the same foot, leaving him in excruciating pain. The foot was never the same, even after five operations, and though it held him back from playing too much golf or tennis, he found other passions. He married especially wisely. His wife, Dorothy Sue Mead, was the daughter of Elwood Mead, the commissioner of the U.S. Bureau of Reclamation, a critical government agency in much of the work Kaiser pursued.

Edgar had one other achievement to boast of to his father. Back in 1938, during the Grand Coulee Dam project, he had arranged for the 15,000 workers on the massive job to get their own private health care plan, building hospital facilities near the site so they would not have to lose time traveling to a faraway hospital when they were sick or injured. So effective was it in the remote desert that the two men tucked away this idea for on-site, prepaid health care as a model to consider on an even grander scale, should the opportunity ever arise. They would not forget.[14]

AS MUCH AS Henry trusted Edgar, there was always one project that Henry Kaiser held up as the model for the type of work he wanted to be most known for, and that was the highway paving work in Cuba. Building two hundred miles of roads on a tiny island, through thick jungles, under brutal heat, with challenging communication issues, while also completing five hundred small bridges to connect the Central Highway, had been a monumental achievement that many had doubted could be done.

Once Kaiser tapped Bedford to lead the Richmond shipyard, he had to find a landing spot for Edgar. The old man hatched a plan. A new order had come in to build thirty-one American merchant ships, but they couldn't be built in Richmond, which was committed to building the British order. Kaiser had several other shipyards underway, including in Los Angeles Harbor, on the Gulf of Mexico in Houston, and six hundred miles north of Richmond, in Portland, Oregon.

The layout and conditions at Oregon Shipbuilding Company, Kaiser's largest shipyard, were almost identical to the Richmond shipyard. Henry put Edgar in charge of Oregonship, as it was called. By putting Edgar in charge of the Portland yard, Henry hoped that his son and Bedford, longtime friends and colleagues, would be motivated to compete against each other in their respective shipbuilding programs. "Competition," Henry Kaiser liked to say, "was more important than compensation."

Sure enough, the moment Edgar got to Oregon, he recognized that Bedford had a month's head start on building his shipyard and preparing to launch his first keel. Edgar wasted no time, hiring workers from local union halls and advertising job openings across the region, emphasizing no experience necessary and listing promising pay scales, knowing that would entice workers still recovering from the Great Depression.

Word of the available jobs spread beyond Oregon and lured people like Joe Dardis and his wife, Edith, all the way from North Dakota. Tired of raising cattle and being at the mercy of the economy and the weather, they packed up their two teenage daughters and took a train for two days to Portland. All four of them eventually found shipyard jobs, wearing heavy protective leather outfits to protect them as they learned to become expert welders.[15]

Edgar set up a school to teach welders how to use the forty automatic welding machines on-site. Within eight months, three thousand welders received training. In no time at all, Edgar had established his shipyard as a model for training workers and ship production.

One of Kaiser's longtime employees, Albert Heiner, remembered the decision to separate Bedford and Edgar as being both deliberate and purposeful. "Kaiser's long construction experience had convinced him that when workers are given high goals," Heiner said, "when they compete with another group, and when they get recognition for their achievements, they are sure to break one record after another."[16]

Henry Kaiser was counting on it.

CHAPTER EIGHTEEN

The Firsts

THE CHERRY BLOSSOMS IN WASHINGTON WERE IN FULL bloom. The president was looking forward to escaping the White House bubble and taking a ten-day fishing trip on Cape Cod.[1] Putting aside his worry about the war overseas, he remained upbeat and confident, and was even willing to take political gambles. The way Roosevelt saw it, if U.S. aid to Britain and Russia could somehow combine to defeat Hitler's Germany, the number of American lives spared and the amount of American money saved would be immeasurable.

Besides that, his emergency shipbuilding program was progressing full steam ahead. Gibbs & Cox, under the watchful eye of Jerry Land and the Maritime Commission, had transmitted the design plans for Liberty ships to shipyards around the country. It was like sending a chocolate chip cookie recipe to a dozen friends and telling them to follow the instructions precisely so that they all made the exact same cookie. Except this recipe called for multiple distribution centers to dole out 250,000 different pieces, parts, and components to construct a single cookie. And the cookie was 441 feet long. And from the bottom of the hull to the top of her tallest mast, she stood over 100 feet tall.

Domestically, he had reason to feel optimistic. A historic vote in March by

Congress had passed the Lend-Lease Act, allowing the United States to lend or to lease supplies for war to any nation considered "vital to the defense of the United States." The act freed up $7 billion of military spending that immediately helped industrialists like Henry Kaiser.

But instead of celebrating, Roosevelt was red hot over a handful of economic issues that were impeding the country's efforts to prepare for war. A labor strike at a California aviation plant that built important twin-engine bombers had to end, peacefully or otherwise. Roosevelt ordered federal troops to march in and break up the strike and retake control of the plant, and within a few hours of his declaration, the workers had returned to their posts and production resumed. A more stubborn problem was that the automobile industry was a roaring success, to the point where car manufacturers were using up the raw materials that the government needed to produce wartime supplies, vehicles, and machinery. Eighty percent of all rubber and 44 percent of sheet steel, two critical war materials, were instead going to automobiles. The suggestion to reduce automobile production by 50 percent was entertained, then dismissed as too radical.[2]

The first lady pushed for a softer touch, believing that Americans would oblige a White House request to save for the future, and to cut their own spending if it meant stronger defense spending. She urged Americans to start imagining their life without "new automobiles and aluminum kitchen utensils when present stocks are exhausted."[3] But her plea went largely ignored. A compromise of a 20 percent reduction in automobile production was reached.

The tension in the Atlantic Ocean was the president's gravest concern. He could not imagine America continuing to maintain the mirage of neutrality while U.S. ships were being attacked by German submarines. His voice had grown weary in recent weeks. He felt himself torn between pleas from Americans to maintain isolation and neutrality from the war in Europe and his own awareness that if he did not help Churchill, and if Britain fell to Germany, the world order could collapse.

———

ON FRIDAY, APRIL 10, an American destroyer in the Atlantic, the USS *Niblack*,[4] came across a trio of lifeboats carrying sixty-one Dutch and two Chinese crew members of a Dutch freighter. Their ship had been sunk by a German torpedo the day before. The *Niblack* collected the souls off the water, but before she could head for Iceland, her sonar detected something that sounded like a German U-boat approaching. Without hesitating, and fearing an attack, she dropped three depth charges. No explosion occurred, and a later investigation determined the *Niblack* had detected a false contact. But merely by firing on what it believed was a German submarine, the *Niblack* became the first American ship to show the world that the United States was no longer neutral. It was ready to fight and it would not wait to be fired upon first.

THEN, JUST FIVE days later, the tense mood in the White House lifted. At 1:30 p.m. on Tuesday, April 15, a group of shipyard workers and representatives from Britain gathered on the shore of the Richmond shipyard to watch the first keel be laid for the British ships. The British version was called the Ocean class. It was a month behind Kaiser's original deadline. The huge plate shop for fabricating the steel was not quite finished yet. Only three of the seven shipways were done, and an enormous clamshell dredging machine was still hard at work on the shoreline creating enough depth for ships to slide into the water safely. But no one was complaining. Kaiser was nowhere to be seen, too busy to bother with ceremonial bluster. And the act itself was anticlimactic, with enormous sheets of steel simply being slipped into place and welded together.

But the symbolism reverberated through the country. In just three months, a barren California mudflat had been converted into a bustling, round-the-clock construction yard, and more work was coming. Two days later, Kaiser got word that Richmond had been approved to set up a second shipyard, to be called Richmond Yard No. 2, to build twenty-four additional ships. Except these ships would be American, not British, and the aim was to have the second shipyard operating by September.

One week later, Kaiser's good fortunes continued. He arrived in Washington for a fifteen-minute meeting on April 22 with President Roosevelt.[5]

Though Kaiser's shipyards were leading the shipbuilding charge across the country, they were hardly alone. And on the afternoon of April 30, a rival shipyard made some history of its own when Eugene R. Grace, the president of Bethlehem Steel and Bethlehem-Fairfield Shipyard, outside Baltimore, helped to center a ship's keel onto its blocks. This was the first keel for a Liberty ship.[6] Of all the contracts issued for American ships, the Baltimore yard, set on a sprawling 174 acres and on its way to employing 35,000 shipbuilders, had the biggest one, calling for the construction of fifty ships and a shipyard with thirteen ways. The original 200 ships that the Maritime Commission had started building under Roosevelt's emergency plan was no longer a sufficient number, and another 112 had been ordered, bringing the new target to 312.

Land and Vickery surveyed the progress at shipyards across the country, and they saw trouble. Portland, Maine, and Richmond were busy building their first ships for the British and it would be months before Richmond could lay its first Liberty ship keel. Kaiser's Los Angeles shipyard was struggling to move quickly, and Maine was also moving far too slowly.

Privately, Newell and the Maritime Commission were feuding, with Newell arguing that every time the commission insisted on adding new shipways to the layout, it slowed the construction of the actual ships already underway. There were also unfounded rumors that the West Coast shipyards were hijacking steel and equipment meant for the East Coast, and even luring workers across the country with promises of better pay and housing. When Newell demanded permission to convert a nearby railroad yard into a steel storage facility, the commission rejected him and instead went forward with decimating 140 homes through eminent domain to create more land for shipbuilding. Newell opposed the move, and when a local congressman blamed him for destroying a community, he was almost tempted to walk away from the whole South Portland operation.

A heated argument erupted in Washington during a committee hearing when Land and Vickery, along with Maine Senator Owen Brewster, studied a chart that showed how far behind South Portland had fallen to the West Coast shipyards. Land and Vickery blamed Newell's operation for not hiring enough shipbuilders, allowing an absentee rate of 15 percent, having a poor shipyard layout, and not doing enough preassembly of certain parts to make construction go faster. Maine, Vickery said, was used to building boats, not ships, and its inexperience was showing. "It is not a real shipbuilding job," Vickery said. "It is a mass-production job of collecting materials. It is an entirely different job than the normal building of ships." While he praised Newell's work in Bath on the Navy destroyers, he said the construction in Portland of merchant ships was unacceptable and had to be accelerated. "The things you normally do in building a destroyer, you don't have to do in building one of the cargo ships," Vickery said.[7]

Newell was livid at the exchange when it reached him, but his patriotism was too strong. His shipyard found its footing and went on to build almost 300 Liberty ships.

But the worst progress was in the southern yards. Delta Shipyards in New Orleans had just signed a contract to build 60 Liberty Ships, but it was already falling behind schedule in construction, as was Todd's Houston Shipbuilding, which had 69 ships to build. Vickery called all of the progress "disconcerting."

Things were becoming so tense that Roosevelt and Land, rarely at odds on issues of strategy, had a strong disagreement over how much they should be helping the British. April was an especially successful month for German U-boats, which sank 195 merchant ships, one of the worst monthly tallies of the war. In early April, Land and Vickery had dinner with the British official Sir Arthur Salter, who had been instrumental in the cargo-ship contract. Land was beginning to worry that the British were relying too heavily on American assistance, and he could not help himself from giving the president a piece of his mind.

"If we do not watch our step," Land wrote in a memo to Roosevelt on April 11, 1941, "we shall find the White House en route to England with the Washington Monument as a steering oar."[8]

Roosevelt, always one to enjoy a good chuckle, replied in the same spirit three days later.

"Here is something to think over," he wrote to Land. "Which would you rather do, give away the White House and the Washington Monument and save civilization including American independence and the democratic system or have the White House and the Washington Monument taken over by people under a different regime? Think it over."[9]

Their relationship was strong enough to survive disagreements, like the one they had around the same time over how far they could push the limits of the Neutrality Act. The president called Land at home one evening and asked that certain American merchant ships be assigned to help the British in emergency situations, an action that would probably exceed the boundaries of what the Neutrality Act allowed. Land told Roosevelt he would not do it.

"Why, Jerry?" Roosevelt asked.[10]

"The action would be illegal, Mr. President," Land answered.

"Jerry, if the attorney general advises you tomorrow morning that the action I want taken is legal, will you take it?"

"Yes, sir!" Land said.

Their spat put to rest, Roosevelt continued to express pleasure at every update Land gave him regarding the shipbuilding progress across the country.

"I cannot stress too strongly the urgent necessity of keeping all of the existing shipyards in continuous operation," the president told Land.

LAND SOON HAD more good news to deliver the president. On May 19, 1941, Edgar Kaiser's Oregonship set its first keel into place, one month behind the first keel laid by Bedford in Richmond.[11] Admiral Vickery visited the Oregon yard and told the young Kaiser that the shipyard was expected to "roll ships out of here at the rate of 45 a year." Edgar heard the challenge and set a furious pace to catch up to Bedford and to meet the Maritime Commission's target.

"Boys, you've heard what they told us," Edgar told his crew of shipbuilders after hearing Vickery's words. "It's our job and we're going to put this ship out and do it fast. Let's go."[12]

Five days later, across the country, another first occurred when prefabricated steel plates were loaded onto flatbed cars in South Portland, Maine, and moved to the basin, where they were placed against the walls of the cofferdam. A pair of aerial cables dangled overhead carrying enough voltage to produce 5,000 horsepower for the welders to do their job. Maine's Hull No. 1 for the British, assigned the name *Ocean Freedom*, was underway.

The *Ocean* ship program was at full speed when Lord Halifax, the British ambassador to the United States, visited several shipyards over the summer to check their progress. In Richmond, Henry Kaiser and Bedford led him around the yard on July 16, and witnessing nearly 5,000 workers in rapid action left him astonished. Halifax asked to deliver a few words of encouragement and, more importantly, of gratitude for their effort in a war that was not even theirs to fight. Before the throng of shipbuilders as they stopped to work and stood there in their hard hats, his rousing speech brought out loud cheers from them. "What has been done here in the last six months is as near a miracle as any other human thing I've ever seen," he said. "To think that last January this place was a mudflat, and a month from now you are to launch your first ship. . . . The joint effort will be good enough to make an end to Hitler. It's wonderful. No job in the war effort is more important than what you are doing here."[13]

ON AUGUST 16, an unseasonably chilly 60-degree Saturday on San Francisco Bay, all of those 250,000 pieces, parts, and components came together in a historic moment. Nearly 10,000 people, most of them employees of the Todd Corporation and their families, gathered at the Richmond shipyard to witness the launch of the first ship under the Liberty ship design. The shipyard employed 4,698 men on the day of the first launching, a sign of what was to come. Humble little Richmond, California, was on its way toward becoming America's shipbuilding capital.[14]

It was only four months to the day from when the keel for the ship had been laid back on April 14, a production timeline that would have been unheard-of during World War I, when ships could take nine months to a year to be completed. Making the speed even more remarkable was how naive, even downright clueless, the newly hired workers were to shipbuilding. One worker in Richmond was overheard in the shipyard's early days asking, "When are we going to pour the keel?"[15] He thought a ship's keel was shaped from poured concrete rather than fabricated steel.

Technically, because it was built for the British, the *Vanguard* was an Ocean-class ship rather than a Liberty ship. She was painted a battle gray and proudly flew American and British flags from her bow.

The editor of the *San Francisco Chronicle*, Paul C. Smith, served as the day's master of ceremonies, and a radio broadcast was arranged for Americans to hear the late afternoon speeches. Half a dozen dignitaries were on hand for the celebration, including Jerry Land, wearing a dark gray pinstripe suit; his wife, the former Elizabeth Stiles from Newton, Massachusetts, with a white wreath draped around her neck; Henry Kaiser; and Sir Arthur Salter, the head of the British Merchant Shipping Commission, which was to take ownership of the ship. Also in attendance was California governor Culbert Olson, who praised Kaiser's operation for a "remarkable job" launching a ship a mere seven months after the mudflat was transformed into a shipyard.

"This is the first of several scores of British-owned ships built in American yards to carry the weapons of war and food for those who use them," Sir Arthur told the audience. "It will be followed by hundreds, and, if need be, by thousands of similar American-owned ships destined for the same service. The Battle of the Atlantic is not yet won. But this ship shows how the battle can be won. Constructive energy can outmatch destructive fury."[16]

He explained the name painted in white on the ship's hull—*Ocean Vanguard*.

"Since America can produce as much steel as the rest of the world together, the key of victory in this war of steel is here. That is why we call this ship the *Ocean Vanguard*—V for victory on the ocean. It is in the van of the vast new merchant Navy which will carry the instruments and sinews of war and then, as the last and greatest of its cargoes, victory itself."

Land followed with his own rousing speech, promising the crowd and those listening at home that producing "two ships a day will keep the Germans away."[17] He reminded Americans that "ships have won every great international war," and he vowed that America was prepared to construct ships twice as fast as it did during World War I.

"This ship, the *Ocean Vanguard*, and the hundreds of her sister ships that will be produced in the shipyards of America and Great Britain, will win this war," Land said. "Of that I have no doubt. The sooner the ships are built, the sooner the war will be won."

Land also provided the audience with some news in his spirited speech. He said America was no longer aiming to build a few hundred Liberty ships.

"Our immediate goal in America's supreme shipbuilding program of all time is to produce more than 1,200 merchant vessels by the end of 1943. That means two ships every day for the next two years!" In a speech a few weeks later, he would provide more details, promising that 130 ships would be built by the end of 1941, an additional 574 by the end of 1942, and 220 more in the first quarter alone of 1943.

For Henry Kaiser, a man not known for emotion and who frequently would skip celebrations that involved his achievements, his mere presence at the launching of the first cargo ship signaled that even he was impressed. Short and potbellied, and wearing a dark gray suit, he stepped to the microphone with a big grin and thanked the crowd for attending "this momentous hour."

"I wish the ship could speak for herself," Kaiser said, beginning a speech that, for him, was unusually poignant.

She would tell you of the strong and capable hands that piece by piece, put together every vital part of her. She would tell you of the inspired coordination and cooperation which cut time to a minimum and made it possible to make her a living thing out of inanimate materials. She would give you her thanks for her life and pledge you faithful service in the fight for freedom. She would give you a message of courage, faith, hope and cheer. To the men who built her and their wives and sweethearts with sincere appreciation and gratitude, this mass of steel, about to become a great ship, says thank you![18]

With the crowd cheering her on, Elizabeth Land stepped forward and grabbed the champagne bottle dangling from a ribbon. Sirens and whistles filled the air, as a band played both the American and British national anthems. But before she swung back her arm, she offered a few final words to the audience.

"*Ocean Vanguard*—the name rings true, and sounds hope for the future, and the freedom of the seas—not the Atlantic alone, but all seas of all the world. All must be left open for free and friendly intercourse among all peoples!"[19]

As she finished, she stepped toward the massive hull, reached back, and, to her surprise, watched as the ship slowly started to slide down the shipway. Inadvertently, the launching crew had sliced the steel rods that helped keep the hull still. Mrs. Land quickly recovered and gently slapped the bottle against the ship's bow to avoid missing the moment, and the *Ocean Vanguard* slid down the inclined shipway and splashed into the water at 5:22 p.m., the height of the heaviest running tide.

"I christen thee *Ocean Vanguard*," she shouted, "and wish good luck to all who sail thee."

A tugboat pulled alongside the *Vanguard* and guided it to nearby docks so it could be fitted with final touches for service. As she faded from their view, the crowd roared its approval at witnessing history.

"They slid down fast after that, the *Ocean Vigil, Ocean Voice, Ocean Venture, Ocean Viking, Ocean Vestal, Ocean Vesper*—and so on, far into the dictionary," one shipbuilder who was there that day said.

AS THE FINAL days of summer wound down, President Roosevelt continued to wrestle with how far America should step to involve herself in an expanding war between Germany, Britain, and Russia. During his fishing trip off Cape Cod while on board the presidential yacht *Potomac*, he managed to slip away from the spying reporters tracking his whereabouts to hold a rendezvous with the British prime minister in Placentia Bay, off Newfoundland. Both men arrived into a mist-filled harbor in clandestine fashion, Roosevelt first in the Navy cruiser

Augusta, and the prime minister a day later on the battleship *Prince of Wales*.[20] The location was one of the bases that Britain had transferred to the United States in the destroyer deal between the countries to get around the Neutrality Act. Churchill used the meeting to press Roosevelt to start allowing U.S. Navy ships to escort British ships traveling through the Atlantic in convoys and to encourage the United States to supply more aid to Russia to use against Germany.

But for Roosevelt, it was all one step too far. He refused to commit to anything that involved U.S. ships in the war. He knew the pulse of his citizens. Congress had just narrowly approved an extension of the military draft—by a single vote. The appetite for war remained low at best. The most that Roosevelt could promise Churchill was that the American military would pounce at the first episode that riled up his people and shifted public opinion in his country away from neutrality. Only then would he feel empowered to act. Their meeting ended with an emotional church service on board Churchill's ship with British and American sailors singing hymns beneath the ship's guns. Churchill cried, knowing that many of those on board could soon die in battle.

"Every word seemed to stir the heart," he recalled later. "It was a great hour to live by."[21]

ROOSEVELT AND CHURCHILL were six hours apart during the summer of 1941 when both men received the same grim news—Hitler had fulfilled a desire he'd held for years with a predawn invasion of Joseph Stalin's Soviet Union, an action of war he had all but forecast in his autobiographical manifesto, *Mein Kampf*, in 1925. "This colossal empire in the East is ripe for dissolution," he wrote. "The end of Jewish domination will also be the end of Russia as a state."

Churchill immediately planned an evening address on the BBC, telling an aide beforehand, "I have only one purpose, the destruction of Hitler."[22]

For Roosevelt, the politics were more complicated. Unlike Churchill, his country was not yet officially at war with Germany. Many Americans saw Hitler's invasion of Russia as validation for staying as far away from the fighting as possible and letting a pair of despised countries led by deranged dictators kill each other. Long live isolationism! Roosevelt knew that position was unsustainable, and his evidence was mounting. Hitler's Russian invasion added another front to the war. Richmond, which already had two shipyards for building the Ocean ships for the British and Liberty ships for America, opened a third shipyard to handle construction of larger naval or cargo ships. Jerry Land sent a memo to Roosevelt expressing the urgency.

"Because of increased shipping requirements, both our own and the British, and decreases in available tonnage due to sinkings, it appears that our present shipbuilding program needs to be expanded," Land wrote. He asked the president for an additional $1.2 billion for new ships and new shipways. The president agreed and went a step further, proclaiming an unlimited national emergency. Shipbuilding across the country began to hum. The yards were now operating around the clock, and not a moment too soon.

ON THE MORNING of September 4, 1941, the destroyer USS *Greer* was on its way to Argentia, the naval station in Placentia Bay, Newfoundland, where Churchill and Roosevelt had met only a few weeks earlier, flying her American flag in broad daylight, loaded with mail and passengers.[23] A British Lockheed Hudson flying nearby alerted the *Greer*'s command to a German U-boat, *U-652*, that had crash-dived ten miles ahead, sometimes an indication that it was preparing for an attack. The *Greer* sped up and used her sonar to spot the submarine and track her for three hours. It seemed as if a confrontation would be avoided, until the pilot of the Hudson dropped three depth charges into the water near the German sub. The explosions did not strike *U-652*, but they shook the water violently, prompting the sub commander to assume the American destroyer had fired upon him. The *U-652* fired a torpedo at the *Greer* and missed, and the *Greer* responded with its own pattern of eleven depth charges. Both vessels evaded the enemy fire and went their separate ways.

When word reached the White House of the encounter, Roosevelt's patience expired. He issued a "shoot on sight" policy toward any German submarines that entered American defensive zones, his strongest statement to date on the war, and one that polls showed was widely supported by the American public.

At a press conference a day after the *Greer* incident, reporters confronted Roosevelt, questioning whether this meant the United States was now at war. When one reporter asked whether it was U.S. policy to fire back at an attacking sub, Roosevelt snapped: "What would you do if somebody fired a torpedo at you?"[24]

Finally, another reporter touched a nerve with the president by suggesting that the whole incident should just be forgotten since neither vessel was injured. Roosevelt chose to respond with a brief allegory.

Once upon a time, he began, some children living out in the country were on their way to school when somebody fired shots at them from nearby bushes. Their father decided to forget the moment and to move on since nobody had been hit. The president said the decision that the father made would not be the position the United States government would be taking. The bushes, he said sternly, were absolutely being searched for the shooter of the *Greer*.

"What would be done if we find the marauder?" a reporter asked.

"Eliminate it," Roosevelt answered.

CHAPTER NINETEEN

Liberty Fleet Day

ON THE MORNING OF SEPTEMBER 27, 1941, MOST AMERICANS were not fretting about imminent war, or nervous that Germany had just commissioned two new submarines while Japan was commissioning a new aircraft carrier. And they were oblivious to the mass slaughter Hitler was ordering, with Nazis wiping out entire villages of Jews, rounding up and shooting them or forcing them into labor camps until they starved to death. Widespread news of the Holocaust was a year away still, which is why, as summer transitioned into fall, Americans were focused on more fun and frivolous matters.

Citizen Kane came out for previews in February to glowing reviews. But by the time it hit theaters officially on September 5, the aging and legendary media titan William Randolph Hearst, who was seventy-eight, was criticizing the little-known twenty-five-year-old director and star of the film, Orson Welles, and Welles was threatening to sue Hearst for attempting to suppress the film. Their Hollywood feud dampened its box-office performance—it bombed—but accolades poured in, and the film would be nominated for nine Academy Awards.

As good as it was, *Citizen Kane* was no match for an epic summer of sports. A cocky, stocky Irishman named Billy Conn nearly shocked the world by outboxing the heavily favored Joe Louis for most of their epic fight. And the baseball season of 1941 began with tragedy and ended with history. On June 2, fans mourned the death at just thirty-seven years old of Lou Gehrig, one of the game's greatest hitters, and a member of the New York Yankees' famed Murderers' Row, who earned the nickname "Iron Horse" for playing 2,130 consecutive games. Gehrig seemed indestructible, which is why fans were shocked when he retired during a game in June 1939, suffering from a paralyzing illness. Two years later he was dead, and his diagnosis of amyotrophic lateral sclerosis came to be known as Lou Gehrig's disease. Fellow Yankee Joe DiMaggio helped lift fans back up during the summer of 1941 when he safely hit in a record 56 straight games.

In any other season, DiMaggio's feat would have been the only story line that mattered in baseball. But another great hitter, and future war hero, the Boston Red Sox slugger Ted Williams, stole DiMaggio's headlines when he entered the month of September with a strong chance to bat over .400 for the season, something that had been accomplished only a handful of times in the game's history. After he walloped three home runs on September 1, Williams's every at-bat became baseball theater, with fans wondering, *Will he or won't he?* On the morning of September 27, the Red Sox had just three games left in their season for Williams to try to hold his average above .400. (He did, and just four months later, he was drafted as a pilot into the Navy Reserve.)

AMID ALL THAT excitement, drumming up public excitement about a fleet of hulking, gray, cargo-carrying merchant ships proved challenging for Jerry Land's Maritime Commission. The few individual recent ship launchings that had occurred elicited little more than a collective yawn from the citizenry. Newspaper editors showed a similar apathy, burying the stories deep inside their publications.

"SHIP FOR BRITAIN GOES INTO WATER," the *New York Times* reported on August 17 to announce the *Ocean Vanguard*'s arrival. It was a historic moment, the launching of the first Ocean-class ship for the British, under the Liberty ship design, from Kaiser's new shipyard in Richmond. Yet the news appeared on page 26 of the *Times*, next to a story about Westchester County elections.

Jerry Land refused to sit by quietly. He decided the Liberty ship program needed a shot in the arm, a boost to make people fully appreciate the manufacturing miracle taking place in shipyards, and to lift the morale of the workers at the same time. He knew that a number of Liberty ships were nearing completion in early September and he did not want the moment to pass with just a series of small, brief, individual ceremonies in various cities. He wanted to make a public relations splash, and he had an idea.

The naming of individual ships, along with the launching ceremonies, would not be boring or routine or small. They would be parties! Morale-boosting celebrations of patriotic symbolism. And they would have touches of real drama and human emotion to poke at the hearts of Americans. Watching a gigantic ship taller than a ten-story building slide down a ramp into the water with a tremendous roar and loud splash felt both dangerous and exciting for the thousands who gathered to witness it.

But for those who handled the launchings, a specially trained crew, it was a delicate and risky feat. They first had to raise the hull and construct a wooden cradle to ready the ship for launching.[1] When the launching moment approached, they would hammer wooden spikes into the ground to create a tiny bit of space between the hull and cradle, so that the ship was resting gingerly on top. At the same time, in the same place, they also welded a series of steel "burn-off" plates. As they listened to the ceremony, waiting for the champagne bottle smashing, they would knock the wooden spikes away, leaving the ship precariously attached to the temporary steel plates. When it was time, they quickly burned off the steel plates until the ship slowly started sliding under its own weight into the water. Sometimes heavy chains helped slow the ship down so that her splash was more controlled, at which point the waiting tugboats dragged her away for finishing. Some ships went so hard and fast into the water it almost looked like they would tip over.

Usually the ceremonial bottle of champagne only added to the excitement of the moment. As it turned out, for some who were asked to perform a ship's christening, the pressure was daunting to not embarrass themselves in front of a crowd by swinging and missing or failing to smash the bottle. When the wife of a shipbuilder, Mrs. Martin Staley, agreed to christen the SS *Nathaniel Hawthorne*, in Portland, Oregon, she spent weeks practicing beforehand by smashing milk bottles against their family's barn in Yault, Washington.[2] When her moment in the spotlight came, she connected heartily. Other times, accidents had nothing to do with the champagne smashing and everything to do with the traffic on the water. One of the British Ocean vessels, *Vigil*, splashed into the water with such speed that she broke her chains and slammed into a Russian freighter. Nobody was hurt and damage to both ships was minimal, but because Henry Kaiser's wife had been the one to christen the *Vigil*, it was an embarrassing mishap for the crew.[3]

The christening of a ship was like a Broadway theater first putting a show's name up in lights on a marquee. Everybody loves that moment when the curtain goes up for the first time—which is why on September 27 Land orchestrated Liberty Fleet Day, a celebration of fourteen opening nights in eleven different cities. Chester, Pennsylvania; Baltimore; Los Angeles; Tacoma; Pascagoula, Mississippi; Kearny, New Jersey; San Francisco; Wilmington, Delaware; Quincy, Massachusetts; Portland, Oregon; and Richmond all made plans to celebrate the day. Three of the ships to be christened would be from the Liberty fleet: the SS *Patrick Henry* in Baltimore, the SS *Star of Oregon* in Portland, and the SS *John C. Fremont* in Los Angeles. Two would be Ocean-class ships for the British, and the remainder would be a mishmash of different-sized American cargo and naval vessels.

Because Henry Kaiser controlled so many Liberty shipyards, Land sought his assurance that he would cooperate and help organize the celebrations. Kaiser agreed, with two stipulations: Always mindful of his budget, he wanted to serve Coca-Cola and other light refreshments to show the workers appreciation. Also, he wanted the government to reimburse his company for the petty charges.

"This is a goodwill program and will stimulate labor-employer relations and is not a private party for a few select friends of the builders," Kaiser wrote to the commission.[4]

But other shipyards wanted even more glitz for their ceremonies, including engraved silver plates, framed photographs from the ceremonies, wristwatches with diamond studs for the main participants, and elegant lunches. The women who christened the ships almost always received a gift, which varied yard to yard, and sometimes raised eyebrows in Washington. When a Senate committee looked into five gifts, like an expensive decorative plate and a silver cigarette box, and discovered that the total value of them was $6,457, and that all the women who smashed the champagne bottles were related to government officials, and that even Eleanor Roosevelt had received a $553 gift, the whole gifting program was reined in. When the Liberty SS *Ernie Pyle*, honoring the famous war correspondent, was launched near the war's end, his widow received $25.[5]

For Land it all became a delicate balancing act. He wanted the shipyard workers and shipyard owners to feel appreciated and important, but without such lavish expenses that made the Maritime Commission appear out of touch with the gravity of the time. Liberty Fleet Day had to be about patriotism, not pomp.

The British felt the same. Britain's minister of war transport, Lord Leathers, sent a cable of appreciation to Land on the morning of September 27.

"Liberty Fleet Day symbolizes for us and our allies the cause for which we are fighting," it read. "Only by the freedom of the seas can the freedom of the world be secured."[6]

It was a brilliant marketing stroke by Land to hold a single day dedicated to launching multiple ships around the country. Being chosen to sponsor a ship became a huge honor. The Maritime Commission chose fourteen women to christen the fourteen ships, from wives of senators and governors and representatives to relatives of the wealthy shipyard owners, to descendants of the famous persons whose names were painted on the ships. But in order to make the day a total success, Land knew there was only one person who could make Americans pay attention for certain and whose mere presence would ensure front-page publicity.

IT WAS A sad time at the White House. Not only was Roosevelt still mourning the death of his mother a few weeks earlier, but the first lady's brother, Hall Roosevelt, had also just died, and on the morning of Liberty Fleet Day they participated in his burial service near their Hyde Park, New York, residence.[7] By then Roosevelt's speech was all finished and special equipment was set up so that his prerecorded words could be played over loudspeakers at all eleven shipyards hosting launchings.

His speech needed to serve a number of political purposes. It would highlight the work being done in the shipyards for the last nine months. It would have to boost the morale of the workers and their families. It would lay the groundwork for him to ask that the Neutrality Act either be modified or repealed, once and for all. And, with the largest single-day launching of new ships since World War I, it would send a message to Hitler, and to the world, boasting of what America was capable of producing in times of great urgency.

Shortly after noon, as thousands of people gathered at shipyards around the country, the president's distinctive voice echoed into the air, transmitted across a nationwide radio network.

"My fellow Americans," he began, "this is a memorable day in the history of American shipbuilding—a memorable day in the emergency defense of the nation. Today, from dawn to dark, fourteen ships are being launched—on the Atlantic, on the Pacific, and on the Gulf, and among them is the first Liberty ship, the *Patrick Henry*. While we are proud of what we are doing, this is certainly no time to be content."[8]

He emphasized the importance of rehabilitating the Merchant Marine at an accelerated speed, which was essential to protecting against Hitler's aggression.

"The ship workers of America are doing a great job," he proclaimed. "They have made a commendable record for efficiency and speed. With every new ship they are striking a telling blow at the menace to our nation and the liberty of the free peoples of the world. They struck fourteen such blows today. They have caught the true spirit with which all this nation must be imbued if Hitler and other aggressors of his ilk are to be prevented from crushing us."

In a spirited closing, he said America must protect its ships from enemy torpedoes.

"The *Patrick Henry*, as one of the Liberty ships launched today, renews that great patriot's stirring demand: 'Give me liberty or give me death.' There shall be no death for America, for democracy, for freedom! There must be liberty, worldwide and eternal. That is our prayer—our pledge to all mankind."

ELEANOR KUNITZ WAS an odd choice to be put in charge of naming some of the most important ships the United States had built in decades. A red-haired, little-known actress, she had been living a quiet life with a poet in Bucks County, Pennsylvania, when he was drafted by the Army and left her behind. In her search for work to keep busy while he was away, she stumbled into a public relations opening with the Maritime Commission.[9]

With construction of 200 Liberty ships commenced, the commission created the Ship Naming Committee, tasked with creating a list of hundreds of names so that a new name could quickly be chosen every time a Liberty was finished and ready to be christened. Kunitz eventually was put in charge of the Naming Committee. It was a quiet role at first, as only a few ships needed to be named. But as dozens of ships moved nearer to completion, and hundreds more were in various stages of construction around the country, Kunitz needed help. Shipyards were granted permission to form their own subcommittees to decide on names for the ships they built, and they submitted their favorite names to Kunitz, whose department held final approval authority.

Once it was decided that all the ships were to be named after the most famous, deserving, and, importantly, dead Americans in history, naming one after the great orator Patrick Henry was an easy decision. With the founding fathers and so many patriots from the Revolutionary War, the Civil War, even the most recent world war, finding three hundred names was not expected to be a challenge. Thomas Jefferson, James Polk, and Calvin Coolidge were all easy choices. Nevertheless, the role of the Naming Committee was to establish categories for names, to make sure they were not all politicians and war heroes, and assuredly not all men. Amelia Earhart, Betsy Ross, and Louisa May Alcott were as deserving of the honor as Daniel Boone, Benjamin Franklin, and Edgar Allan Poe.

As the Liberty ship program would grow during the war, so did the list of names, and their backgrounds. Schoolchildren were asked to suggest names for ships. Authors and poets, athletes and actresses, scientists, painters, explorers, congressmen, railroad builders, college presidents, historians, doctors, social reformers, singers, abolitionists, were all put on to the growing list. At first only Americans made it. But it was not long before prominent foreigners whose ties to America were deemed profound made the list as well.

Another consideration was making sure two ships were not named after similar-sounding or similarly spelled names, to avoid confusion if they were both out at sea, and one of them was in distress. There would be 193 cargo ships with the first name *William*, and 11 with a last name of *William*, *Williams*, or *Williamson*. And, naturally, there was the SS *William Williams*, to honor the Connecticut delegate and founding father who signed the Declaration of Independence. In the end, some confusion was inevitable. There were too many Johns in history, and far too many with the last name Brown, Johnson, Jones, or Smith.

Some ships were named with good public relations in mind. The SS *Davey Crockett* and SS *Sam Houston* were both built in Texas. And there was unanimous agreement that all ships were to be named after dead people. That took egos out of the conversation.

"We couldn't get into any hassles with VIPs who wanted ships named after themselves or members of their families," Land said in explaining the decision. When it was suggested that Land himself was deserving of a ship in his name one day, he squashed the idea, instead agreeing to a ship in his father's name, Scott E. Land.

But even the decision about only using dead people occasionally got messy. When a politician on the West Coast learned there was a ship in his name, he wrote discreetly to the commission to inform them he was, in fact, not dead.

"I'm not in dry dock and I don't need my bottom scraped," he wrote. "Please change the name."[10]

The commission wrote back, explaining that the ship was not named for him, but in honor of an individual with the same name who died years ago.

SHE WAS ALL dolled up for her big day, America's first Liberty ship, resting in shipway No. 1 at the Bethlehem-Fairfield Shipyard in Baltimore. Her gray hull glistened, her bow was decorated in red, white, and blue bunting, and her rainbow of colored code flags flapped in a mild-September breeze. Liberty ship SS *Patrick Henry* was ready.[11] Roads leading to the yard were bumper-to-bumper with cars as thousands of people came to watch her christening. They erupted in cheers when President Roosevelt's speech recalled the stirring words of Patrick Henry, "Give me liberty or give me death."

Jerry Land was there too, and his remarks seemed to be aimed not only at the audience at the shipyard, but to every Liberty shipbuilder from Maine to California, from North Carolina to New Orleans. Even though the shipbuilding program was moving swiftly and ahead of the president's desired schedule, it was not enough. Since the president's announcement back in January, not even a half-dozen new ships had been launched. He said the shipyards must continue to accelerate, striving "for more speed, and still more speed." Today's Americans, Land urged, "must almost attain the superhuman," just as their forefathers once did.

The event was choreographed down to the minute, with the agenda calling for the ship's ties to be snipped at 12:30 p.m. But at 12:19, Mrs. Henry Wallace, the wife of Roosevelt's vice president, stepped forward carrying a large bouquet of three dozen roses. She set the roses aside and reached out to grab the traditional bottle of champagne to be smashed against the hull. Just as Land was finishing his speech, and blasts from harbor whistles drowned out his closing words, the vessel unexpectedly started to slide down its ramp, catching everyone by surprise.

Somebody grabbed the bottle dangling off the hull and thrust it into the vice president's wife's hand. Just as a voice shouted, "Now!" she leaned as far over the rail as she could and slugged the bottle against the moving hull, interrupting Land's speech. The ship continued down its ramp, fresh champagne droplets dripping off its nose, and splashed into Chesapeake Bay, where waiting tugboats pulled up alongside it.

The Baltimore Civic Band broke into song, playing the "The Star-Spangled Banner," cheers erupted, and a flock of twenty pigeons was released in honor of the moment. The celebration continued nearby with a buffet lunch of lobsters and crabs at the Belvedere Hotel. But back at the shipyard, with the *Patrick Henry* safely away, only minutes passed before it was time to get back to business. The shipway was greased once more in preparation for the next keel to be laid, the next Liberty to be built.

Across the country, the day's thirteen other ceremonies went off without a hitch.[12] Fittingly, the last ships to splash into the water on Liberty Fleet Day were Kaiser ships—the SS *Star of Oregon*, built at the Oregon Shipbuilding Corporation in Portland under Edgar Kaiser's watch, and the British ships *Ocean Voice* and *Ocean Venture*, built under Clay Bedford's leadership in Richmond.

With 25,000 people watching, and American flags dangling off its stern, the *Venture* was christened by Clay Bedford's wife and the *Voice* was christened by the wife of a London official on hand to take ownership of both ships. Godfrey Fisher, a British consul general to San Francisco, praised the American workers for building ships that were "desperately needed" and that served as a warning to aggressor nations.

"There seems to be no limits to American enterprise and ingenuity," Fisher told the cheering crowd. "To have contrived within the space of a few months to convert derelict mudflats into a thriving shipyard launching a steady stream of ocean-going vessels is surely a phenomenon without precedence even in this age of miracles."

But the last words of the ceremony belonged to Henry Kaiser.

"Today we would not be privileged to gather here but for cooperation—many working as one to fulfill our promise," he bellowed. "So we as a nation must above all cooperate one for all and all for one."[13]

BY ALMOST EVERY measure, Jerry Land's Liberty Fleet Day was a resounding success. Newspapers around the country carried stories of the launchings on their front pages, the individual christenings were attended by thousands and sometimes tens of thousands of people, and the complete transcript of President Roosevelt's fighting words appeared verbatim in publications. His speech could be heard across the country, starting with a 6 a.m. launching in Chester, Pennsylvania, and concluding at 8:30 p.m. with the ceremonies in Richmond, California. One line in particular from the president called out the shipbuilders in the country, as he implored them to not let the excitement of the day permit them even one minute of relaxing their efforts.

"We must build more cargo ships and still more cargo ships—and we must speed the program until we achieve a launching each day, then two ships a day, fulfilling the building program undertaken by the Maritime Commission," Roosevelt said.[14]

The *Patrick Henry* had taken 150 days to complete, or five months, from the time her keel was laid on April 30, 1941, until she was christened on September 27. Kaiser's Richmond shipyard, meanwhile, had finished building the *Ocean Vanguard* for the British in four months and launched it in August, an equally remarkable pace considering the Richmond shipyard hadn't existed at the start of the year.

ON THE SAME weekend that America celebrated Liberty Fleet Day, Germany's atrocities continued. While Roosevelt was proclaiming the launching of fourteen ships in a single day as a "telling blow" against Hitler, the Nazis executed more than thirty thousand Jews just outside the city of Kyiv at a ravine called Babi Yar.

At sea, German U-boats continued to pummel British and Allied ships. Just three days before Liberty Fleet Day, on September 24, a single German sub, *U-107*, managed to attack three British vessels within hours of each other. All three cargo ships were sunk, three sailors were killed, while the others were rescued by nearby ships, and the British Admiralty was forced to begin diverting its convoys toward new and safer routes. The *U-107* was not just any German sub. It was commanded by the son-in-law of Admiral Karl Dönitz, who had been one of Germany's leading U-boat commanders in World War I and earned the trust of Hitler to lead the country's U-boat attacks two decades later.[15] Dönitz's strategy revolved all around tonnage of ships—he had calculated that if Germany could sink 700,000 tons of shipping per month, there was no possible way that American and British shipbuilders could replace those tons at the same speed. It would only be a matter of time, he reasoned, before Britain would succumb to his relentless U-boat attacks, like the ones perpetrated by his son-in-law in *U-107*.

CHAPTER TWENTY

Launching and Loading

AS JOYOUS AS THE LIBERTY FLEET DAY CELEBRATIONS HAD been, they had painted a picture of a half-truth to the nation. The three Liberty ships and two Ocean-class ships for the British, along with the other nine vessels launched on September 27, did not sail off heroically into war the moment they hit the water with a celebratory splash. Launching a Liberty ship merely sent it a few hundred feet downriver, or a few miles up the shore, depending on its shipyard. And that's where a new crisis was emerging.

A newly launched Liberty ship was still the property of the yard that built it, and it could not be delivered and transferred as a finished product to the United States government because it wasn't done yet. It was just a shell, an empty hull with an empty deckhouse, lacking the organs, guts, and arteries to give it life. It was a car without a transmission or brakes or a steering system. But the shipways were far too valuable to hold a Liberty for weeks after it was completed, just so its final touches could be applied. That's why christenings occurred the moment a ship was deemed sailable, allowing a shipway to be cleared and prepped for the next keel to be lowered into place.

"Finished" Liberty ships went to their outfitting docks. From the early days and months of the shipbuilding program, outfitting quickly became the weak link and source of major frustration for the Maritime Commission. Too often, once a ship was launched, outfitting took just as long as the construction time, and even longer. That meant a three-month ship was, in real terms, a six-month ship by the time it was delivered to the Maritime Commission, hardly the sort of speed and urgency that Roosevelt had in mind when he announced the program back in January. Launching ceremonies gave the false impression of a finished product, like baking a birthday cake for a party, but leaving the frosting to be done weeks later. Everything seemed to be happening at record speed—the erection of the shipyards, the addition of new shipways, the laying of keels and the building of the ships, and the launching ceremonies. Yet none of it was happening fast enough.

Within days of Roosevelt issuing his "shoot on sight" order for American naval vessels on September 11, 1941, Germany had flouted the warning and taunted the president. Six American cargo ships were quickly sunk, and the SS *Pink Star*, a small American cargo ship flying under the Panamanian flag, became the seventh.[1] It was sunk by a German sub in North Atlantic waters near Greenland. In addition to the loss of life—thirteen of her thirty-five crew members perished—the sinking sent a vast supply of evaporated milk and enough cheddar cheese "to feed more than three and a half million laborers in Britain for an entire week" to the bottom of the ocean.[2] Because the commander of the *Pink Star* had been Canadian, Canada's newspapers took special interest in the sinking, and they were blunt in their assessment of what was taking place. "Hitler has fired first—the shooting has started," the *Ottawa Citizen* reported.[3]

THE LIBERTY SHIPS were supposed to be the solution to America's and Great Britain's desperate need for more cargo ships by filling the oceans with so many of them they would overwhelm Germany's vaunted U-boat fleet. Instead the production of war supplies was outpacing the production of the ships to transport them, a point that *Fortune* raised with urgency under the headline "The No. 1 Bottleneck Now Is Lack of Ships."[4] The *Patrick Henry* became the unfortunate symbol for the woes of outfitting—its keel was laid April 1941, it was launched five months later on Liberty Fleet Day, but it was not scheduled to be delivered to the Maritime Commission until December 31, 1941, eight months in total from start to finish. "From one great crisis we have lunged into another," *Fortune* wrote. "The 1941 crisis of production and materials has been succeeded by the 1942 crisis of shipping."

During the early days of the Liberty ship program, outfitting a ship was taken for granted, thought to be little more than final housekeeping touch-ups that could be handled in a week or two. Instead it became a daunting, tedious, time-consuming journey, which the magazine at the Marinship shipyard in Northern California described as "500,000 things to do in 45 days."[5] Outfitting included installing electrical systems, the propulsion machinery, and ventilating equipment and getting in all of the pipes and plumbing, and if any of those parts were held up by a steel shortage, or a shipping delay, or a bookkeeping snafu, a 441-foot cargo ship that was 95 percent completed could sit for weeks or longer as war raged overseas.

"Seven Liberties . . . were held in the fitting basins for want of valves, fire-control apparatus, radio equipment, piping," *Fortune* wrote. "A few yards have no criticism of steel deliveries, but in some the flow is described as 'jerky,' and in others as being 'too late and too little.'"

THE MOST IMPORTANT step at outfitting was testing the hull for water-tightness.[6] Every weld was inspected belowdecks to make sure there were no leaks. Electricians, pipefitters, burners, welders, machine operators, painters, riggers were all waiting at outfitting for a new ship to arrive, and the moment it docked, they pounced. Officers' quarters still had carpentry that needed finishing. The telegraph still required electrical work. Pipes still needed asbestos insulation. There was no waiting for one task to be completed before another started.

In addition to inspecting the hull, one of the first tests run on a finished

Liberty was checking the steam-driven cargo winches, booms, and the three Whirley cranes so that cargo could be loaded. The cranes, each one operated from an individual mast house on deck, would have to lift tanks, jeeps, ambulances, and boxed-up airplanes, not to mention hundreds of boxes of supplies and ammunition. They had to be tested to make sure they were secure and up to the task. A flat barge would pull alongside a Liberty, carrying four enormous blocks of concrete weighing a total of 62 tons. The strongest crane was designed to lift 50 tons, but for the test more weight than the maximum was used. Once all four concrete blocks were wrapped and hooked to the winches, a boom tester gave the signal for crane operators to begin, and four different winches lifted the blocks for the test hoist. The blocks were positioned directly over the cargo hold to make sure that the cranes and booms were secure, and the weight could be safely lowered. It took about an hour and a half per Liberty ship to test its 50-ton, 15-ton, and 5-ton booms. There could be no chance of dropping a 60,000-pound Sherman tank into a cargo hold, where it would crush dozens of other vehicles or boxes and delay a ship's loading by days or weeks.

The very final step before a shipyard handed over a Liberty to the Maritime Commission was the sea trial. This test drive allowed a small crew to put the ship through all of its paces, pushing the propulsion system, testing the steering mechanism, making sure the fuel use was appropriate.[7] A group of data analysts went on every sea trial to read the gauges and record the numbers to make sure the computations added up. Even the mess halls on a ship got tested by a chef to make sure that twenty-four hours into a journey, the kitchen remained functional so it could continue providing meals for eighty hungry sailors. Test meals were not scrambled eggs and toast, but such elaborate servings as grilled lamb chops, Kennebec salmon with Béarnaise sauce, Yorkshire pudding, or poached filet of sole. A single sea trial could take half a day; it left its dock in the morning and returned by dinnertime, and the moment a ship was deemed seaworthy, there was no waiting around for it to join the fight. Hitler was showing no fear, boasting in a radio interview, "I can beat any other power in the world."

CHAPTER TWENTY-ONE

Neutral No More

ONE MONTH AFTER LIBERTY FLEET DAY, ON THE EVENING of October 23, 1941, moms and dads and the young children of New York City flooded into the Broadway Theatre at the corner of 53rd Street to meet an animated, big-eared, flying elephant named Dumbo. The *New York Times* gushed the next day, "Never did we expect to fall in love with an elephant. But after meeting up with Dumbo at the Broadway Theatre last night we have thoroughly transferred our affections to this package of pachyderm." At just sixty-four minutes, it was short for a feature film, but nevertheless, a flying cartoon elephant was exactly what Americans needed that fall. It was, for everyone, a perilous time.

Only a few hours earlier, the USS *Reuben James*, a Navy destroyer, pushed off from the Canadian coast of Newfoundland.[1] She'd had an unremarkable existence up until this day. First launched just after the end of World War I, she spent the 1920s mostly patrolling the safe coast off South America until being decommissioned in 1931, with little need for her services. Eight years would pass until, with tensions rising around the world, the Navy returned the *Reuben James* to its Atlantic Fleet.

In command of her was a broad-shouldered, thirty-five-year-old blond Texan with the clean-shaven face of a teenager. Heywood Lane Edwards was a rising star in the U.S. Navy thanks to his wrestling exploits in the 1928 Olympics. After serving on half a dozen submarines and destroyers for more than a decade, he had assumed command of the *James*.

Departing from Newfoundland on October 23, Edwards's mission was to help escort a convoy of forty-two British merchant military ships headed for home through neutral waters. Ordinarily it would have been a safe and routine voyage, but as Hitler had shown, no waters were safe anymore. That same morning, a German U-boat, the *U-563*, torpedoed the British destroyer HMS *Cossack* in the Atlantic Ocean. The *Cossack* was wounded so badly she would sink in bad weather four days later.

On October 25, two days after the *Reuben James* left Newfoundland, a German submarine, identified only as *U-552*, left its French port of Saint-Nazaire. Its mission was to patrol the waters of the North Atlantic and eliminate any threat in the war zone. The *U-552* was notorious in its homeland for its nickname, Roter Teufel, meaning "Red Devil," and for the devil-like figure painted on its conning tower. It had already accumulated a fierce and merciless battle record, having sunk a dozen British and Norwegian tankers and freighters in recent months and even taken down an innocent Icelandic trawler that found itself in the wrong place at the wrong time.

For one week in late October, the *Reuben James* and the Red Devil navigated the Atlantic, one traveling on the surface, one below, both slowly making their way in the direction of the western coast of Iceland. Dawn approached on the morning of October 31 when the *Reuben James*, moving steadily at 10 mph, turned to investigate a bearing that it had detected just after 5:30 a.m. Sensing that a U-boat attack was imminent, Edwards positioned the *James* between the submarine and a British civilian ammunition ship. With no warning, a torpedo intended for the British ship ripped into the port side of the *Reuben James*. The destroyer's entire bow was aflame in minutes and sinking into the dark waters. The ship's stern followed five minutes later, with her own depth charges blowing up as the pieces sank, killing survivors as they desperately tried to swim away from the wreckage. With three lifeboats carrying away the few dozen survivors, a plume of orange flames and black smoke could be seen for miles. There had not even been time to issue an "abandon ship" order, and in the blink of an eye, all 314 feet of the American destroyer disappeared, and 115 of the 160-man crew were gone, including Commander Edwards and every officer on board. The *Reuben James* was not the first U.S. destroyer torpedoed by enemy fire in World War II. But it was the first to be sunk. The Red Devil slipped away into the black nighttime sea.

"Whether the country knows it or not, we are at war," said Harold R. Stark, chief of U.S. naval operations.[2]

CERTAINLY, ROOSEVELT WAS fed up with American ships taking punch after punch from Germany without punching back. There may have been a time, he acknowledged, when the Neutrality Act had good reason for existing. But those times had changed. He sent a stern message to Congress arguing that America was anything but neutral in this war and needed to stop pretending that it was. Congress, he wrote, needed to repeal the Neutrality Act. He said it was imperative to arm merchant ships against "the modern pirates of the sea who travel beneath the surface or on the surface or in the air destroying defenseless ships without warning and without provision for the safety of the passengers and crews."[3]

Roosevelt understood what made Hitler's U-boats so effective and cargo ships so vulnerable. The U-boats could surface close to cargo ships without fear of being attacked, allowing them to fire their torpedoes at close range and with great accuracy. But if the new Liberty ships had greater freedom to fire back, it would force U-boats to fire while submerged at a greater distance, a much harder shot to fire with accuracy.

"A vast number of ships are sliding into the water from American shipbuilding ways," the president wrote. "We are lending them to the enemies of Hitlerism and they are carrying food and supplies and munitions to belligerent ports in order to withstand Hitler's juggernaut. Most of the vital goods authorized by the Congress are being delivered. Yet many of them are being sunk; and as we approach full production requiring the use of more ships now being built, it will be increasingly necessary to deliver American goods under the American flag."

Three weeks after the sinking of the *Reuben James*, Congress agreed to repeal three sections of the Neutrality Act and Roosevelt immediately signed the measure.

He was not the only political leader facing pressure to act within his country. Hitler's highest admirals, including Dönitz, were insisting that America was going to begin offensive war measures. Germany, they told him, could no longer treat United States ships as neutral bystanders, even if they were not officially at war with the United States. Hitler's grand admiral Erich Raeder told the Führer that in his mind, the war in Europe had a new player: "There is no longer any difference between British and American ships."

If Germany was going to open fire on American ships with the same frequency and ferocity with which it had been attacking British ships for two years, America's shipbuilders were about to become the most important manufacturing industry in the country—if not the world.

CHAPTER TWENTY-TWO

"A War of Transportation"

THE PRESIDENT WAS RELAXING IN HIS STUDY AT THE WHITE
House with his aide Harry Hopkins on the morning of December 7, 1941, when
his secretary said she had Frank Knox, Roosevelt's secretary of the Navy, on
the phone, demanding to speak with him immediately.

"Mr. President, it looks like the Japanese have attacked Pearl Harbor," Knox
said.[1]

More phone calls came in the next few minutes, confirming the news that
bodies were everywhere, trapped inside of sinking ships, floating in the waters,
blanketing the ground that had been shredded by bullets and bombs. The grim
news would come soon, that 3,500 soldiers, sailors, and civilians were dead,
making it the deadliest disaster in American naval history.

It was news the president had dreaded—an attack on American soil. But
this attack was especially unnerving for Roosevelt because it did not come from
where all eyes had been watching—on the Atlantic Ocean side of the country. It
came from the Pacific Ocean. While most of the nation's attention had been on
Hitler, Churchill, and the war in Europe, Roosevelt knew that U.S. attempts to
slow Japan's global expansion through sanctions and embargoes were angering
officials in Tokyo. He had been holding out hope that ongoing talks between

envoys from the two countries might prove fruitful, but he underestimated just how determined Japan was to claim status as a world power.

As the president absorbed the morning's news, Eleanor, who had just finished a luncheon, walked past and saw the look on the faces of the men and the secretaries with the president. She was struck by the panic and anger in everyone's demeanor—except for her husband, who she recalled had a "deadly calm" about him as he sat at his desk, taking one call after another, each one delivering worse news than the last. She paused only briefly enough to hear some of the conversation, and she knew what had happened. "I said nothing because the words I heard over the telephone were quite sufficient to tell me that finally the blow had fallen and we had been attacked."[2]

With the country a decade removed from the start of the Great Depression, Roosevelt knew the perilous state of the Navy, as well as the depleted fleet of cargo ships. It was what prompted him eleven months earlier to announce his emergency shipbuilding effort. Only now he had to wonder if it was enough.

"I never wanted to have to fight this war on two fronts," the president told Eleanor. "We haven't got the Navy to fight in both the Atlantic and the Pacific."

It was purely by coincidence, but on the same day as the attack at Pearl Harbor, Edgar Kaiser's Oregonship was busy celebrating. Henry Kaiser joined his son for the ceremonial christening of the Liberty ship SS *Thomas Jefferson*. Bess Kaiser had the honor of cracking the champagne bottle on the ship's nose and sending it sliding down its ramp into the Willamette River. When it hit the water, it was armed with a single 4-inch gun and two .30-caliber Marlin machine guns.

THAT EVENING, GRACE Tully, Roosevelt's private secretary, walked into his study a few minutes before five o'clock. He was by himself for a few moments and his desk was neatly organized with stacks of his notes from throughout the day.

"Sit down, Grace," he told her in a calm voice. "I'm going before Congress tomorrow. I'd like to dictate my message. It will be short."[3]

He was comfortable dictating; it was how he wrote his letters. But in this moment, he spoke more deliberately than his usual cadence, putting emphasis on every mark of punctuation, to make sure his pauses during his speech carried their intended effect.

"Yesterday, comma, December 7th, comma, 1941 dash a day which will live in world history . . ."

That evening, surrounded by congressional leaders and his cabinet, Roosevelt shared that he would deliver a brief message the following day, calling for a declaration of war. As he described the details of the attack at Pearl Harbor, the gathering sat in total silence, even after he had finished. Texas senator Tom Connally finally broke the silence with an angry question while banging his fist on the desk in front of him.

"How did it happen that our warships were caught like tame ducks in Pearl Harbor? How did they catch us with our pants down?"

Roosevelt, his head bowed, could only wonder the same question.

"I don't know, Tom. I just don't know."[4]

THE FOLLOWING DAY, the president sent off a letter to Admiral Land. As much as Roosevelt was intensely focused on the devastation to his Navy warships, he immediately recognized that in order to win a war, it would be about much more than who had the most firepower. Just as important, America would need cargo ships to supply troops with the food, weapons, tanks, gear, and supplies they needed anywhere in the world.

"I am concerned with the necessity of securing the most effective use of the Merchant Marine to carry out the war effort and maintain the flow of military and civilian shipments," Roosevelt wrote to Land. He explained that he was establishing a Strategic Shipping Board composed of the chairman of the Maritime Commission, which was Land, as well as the president's chief of staff, chief of naval operations, and his favored assistant, Hopkins. "It should establish policies for and plan for the allocation of merchant shipping to meet military and civilian requirements."

He wasn't done. The following day, December 9, a day after Roosevelt declared war on Japan, and two days before he would declare war against Germany and Italy, the president called his wartime chairman of production management, Bill Knudsen, to the White House. Earlier in the year, Knudsen had delivered a report to Roosevelt outlining the impressive rate of American manufacturing for 1941, including 19,290 planes, 97,000 machine guns, 3,964 tanks, and 1.1 million tons of Liberty ships. But now, in the aftermath of Pearl Harbor, those figures were all irrelevant. Roosevelt told Knudsen every category needed to be accelerated—now he wanted 30,000 planes, 45,000 tanks, and 8 million tons of Liberty ships in 1942.

"Can we do it?" Roosevelt asked.

"Yes, sir," came the answer.[5]

A SHIPBUILDING PROGRAM that began with modest ambitions back in January 1941, with plans to open a couple of new shipyards and build five dozen cargo ships for the British, and then two hundred more for America, now carried the fate of American democracy on its back. The president no longer merely wanted a few hundred Liberty ships. He needed a few thousand of them.

The only way that many ships could be built in a hurry was if more shipyards were opened, more shipbuilders hired, and existing shipyards were expanded. Admiral Vickery sent out a series of telegrams, seven in all, to Henry Kaiser and to the rest of the leaders at Six Companies. He was desperate to meet the president's outrageous tonnage demand, and he asked them all to write back as quickly as possible with a proposal to build a new shipyard from scratch that could be operating within months.

"The emergency demands all within your power to give your country ships," Vickery wrote.[6]

———

EARLY IN 1941 after the British came calling for help building ships, the government had estimated that American shipyards would need to hire roughly 260,000 new employees, the majority of them to work throughout New England and into the mid-Atlantic region down to Philadelphia.

Then Roosevelt asked for a few hundred American cargo ships.

Then the Japanese attacked Pearl Harbor.

Then the United States went to war in both the Pacific and Atlantic Oceans.

Then Roosevelt changed his demand from a few hundred ships to a few thousand ships, as American troops were needed in Europe and East Asia, on islands and on mainlands.

Just like that, 260,000 shipbuilders were not nearly enough. The government released a new estimate, saying it needed twice that number, more than 550,000 shipbuilders—and they were needed from East Coast to West.

"We are in a war of transportation, primarily salt-water transportation, a war of ships," Jerry Land said in a speech that he delivered. "It's no damn sense making guns and tanks to be left in the United States."[7]

IT WAS SHAPING up as a grim Christmas Eve in the White House. But at least the president had company. Winston Churchill and his staff of war advisers were visiting Washington for a summit conference, to make sure the two countries were aligned on how to confront both Germany and Japan. The conference, which was code-named Arcadia, was scheduled to run for at least three weeks, into mid-January, but it was unclear how long Churchill would stay.

In the nights leading up to Christmas, the president and prime minister sipped brandy, smoked cigars, and stayed up talking until 2 or 3 a.m. Roosevelt, normally in bed by 11 p.m., would occasionally nod off in his chair until one of Churchill's rousing stories stirred him back to life. But for Churchill, a notorious night owl, his requisite afternoon naps gave him the energy to last long into the evening. Eleanor would occasionally interrupt the leaders and suggest they retire for the night, only to be rebuffed.

Despite pressure from the American public to seek revenge on Japan for Pearl Harbor, both Roosevelt and Churchill agreed that Hitler posed the greater threat and must be their priority. After one particularly feisty argument that one bystander described as "a hell of a row," the two leaders decided that their combined war effort would be based out of Washington, not London, with combined resources and communications staff.

"We live here as a big family, in the greatest intimacy and informality," Churchill wrote in a telegraph back home, "and I have formed the very highest regard and admiration for the President."[8]

The feelings were mutual. Roosevelt had become especially enamored with a map room that Churchill arranged in the White House that allowed the prime minister to see in front of him where the war was progressing well, and where it was not. Roosevelt demanded his own map room and one was quickly set up in an old coatroom on the ground floor. Fiberboards covered the walls and each one had charts of the Pacific and Atlantic Oceans that were updated throughout the day with ship locations, enemy movements, and battle lines.

One day, when Eleanor walked past the president's map room, she glanced inside and saw the world's two most powerful men waving their hands in conversation and pointing at the maps and charts, as if they were young boys playing soldier.

"They seemed to be having a wonderful time, too wonderful in fact," she noted later. "It made me a little sad somehow."[9]

WHEN CHRISTMAS EVE arrived, Churchill joined the president and first lady outside under a crescent moon for the ceremonial lighting of the National Christmas Tree. The Secret Service, worried about the tree's bright lights making the White House an easy target, had tried to cancel the celebration, but Roosevelt refused their wishes and agreed to instead move the tree from Lafayette Park to the South Lawn. Armed guards surrounded the White House and used ropes to keep the throng of invited onlookers a hundred yards back, while 15,000 people watched from outside the gates.

As the Marine Band played "Joy to the World," Roosevelt lit the tree with the push of a button. In brief remarks, Roosevelt called Churchill "my associate, my old and good friend," before stepping aside to let his British guest add his own thoughts on the emotional moment.

"Here in the midst of war," he began darkly, "raging and roaring about us over all the land and seas, creeping nearer to our hearts and homes, here amidst all these tumults, we have the spirit of peace in each cottage home and in every heart."

Polite applause interrupted him before he turned to leave the crowd with a lighter note.

"Let the children have their night of fun and laughter. Let the gifts of Father Christmas delight their thoughts," he said. He assured those listening that "these same children shall not be robbed of their inheritance or denied their right to live in a free and decent world."[10]

The ceremony concluded and both men immediately ducked back inside to get to work.

"Xmas was a very sad day for me," Eleanor later admitted to her daughter Anna. With her four boys all in the service, and Anna back home in Seattle, it was the first Christmas in years that none of the Roosevelt children were home.

On the last day of 1941, Richmond launched the SS *James Otis*, its first Liberty ship, into the water after spending much of the year building Ocean-class ships for the British. Building for Churchill had not been a waste of time for Kaiser's shipbuilders. Even though those sixty ships they were building would not carry American supplies, they were already transferring the lessons they learned into Liberty ship construction. And now they had extra incentive—revenge.

"Twenty-four days of avowed vengeance following December 7 were built into her on the ways," a reporter observed of the *Otis* launching after Kaiser invited her to watch his shipyards in action.

ON NEW YEAR'S Day, Churchill joined Roosevelt for a solemn drive into the Virginia countryside to visit Mount Vernon and lay a wreath on the tomb of George Washington. As the Arcadia conference began to wind down, the advisers devised strategies to play offense against the enemies, not defense. It was the only path to victory, according to the deputy in the War Plans Division of the War Department General Staff, Dwight D. Eisenhower. "We had to attack to win," he told the conference.

The more the two sides worked together, the more disagreements began to surface and tempers started to flare. Eisenhower used his personal diary to vent his frustrations about what the Allies needed more than anything else.

"Tempers are short," he wrote on January 4. "There are lots of amateur strategists on the job and prima donnas everywhere. I'd give anything to be back in the field. . . . We're trying to ship staff and personnel needed. But we've got to have ships and we need them now!"[11]

With the conference in its final days, he wrote about his excitement to ship 21,000 men off to Australia. But he added his concern about when those men would be able to get their equipment and supplies to wage war.

"Ships! Ships! All we need is ships!"

When Churchill finally returned home, he was greeted by a pleasant note from his host in Washington. "It is fun to be in the same decade with you," the president wrote.[12]

IF, AS JERRY Land insisted, America was entering into a "war of transportation," Henry Kaiser believed he was positioned better than any man, even Henry Ford, to provide the nation with the two most important elements necessary to win that "war of ships." Kaiser was building an army of loyal, skilled, and motivated shipbuilders. And he had a vision to produce mountains and mountains of steel. Without an overflowing abundance of workers and steel, Kaiser knew there would be no more Liberty ships.

On January 6, 1942, the president shared with the nation what he had told Knudsen in the days after the attack. America was going to produce an arsenal of tanks, warplanes, jeeps, and guns that could hardly be imagined. He rattled off numbers not to impress his own citizens, but to warn the enemy of what they had unleashed. Instead of taking ten years to build 500 vessels, the Maritime Commission assured the president, it would launch almost 600 ships in 1942 alone.[13]

"These figures will give the Japanese and Nazis an idea of what they accomplished in the attack at Pearl Harbor," Roosevelt said.[14]

He listed the four priorities he had outlined for Congress: more airplanes; more tanks; more guns; and then he came to his fourth and final directive: "To increase our production rate of merchant ships so rapidly that in this year, 1942, we shall build 6,000,000 deadweight tons as compared with a 1941 completed production of 1,100,000. And finally, we shall continue that increase so that next year, 1943, we shall build 10,000,000 tons of shipping."

If there were any question about the heart of the nation's wartime manufacturing effort, Roosevelt reminded Americans that without these huge cargo vessels, none of the other supplies would ever reach American troops. "We must raise our sights all along the production line," he stated. "Let no man say it cannot be done."[15]

Finally, after so much frustration, Dwight Eisenhower expressed relief that his pleas were no longer being ignored. "Had a meeting with the Navy," Eisenhower wrote in his diary on February 19. "One encouraging sign was that they have come to recognize the need for cargo ships."

CHAPTER TWENTY-THREE

Nerves of Steel

WAR CHANGED THE WAY AMERICANS WENT ABOUT THEIR
lives. Everyday household items, from batteries to paper clips to hair curlers
to forks and spoons to pie tins and sewing needles, all became hard to find.
Women were told to bring their own bobby pins when they visited their hair
salons. The military, so heavily dependent on typed paperwork, asked the
public to donate any nonessential typewriters so that the manufacturing of
new ones could be reduced. Even the Academy Awards stepped in to help. The
normally gold-plated official Oscar statuette was made of plaster in 1942 and
sprayed over with a bronze lacquer. The War Production Board took the drastic
measures of ordering manufacturers to reduce the amount of tin they used in
packaging products and requiring Americans who wanted to buy a tin tube of
shaving cream or toothpaste or ointment to first turn in their old, used tube.

Kaiser paid attention, and once again in chaos and crisis, he saw oppor-
tunity. Seven months before Pearl Harbor, on the morning of April 22, 1941,
Kaiser's foresight had him standing inside the White House with Utah senator
Abe Murdock, waiting to meet with President Roosevelt.[1] It was a busy few
days for the fifty-nine-year old president, who just returned from his home in
Hyde Park the previous day and had been up past eleven at night monitoring

the war in Europe, where England's losses were mounting. After his 11:15 a.m. meeting with Kaiser and Murdock, the president had a full day of meetings ahead, including lunch with his cousin Kermit Roosevelt.[2]

Kaiser was eager to have the president's ear and had no intention of wasting his fifteen minutes. He recognized that he was not yet a household name, even despite building the Boulder Dam, and holding the nation's largest responsibility for cargo ship production, so this meeting presented him with a rare and precious opportunity. He was a regular visitor to the hallways of Capitol Hill, lobbying for one project or another, but face time with the president was different.

In fact, at the time, Kaiser's most important East Coast connection was not a politician. It was a fellow Henry. Media titan Henry R. Luce owned the triumvirate of *Fortune*, *Life*, and *Time*, and by one estimate, the words in his magazines reached one-third to maybe one-half of the country's literate population. In 1941 perhaps no man could shape public opinion more than the dapper, fabulously wealthy, silvery-haired forty-three-year old Luce. He and Kaiser were more pen pals than friends, trading letters and occasional phone calls. They had only met a few times. Kaiser kept their relationship on a business casual level, always opening his letters to Luce with "Dear Henry."

When *Fortune* began an April 1941 article by describing "the fabulous Henry J. Kaiser of Boulder Dam fame," and when *Time* referred to him as "fabulously successful" and compared him to folk hero lumberjack Paul Bunyan, it was only natural that Kaiser's public profile began to soar. Nicknames like "Hurry Up, Henry" and "Sir Launchalot" became part of his legend, even as critics scoffed that his public relations machine was earning him more credit than he deserved. But the attacks rarely stuck.

"Bald, tight-lipped Henry J. Kaiser is one of those American industrial geniuses that average Americans are prone to take for granted until the country gets in a jam," *Time* wrote in March 1941. Other media jumped on the Kaiser bandwagon, perhaps inspired by the glowing magazine coverage. The *Wall Street Journal*, known for its straight-as-an-arrow writing, gushed about "Fabulous Mr. Kaiser" and wrote, "Everything Mr. Kaiser does is tremendous."

As he stepped into the White House for his meeting with Roosevelt, Kaiser's rising popularity could not have come at a better time. The United States president for the first time in his unprecedented nine years in office had recently seen his approval rating surpass 70 percent. He was keen on making sure it never dipped below that threshold again, and he was beginning to recognize that he would need Kaiser just as much as Kaiser needed the president. Their individual successes were undeniably linked to each other—Roosevelt needed Kaiser's ships, and Kaiser needed Roosevelt's support and his contracts.

WITH THE CONSTRUCTION of his Richmond shipyard complete, Kaiser saw trouble brewing for Roosevelt's emergency shipbuilding program. American steel manufacturers were reporting a backlog of four million tons, a figure that was only going to grow with the construction of Liberty ships. With the bulk of those steel producers on the East Coast, mainly in Pennsylvania, where U.S. Steel produced more steel during the war than all the Axis powers combined, Kaiser's West Coast shipbuilding operation stood to be hit the hardest. The bulk of the steel would land in states along the Gulf of Mexico or the Great Lakes before finally reaching California, Oregon, and Washington, the states poised to produce the most ships.

A steel shortage would cripple shipbuilding, among other industries. Constructing a single Liberty ship required 3,425 tons of steel for the hull, 2,725 tons of steel plates, and an additional 700 tons for various sizes and shapes of castings.[3] Flame-cutting equipment that could take a fifty-foot piece of steel and cut it to a precise measurement in seconds was vital to the construction of Liberty ships. The torches were mounted on tracks that could easily circle around a piece of steel and trim every corner and side to fit a template. Just as important as the cutting torches were the furnaces and bending slabs that allowed the steel to be shaped.

But with no steel, there would be no ships. And a slowdown or stoppage in production of Liberty ships would be catastrophic to Roosevelt's war strategy. It was paramount to both men to avert any kind of steel crisis. That is why instead of panicking, Kaiser saw an opportunity. At his meeting with Roosevelt, Kaiser proposed that the government help him build a $150 million steel plant in California, which he would power by means of his hydroelectric dams. Roosevelt was intrigued. He had recently been given an eighty-page report saying the country's existing steel plants were up to the task of handling increased production from a possible war, and they had room to handle excess capacity. But Roosevelt doubted the findings. He knew that steel output was running at more than 90 percent of capacity, yet he kept his thoughts private, mostly out of fear of causing panic in the country and a run on steel.

The press, however, and especially Henry Luce, showed no such kindness, blasting the report as overly optimistic.

"In its cozy assumptions, it ignores what is actually happening in steel *now*," *Fortune* wrote, "and what will inevitably happen if the nation ever goes full out on a war program."

Kaiser agreed with *Fortune*. He knew about the report. And he insisted to the president that its arithmetic was deeply flawed, that a steel shortage was an almost certainty, and that his proposal for a new plant in California was a surefire way to avoid it.

"I believe I have had sufficient raw materials studies made to insure the plan," Kaiser told the president.

He was bluffing. In fact, Kaiser had no such studies. He just had a hunch that he was right about the looming steel shortage. After the meeting, Kaiser met with the press and spoke with his typical arrogance.

"If we get a green light, we will be under production from scrap in eight months, and from ore in twelve," he boasted.[4]

A few days later he politely wrote to Roosevelt, thanking him for "your gracious reception."

With the president's encouragement from their meeting, Kaiser spoke with government engineers about his proposal. But instead of gaining momentum, his plan started to fall apart. The engineers, armed with their own intelligence, poked one hole after another in Kaiser's grand vision. In a series of meetings, Kaiser admitted he did not have the land for a steel plant. Nor did he have financing lined up. He also had no thoughts on its usefulness once the war was over. And when members of the War Production Board asked him what he knew about the complexities of steel production, he confessed it was very little, even while assuring them he could figure it out. When he was told he would need to acquire a turbo-blower, an enormous piece of equipment that helps fan the fires that smelt the ore in the metalmaking process, Kaiser insisted no obstacle would stand in his way. He didn't care that all the manufacturers of turbo-blowers were beyond capacity to build another.

"We can build our own," he told the board.

A few minutes later, out in the hallway after the meeting, he was overheard asking, "What's a turbo-blower?"[5]

It was typical of Kaiser's style. Identify the problem. Propose a solution. Figure out the details later. Despite his confidence, Kaiser received disappointing news a month after his White House meeting. The president did request an increase in steel production capacity—but only for five million more tons in the West, compared to ten million more tons in the East. As if that were not painful enough, the western plant would be in Geneva, Utah, the home state of the senator who had accompanied Kaiser to the meeting with Roosevelt. Kaiser's name was not even mentioned in the president's request. But as Roosevelt would learn, Kaiser did not take losing lightly.

He steamed for months about losing out on a California steel plant. He viewed it as an essential piece to his production puzzle. Throughout the spring and summer of 1941, Kaiser watched as his prediction proved correct. Production of structural steel fell two months behind schedule, and new orders were backlogged for five months. Shipyards were forced to slow their production and watch in frustration as more steel went to munitions plants and even automobile factories—both longtime customers of the steel industry.

Finally, on May 22, the steel report by Gano Dunn, the president of the engineering firm that issued it, was revised, acknowledging that 1941 would end not with a steel surplus, but with a steel shortage of 1.4 million tons.

"Mr. Dunn had to eat his own words," one journalist wrote. "But he ate them very gingerly."[6]

SEVEN MONTHS LATER, Kaiser's patience paid off. When war broke out, Kaiser went right back to Washington. He was interested in a little gloating, but far more invested in securing the steel plant he'd been chasing for almost a year.

The attack on Pearl Harbor created the crisis in steel production that Kaiser had been warning of for months. It threatened to slam the brakes on everything Roosevelt wanted to build—tanks, ships, engines, jeeps, ammunition, guns. The president's advisers told him that a nation at war would need to produce a minimum of 80 million tons of steel a year. In the decade after the Depression, steel production had plummeted from more than 60 million tons in 1929 to 30 million tons by the end of the 1930s. The gap between 30 million and 80 million sounded unachievable, except to Kaiser.

For weeks, as 1941 bled into early 1942, Kaiser pestered Houston businessman Jesse Jones with calls, letters, and visits, pleading for $100 million to open a steel production facility in Southern California. Jones ran the Reconstruction Finance Corporation for Roosevelt, which meant that no major government expenditure would happen without his blessing. And Jones did not like the idea of a steel plant on the California coastline, fearing it was too vulnerable to a Japanese air attack in the early weeks of the war. As soon as Kaiser compromised and agreed to a safer inland location in the town of Fontana, about fifty miles east of Los Angeles, he got his $100 million and permission to build Kaiser Steel.

Kaiser immediately called another of his most loyal employees—his chief engineer, George Havas. No contract had even been signed yet, but Kaiser was done waiting. Havas, like Clay Bedford and A. B. Ordway, was another loyal lieutenant to Kaiser, who had stayed with him for decades. Kaiser first recruited Havas in the late 1920s while building the highway in Cuba. Havas was a young businessman from Budapest, Hungary, running a banana plantation in Cuba, when Kaiser poached him to work on the Cuba road project. Nearly two decades later, Bedford, Ordway, and Havas had become three of Kaiser's most trusted senior leaders.

"George, you're going to build me a steel mill," Kaiser told his engineer.

"What kind of steel mill?" Havas asked, since he knew as much about steel as Kaiser did.

"Oh, just a small one," Kaiser answered. "At least at first."[7]

KAISER'S GRAND VISION was coming together. He already had the largest government contract to build Liberty ships. Now, with Roosevelt's blessing, he had permission to build the largest steel plant on the West Coast to meet the demands of the Liberty ship program. But he still wasn't satisfied. In order to win the "war of transportation" that Jerry Land had spoken of, Kaiser understood that steel was only one half of the necessary equation. Somebody had to smelt, rivet, and weld that steel into the shape of a Liberty ship. No machine could do that by itself. And with America now at war in two oceans, not just one, it had to done faster than anyone dreamed possible.

A decade earlier, Henry Kaiser had been presented with a strange business opportunity to own half of a cemetery in Berkeley, California. He was told it was a chance to break into a field that "keeps growing"—the business of death. Kaiser wanted no part of it. He explained that he didn't want to wait until someone's funeral to start making money off them. He was far more interested in finding a way to make business opportunities out of keeping people healthy. It was time to start revolutionizing the American workplace.

PART V

Building a Workforce

CHAPTER TWENTY-FOUR

"Avalanche of Humanity"

ON A WINTER DAY IN EARLY 1942, TWENTY-ONE-YEAR-OLD Stanley Nystrom strolled to the post office on Nevin Avenue in downtown Richmond to mail a letter. It was a fifteen-minute walk from his house. He expected his errand to be quick, but when he arrived, a stranger approached him who said he also wanted to mail a letter to his family back home, to tell them that he had arrived safely in Richmond. Except he didn't know how to write.[1]

"He asked me if I would write the letter for him," Nystrom said.

He did. But as he walked back home, Nystrom thought about how surprised he was to encounter an illiterate stranger not the least bit self-conscious or embarrassed. He had been noticing a lot of changes of late in the town where he'd lived his entire life.

Richmond's nightlife used to end early. But restaurants were staying open past midnight, movie theaters adding late shows, the dance halls were packed every night, and the sidewalks bustling like a major metropolis. The streets were filled with workers in heavy riggers boots and hard hats on their heads. Weekends and weeknights blurred together, with Tuesday feeling no different from Saturday. Shopping in Richmond had always been easy and familiar for Nystrom, but now he was seeing a lot more unfamiliar faces. And there was something else—the faces in town looked different. Nystrom was noticing more Black people and more women, not to mention more funny accents, than he'd ever seen or heard.

Incidents of crime were soaring. The Richmond city jail, built to hold twenty-nine prisoners, was often packed beyond fifty. The number of available beds, rooms, and homes for everyone in Richmond to sleep was woefully inadequate. Almost five thousand Richmond residents were renting out rooms to make up income lost during the Depression. Sometimes they even rented out "hot beds" in which one person used it for a few hours and then it turned over to a new person. One landlord was punished for having sixty-five people in a single house. When federal housing inspectors visited San Pablo, two miles up the road from Richmond, they found hundreds of families living in converted garages and sheds that were so horrendous they recommended burning the dwellings down. They found one family—a shipyard welder, his wife, and five children—living in a windowless chicken coop.

"Three of the children sleep on a thin concrete floor less than twenty feet from the muddy banks of the San Pablo Creek with drainage from a privy and a garbage pile toward the house rather than toward the Creek," the investigators wrote in their report.

This was not the Richmond that Stanley Nystrom grew up in. He knew the reason why. Everybody did. And it wasn't just happening in Richmond. From downtown Portland, Oregon, to coastal Maine to the harbor of Baltimore to the Gulf Coast in Alabama to the bay waters off Houston to the coast of the Carolinas, small towns and midsize cities were exploding in a shipbuilding bonanza. In December 1940, a year before the Pearl Harbor attack, approximately 228,000 workers, almost all of them men, were employed in the shipbuilding industry. Less than two years later, it was 1.2 million.[2] On the East Coast, the new shipbuilders were mostly locals, trickling into shipyards from nearby towns, cities, and neighboring states in search of jobs. Many of them didn't need housing, as they were able to commute from home. But the West Coast was different. It became a magnet for thousands upon thousands of poverty-stricken migrant families who left behind their dried-up Oklahoma farms just like Tom Joad did in John Steinbeck's 1939 novel, *The Grapes of Wrath*.

When Nystrom's widowed mother needed a way to keep food on the table, she packed up her belongings from her bedroom and moved to the back of the house. In a matter of days, a married couple from the Midwest was renting the room. Sure, it was more mouths to feed, but it was also a steady source of income. As full as the Nystrom house was, it was nothing compared to Irene Bianchini's. She welcomed seventeen boarders into her home, and handled all their laundry too.

"When the first shipyard hit, it turned the town upside down," Nystrom recalled. "All of a sudden there were too many people in town, and it was a 24-hour a day business area. People just seemed to come from everywhere. I remember being kidded about the way I talked, because I didn't talk with a Midwest or Southern accent. They said I talked funny. To me, they talked funny."[3]

Those funny-talking Arkies and Okies were flooding the entire West Coast and breathing new life into the nation's once-moribund shipbuilding industry at a moment when shipbuilders were needed the most.

WHEN THE END of the Great Depression in the late 1930s collided with a crushing drought in America's Southwest, the Dust Bowl wreaked chaos on the farmers and the agricultural economies of Missouri, Texas, Arkansas, and Oklahoma. But when those migrants flocked west to California, Oregon, or Washington for a fresh start, they were not exactly embraced. Californians were protective of their own fragile economy and feared an invasion of newcomers with little money and big families who would overwhelm their communities. But when war erupted and West Coast shipyards, airplane factories, steel plants, and government agencies needed to hire tens of thousands, no group filled the need more than the Okies. They were white, they were skilled in using industrial equipment, and they spoke with a distinct dialect that wasn't quite Midwest twang and wasn't exactly Deep South drawl. And just like the women and Black people signing up for work in shipyards, Okies absorbed their share of antagonism and abuse. Shipyard urinals were often labeled with graffiti that said, "Okie drinking fountain," and sometimes over an open passageway on a ship was the scribble, "Okie, this is a door." While most of the Okies took it in stride, some could not understand why Californians, whom they derisively called Calies, felt so superior considering that most of them had migrated to the state only a few years earlier themselves. "Why, back in my hometown, we treat stray dogs better than they treat men out here," one Okie confided.[4]

There was even a crass little poem heard on the streets of San Francisco that some Okies liked to mutter as way of reminding Californians they were once migrants too.

The miners came in forty-nine,
The whores in fifty-one;
And when they bunked together
They begot the native son.

Native-born white Californians didn't bother hiding their prejudice against the newcomers. Denise Fleig, a welder in Henry Kaiser's Richmond shipyard in early 1942, said that anyone who didn't talk with a California accent was shoved aside. "They're dumb for one thing. They're farmers, for one thing, so they're not urban dwellers, like us, who are several stages above rural people," Fleig said. "They're ignorant, they're unschooled, none of them ever went to college, that's for sure. . . . I thought they were all hillbillies, and hillbillies are rude, uneducated, boorish, no manners."

Fleig began to soften on the Okies, however, as she got to know a woman welder from Arkansas she nicknamed Tiny. The two women hit it off, and as Fleig got used to Tiny's accent she began to see they were more alike than different, and before she knew it, the Okie and the Calie were friends. But to win that acceptance, the Okies had to be strong.

Laura Fortier was a single mother of four kids, holding down two jobs and living in a suburb of Oklahoma City, when she tired of her meager pay and tiny house and decided she wanted to help in the war effort. In early 1942 she heard the shipyard in Portland, Oregon, where she had a brother living, was hiring and she already had experience driving farm tractors. She moved west and was quickly hired as a truck driver at Oregonship. She waited for a dispatcher to give her an assignment, figured out the directions on her own, and drove her truck around the city to collect various supplies, like kegs of nails and bolts, to bring back to the shipyards. Even though some of the other women drivers needed help with their loads, Fortier insisted on handling it herself, even while working the graveyard shift.

"I was strong," she said. "I could pick up a hundred pounds easily, throw it over my shoulder, just like that. I could throw a man over my shoulder."[5]

THEN THERE WERE the Okies and Arkies who came with hidden talents that quickly won them friendships and respect. Lewis Van Hook was thirty-seven years old with eight children at home in Arkansas when the war began. He'd grown up farming, feeding pigs, and getting kicked by the family mule, and he knew that wasn't his future—he wanted to build things and as soon as he was old enough, he joined the carpenters' union. He registered for the draft, but because he had so many children, he was passed over. When he started to hear about shipyard jobs in California, offering good pay and housing, he went and visited his father to have a conversation.

"I've made up mind," he told his father. "I'm going."

"I hear that there's no place out there to live," his father told him. "People that are working are sleeping in tents and whatnots. There's really nowhere you can stay. So I just don't think you ought to go."[6]

Lewis listened, and then the next day he went down to the bus station, bought a bus ticket to San Francisco, and left. He arrived the next day, found a bed to sleep in, and made his way to a state employment office, where he stood in a long line until he got to the front window. He didn't know much about the Richmond operation, and so when the lady said to him, "Yard three?" he just nodded his head and went off to start his new life—as a driller in a new California shipyard, and as an Arkie living on his own.

With eight kids back home, and a constant need to bring home extra money, he learned how to cut hair and started a little barbershop business in Richmond on the side of his shipbuilding job. When he was finally able to bring his family to Richmond, he got his wife a job as a welder, and they were officially transplanted Arkies. "We were working together and drawing our pay," Van Hook recalled. "We cashed our checks together on Tuesday mornings, I believe it was. We had our money, saving our money. That was quite a thrill."

But the thrills were mixed with tensions. Van Hook hung out most nights with fellow migrants, mostly from Texas and Arkansas. But one night his wife came home crying, complaining of the men in her welding group harassing her, and she said that she'd been transferred to the worst spot, the double bottom, which was the floor of the ship. He went straight down to her supervisor to complain and got her moved back up to the plate shop. Another night at the shipyard's tool shed he saw a fight break out between a Black man and a white southerner when the white man's hammer fell and landed right near his coworker.

Van Hook stumbled into a surprising way to help ease some of the shipyard tensions he was seeing between Black and white people, men and women, and Okies, Arkies, and Calies. When a neighbor stopped by for a trim one afternoon, he mentioned that he sang in a quartet, which Van Hook had done back home in Arkansas. "He said to us that he was trying to find fellows to start a quartet, and that's the way it got started," Van Hook recalled. The next thing he knew, their quartet's songs, in perfect harmony, were being played on the local radio station KRE and they began to call themselves the Singing Shipbuilders. Any chance they got, they dedicated songs to their fellow workers and supervisors, and their popularity took off. They began singing at lunchtime, during breaks, and they practiced any free time they could find. When a Liberty ship was launched, the Singing Shipbuilders were invited to the ceremony to lend a friendly touch. "A nation singing, fighting, working toward victory," *Fore 'n' Aft* wrote of the Singing Shipbuilders.[7]

One of Lewis's sons, Clarence Van Hook, joined the quartet and years later remembered his father boasting about how the singers helped ease strife among shipyard workers. "There were people here from all over the country and there was a lot of racial tension," Clarence said. "People were getting into fights. But when the Shipbuilders sang, everybody would go and listen. They played a great role in keeping race relations calm."

UNLIKE THE MILITARY, which had been building its ranks through a draft, Jerry Land's Maritime Commission had no powers to pull people into shipbuilding. It needed volunteers to build its ships. Initially the call went out for skilled workers only, tradesmen like plumbers, electricians, welders, engineers, construction workers. The California Federation of Labor went so far as to discourage unskilled laborers from bothering to apply for shipyard jobs, worried that a glut of handyman-wannabes would slow down the emergency efforts.

"The man who thinks he will get a job building ships because he built a woodshed somewhere is doomed to disappointment," the labor federation said in a public relations campaign notice.

That recruiting tactic lasted all of a few months. The shipyards were in no position to be choosy about the workers they hired.

But then for a moment, the hiring at some shipyards almost swung too far in the other direction, with an open call to anyone and everyone. A "work for drunks" program was started in Los Angeles, with judges suspending the sentences of vagrants and small-time criminals if they agreed to go to work at the shipyards. But when a bus showed up in Richmond one afternoon full of seventy-four drunks, and three of them were arrested almost immediately for public intoxication, the flaws in the program were exposed. Richmond police chief L. E. Jones said his jail was far too small to handle an influx of slackers who might, or might not, be suited to work on the ships.[8]

Kaiser suspended the program and agreed to look beyond California for his workers. He hired two hundred recruiters, put them on trains bound mostly for the Midwest and the South along with a few who traveled east of the Mississippi, gave them enough money to pay the train fares of anyone who agreed to come back to build ships, and told them what their primary recruiting tactic should be: appeal to their sense of duty, their patriotism, their desire to help U.S. troops fighting to defend democracy.

The U.S. military had drafted 18,633 men in 1940, followed by an additional 923,842 in 1941. In 1942 and 1943 together, it would induct six million men. When they were shipped off to battle, they were going to need guns, food, bombs, tanks, jeeps, ambulances, uniforms, ammunition, tents, sleeping bags, canteens, and much more. And the only way those supplies were going to reach them was on board giant cargo ships—ships that hadn't yet been built.

Kaiser knew that appealing to Americans' patriotism would not be enough. He told his recruiters a few other tactics they should use to entice workers—the West Coast weather, the steady work, and the almighty buck.

THIRTY BUILDINGS. FOUR shipyards. Twenty-seven shipways. Nine hundred acres of boggy tideland had been transformed into a sprawling, round-the-clock construction operation. Once-sleepy Richmond was now America's shipbuilding capital. No longer was it an anonymous, coastal town with 23,642 people and a single busy thoroughfare, Macdonald Avenue, running through its heart. Richmond had become one of the nation's most important industrial hubs, just as vital to President Roosevelt's Arsenal of Democracy as the Motor City of Detroit or the airplane capital of Seattle or the torpedo hub of Newport, Rhode Island.

Rather than try to draw workers from big cities, Kaiser targeted smaller cities in the South and Midwest, as well as a few cities east of the Mississippi. The recruiters fanned out with thousands of jobs to fill at his West Coast shipyards. Armed with train tickets to give to the workers who signed on, the recruiters found the most success in places like Omaha; Minneapolis; Memphis; Phoenix; St. Louis; Chattanooga; Little Rock and Fort Smith, Arkansas; Chicago; and Kansas City, Missouri. Knowing there were no shipyards in the most populous city, New York, he dispatched two trains there with recruiters and both trains, dubbed "Kaiser Karavans" and "Magic Carpet Specials," returned to California completely full with almost 500 workers. For "Texies" and "Okies" and "Arkies," the opportunity was too hard to pass up.

Kaiser also capitalized on his own good name with the public. He positioned recruiters along the California border to point anyone who they came across toward the shipyards. Kaiser was not the only one with the same idea; recruiters for other shipyards in Southern California and aircraft plants tried the same tactic, but they didn't have the Kaiser name to sell.

The working migrants came to Richmond with three expectations: to land good jobs, to earn good money, and to find good housing. They found the good money and good jobs in the shipyards, which is why historian Gerald Nash later described Richmond as the "quintessential war boom town in America." Boom town, however, implies thriving. The city manager of Richmond, J. A. McVittie, lived through the wartime surge, and he painted a different picture, calling it "an avalanche" of humanity.[9]

The outbreak of war brought a flood of new children into Richmond's school system. Class sizes became unmanageable while a teacher shortage quickly reached crisis level. The number of students in the Richmond Union High School District more than doubled, from 3,430 to 7,921. But the elementary-aged children caused the biggest problem, as their numbers soared from 2,987 to 13,112. Attempts to stagger students in double, triple, or quadruple shifts throughout the day failed. Wives of some of the new shipyard workers, some of whom were barely literate, were hired as teachers.

Marian Sauer, a teacher at Woodrow Wilson Elementary School in Richmond, noticed how diverse her classrooms suddenly were in 1942. She worried about the mixing of students, not just Black and white, but shy Okie kids with brash southerners and established local kids. But they got along beautifully, other than occasional name-calling. When she put them in a circle and asked them to hold hands, she noticed one white child staring at the Black hand he was holding.

"I guess he thought it was chocolate or something, because he looked close, and then he was perfectly happy," she said.[10]

Some parents didn't adjust so easily. Another teacher, Evelyn Haag, received an upsetting note from a southern white parent.

"Don't let my little boy sit next to that n---er," the note said. Haag didn't understand. The children were so happy playing together, oblivious to skin color.[11]

Alice Brimhall couldn't believe what she saw on her first day teaching first and third grade. The teachers all stood out in the yard holding up signs for their children to follow like herding cattle, but as she walked her students back to her classroom she didn't glance back to see how many were following her.

"When I got to my room I had 112 children, and 50 desks," she recalled. "So we took turns who would sit in the desk and who would sit on the floor."[12]

The Richmond schools superintendent, Walter Helms, pushed for federal funds to build additional schools, and when that didn't happen quick enough, he built portable, temporary classrooms—entire new schools of them. Before the war the average enrollment in most Richmond classes was about twenty-three children. After Pearl Harbor, many classrooms had sixty or seventy.

LOCAL RESIDENTS TRIED in vain to cling to their small-town flavor, maintaining personal farms on their properties with chickens and pigs to provide food for their dinner tables and occasionally money for their pockets. But their days of enjoying peaceful evenings on their porches were gone. Twenty-four hours a day, seven days a week, the glow of lights from Kaiser's shipyards lit up the sky over Richmond and could be seen from miles away and across San Francisco Bay. New businesses popped up, many of them using the same word to draw in customers. Victory Cafe stayed open from 5:30 a.m. until 2:30 a.m. the next day to capture as many shift workers as possible. Victory Liquor, a small, boxlike building, served a steady flow of customers well into the evening. A cacophony of sounds echoed through the town, rattling windows, vibrating the roads, and shaking the countertops where cups of coffee rested all day.

With the influx of workers, no place in town served more coffee than Leo's Defense Diner. From sunrise to sundown, a nonstop flow of customers strolled in and out of Leo and Mary Lockshin's cozy diner inside a small Pullman railroad car along Cutting Boulevard, a few steps north of the Richmond shipyard. The smell of fresh, homemade donuts wafting out of the diner was irresistible to hungry shipyard workers. The breakfast counter filled up every morning with new arrivals to town eager for a hearty breakfast before a long day ahead. And the diner stayed open to feed workers from all the shifts. The milk shake maker and the donut machine never rested. Most mornings at least a handful of workers came in requesting twenty or thirty donuts for them to bring to the shipyard.[13]

Marvin Foster was a regular. He noticed how hard the women worked there, busing tables, manning the ice cream fountain, washing dishes, and he came home one night to tell his wife, Selena, about it. He told her he spotted a sign saying the diner needed a fry cook. Growing up in Texas, the second of nine children, Selena had always been comfortable in the kitchen, making breakfasts for her younger siblings, and she got excited about the possibility of a kitchen job. She and Marvin didn't have children of their own, so she was flexible about what hours she could work.

"You should go down there and talk to some of those girls and you might get on," he told her. "They work awfully hard, and they don't look like they have enough help there. And they have a night shift."[14]

She went down right away and met with Leo, and before she knew it, she had a white uniform and a steady job working a night shift that started at nine o'clock. But Leo and Mary, after watching Selena work, thought she'd be better for them working at the fountain, where the popular milk shakes and donuts were served along with the never-ending supply of hot coffee. Soon enough, Selena was managing the fountain, and all the workers knew her name. Between her job at Leo's and Marvin's job at Kaiser's shipyard, the couple epitomized the new workers who transformed Richmond almost overnight.

SHORTLY AFTER THE holidays, in early 1942, the British American journalist Alistair Cooke set off on a road trip to see firsthand how Americans were handling the war. He was only thirty-four years old, but he had already been the London correspondent for NBC and the film critic for the BBC. Just six days before the attack on Pearl Harbor, he had taken his oath as an American citizen, and soon after that he set his sights on exploring the country and finding compelling stories to tell. By the time he arrived in Richmond to see Henry Kaiser's shipyards, he had heard all the cynical words about how Kaiser called a ship's bow the "front end," and that he was nothing more than a glorified contractor, and he was receiving more credit than he deserved. Cooke walked into Richmond a skeptic. He walked out a believer.

"The Kaiser yards look like something out of Disney. They were absurdly clean and neat," he would go on to write in his book *The American Home Front: 1941–1942.*

He wrote how "Innumerable cranes swing through the air," clutching items off piles of steel, depositing them at plate shops or heaving them down to the shipways. "Small armies of Disney characters rush forth with welding guns and weld the parts into a ship as innocently as a child fits A into B on a nursery floor and confronts a destroyer made with his very own hands."

But the observant Cooke also noted a growing problem. He wrote of rampant absenteeism and loafing in the shipyards, from those dealing with a sick baby at home to others hungover after a long night of poker playing on the graveyard shift. None of it was surprising given the crush of newcomers who had flooded into town, but it was a problem that the Maritime Commission had also been hearing about. And it needed to be addressed.

Across all shipyards in the United States—Maritime Commission, Navy and repair yards—total employment in the summer of 1940 was about 168,000. After Pearl Harbor, that number soared every month up to a peak of 1,500,000. Richmond was a microcosm of that spike. After employing 4,000 people in late 1941, by the spring of 1942, Richmond's shipyards had more than 50,000 workers, with a path toward 80,000 by year's end—and more than 100,000 in early 1943. Not surprisingly, the rise of Richmond was anything but smooth.

It was as if an ocean liner pulled up alongside a rowboat and tried to unload all its passengers—there was simply no place to put everybody.

The rise of Richmond pitted small businesses against big-city industrialism, forced rapid integration of Black people into a population that was not ready for the change, overwhelmed taxpayer-funded city services like water and sewer lines, and created a deluge of workers that piled into already-dense housing. Richmond residents embraced the new arrivals for helping grow the city base they had long desired but also resented them for their impact on Richmond's sleepy way of life.

A representative from Massachusetts, George J. Bates, served on a congressional committee studying congested areas during the war. He described Richmond as the most overwhelmed city the committee had run across in the entire country. "I don't think there is any comparison between your problems in Richmond," he said, "and any other city even though the other cities are bad."[15]

CHAPTER TWENTY-FIVE

Revolutionizing the Workplace

DR. SIDNEY GARFIELD WAS IN HIS OFFICE AT THE UNIVERSITY of Southern California when his phone rang. The medical community was grappling with the possibility of epidemics of influenza, pneumonia, or measles. "Flu Epidemic Is Feared," a *New York Times* headline read. There had been surges starting in Hawaii that were making their way to the mainland, but it was not clear how bad the outbreaks might be yet. Garfield's mind, however, was elsewhere.

A first lieutenant in the U.S. Army Medical Corps, he was awaiting the official order for his Army unit in the 73rd Evacuation Hospital. He wondered if this might be the call telling him it was time to ship out. It was a mid-December day in 1941, and all he knew was that his unit was headed for Southeast Asia to set up a field hospital and help protect the Burma Road, a seven-hundred-mile lifeline that Allied troops were using to move supplies from India to southwest China. When he answered the phone, he braced himself for the news.[1]

Instead, he heard the familiar voice of an old friend. Clay Bedford sounded desperate. The two men had worked together a few years earlier at the Grand Coulee Dam near Spokane, Washington, one of Henry Kaiser's biggest projects. Bedford never forgot Garfield's compassion for his patients and his ingenuity in treating five thousand workers under stressful and remote conditions. Now he was hoping to lure Garfield north to Richmond to re-create his medical magic, and more importantly, to reduce the alarming rates of absenteeism and turnover that were plaguing shipyards.

"Look, Clay, I'm in the Army too," Garfield responded to the invite, with his warm and friendly drawl. "And I'm leaving in a month for India."

A month. Bedford sensed an opening and he jumped at it.

"Well, you've got a month. Can you come up and advise me what to do? It's a desperate situation."

"Sure, I could do that," Garfield said.

FOR A BUSINESSMAN, a husband, and a father, Henry Kaiser had come to understand that in order for his workplaces to thrive, his workers first had to be happy. If he wanted to revolutionize shipbuilding, he would have to revolutionize the shipyard at the same time.

As with everything he did, Kaiser saw chaos as opportunity, and he viewed one project as his gateway to the next. From paving roads he moved on to building bridges. From building bridges came the construction of hydroelectric dams. His dam work helped land him in the shipbuilding business. That paved the way for a steel plant and concrete enterprise. Now, with the nation at war, his brain was churning once again, in search of ways to capitalize on the Liberty ships and to use them as another stepping-stone.

Roosevelt's emergency shipbuilding program, not even a year old, was at risk unless the well-being of the shipbuilders—and their children—was a priority, not an afterthought. The Maritime Commission had already acted, moving to hire Dr. Philip Drinker, an expert in industrial hygiene at the Harvard School of Public Health, to study the health and safety issues in the shipyards.[2] But Kaiser didn't need some wonky government report to tell him what he already knew—America's newest shipyards were hazardous, dangerous, and cesspools for viruses to spread. And they were especially unfriendly workplaces to women with children.

Kaiser needed women. But the round-the-clock workload necessary for building Liberty ships was unsustainable for women with children. And the War Manpower Commission was discouraging young mothers from working, insisting they should be raising them at home and not hiring daycare. Kaiser saw the dilemma up close. The shipyards did not want to hire older women. But young mothers were reluctant to sign up knowing the sacrifices they would have to make. If the communities around the shipyards would not provide enough daycare for his women welders, Kaiser decided he would just do it himself.

"Factories should be equipped with childcare centers, health clinics, shopping centers, food dispensers, banking facilities, dry cleaning, shops, recreation centers, comfortable lockers and restrooms," he told the *New York Times*. These were not benefits or perks, in his mind. They were examples of "the factory of the future."

When a group of thirty women welders walked into Oregon Shipbuilding one day and told a counselor there named Eleanor Niemi they were fed up, Kaiser's idea took off. The appeal of West Coast shipbuilding had lured these women from their homes in the South and Midwest, but they would no longer build Liberty ships until they found appropriate daycare for their children. They were done leaving their kids with neighbors, friends, families, or sometimes random strangers who volunteered to help them, just so they could go off and work a midnight shift to weld a hull together. One mother said she had to change her childcare arrangements eight times until she found a stable situation.

"We paid strangers to take care of the kids, and of course we got ripped off plenty on that," welder Nona Pool, who came to Oregon with her husband and two children from Nebraska, griped. "I had to furnish their food and furnish their washing and everything, and I found them putting the kids to bed without their supper and eating the kids' food."[3]

The stories kept pouring in. Rosa Dickson said she preferred the graveyard shift because it was the only way she and her husband could juggle parenting. "I could put everything away nice, I could slip out and be there at twelve at night and they was all in bed and my husband would be there at twelve," she said.[4] Marie Merchant came from Kentucky and found that nobody wanted to rent an apartment to a Black woman with children, so she sent her kids to live with her parents.

Kaiser applied for funding from the Maritime Commission, knowing how important the Liberty ships were to the administration and how important women were to his shipyards. He also managed to land the one advocate who would give him all the support he needed. Kaiser shared his plans with Eleanor Roosevelt, who wasted no time in bringing them straight to Jerry Land at the Maritime Commission with her message: do this now.

"I have long known that the only way we could possible [sic] get the women that we need to take jobs was to provide them with community services," she wrote to Land. "If the shipbuilding companies will recognize this fact, that it is a part of being able to do their jobs to render these services, it may spread to other industries."5

Land agreed, Kaiser got his funding, and the Kaiser Child Care Service Centers that eventually opened in both Richmond and Portland became models for the country, and helped fuel new research into early childhood education for generations. They were open twenty-four hours a day, serving more than a thousand children each, and another *New York Times* article gushed about it, describing Portland as "the focal point of the nation in the care of working mothers of preschool children."

AS REVOLUTIONARY AS providing childcare was for working women of the shipyards, providing health care for his workers became Kaiser's newest and most serious passion.

His shipyards, like those around the country, were overflowing with inexperienced, accident-prone workers. The stories circulating sounded like bad jokes. One worker wasn't sure which end of a screwdriver to use. Another had no idea how to remove a drill bit from the drill guide. Men would carelessly light up their welding torch before sliding on their goggles, or fall from a perilously placed ladder, or lift a heavy, sharp piece of steel and throw out their back or slice open their hand. Some showed up to work exhausted, others came drunk, and still others just blew off their shifts without telling anyone. Pneumonia was rampant. Terms like "welder's cough" became commonplace, as more workers inhaled toxic fumes and began spitting up blood.

When a clip eight inches long and made of three-quarter-inch steel dropped thirty feet over the edge of a Liberty's hatch and into the cargo hold on a December day in Richmond, it was precisely the sort of careless accident that could cause a devastating injury. It might have been dropped or kicked, nobody knew, but it slammed into the black helmet of a bespectacled electrician named W. D. Scott with such velocity that it went clear through the helmet and wedged itself into the fibers. "Instead of taking a ride in an ambulance," the shipyards newsletter reported later, "Scott ambled over to the safety office for a new chapeau."[6]

Injuries could be serious, thanks to the heat of the welding torches, to the respiratory effects of inhaling fumes off burning steel or toxic paints, to falling objects that could easily break a limb or crush a skull, and to the narrow spaces that could trigger vertigo or claustrophobia. A single tiny splinter of metal from a piece of burning steel could pierce an eye or embed into a leg and send a worker off for emergency treatment.

Even with workers often dressed in heavy leather outfits, head to toe, and welders wearing goggles and helmets that made them look like astronauts, injuries were part of the shipyard life, striking almost one out of every ten employees in 1942. All too often, an injured worker was showing up drunk or hungover to avoid missing a paycheck only to trip and fall or forget a critical piece of safety equipment. Fatal accidents, though not frequent, were accepted as the risks of the job. Ambulances were making daily trips through the Richmond shipyards, collecting workers and rushing them off for treatment, not exactly a strong selling point for Kaiser's recruiters.

Beyond the rampant sickness and injuries, many of the newly hired shipbuilders came with infants, or with pregnant wives, or sick children, all of which put strains on how much time off they needed to care for their families. Not surprisingly, when Oregon Shipbuilding surveyed one thousand women office workers and welders, it found that those women with children missed far more work than the women without children. And the welding women lost more time than the office workers, since they often faced overnight shifts and took on overtime hours. Absenteeism due to sickness, loafing, fatigue, or general malaise was running at around 7 percent. Every day off requested stretched the production of Liberty ships at a time when every minute in every hour in every day mattered.

SIDNEY GARFIELD WAS standing in Richmond a few days after Bedford's call. It was the middle of December 1941; the shock from Pearl Harbor was still raw. He explored the shipyard to get an understanding of the type of medical care that was needed. He visited hospitals and met with doctors in group practices, hoping to recruit a handful to treat shipyard workers. He also scoured the area for facilities with beds where sick or injured workers could stay.

The problem as Garfield saw it was that the workers typically fell into three categories—too young to serve, too old to serve, or unfit medically to serve. He called the scene a "walking pathological museum," even as he was impressed with the speed they were building ships. The problem was that most of the doctors around Richmond were going off to war, and all the sick and injured workers were landing in hospitals that didn't have the manpower or the beds to treat them.

But what Garfield didn't know is that while he was distracted with finding solutions in Richmond, Bedford had quietly dispatched A. B. Ordway, Kaiser's most loyal employee, to Washington, D.C., so he could explain the medical crisis facing Richmond, along with many of the other shipyards. Kaiser's instructions were for Ordway to impart this message throughout the halls of Congress, without any hint of ambiguity or soft shoeing: *A healthy workforce is no less vital to the Liberty ship program than an abundance of steel.*

Whatever Ordway said must have worked. When he returned to Richmond a few days later, he handed Garfield a letter. The doctor was stunned that it was from the White House. He opened it up and saw that Roosevelt's administration had granted a request from Kaiser to release him from his Army obligation so that he could begin to provide medical care for shipyard workers.[7]

Bedford and Ordway expected Garfield to be relieved to not have to travel to Southeast Asia. Instead he was upset at the surprise intervention. He worried that his colleagues in the 73rd Evacuation Hospital would think that he sought out special treatment to avoid the war. He called back to USC to ask one of his supervisors what he should do.

"For God's sake, take it," he told Garfield. "You will be doing a hell of a lot more than we will be doing in Burma, I'm sure."[8]

BEDFORD NEEDED A miracle worker. He envisioned Sidney Garfield becoming to health care what Henry Kaiser became to building things—a relentless innovator. Bedford thought that Garfield and Kaiser would be kindred spirits. As one doctor who knew both men said, "Sidney was a dreamer and Henry Kaiser was a dreamer, so they dreamed together."

Beyond his medical bona fides, Garfield carried a certain Hollywood glamour that Bedford thought might prove useful with the challenge in Richmond. Garfield was no fuddy-duddy, rumpled doctor. He had an air of mystery about him, wearing sharp, tailored suits with dark shirts and white ties that complemented his gray-green eyes, closely cropped red hair, and chiseled cheekbones. He drove a Cadillac that impressed his younger residents and interns, who followed him around like puppies chasing their mother and listened raptly to his surgical lectures. When Garfield was a young boy growing up in Elizabeth, New Jersey, his hardworking father preached one lesson to him over and over: "It is much better to work for yourself and make ten dollars, than it is to work for someone else for one hundred dollars."

That message would drive Garfield throughout his career, starting around the time he finished his residency in 1933 at a time when 15 million Americans, about 1 in every 4, were unemployed. Rather than forge a traditional career at a hospital or in a group practice, he found satisfaction in experimenting, always with an eye on the patient and society's larger health care needs.

HOW HE EVENTUALLY found himself side by side with Kaiser is a story that seemed scripted by fate.

Kaiser believed in the premise that a happy worker is a more productive worker. It was a major reason why people like A. B. Ordway and Clay Bedford and George Havas stayed with him for decades, and why hundreds of ordinary construction workers, engineers, and midlevel managers followed him from one job to the next. They knew he'd take care of them.

Now as he neared sixty years old in the early days of 1942, Kaiser was telling anyone who would listen that poor medical care had caused his mother to die in his arms when he was sixteen and improper treatment contributed to his father going blind. In marriage, he and Bess lost a daughter in childbirth and their younger son Henry Jr. had multiple sclerosis. Health care was consuming him, and he vowed that one day he would find a way to create a health care system for millions, not just hundreds or thousands. Nobody knew if all the details from his life story were actually true, but nobody doubted his determination.

On earlier projects, Kaiser merely complied with the laws required of him, like sharing half the cost of treating injuries that employees suffered while at work. But his attitude toward the importance of good health care began to shift in the early 1930s.

While building the Boulder Dam, Ordway heard about a young doctor working in the middle of the Mojave Desert who had somehow arranged for workers building the Colorado River Aqueduct to have a prepaid health care plan.

Starting with just $2,500 of his own savings, Garfield borrowed money to build and manage a twelve-bed mobile hospital in the middle of the Mojave to treat workers on the aqueduct job. The hospital buried the doctor in debt, and he was unable to pay his three-person staff for half a year. Creditors threatened to shut it down and even repossess the ambulance he was using. What kept his hospital afloat was the outstanding medical care. Aqueduct contractors arranged for their workers to get treated at the hospital by having a few pennies a month deducted from their paycheck. And the money not only covered their on-site injuries; for an additional nickel every month, they could be treated for all their health care. It was a brilliant stroke because it encouraged workers to get preventative wellness checkups, and it kept them healthier and on the job longer. Importantly, it also guaranteed income to Dr. Garfield regardless of how many workers got hurt.

When the Boulder Dam job was finished, Kaiser and Six Companies pivoted toward building the Grand Coulee Dam. The Grand Coulee was built in a remote and rugged tract almost a hundred miles west of Spokane, Washington. Kaiser, who was the lead contractor on the $41 million project, had decided it was too costly to keep losing workers for days while they traveled back and forth between Spokane for medical care. He also noticed that workers who were very ill would avoid the hospital trip altogether, only prolonging their illness and making them more expensive to treat in the end. Kaiser told his son Edgar to figure out a better plan for health care.

Edgar had gotten to know Garfield while the two of them worked on the Grand Coulee project. He convinced Garfield to visit them in Spokane, and in a matter of months, Garfield had set up a remote hospital that served the 15,000 dam workers as well as their families. Garfield settled on a prepayment fee of fifty cents for adult dependents and twenty-five cents for children. But he only knew his plan was really working when he began to notice that residents of the nearby community were walking in and willing to pay for reliable health care out of pocket.

Henry Kaiser let his son run the Coulee Dam project and only visited every two or three months. Edgar decided to wait until the hospital was fully set up and humming before he finally let his father meet the doctor for the first time. Garfield and Henry Kaiser spent an entire day together, with Kaiser peppering Garfield with questions about how he had set up medical care in a desert and how the newest project was coming along. As they parted company at dinnertime, Kaiser leaned into Garfield.

"Young man, if your plan does half the things you say it has done, it should be made available to every person in the country," Kaiser said.[9]

Garfield was taken aback. He had always struggled for resources and support and here was one of the nation's biggest contractors practically begging to partner with him.

"Mr. Kaiser," Garfield responded, "I have had a hell of a job just getting the services for this little job, which will take care of about 20,000 people. How do you expect to cover the rest of the country?"

Kaiser laughed.

"Don't worry, young man, you will have plenty of help," he said. "You will have plenty of competition, people will want to do the same things that you are doing, if it works that well."

When the Hoover and Grand Coulee dams were finished, those thousands of workers went looking for their next paycheck and in the early days of 1941 they flocked to the shipyards in Richmond and elsewhere. Kaiser realized the health care experiment at Grand Coulee was attractive bait for the workers, and he knew if he could somehow bring it to Richmond, the potential after that was limitless. One year later, Kaiser and Garfield were reunited in Richmond.

AFTER ANOTHER MONTH of searching for a hospital around Richmond, Garfield set his eyes on a crumbling, four-story building in downtown Oakland. At one time it housed the maternity wing of Fabiola Hospital. It was twelve miles from Richmond. Garfield estimated that restoring the space would cost $250,000. When he told Kaiser about it, Kaiser arranged a meeting in February 1942 with a Richmond banker named Amadeo Giannini. He had started up the Bank of Italy in San Francisco in the early 1900s, and Kaiser knew Giannini had a solid reputation for loaning money to local businesses to help them get off the ground.

But when Garfield and Kaiser visited Giannini's office in San Francisco, they discovered he was no pushover. Helping a cobbler or a grocer open a small business was one thing for Giannini. A hospital? That was far riskier.

"I can't lend you a penny," Giannini told the men. "The hospital is absolutely no good to loan money on, because if anything happens and you go in default, there is nothing we can do with a hospital."

He explained to them that an office building is easy to flip and find a new tenant for, but flipping a converted hospital building was near impossible.

"Hospitals just lose money, and they are no good to anybody," Giannini said. Garfield objected.

"We don't lose money," Garfield said, even though he knew it was a lost argument.

Giannini was stubborn. But he was no dummy. He turned to Kaiser.

"Henry, if you will guarantee the loan, I will let him have it."

"I'll guarantee it," Kaiser answered.[10]

Garfield had his space, and they called it Permanente Hospital, named for Permanente Creek that flowed near another Kaiser business in Cupertino, California. (If you are wondering if the name of the modern health care giant Kaiser Permanente derives from all this, rest assured that it does, as we will see later.) Then he went shopping. Kaiser told him to spare no expense, and Garfield set out to purchase the best X-ray equipment, medical and surgical tools, and the finest laboratory necessities, while at the same time lining up a team of top surgeons and physicians to staff the facility, offering them generous salaries ranging from $450 to $1,000 a month. By the summer of 1942, the operation was humming, and to no one's surprise, with just 70 beds, it was immediately overwhelmed. Almost overnight, Garfield's team was inundated with five hundred cases of pneumonia just in their first six months.

Hundreds of cases that would have cost patients between $500 and $1,000 for a private doctor were being handled for pennies on the dollar. One girl, deathly sick from a case of staphylococcus pneumonia, required special nursing of three shifts per day for three months to handle transfusions, medications, and serums. Her treatment cost more than $7,000, but she pulled through.

———

HE SET UP an ambulance system, so that Permanente Hospital could handle the shipyard emergency cases, and area hospitals could take their overflow, nonemergency cases. It didn't take long for the word to spread about the health plan's benefits. Like most of the shipyards around the country, Richmond had started an in-house publication that had become must-read material for its workers.

Richmond's *Fore 'n' Aft* was published weekly in various lengths, from eight or ten pages to twenty or more at times. Portland, Oregon, had its own, called *The Bo's'n's Whistle*. Portland, Maine, had *Keel*, a weekly newspaper. All of them served the same purpose: build morale to build more ships. Articles profiled shipbuilders, interviewed shipyard managers or wartime officials who visited, shared updates on new policies, reminded workers about safety tips, and boasted of new innovations being tried that made their jobs more efficient. If there was a marriage, or a birth, or an award, it was ripe for celebrating in print. As the word of the Kaiser health care plan spread, the newsletter boasted how members "can afford to have eyes examined, colds treated, cuts bandaged, tonsils removed, or treatments for that run-down feeling," all for the cost of "one-half the cost of a pack of cigarettes."

That's not to say it was flawless. The ambulance drivers were just as interested in their next drink as their next patient and were frequently delayed on their rounds by a stop at a Richmond tavern. There was a report of a driver raping a patient, and another report of a stretcher with a strapped-down patient flying out of an ambulance climbing a steep hill. But Kaiser pledged his support to Garfield with a steady stream of funding, using shipyard earnings to help establish the Permanente Foundation.

In addition to opening the hospital, Garfield got six first-aid stations launched in weeks at the shipyards in Richmond. Nurses, doctors, and novice first-aid workers played the role of a frontline crew, treating sniffles and coughs and broken limbs and bloody scrapes with the goal of patching up those who could be patched up and returning them to their work. Those who needed more treatment were rushed into a waiting ambulance and brought to Permanente Hospital, where the normal red tape of a medical facility was nowhere to be seen. A long desk was staffed with pretty and polite young women, whose job was not to ask if someone was eligible for care, but to presume that they were. Patients who walked in waited; if they were on a stretcher, they got priority.

A FIRSTHAND STORY of one shipyard worker's experience with the new medical care circulated widely as testimony to the miracle that Garfield and Kaiser had pulled off. She said her name was Mrs. Rice and that she was a former trained nurse turned shipyard welder. She had fallen off a ladder and shattered her pelvis, and was in searing pain at the shipyard. Within a half an hour of her fall, she'd been brought by ambulance to Garfield's hospital and been seen by a surgeon who gave her a preliminary orthopedic examination. She later said he had the "hands of God." After an X-ray and receiving an opiate, she was resting comfortably barely an hour after the entire incident began.

In her retelling of the story, through tears, she described how quick response time was to her pain needs. "These are not on call by a button that you push for long in vain," she said. "You get them over an intercommunication system that brings quick answer from a nurse at a central desk."[11]

When she asked how long she could remain in her hospital bed, worried the answer would depend on how much money she had, she was told the orthopedist would release her only when her treatment was finished. Not one day sooner. It seemed too good to be true. Her light green room was bright and cheerful, the Venetian blinds protected her from a glare, and she shared the space with only one other patient.

She had traveled the world as a nurse on luxury liners and experienced hospital care of all levels. Nowhere, she said, did any care that she received compare to the type of unlimited, thoughtful attention she got after injuring herself while working in Henry Kaiser's Richmond shipyard. It astonished her that the same level of care was being afforded to almost 100,000 of her fellow shipyard workers, and for just seven cents a day.

———

AS IT TURNED out, it almost was too good to be true. The standard of care Garfield and Kaiser always wanted, which included private rooms rather than cavernous hospital wards full of cots, was impossible to sustain after only a few months with so many injured workers. Garfield suggested renting out a nearby country club and converting it into a makeshift annex to their hospital, but his boss refused.

"No, sir, we'll not hospitalize them in such barracks," Kaiser barked.

"Then we'll have to enlarge Permanente Hospital," Garfield told him, seeing no alternative.

Kaiser agreed. He went back to visit Amadeo Giannini. Only a few months earlier, the Italian banker had reluctantly signed off on Kaiser's original $250,000 loan to open the hospital, by forcing Kaiser to personally guarantee the loan with his signature. Now Kaiser was back, explaining that he wanted to build a 100-bed addition to his hospital and he needed an extra $300,000 loan.

"All right," the bankers said to him, "and of course you'll sign this note, too?"

This time, Kaiser shook his head. He knew the numbers. His shipyard hospital was a roaring success, too successful in fact, and had proven the bankers wrong. The original loan was being paid off at the astonishing rate of $25,000 a month thanks to the prepaid contributions to the health care plan of his shipyard workers.

"No," Kaiser said to the question about securing the new loan. "I signed the first one in the interest of the health of this community. Now it's time for you fellows to get medically community-conscious, too."[12]

Giannini did and Garfield got his addition.

WITH EACH MONTH, injuries in the shipyards mounted, even while safety standards around the country improved. All new employees began to receive physicals before being assigned to jobs. Yards were recommended to have two full-time doctors for every 5,000 employees, plus one additional doctor for every additional 5,000 workers. Inspections of food and water supplies became more regular. Preventative measures were put in place to reduce the volume of the two most common ailments—eye injuries and respiratory issues. Welders were instructed to look like "a man from Mars" when they got down to work in order to protect their eyes and lungs. Even still, for every 100 employees, there were 9.2 injuries in the shipyards, a rate that ensured nearby hospitals would remain busy throughout the war.

Corporal Wilmer Patrick Shea of the U.S. Marine Corps was one of those injured. In the immediate hours after Pearl Harbor, the war in the Pacific had shifted five thousand miles to the west of the American naval base in Hawaii, to Cavite Naval Base in the Philippines. This was the operational base of the United States Asiatic naval fleet, and it was here, during another attack by Japanese planes that killed more than 500 soldiers and approximately 1,000 civilians, where Shea, a tall young man from Alhambra, California, twenty-two years old with tousled brown hair and a narrow, chiseled face, saw his right arm shot clear off during battle. The ensuing hemorrhage and infection nearly killed him. He took his pension, eighty dollars a month for life, and set out to find a new journey.

"I wanted to really help build boats to take the stuff to our fellows out there," Shea said.

So he did. "Believe it or not, they taught me to be a one-armed welder."[13]

But after he'd been trained to work in the shipyard, he slipped on the deck of a boat and broke his arm. He was rushed to the Richmond Field Hospital, his arm put in a sling, and told to sleep in his dormitory, and to return every day so he could be sure and get three meals a day and meet with a nurse. As he watched the care being given to his fellow shipyard workers, under the care of Garfield and the staff there, he could not believe their kindness. Head injuries were not just treated as bumps so that a worker could be rushed back to the yard, but instead they were kept under close observation. Shea's transition from battle-tested Marine into a skilled and dedicated shipbuilder became a widely told story of how Henry Kaiser was doing a lot more to help the war effort than building Liberty ships.

"They don't bargain about the care you ought to get," Shea explained later. He recalled befriending another patient who'd been hurt in a car crash. He came to the hospital for his injuries, and was found to have cancer on his lips, so they treated that, too. "All for seven cents a day," Shea said in wide-eyed amazement.

He came to understand that the seven cents a day they were all paying was not about healing them, it was an investment to protect them from future injury. The slightest sneeze or sniffle was encouraged to be treated, not ignored, and not just treated with two aspirin, but with chest X-rays too.

"You see, the way they treat us fellows at the shipyards keeps a lot of us from dying," Shea said. "Out of all the pneumonias, over half of them wouldn't have got any treatment, if we hadn't had the health plan. And half of that fifty percent would have died."

When he was asked by a writer named Paul de Kruif, who was also a micro-biologist conducting research for a book, to put his opinions of the hospital in writing, his left arm had been out of its sling for only one day. Shea managed to scrawl a few words on a slip of paper.

"I as a shipyard worker think the Field Hospital and the health plan are tops. Because you get the best that science can give. I think the rest of the shipyard fellows feel the same." Then he scribbled his name, "Shea."

Handing the paper over to de Kruif, his face went from stern to smiling. "I don't see why this can't be done everywhere, for everybody," he said.

The workers were not blind about who was responsible for making it happen. Dozens of workers came in with skull fractures, broken ribs, pneumonia, and other ailments, and they said they could never remember feeling happy being inside a hospital. One woman, short of breath because of an injury to her sternum, said to the same journalist who interviewed Shea that she was going back to her Richmond shipyard to tell everybody about the care she received.

"This should be for everybody," she said. "We must organize and demand this not only for us workers but for all their families. It should be for everybody in America."

Another worker, a burly shipbuilder recovering from injuries, said he was being treated so nicely he didn't want to leave. "Henry Kaiser's a big man, but, by God, this is the best thing he ever did."

De Kruif left the hospital in awe. He said his research found that only 1 out of every 500 workers refused the Kaiser plan health care offer.

"Talking to these witnesses you could read this in all their faces," he later wrote. "Pride that this was no charity they were getting. You could see they felt they owned this health plan. Pondering their unanimous testimony, you felt a tingle down your spine, a lift to make you forget the world's death and sadness."

The Permanente Foundation that Kaiser set up with Garfield would go on to revolutionize health care in America. But in its infancy days of 1942, when the Richmond shipyard workers were just beginning to understand the value of paying seven cents into a system for better treatment, it did something far more important. It confirmed Henry Kaiser's long-held belief—happy workers are productive workers.

"It stirred the worker-army to a roaring chant of *Praise the Lord—Pass Another Section*," de Kruif wrote. "This was their battle hymn as they slammed and banged and hoisted and welded giant sections of Liberty boats together. This was their theme song as they built boats in days where they used to be built in months."[14]

The chant was a reference to a popular verse said by a Navy chaplain at Pearl Harbor. Sensing how exhausted some of the sailors were, he uttered a spontaneous phrase while patting a few of them on the back: "Praise the Lord and pass the ammunition," he told them. What started as a rallying cry for soldiers and sailors was now an inspiring cheer for America's shipbuilders.

CHAPTER TWENTY-SIX

The Map Speech

BY EARLY 1942, THE LAST OF THE OCEAN-CLASS SHIPS FOR the British was nearing completion, an accomplishment that opened the door for dramatic change in Richmond and across America's shipbuilding landscape. In mid-February, representatives from Kaiser's company and Todd Shipbuilding met in New York City to hash out their breakup. They agreed that Kaiser would maintain control over the western shipyards, in Portland, Oregon; Richmond, California; and Los Angeles, while Todd would take Seattle-Tacoma Shipbuilding and Houston Shipbuilding, along with controlling interest in the South Portland Shipbuilding and Todd-Bath Iron Shipbuilding Corporation in Maine. With the British ships mostly behind them, it was time for America's most productive shipyards to devote their resources to building America's Liberty ships.

"It is believed that by more intensive concentration in definite areas, the individual organizations can more effectively speed up construction programs of the Maritime Commission and the Navy," John Reilly, the president of Todd Shipbuilding, explained in announcing the split.[1]

Nobody was pushing them harder to speed up than Admiral Vickery. At every chance he got, Vickery needled the managers of shipyards across the country about how fast another shipyard had completed a Liberty ship. When the shipyards were expanded to accommodate more shipways, he issued them a blunt challenge.

"I consider you are all in competition," he said.

When he learned that Edgar Kaiser's Oregon yard had set the new speed standard for construction, he telephoned the manager of a competing yard to make sure he knew this was a rivalry. And there were winners, and losers.

"You haven't matched that. And you're supposed to be a shipbuilder!" he shouted.[2]

Nobody took his prodding too seriously. In February, Clay Bedford sent Vickery and Land safety hats with the Richmond shipyards logo. But on Land's hat, Bedford put a crown, and on Vickery's he put a broadax, and both hats carried four stars to signify "Big Chief." Anything to help ease the tension.

THE WAR WAS going badly for America. Germany was pumping out new submarines aggressively. Sadness and grief still lingered two months after Pearl Harbor. Families who said goodbye to their soldiers nervously awaited word that they had safely crossed the Atlantic and arrived in Europe. British intelligence warned the U.S. Navy that a flotilla of German U-boats appeared headed straight for the eastern shoreline, somewhere between New York City and Portland, Maine. Was an attack imminent? Was Hitler really going to invade the United States?

A twenty-eight-year-old U-boat commander showed how easily an attack could have been carried out, if Hitler had so desired. In January 1942, Reinhard Hardegan navigated his submarine with zero interference directly past Coney Island, where Brooklyn meets the Atlantic. He had visited New York as a young boy and could not believe now he was staring at it through his periscope.

"I cannot describe the feeling with words, but it was unbelievably beautiful and great," Hardegan wrote a year later in a memoir. "I would have given away a kingdom for this moment if I had one. We were the first to be here, and for the first time in this war a German soldier looked upon the coast of the U.S.A."[3]

Hitler would have been proud. Roosevelt, if he knew, embarrassed.

The Battle of the Atlantic intensified with disastrous results. It started when a British freighter called *Cyclops*, carrying Chinese cargo and Chinese sailors, took a series of torpedo hits from a German U-boat that tore the ship in half off the coast of Nova Scotia. In less than ten minutes, the *Cyclops* was gone and nearly a hundred seamen on board drowned. It marked the beginning of Operation Drumbeat, a coordinated series of unrelenting attacks by German subs on Allied shipping. German U-boats had already sunk 1,124 Allied ships, and that was only the beginning.

Finally, in February, a flurry of shipbuilding activity reflected the desperation sweeping across the country, and through the halls of the White House. Vickery, speaking to a group of California steel and iron workers, uttered a surprise proclamation. He said Liberty ships would soon be constructed in 105 days, "a new record for shipbuilding construction," the *New York Times* reported, and half of the current 210-day average. The statement hit newspapers the next day, and Vickery reached out to his shipbuilding kingpin to explain that 105 was the new goal, and it was only going to get faster. Even for Kaiser, who rarely lacked confidence, it felt unrealistic.

"We can't do it!" the shipbuilders responded when they learned the news. "It's impossible!"[4]

For a week, as Kaiser weighed the demand from Vickery, he endured criticisms from his own employees and from the usually adoring press that had dubbed him Sir Launchalot. He finally relented.

"All right," he conceded to Vickery. "If you think it can be done, we'll try. We'll get you your hundred-and-five-day ships!"

Vickery immediately began to spread the word to shipbuilders across the country. He wanted them to know Henry Kaiser was going to build Liberty ships in a little more than three months. He dared them to keep pace.

"That hurt," the *Saturday Evening Post* reported. "As a shipbuilder Kaiser was only a novice from the West Coast, and his name was already rasping and grating on sensitive prides. The Eastern builders, with their long tradition of shipbuilding, couldn't afford to be outclassed. And all over America, from general manager down to the lowest laborer, the heat went on."

That 105 days was broken down into 60 days to complete the vessel, plus another 45 days to outfit it with gear for the crew and cranes to load its cargo, and to set it sailing. It was a breathtaking demand, because up until that point, through 1941, the building of most Liberty ships took more than 200 days. It had come down slowly, with some ships being built in 150 days, or five months, and a few ships coming off their ways even faster. But three months represented a new aggressiveness. Vickery and Land both believed it was essential for shipyards to begin producing five or six Liberty ships per year, per shipway, instead of four.

In fact, Richmond, under Clay Bedford's leadership, had already cut its production time of launching a Liberty to 80 days. And up north in Portland, Oregon, Edgar Kaiser was even faster, reducing the average time to 71 days. The problem Vickery faced was that across the country and down south, important shipyards at Bethlehem-Fairfield and Houston and Mobile, Alabama, needed more time, closer to 150 days total rather than 105.

Feeling the pressure from the Oval Office, Vickery saw only one solution in order to please the White House demands: more shipyards. Between the new shipyards and the faster production speed, Vickery expected nothing less than a 30 percent increase in Liberty ships launching into the waters around the country throughout 1942 and into 1943. Jerry Land framed the state of shipbuilding as a warning to the president to resist any more bold or outrageous demands. "The shipbuilding cup is full to overflowing," he declared.[5]

Meanwhile, the toll from the war was growing. Operation Drumbeat was going better than the Germans could have hoped. By early spring, only seven U-boats had been sunk since America entered the war, while the Allies lost 397 ships, almost all of them tankers. And of those 397, eighty-two were sunk off the coast of North Carolina and southern Virginia. Residents who lived along the Outer Banks, especially Topsail Beach, would watch from their beach houses as flames erupted on the horizon, and a few days later they would stumble upon oil slicks, or in some instances, burned and decomposed bodies onshore.

As the numbers mounted, both Vickery and Land realized that to build more ships, the solution was more complicated than building more shipyards. They were going to need to hire and train more shipbuilders. In a hurry.

ON FEBRUARY 19, a tired and sick president invited Land to his private quarters at the White House. Roosevelt was in no mood for debate or dialogue. He had an emotional day in front of him and he wasn't feeling well.

That very morning, Roosevelt's chief naval officer, Admiral Harold S. Stark, had driven his personal car downtown with a plain black briefcase beside him on the passenger seat filled with $500,000 in high-denomination bills.[6] After parking outside Riggs National Bank, Stark, a short, silver-haired man in non-descript clothes, walked inside and handed his briefcase to a bank officer with instructions to open a new account that he could easily transfer money into and out of with no holdups. Once all the papers were signed, Stark drove home, changed into uniform, and took a chauffeured Navy car to his office. Everything was now in place for a highly secretive plan hatched by Roosevelt. Following the president's orders, there were no records of the deposited funds, no paper trails. Under Project LQ, and with the cooperation of Jerry Land's Maritime Commission, giant tankers and freighters were being converted into armed merchant ships so they could be used as decoys to lure German submarines into making a torpedo attack. The ships were to be filled with buoyant cargo to make them difficult to sink, and when a U-boat surfaced to finish off the attack, the crew on board the ship, standing behind hidden four-inch barrel guns, would open fire in a surprise assault.

Project LQ represented the desperate state of the war two months after Pearl Harbor. In 1939, after World War II broke out following the Nazis' invasion of Poland, a strategic assault by German U-boats was referred to as the "Happy Time" by the Germans. Now, two years later, German sub commanders were parking their U-boats along the East Coast of the United States, especially along Long Island and off the coast of New Jersey, and opening fire on American and British tankers. U-boat crews dubbed it their "Second Happy Time."

Roosevelt hoped his top-secret plan might slow the Germans, but that wasn't the reason he had summoned Land to the White House. He told Land that the Allies needed the United States to build 9 million tons of Liberty ships in 1942, instead of 8 million, and a staggering 15 million tons in 1943. Land, never without words, was speechless. It was as if the success of the shipbuilding program in its first year set up unrealistic expectations.

Roosevelt explained later in a letter to Land that "the great enemy left no options." But he added, "I feel certain that in this very great emergency we can attain it."

His words were of little comfort to Land, who reached out to Vickery with the news. Vickery was already traveling the country in search of new possible shipways to construct.

"You know it is impossible to get nine million tons in 1942," Vickery told his boss.

"Yes, and I have so informed the authorities," Land replied. "All I said was we would try."[7]

MORE THAN TWO months had passed since Pearl Harbor. With each passing day, Roosevelt had a greater sense that Americans had no idea of the military challenges that lay ahead. Or of the vital role that Liberty ships were going to play and why he was insisting that thousands of them be built. After eight years in office, Roosevelt had mastered the art of being a reassuring voice without sounding rosy and overly optimistic.

"I want to tell it to them in simple terms of ABC so that they will understand what is going on and how each battle fits into the picture," he told his speechwriters. "If they understand the problem and what we are driving at, I am sure that they can take any kind of bad news right on the chin."[8]

It was time, he told his staff, to give Americans a geography lesson. In the final dark days of February, Roosevelt decided he needed this fireside chat to feel different from his others. The moment was too important for it to feel ordinary. As he started drafting his remarks, he grew determined to find a way to strike a balance in boosting the nation's morale while being realistic, not overly optimistic. The message he wanted to send was that America was up to the task—no matter how daunting it seemed or how evil its enemies. He just needed a gimmick.

AS A BIT of a geography buff, Roosevelt informed his staff that in order for his speech to work effectively, he wanted Americans listening at home to understand the complex geography of a world war. And in order for them to understand it, he wanted them to have a map of the world in front of them.

"I'm going to speak about strange places that many of them have never heard of—places that are now the battleground for civilization," Roosevelt told his speechwriters. "I want to explain to the people something about geography—what our problem is and what the overall strategy of the war has to be."[9]

The president hoped that if others could see the problem in front of them just as he did, it might change the way they processed news about the progress of the war. Word was sent out through his staff about the maps, and within days Americans were stampeding through their local stationery, convenience, and department stores to clear shelves of all the maps they could find. When the maps were gone, people snapped up globes instead. The weekend just before the speech became a frenzy. On Forty-Third Street in New York, at C. S. Hammond & Company, the sales manager, E. G. Schmidt, heard the news about Roosevelt's speech and rushed down to his warehouse on Saturday to collect two thousand copies of the newest atlas to keep on hand in the store. All two thousand were gone by day's end. Every time he tried to close his store in the afternoon, another customer pleaded with him to open up.

"Why even last night when I went home," Schmidt told a reporter for the *New York Times*, "my wife, who has never particularly cared about maps, asked me to put up on the wall a large commercial map I've had for years."[10]

———

AT 10 A.M. on Monday, February 23, 1942, President Roosevelt, battling a mild cold but still wearing a dark suit and tie, took a seat in front of a microphone with his own map of the world mounted on the wall behind him. More than 61 million adults, almost 80 percent of the possible audience, sat beside their radios with their maps spread out in front of them, just as their president had asked of them. He began with a history lesson, reminding people that George Washington had run out of supplies at Valley Forge, Pennsylvania, but refused to back down until the American Revolution was won. He talked about the paths the pioneers took to climb the Rockies and push westward. Then he transitioned to why the current war was unlike any that preceded it. It wasn't being fought in one country, or across one ocean, he said.

"This war is a new kind of war. It is different from all other wars of the past, not only in its methods and weapons but also in its geography. It is warfare in terms of every continent, every island, every sea, every air lane in the world."[11]

Referencing the maps in front of his listeners, he explained the four ocean shipping routes that were essential to the war, and to America's survival. At one point he addressed his audience as if he were a professor and they were his students sitting in front of him.

"I ask you to look at your maps again, particularly at that portion of the Pacific Ocean lying west of Hawaii," he said.

He explained how the tiniest dots on their maps might seem inconsequential, but in fact represented key strategic islands, such as Guam, because of their positions along vital shipping routes. And throughout the speech, he went out of his way to reference the importance of cargo ships in particular.

These routes are not one-way streets, for the ships that carry our troops and munitions outbound bring back essential raw materials which we require for our own use. The maintenance of these vital lines is a very tough job. It is a job which requires tremendous daring, tremendous resourcefulness, and, above all, tremendous production of planes and tanks and guns and also of the ships to carry them. And I speak again for the American people when I say that we can and will do that job.

Airplanes can't do it alone, he said; not when the war is being fought across oceans.

"Heavy bombers can fly under their own power from here to the southwest Pacific, either way, but the smaller planes cannot," he explained. "Therefore, these lighter planes have to be packed in crates and sent on board cargo ships."

That's why, he continued, "our first job then is to build up production—uninterrupted production—so that the United Nations can maintain control of the seas and attain control of the air." In concluding, he asked Americans to appreciate the effort underway to protect them, and the speed at which it was moving.

"Never before have we had so little time in which to do so much."

Close observers of Roosevelt hailed the speech, with the *Times* calling it "one of the greatest of Roosevelt's career."

WITH HIS CONFIDENCE growing about the state of shipbuilding and feeling pressure from Winston Churchill to help with Britain's relentless shipping losses, Roosevelt once again upped his demand on the U.S. Maritime Commission. He told Land and Vickery that his request for 9 million tons of merchant ships in 1942 needed to be more than doubled, and now he was demanding a combined 24 million tons for 1942 and 1943.

Instead of panicking, the Maritime Commission leaders took heart. They believed a production increase was achievable. They were not saying so publicly, but the success of the current shipyards, from Maine to Washington, from North Carolina to Northern California, and from Maryland to Southern California, had made the need for building another costly, enormous shipyard in New Orleans less critical. A $29 million contract they were about to sign with a shipbuilder there named Andrew Jackson Higgins to build 200 Liberty ships was canceled.

At the beginning of March 1942, one year after Kaiser's operation began in Richmond, just 17 Liberty ships had been completed nationwide, and the average length of time it was taking to build them was 217 days, or more than seven months. But in the weeks surrounding the debate over whether to approve or cancel the Higgins contract, the pace picked up. In March and April combined, another 52 ships were launched, and in May 43 more, putting the total over 100 by the spring. And from seven months, the average time to build a ship was dropping with each week, down below five months by May and four months in June, with some yards closing in on three months.[12]

When Land was brought before the House of Representatives committee investigating the Higgins canceled contract, he boasted of the Liberty ship program's success as the reason why the new shipyard was not necessary.

"We definitely . . . will meet the President's program irrespective of this cancellation," Land said.

WITH SUCCESS CAME added pressure. An order from United States Naval Intelligence about the United States Censorship Code gave shipbuilders a new reason for worry. "No Admittance!" the memo read, reminding everyone of the fear of espionage or spies. Future public launchings of new Liberty ships would be private, with no public attendance allowed, other than the sponsor of the ship and shipyard managers and employees.

"The order is designed to make it impossible for details about the shipyard to leak out into unfriendly hands," the Richmond shipyard newspaper *Fore 'n' Aft* reported. "You know you can be trusted, and every man on your crew, but public launchings might permit unfriendly persons to plan or commit sabotage in our yard. This is war and no admittance must be the rule!"[13]

Then, in mid-March 1942, only a few weeks after Roosevelt's map speech, a rumor began circulating among some disgruntled shipyard employees. At first it was only gossip. But as the word spread and took on a life of its own, not only did it threaten to derail the shipbuilding momentum that Land was boasting of, but if it turned out to be true, it could also halt shipbuilding in all of Kaiser's shipyards. And maybe endanger the Liberty ship program across the country.

CHAPTER TWENTY-SEVEN

Strikes, Safety, and Sexism

ON WEDNESDAY NIGHT, MARCH 18, 1942, FIFTY MEN GATH-
ered outside the gates of the Richmond shipyards, chanting and yelling for
other workers to join them in a strike. Tensions in the shipyards had been
building for months.[1]

For as long as America had been building ships, American shipbuilders
had been white and male. They saw themselves not only as patriots but as
soldiers of shipbuilding who were working with their own dangerous weapons—welding torches, industrial chemicals, huge cranes. And then overnight,
the war changed everything. The white male shipbuilders found themselves
working alongside Black people from all corners of the country talking with
funny accents, and next to women young enough to be their daughters or old
enough to be their mothers. The blending of the workforce under tense, wartime conditions did not go smoothly. The old guard was jealous, suspicious,
defensive, petty, and mean. They would crowd around the women to intimidate
them while they worked. They would accuse them of being more interested in
socializing than working. When the men didn't get what they wanted, they just
slacked off, dozed off, or walked off the job. They did whatever they could to
prevent Black people from taking their jobs, joining their unions, or squeezing

them out of higher-pay opportunities. They fought to keep even the most experienced Black people from joining the unions.

Black people should "look before they leaped" into temporary defense jobs, wrote Louis Campbell, a columnist for *California Voice*. He wrote they would be "cast adrift in the army of the unemployed as soon as white employers got the chance to discard them."[2]

ONLY A FEW days before the walkout at the Richmond shipyard in mid-March, Roosevelt's administration had reached a labor agreement for shipyards across the country. The new plan called for twenty-four-hour workdays, seven days a week, broken up into three, eight-hour shifts. It was intended to make the shipyards more efficient and safe. It also called for time-and-a-half pay on a worker's sixth day of the week, and double pay if they worked a seventh day, regardless of whether those extra days fell on a Saturday or Sunday. The new plan made sense. Yet it overlooked one key element for the workers—it eliminated consistent and valuable overtime pay they could earn, and it blurred the line between an ordinary daytime Tuesday shift and a late-night Saturday shift. Some workers had managed to increase their wages by as much as 40 percent with overtime hours, and now that opportunity was gone.

When word on the streets of Richmond began to circulate that some shipyards in other locations were operating with two, ten-hour shifts per day, plus offering double time pay for extra hours, the anger was swift. If it was true, it would not only be better pay than the Richmond workers were earning, but also would violate the labor agreement that came straight from the White House.

The Richmond workers who gathered outside the gate were determined to put pressure on those inside to join them. It worked. Slowly at first, but then in increasing numbers, the workers inside started to walk off their assigned jobs and make their way toward the exit. At first it was only a few dozen. But then a hundred joined them, and by the end of the night, one thousand workers at the Richmond shipyards walked off the job, most of them union members of the International Brotherhood of Boilermakers. It was a swift and sudden job action by workers mostly assigned to the late afternoon and graveyard shifts who were convinced there was better pay out there to be had.

They wanted assurances that the new labor plan was not about saving money, and that it would not enrich men like Henry Kaiser at the expense of their laborers. The morning after the strike began, back in Washington, Paul Porter, the chairman of the shipbuilding stabilization committee of the War Production Board, got word of what happened in Richmond and immediately sent a telegram directly to the workers to vent his disgust.

"They are stabbing their country in the back," he wrote. "If they don't yet know there is a war going on, they should be escorted by loyal workers to the nearest Army recruiting station before the day is over and given a chance to get into the fighting zone."[3] He called on the workers to return to their shift immediately and to ignore the rumors they were hearing.

Nazi submarines were busy sinking American ships so close to the New Jersey shore that their flames could be seen from the beaches at night. The Army was ordering that the bright neon lights from the Jersey beach resorts be blacked out, because the lights were helping enemy subs spot the silhouettes of ships backlit against the shore. This was no time for Liberty ship production to be threatened by a work stoppage, Porter said.

"The president's request for 24-hour operation, seven days per week, will not result in one cent more profit to any shipbuilding company," Porter said. "Any such false report used to create dissension between employees and shipyards is the work of subversive elements."

Henry Kaiser, aware of a potential public relations nightmare to his business and growing popularity, chimed in too. He had dismissed the reports of growing absenteeism in shipyards as "grossly overdone." But now, knowing that the country could ill afford any slowdown in the production of Liberty ships, and that he controlled the most productive shipyards, he had to speak out again—or else risk a backlash. He published advertisements in which he explained that all profits from his Richmond shipyards went straight to the Reconstruction Finance Corporation, not into his pockets.

"We must get production," Kaiser said in an interview. "A lot of people don't believe the sole aim of this company is to win the war, not to make profits. Winning the war is our only aim."

The quick and decisive responses from Land, Porter, and Kaiser worked. The striking employees and their unions accepted that the rumors about fewer shifts were false and they returned to work. But if anyone thought that would end any shipyard tensions, they were mistaken.

WOMEN, ESPECIALLY BLACK women, suffered the worst—both racism and sexism—accused of being distractions and undeserving of good-paying jobs. Whispers permeated some shipyards that women were selling their sexual services in warehouses and remote compartments inside the ships. But prostitution wasn't the problem. Men just wanted to discredit the women as serious workers, and when an article appeared in *BusinessWeek* about an alleged prostitution ring in Portland's shipyards, it nearly worked.

Three Black women—Flora Hilliard, Elmira Ake, and Frances Mary Albrier—decided to take on the hiring practices of the unions, especially the most powerful one, the Boilermakers. They were fed up with being cast aside when they were just as hungry to work in the shipyards and just as capable as men to handle both menial and hard labor jobs like welding.[4]

Hilliard caught the attention of California's War Manpower Commission, which assisted her in getting admitted into the Oakland Shipfitters & Helpers Local 9 union in Richmond Yard No. 3. The union had told Hilliard it lacked any guidance from its national organization on "how to handle this type of membership," but once the Manpower Commission intervened on her behalf, the union suddenly found a way to welcome her.

Elmire Ake, a resident of Oakland, went to a higher power for her case—the White House. Her husband was of draft age and her son was about to join the armed forces. She had managed to get hired in Richmond as a laborer, but she wanted work as a welder or a burner, both higher-paying jobs. When she tried to join the Boilermakers, they responded matter-of-factly that they "[d]id not take negro women in the Boilermakers union."

She decided to write to President Roosevelt.

"Why can't I have a [decent] job as other american Citison [*sic*]," she wrote. She asked that he reply to her and to "rite me and tell me why cant [I] become a member."[5]

Moved by her plea, the White House passed her letter to the Fair Employment Practices Commission. But the help ended there when it informed Ake that unless she could prove that lack of membership in the union was preventing her from getting a job or improving her wages or opportunities for promotion, it could not do anything.

Occasionally, the threat of a lawsuit worked, which is how Frances Albrier, a longtime community activist in the San Francisco Bay Area, became a trailblazer for Black women. Like Ake, she landed a shipyard job in Richmond and she even completed more than sixty hours of training to be a welder, passing the welding test "with flying colors," in her eyes. Still, her application to Local 513, an all-white, predominantly male union, was rejected, a decision that prompted her to threaten to sue.

The union said it would take her union dues in Richmond, then transfer them to its nearby and smaller Oakland auxiliary shop until the more prominent Richmond shipyard had formal protocols in place to accept Black women. It was a weak compromise, but a first step. When Albrier showed up for work in her all-leather, full welder's outfit, other Black shipyard employees stared at her in amazement.

"How did *you* get in here?" they asked.

She responded, "Well, I just happened to bust my way in here!"[6]

Most Black women were excluded from full membership throughout the war as the unions maintained their racist and sexist bias. But they never stopped fighting. While the government's intervention with the unions should have been stronger, it worked in other ways to recognize the value and contributions of Black Americans to the war. None of the attacks could keep them away. Women knew they were needed. Their husbands, boyfriends, fathers, uncles, and brothers were all going off to fight, and if the men weren't around to build Roosevelt's Arsenal of Democracy, women had to step forward. Women got their own instructions when they arrived in shipyards. No floppy bandanas or loose clothing. Low heels and full-toed shoes. No rings, necklaces, or bracelets. "Weights over twenty-five pounds shall not be lifted!" *Fore 'n' Aft* warned.

UNLIKE THE RACIAL tension that arrived with the influx of Black people in shipyards, the misgivings about women working on Liberty ships were different. There was some anger and animosity toward them from the traditional white male shipbuilding guard, but there was also concern for their health, safety, and well-being along with disbelief that they could actually perform any tasks beyond the menial. The concerns, of course, were woefully misguided and overtly sexist, and no action was more offensive than when a white woman welder dared to socialize with a Black coworker, earning her the label "n---er lover" inside the shipyard. The "Okies" and the "Arkies," the white southern shipbuilders, were most offended by the idea of Black men with white women.

Much of the progress toward independence that women enjoyed during the Roaring Twenties vanished in the sadness and bread lines of the Great Depression. The 1930s mostly resolidified the role of women as chief executive of the home. With money tight, they were sewing clothes, canning fruits and vegetables, baking bread, cooking with time-consuming coal or wood stoves, and laundering heavy loads of bedsheets and clothes outside or in hand-cranked machines. From the farms to the cities, women were spending fifty hours a week just on routine household tasks and chores.

Those who did manage to work, about one in every ten women during the decade, rarely earned more than two hundred dollars in a year in feminized clerical or service jobs, while their husbands were lucky to take home six hundred. And if the puny paychecks were not enough of a deterrent for women, many of them were shamed if they worked. A study in 1936 found that

72 percent of the population believed wives should not work if their husbands held jobs, and some even wanted federal laws passed that would ban women from working.[7]

Then came war. Before 1940, women who worked in shipyards were sewing by hand, working on machine sails and flags. That was their job. The wartime economy opened up new good-paying, government jobs dominated by men, until they started disappearing into military service. Recognizing that something had to change, Roosevelt told his citizens it was time they set aside their old biases and traditions.

"In some communities, employers dislike to employ women," he said in his twelfth fireside chat. "In others they are reluctant to hire Negroes. In still others, older men are not wanted. We can no longer afford to indulge such prejudices or practices."[8]

For shipyard managers, that was far easier said than done. They treated women like porcelain dolls in the early days of the war. In a report undertaken by the Women's Bureau of the Department of Labor, shipyards were warned of a woman's physiological differences and to avoid assigning them too much strenuous work. They were told that "the frame of a woman is such that it is more difficult for her than for a man to maintain her balance," and that her heart beats faster and she will tire more quickly than a man. "And because they are more likely to get varicose veins and tire more quickly, constant standing is more difficult and harmful for them."

Even their smarts and toughness were questioned, with questions raised about their ability to tell the differences between hoses and cables lying around, and whether the din of the chipping and welding combined with the extreme weather elements would overwhelm them. And then there were the morality concerns, of women being more interested in socializing than working and unintentionally, or perhaps intentionally, distracting men from their jobs.

"Night work should be assigned only after careful investigation to make sure that the woman worker's health will not be endangered," the Women's Bureau report said.[9]

When women asked sensible questions, they were treated as if their logic was yet another sign of their weakness. "We were given no advice on clothing and many of us had flash burns and slag burns on our necks," one woman told the Labor Department's agents for the report. "Our slacks were perforated with small burns and some caught fire and burned sizeable holes. Those who wore low shoes frequently had ankle burns. My glasses were well pitted by slag before the matron in the rest room told me to ask for goggles in the office. We still had many questions unanswered and would have welcomed a chance for class discussion."

When the women in one shipyard complained that the toilet doors had been removed in their washrooms because they were suspected of lingering there too long, new doors were installed that were only three feet high, barely affording them any privacy.

THE LIBERTY SHIP program was only a year old, but Jerry Land was worried that workers were starting to get a little too comfortable. He blamed shipyard managers for poor oversight as much as he blamed lazy workers, who he heard were hiding in watertight compartments to avoid their jobs. Report after report that landed on his desk stated that attendance at shipyards around the country was down. And he was told it was only getting worse, with increasing reports of all-night craps games, hulls being left unfinished, and rampant absenteeism.

Fed up, on March 24, one week after the brief strike in Richmond, he took to the radio airwaves.

"It is pleasant to report that the strike problem—formal strikes—is not a serious one at this time," the admiral said in his address. "Last year strikes cost us eight to twelve ships. But what is serious, and serious right now, is loafing."[10]

The word *loafing* made Land cringe. He had been embarrassed to go before Congress and sheepishly explain why strikes had disrupted shipbuilding so much that they cost the U.S. Maritime Commission as many as a dozen ships in 1941. To Land, strikes were bordering on treasonous.

"There is too damn much loafing going on," he said.[11]

When the Maritime Commission investigated loafing, it rated eight ship-yards in good shape and seven as fair. But it also found eleven of them "unsat-isfactory" or "downright disgraceful." At those worst yards, the inspectors found examples of men just sitting around waiting for crane lifts, wandering aimlessly, and even sleeping or playing craps during their shifts. The biggest cause of loafing pointed at the combination of inexperienced workers under inexperienced managers.

When Land fired off a scathing letter to John Pew, the president of Sun Shipbuilding & Dry Dock Company in Chester, Pennsylvania, he did not hold back his ire.

"Here is the largest shipyard in the world whose record of deliveries shows that only one vessel this month is being delivered during this crucial period," Land wrote.[12]

The blame game continued, with union leaders pointing the finger at shipyard managers and managers blaming unions. Land had no tolerance for any of it.

"They do not always do it deliberately. I am criticizing management as well as labor," he wrote to Pew. "There is deliberate loafing on the part of some of them and there may be some deliberate bad management."

AMERICA WAS INTEGRATING—SLOWLY and not necessarily willingly. Prodded by the passage of the President's Committee on Fair Employment Practice, and boosted by the opportunities of wartime employment, the face of the American workforce began changing, and the biggest change was hap-pening out west. Starting in 1942, nearly 500,000 African Americans flooded into California, the largest westward migration of Black people in the country's history. One-quarter of those arrivals moved to the San Francisco Bay Area, drawn by the shipyard work even though the shipyards did not embrace their arrival. When some of the Black workers tried to get the International Broth-erhood of Boilermakers local union in Portland, Oregon, to stop ignoring and excluding them, they were told that the "available supply of Negro labor . . .

could be absorbed as janitors."[13] Only after President Roosevelt intervened personally did the West Coast shipyards, led by Henry Kaiser, begin to hire Black workers in large numbers.

He sent his labor recruiters to the deep southern states to specifically find Black workers. They posted and handed out brightly colored circulars boasting of temperatures more pleasant than the steamy South, of competitive pay and strong benefits. They stressed that these were patriotic jobs. And it worked. For Black migrants tired of the social and political climate in the Deep South, an adventure west was a temptation hard to resist. They did not always get the pay equity they deserved, but just the mere dream of economic prosperity and independence was enough to lure them. In Memphis, Tennessee, William McKinney saw an advertisement in a newspaper for welders, so he took a welding course in three months, along with a group of other men, and they all got offered jobs in Richmond and drove there together for three days straight. "We didn't stop for nothing but the gas and to eat," McKinney said.[14] In Pine Bluff, Arkansas, Margaret Starks caught wind of the recruiters and told her husband to go to California, and to call for her when he was settled.

Federal law stipulated that the shipyards had to be closed shops, meaning they could only hire union members. And the largest shipyard union, the International Brotherhood of Boilermakers, Iron Ship Builders & Helpers of America, refused to allow Black shipyard workers into their shops as equal members. They considered them the "dregs of the recruitment barrel" and relegated them to "auxiliary" roles that hindered their ability to be promoted, to file grievances, and to have a voice in union business. The union made no effort to hide their disdain, using an official publication to describe the new recruits as a collection of "shoe clerks, soda jerks, professors, pimps and old maids."[15] Not only did the limitations anger the Black shipyard workers and create animosity in the shipyards, but they also didn't sit well with Henry Kaiser.

Kaiser had spent the last thirty years of his construction business building strong ties with organized labor, and now he faced an urgent hiring need. He couldn't be bothered with union rules that froze out huge blocks of potentially valuable employees, so he decided to hire workers without going through the union. And he made sure Clay Bedford in Richmond and his son Edgar up in Portland, Oregon, followed his lead.

WHEN THE WAR Manpower Commission supported Kaiser's effort to recruit and hire workers without union clearance, it opened a floodgate of new arrivals out west who were immediately assigned to shipyards in Richmond, Los Angeles, Oakland, Portland, and Vancouver, Washington. Leading the way were mostly unskilled Black people, hungry for work and willing to ignore the warnings sent their way.

When Edgar Kaiser's Portland shipyard promoted eight Black shipyard workers to skilled trade positions from common laborers, the Boilermakers Local Lodge 72 exploded, threatening to "take matters into its own hands" if the promotions were not undone. The same union refused to hire thirty Black workers who had arrived from New York for any job other than menial or custodial work. After tense negotiations, the shipyard manager and the union finally agreed to let Black workers be hired based on their "highest skill." But even that compromise still favored the white workers, since the union was allowed to determine the Black workers' skill level.

To no one's surprise, Black women were refused union membership, were assigned to lower-paying jobs, and were denied promotions more frequently than both their white and Black male coworkers. But not all of them took their lesser standing quietly.

When Margaret Starks joined her husband in Richmond from Arkansas and landed her own job in the shipyard, she felt good about their situation. Then she found out her husband was cheating on her and that she was pregnant. She refused to go back home to her cooking job in Pine Bluff. "I had an abortion, divorced him and with the money I earned from the shipyards I started a life of my own," she said years later.[16] That life included keeping her shipyard job and publishing the first Black newspaper in Richmond, the *Richmond Guide*, which reported on life both inside and outside the shipyard where she worked.

Starks overcame her own frustrations and disappointments and instead became a symbol of the Black working women of America's shipyards—skilled, patriotic, independent.

RACISM, SEXISM, AND strikes kept shipyard managers busy. But two weeks after the brief strike, and one week after Land's radio tirade, a new crisis surfaced on a bright and crisp Saturday morning that would have to be addressed just as swiftly.

On March 28, 1942, the wife of George Havas, one of Kaiser's most loyal engineers, made her way down to a Richmond shipway where the SS *Timothy Pickering* was waiting. A huge American flag was draped loosely over her stern. The ship had been finished in a little more than five months from the time her keel was laid back in October 1941. It was named after the third U.S. secretary of state, who served under both George Washington and John Adams.

Preparations for the launching were just about done, and people were moving into place, when shouts erupted. Fifteen minutes before Mrs. Havas was supposed to smash her ceremonial bottle on the hull, she jumped back as the ship began sliding down its rails, perhaps greased a little too well. Screams pierced the air, directed at the half-dozen workers who were standing down toward the water, directly in the ship's path on the rails.

With seconds to spare, four of the six workers leapt out of the way, suffering only cuts and bruises. A fifth worker to the side was slightly injured, and the sixth miraculously skirted a gruesome death by falling to the ground between the rails and allowing the 441-foot ship to pass over him with a thunderous rumble. The moment the *Pickering* splashed into the water, he stood up, stunned that he had somehow not been flattened, and brushed the grease from his uniform that had rubbed off onto him from the ship's keel.[17]

The small article that appeared in the following day's Santa Rosa *Press Democrat* no doubt gave pause to any newly arriving workers in town who were considering applying for jobs at the shipyard. Safety in the shipyards was a never-ending topic of conversation, and a regular subject in *Fore 'n' Aft,* the printed newsletter that circulated regularly in the Richmond shipyards with articles written and edited by the workers. A few weeks after the near tragedy with the *Pickering*, a *Fore 'n' Aft* issue appeared full of safety tips and advice. One article was headlined FREE JOB INSURANCE . . . SAFETY!

But it was easier to write it than to practice it. The moment a Liberty ship's last bolt was welded, there is a certain urgency and excitement to launch it, so that its shipway could be freed up for the next keel to be laid. The rush to lay keels led to the rare tragedy—but more often to occasional dangerous lapses and mishaps.

Only a few weeks after the *Fore 'n' Aft* warning, a strong breeze caused fifty-six-year-old Ray Lane, working as a rivet heater in Richmond, to lose his balance while standing on a platform on top of a roof. He died later that day.[18] Just as Boulder Dam required a near-constant flow of concrete, building Liberty ships demanded a never-ending supply of steel. The largest steel plates were ten feet high and twenty feet long. They were usually stacked flat, while smaller plates stood on their ends, leaning in a precarious manner. When a plate toppled, an occasional but rare occurrence, it could squash a leg or crush a worker to death, as happened to Charles Ersner just fifteen minutes before the end of his shift.

"A man's job is his best insurance," the article in *Fore 'n' Aft* read later. "It feeds and clothes his family, pays rent, and supplies him with the necessities of life. The least a man can do in return is to respect his job and the safety of his fellow workman. . . . Each of you should remember you do not know what the workman next to you or above you is doing. So we must keep an eye on him. It is often the case where the injured man was possibly the safest workman on that job, but the man next to him was careless."

In order for the construction of Liberty ships to continue accelerating, this mishmash collection of Ivy League graduates and PhD students, Wall Street bankers and small business owners, jockeys and clergymen, chicken farmers and barbers, busboys, wrestlers, waitresses and chefs, lawyers, electricians, artists, and actors had to learn to operate their tools safely. There were as many ballet dancers among the new shipbuilders as there were anthropologists, making it one of the oddest collections of workers ever assembled. Some of the new workers arrived with enough life experiences that they were comfortable wielding a welding torch or a riveting gun, tightening a bolt, or wiring a light fixture. But far too many arrived having never swung a hammer in their life.

In June 1940, shipyards across the country employed 168,000 people. In two years, that number would be 1.5 million. Finding bodies wasn't the problem. Finding experienced bodies was.

"If a fellow knows one end of a monkey wrench from another, he goes in as a helper at ninety-five cents an hour," one hiring manager said of his challenge. "If he doesn't know one end from the other, we'll label the ends for him. We want men and we want them now."[19]

CHAPTER TWENTY-EIGHT

Building the Builders

AS WINTER GAVE WAY TO SPRING, THE COUNTRY'S MOOD
was still on edge five months after Pearl Harbor. The president's map speech
helped put the war in perspective, but it also struck fear in Americans. Even
though the White House was doing its best propaganda effort to hide from
the public the reality of what was happening out at sea, news stories about
sinkings were leaking out every day. German U-boats were having success not
only sinking Allied vessels, but also vanishing into the dark ocean like ghosts.

From January into the summer, Germany would sink 585 ships in U.S.
waters—while losing just 6 submarines. George C. Marshall, the Army Chief of
Staff, wrote to his Navy counterpart, Admiral Ernest J. King, that unless more
cargo ships were put to sea carrying supplies to bring to the fighting troops, he
didn't know how much longer the war could drag out at that staggering rate of loss.

"Another month or two of this will so cripple our means of transport that we
will be unable to bring sufficient men and planes to bear against the enemy . . .
to exercise a determining influence on the war," Marshall wrote.[1]

The average time to build a Liberty ship dropped from 210 days in January
to 156 days by May, cutting off almost two full months. But Land's Maritime
Commission was still facing criticism, and some were even calling for his head.

"Damn it," he grumbled. "A man can't do any more than his best."[2]

The shipyards were feeling the pressure too. When a workman in Richmond dragged his broken bolting tool into the repair shed one spring morning, he asked if it could be fixed.

"Take about an hour and a half," the repair worker told him. "Leave it here and check out a new one from the supply room 'til I get it going again."

Instead, the worker leaned lazily against the building and signaled that he'd just wait until it was fixed. That didn't sit well with the repairman.

"Do you realize that while you are waiting for me to fix this thing, the Japs are turning out 243 machine guns to blow you and me and our families clear off the face of the earth?" he snapped at him. The worker paused, grabbed a new tool, and returned to his work.

THE BIGGEST CHALLENGE facing shipyards was not building the ships. It was hiring a large enough labor force, knowing that none of the workers available would have actual, firsthand shipbuilding experience. The workers who had joined Kaiser's company in building roads, bridges, and dams across the Pacific Northwest were known as "sandhogs." Their skills were useless in shipyards. They needed to be trained as "seadogs."

Back in Washington, William F. Patterson had the responsibility of overseeing the Apprentice Training Service of the War Manpower Commission. What he knew frightened him. Germany, as he learned during a visit, had more than 800,000 indentured apprentices, young men trained in various labor skills and able to contribute to any emergency building effort.[3] All German boys, no exceptions, were forced to complete their apprentice training, were forced into certain trade industries, and were forbidden to leave them for other jobs until their apprenticeship was done. That was life under a dictatorship, and Patterson was not envious of that. But now that his own country was at war, he was jealous of Germany's reserves of trained young men with hard labor skills, because in the United States in early 1942, he had barely 100,000 young men trained in apprentice programs.

When he spoke to a graduating class of twenty-one apprentices from Bath Iron Works in Maine, Patterson implored the veteran shipbuilders to help mentor young men into the industry. "Take the mystery out of shipbuilding," he told the crowd, before sending them off to celebrate with cake and ice cream. "Make them feel at home, pass on knowledge you may have to them and assist them in every way possible." He closed by calling the students up to the stage to receive their diploma and congratulating each one, telling them he had no doubt they would "discharge your duties with glory."[4]

AS LIBERTY SHIP production accelerated, the Maritime Commission helped set up 750 welding schools around the country, borrowing space from local colleges, trade schools, and public schools to handle the training of more than 50,000 new welders per month. Each Liberty ship had 250,000 individual pieces and parts, and pulling all of them together in a matter of months took a monumental effort. Welding was the most important skill, of course, but for those who had no interest in welding jobs, there was no shortage of opportunities.

Workers were needed to operate band saws and table saws; install insulation, refrigeration, and furniture; hang doors and seal windows; make the wire and manila rope for mooring lines and rig those lines on the ship; erect and dismantle scaffolding around the hulls and on the deck; and operate the cranes that lifted the boxes of supplies, the tanks, the jeeps, and everything else into the cargo holds. Then there was all the steel. Plate hangers were needed to move the steel plates into place to be positioned on a ship's hull.

In Richmond, veteran shipbuilder Otho Moore was put in charge of training and his job was to fill every available room at Richmond Union High School. More than one thousand pupils, men and women, stuffed into the classrooms, from sturdy teenagers to weak-kneed retirees. Moore set up 115 different classes, all led by experienced mechanics, where trainees worked with pipe benders, welding machines, drill presses, sheet metal, and acetylene burning. The students wore insulated helmets and heavy leather suits in most classes to avoid injuries. Space was at a premium for training. While many classes were held at the shipyards, and others in off-site buildings, for some workers their training occurred during their commute.

The hourlong ferry ride some workers took from San Francisco to Richmond each day became known as the "Ferryboat College." As they boarded their ferry, workers were greeted by a sign listing that day's subjects: "Attention! Classes Today! Upper Deck."[5]

Once on board, they would settle into a space laid out like a classroom, and the classes unfolded more like team-building exercises than lectures. Shipyard foremen opened up discussions on pipefitting, welding, shipfitting, blueprint reading, marine electricity, and even first aid. He would present a problem and then help the trainees work together on the solution. One day they would tackle the ratios of diameters and perimeters, and another day the magnetic forces of attraction and repulsion. If a subject wasn't offered and a trainee requested it, it was added as soon as an instructor was identified. The ferryboat classrooms were more than lectures. The instructors used images and government-produced motion pictures displayed on a screen, blackboards to write their lessons, and they handed out mimeographed lesson sheets.[6]

SPEED WAS THE great motivator for shipyard managers. The Maritime Commission was paying a $400 bonus for each day's increase in a shipyard's production speed, and each ship launched was rewarded with $120,000.

In a spring 1942 survey of the work being produced at shipyards across the country, the Maritime Commission anointed Kaiser, a man who only a few months earlier didn't know a keel from a bow, as the shipbuilding king. The commission's survey rated Richmond Yard No. 2 as the fastest producer of Liberty ships anywhere, claiming it churned out 13 percent more work than its contracts demanded, and that it was producing a new ship almost once every week. On top of that, the commission listed Kaiser's Portland yard, the one run by his son Edgar, as the second fastest, and his CalShip in Los Angeles as the fourth fastest.

Even though his office was in Oakland, just ten miles south of Richmond's four shipyards, Kaiser didn't spend much time at any of his shipyards. He preferred instead to stay in daily contact by phone. Between Richmond and Portland, there were 58 individual shipways, allowing for an enormous volume of ships to be produced. Kaiser, who was satisfied with four hours of sleep a night, would call Clay Bedford and his son Edgar at all hours to check up on their progress. Edgar acknowledged his father's role in a speech he made at a banquet.

"I never make a major decision without conferring with him, by phone, wherever he may be," Edgar said.[7]

A WORKER WHO took night classes after a day shift might need five or six months to finish training, while another might train in six weeks with more intensive classes. On average it took sixty to eighty hours to learn burning, where a worker used a torch to cut sheets of steel and prepare it for welding; and eighty to one hundred hours to learn welding. But workers rarely waited until their training was completed before they were assigned a shift. The new Marinship yard encouraged workers to take their training home, with paperwork like "Flow of Materials, Safety and Constructive Thinking, Blueprint Reading, Methods of Laying Out, Setting and Scribing Foundations, Fundamentals of Welding Theory, Heat Distortion, and a brief study of each craft." The more that workers understood how a ship was constructed, the more paths they opened for their growth in the shipyard.

Trainees started work at 95 cents an hour and climbed by 5 or 10 cents per step, up to $1.20 per hour once they reached journeyman. And everybody worked 48 hours over six days, drawing time and a half for the extra hours, and double time if they took on a seventh consecutive day. A weekly paycheck of $62.40 was typical for a journeyman, but those who worked the graveyard shift collected more, as much as $250 a month.

Every new trainee was supplied with the clothing, tools, and necessary equipment, but some griped about the $50 union initiation fee they had to pay. One worker who had fought for the French in World War I felt that the unions were destroying worker morale and the spirit of patriotism. He took his complaint all the way to Jerry Land, calling the union fee "an outrageous system of extortion."[8] Most, however, just accepted the fee as a necessary inroad to good-paying work.

Those who arrived with experience were immediately appointed as supervisors, and they in turn identified the best pacesetters among the raw recruits who walked in having never lifted a hammer. They were called trainees or learners, and their training was brisk to help them quickly become handymen or helpers and eventually mechanics. As it turned out, the biggest challenge shipyards faced was not training their inexperienced workers—it was training the supervisors how to manage and instruct those beneath them. They received help in how to teach a particular skill, and they also learned what it meant to show empathy and human relations.

The training at Bethlehem's shipyards in Baltimore became a model, and the Maritime Commission distributed its training booklet to shipyards around the country. Bethlehem's system was simple, which is why it was able to train 1,400 shipbuilders in its first six months: one hour of classroom time a day, followed by supervised production work.

Kaiser's shipyards took a warmer, less methodical approach to training, publishing its own manual in which it devoted only one page out of more than a hundred to the actual "ABC of shipbuilding." Instead Richmond spent more energy helping recruits acclimate to life in the shipyards, from first aid to personnel issues to payday. The various jobs were described in such a way as to emphasize the teamwork necessary to build a ship.

There was another incentive for workers who could look past the war and imagine their postwar careers. Colleges were offering opportunities to move into engineering fields through their wartime training. The University of

California offered one course, Shipbuilding and Ship Design Practice, which met for sixteen weeks. High school graduates who had taken at least trigonometry and had experience in engineering drafting, hand computations, or construction could take the class and learn from Richmond shipyard workers. Not only did the course pave a path toward a shipyard job, but it guaranteed work outside the shipyards once the war ended.

THE MARITIME COMMISSION did not want to take over the training of shipbuilders. But it could not afford to have workers in Maryland or Maine learning to build Liberty ships one way, while workers in California and Alabama learned a different way. It spread the message of its expectations in a dryly worded pamphlet that emphasized training should be completed in a short time period—days or weeks, rather than months. After that, a worker could receive supplemental, on-the-job training before joining the workforce as a full-time employee.

The efficiency of Richmond's training program caught the attention of the commission, which wanted one leader to ensure that its "Basic Principles" messaging reached every corner of every shipyard. Jack Wolff, who had been director of personnel training at Richmond Yard No. 1, was appointed as training director. One of his first messages to shipyard managers was that they were going to lose more and more of their workers to the draft and they could not afford to let slow training interfere with fast shipbuilding.[9]

Wolff, who had spent two decades in management with Standard Oil and taught management courses at the University of California, spared no criticism of the shipyards. His experience taught him that managers who were trusted saw increased productivity from their workers, and managers who communicated poorly were rewarded with frustration and apathy.

———

ACROSS THE COUNTRY from Richmond, on a sprawling campus looking out on Chesapeake Bay, a fifty-year-old, square-jawed engineer named Gilbert Guy Via was leading the best-known apprentice shipbuilding school in America. At the Newport News Shipbuilding Company in Virginia, the apprentice school had been awarding graduation certificates for decades.[10]

Both Jerry Land and Howard Vickery were familiar with the school, as they had visited it on a summer day in 1938 to drive a pair of rivets and signal the beginning of construction on a new luxury passenger liner. Land, coatless but in a tie, took a lesson from a riveter in how to operate the compressed air gun. A front-page story in the *Newport News Daily Free Press* the next day celebrated the visit by Washington dignitaries but appeared directly above an ominous report: "Hitler Exhibits Nazi Naval Might" described a parade of 117 German naval vessels, from battleships to cruisers and ending with 37 heavily armed submarines. "It was as if Hitler were notifying the world Germany once again was a formidable Naval power," the story read.[11]

During their brief visit, Land and Vickery got a glimpse of the training methods Newport News shipbuilders went through and the rigorous standards the school demanded. Even Land's celebratory rivet was tested to make sure it was firm and tight. The day left an impression on the heads of the Maritime Commission. The yard's founders had created a new method of training shipbuilders. They called it "over the shoulder," and it simply meant that an experienced craftsman lurked over farm boys and other trainees until they learned the precise skills necessary to see a ship to completion. What began in 1886 as an informal training program was by 1890 a full-fledged, four-year apprenticeship program.

That was the year Guy Via was born, a few miles from the shipbuilding school. He went to school in town, studied electrical engineering at nearby Virginia Polytechnic Institute, briefly left to work at Westinghouse, and then returned home to teach at his high school. He joined the shipbuilding company's material department in 1914, when he was twenty-four, and quickly rose to be supervisor of training and director of education. Five years later he was one of the founding leaders of the Newport News Shipbuilding & Dry Dock Company Apprentice School.

Under Via's direction, apprentices at the school had to be sixteen years old, and they came to the school to work forty-hour weeks, all paid, including their time spent in classrooms. Students learned twenty different crafts necessary for shipbuilding, but in order to become expert at just one craft there were more than fifty skills an apprentice needed to study and master. They were taught to be versatile, to use a range of tools, and to understand basic ship construction so that their overall skills could just as easily be used to construct the deckhouse or the hull, to work on plumbing or electricity, to weld or to rivet.

By the late 1930s, the shipbuilding company had built a sterling reputation. The Maritime Commission in 1937 awarded it the contract to build the largest passenger ship ever built in the country, at 723 feet, the SS *America*. Described as "the queen of the American merchant marine," the *America* solidified Newport News Shipbuilding along with Guy Via's apprentice program as the company and the school with the necessary tools, training expertise, and facilities to most help Roosevelt's emergency Liberty ship program.

With the opening of a colonial-style, red-brick, three-story dormitory in December 1941, the Newport News campus rivaled nearby colleges for living quarters. Designed for 202 boys to live in 110 shared bedrooms, it was quickly overcrowded with 250 apprentices. Even the school's classrooms were considered state-of-the-art, with blackboards made of fused green plate glass that resisted wear and chips and retained an easy writing surface that did not fade or become glossy. Those were the details that separated Newport News Shipbuilding from its competitors, and when the war broke out, Guy Via used every opportunity, through speeches and papers, to tout his school and others like it. In one journal article titled "The Wartime Training of Shipbuilders," he emphasized the role they would play in winning the war.

"Ships, more ships and still more ships are demanded to transport huge quantity of war materials to distant war fronts, and ships, more ships and still more ships must be built to protect these precious cargoes and finally, to destroy the threat of our enemies at sea."[12]

CHAPTER TWENTY-NINE

Speed Kings

ON A WINDY, DUSTY DAY IN APRIL 1942, THE NOON WHISTLE
blew at the Richmond shipyards to signal lunch. Workers trudged out of their
machine shops, came down off the ship bows, climbed off their cranes, and
were opening up their lunchboxes when a voice boomed out from conveniently
placed loudspeakers. The voice of Henry Kaiser was not instantly recognizable
to them, even if they did know his roundish build, oversize eyeglasses, and
floppy hat. But when he started to speak, the forceful words left no doubt who
was delivering the message.

"Hello, Speed Kings!" he bellowed.

I know that's an unusual salutation, but that is just what you've proved to be.
You are the fastest shipbuilders in the United States today. You boys launched
the first ship faster than any other maritime yard. Your first ship was built faster
than any other yard's first ship. Your tonnage records are higher. The pride
of doing a good job has its own reward in the thrill of achievement. Together
we are shipbuilders. We—labor, management and government—stand on
trial as to what we can do. The fate of our own country is in our own hands,
where it belongs.[1]

In fact, the hands of each worker were valued at $250 apiece by government analysts. That's how much they estimated it cost, $500, to train one individual shipyard worker to perform their job. There were almost fifty different shipyard job classifications, and workers were trained in four or five different classifications apiece until they were so adept at the skills they could close their eyes and complete a task. For shipyards that were hiring 10,000 employees, it was expected to be an investment of $500,000 in 1942 alone.

The occasion for Kaiser's midweek, rah-rah speech came three days later. On April 13, almost precisely one year to the day when the Richmond shipyard first opened, Yard No. 2 launched the SS *Zachary Taylor* forty-four days after laying her keel. It was the fourth Liberty ship to come off a shipway at Yard No. 2, and by far the fastest. Over the course of a year, Kaiser's shipyards had managed to whittle the average time it took to produce a single ship from 241 days, or approximately eight months, down to 44 days, or a month and a half.

"'SPEED KINGS' BECAME more than a title to a gang of men on a new assembly," the writers of *Fore 'n' Aft* said in a spring edition.

With each new ship, the workers began discovering improvements they could make to go even faster on the next one. Irvi "Curly" Taylor, a Richmond steamfitter, noticed that too much time was being spent by pipefitters searching for the right-sized pipe for their job, so he designed a neatly organized pipe hanging shop to help pipefitters and steamfitters find their exact piece quicker. It saved more than three hundred man-hours per week. He was rewarded with a promotion to leaderman and helped train his son to join him as a steamfitter. W. B. "Bill" Stone, an equipment maintenance supervisor, saw that writing individual job assignments for thousands of workers each morning on sheets of paper was time-consuming because too much was wasted sorting through the pile. He devised equipment dispatcher boards big enough to list forty pieces of equipment and two hundred names. Jim Wall's invention was so smart it was nicknamed the Jim Wall Jack. He looked at the way kinks in metal floors and vertical keels were flattened out with sledgehammers and knew there had to be a better way. He told his manager he had an idea to simplify metal straightening, and got permission to design his invention, which took just two hours to create. It was so effective that twelve more were made to be used across all the Richmond shipyards. A pipe burner named John Lima noticed that the burning machines were stationary and that to move one also required moving a track, a time-consuming effort. He created adjustable track gauges that were easily attached to the machines.[2]

SIGNS STARTED CROPPING up all around the Richmond shipyards, carrying a new slogan that workers had taken to shouting: "Get the Job Done." Bill Blodgett, who ran the Richmond sign shop, had been busy painting signs with all sorts of messages for months. "Share Your Cars" was one. "Slap a Jap" was another, and "Work till the Whistle Blows" was a popular one. But the newest one carried extra significance; it was a phrase borrowed from a speech Clay Bedford had made at a recent ship launching, and his workers wanted it plastered all over the shipyard:

> The spirit which says, if you can't go under, go over; if you can't go through, go around; if you can't go right, go left; if you can't get angle, take two plates and make it; if you can't get a quarter-inch rod, take five-sixteenths inch; if you haven't got material, go get it; if you can't find it, make substitutions; if you can't substitute, improvise; if you can't improvise, make an innovation, but above all, GET THE JOB DONE.

From the day they were hired, America's shipbuilders had been encouraged to submit suggestions to their managers if they had an idea that might save on material costs, especially on steel, or man-hours, or general resources. All they had to do was write it up with as much detail as possible, include their name, and drop it into a shipyard suggestion box.

———

THE MARITIME COMMISSION made its suggestion program more official with some concrete incentives. If a suggestion was adopted, it would be shared with other shipyards to maximize its impact across the country. Shipyards were given $187.50 monthly in war bonds to disburse to workers for the best suggestions. Within days, suggestion boxes at shipyards around the country began to fill with dozens of slips of paper, and managers were passing along the best suggestions to the commission.[3]

As one more incentive for the workers, they could almost be guaranteed that their shipyard's newsletter could write up their idea and maybe even display a picture for all of the shipbuilders to see them. "If it works, you and America are ahead, and you have become one of the legion of men to whom work in the shipyards is more than just a job," *Fore 'n' Aft* wrote of the suggestion program.

The Maritime Commission created a catalog of ideas, many of them trivial but effective, like adding a plastic bushing to an automatic welding machine or designing a new plug on the main hand tool used by welders, or making it easier for cranes to lift multiple welding machines at once by arranging the machines in big racks first. One worker who grew frustrated with having to find a second worker just to help mark a chalk line on a steel plate devised a clamp to do the job instead. Rejected submissions were usually dismissed out of hand for being critical of a boss or too costly or time-consuming. But by the end of the war, it was estimated the suggestions saved $45 million and 31 million man-hours.[4]

The Speed Kings did not go unnoticed by America's enemies. As orders for new Liberty ships piled up, German intelligence, perhaps hearing of the Maritime Commission survey, reported in early 1942 that the United States was building ships three times faster than had been anticipated. That prompted a message to Admiral Dönitz, telling him that his submarine commanders needed to increase their sink rates in order to keep pace with the ships America was producing. The strategy that Roosevelt and Land had laid out, that America must outbuild Germany by launching cargo ships faster than the U-boats could sink them, was slowly beginning to pay off.

MORE THAN ANYTHING, what set the Newport News school apart was its apprenticeship program. Its official seal embodied the tradition of its training methods—"the head, heart, and hand." Guy Via believed that if a trainee had those three qualities, smarts, heart, and skill, they could achieve anything. The qualifications to become a skilled shipbuilder were simple in his view. "We have added to our rolls thousands of ex-farmers, ex–school teachers, ex–anybody with legs, two arms, and let us hope, willing hearts and functioning brains," he said in 1942. "These thousands must be taught to work more and more efficiently."[5]

He also recognized that many shipyard jobs required almost no skill at all. His apprentices would learn basic ship terminology to help them move about a ship easily without having to ask basic questions, but they did not have to become experts in naval vocabulary. And reading blueprints was not to be part of their training. Their job was to fit together the pieces that someone else—in this case, William Francis Gibbs—designed. They were not designing the puzzle. They were completing it.

"There are miles of cables to be hung," Via explained, "thousands of holes to be drilled, hundreds of lengths of pipe to be cut, threaded, and installed; numberless joints to be made up; hours of filing, chipping or reaming; millions of bolts to be put in place."

He believed that if the employees were trained to do these skills, it would free up the more expert mechanics to focus on their more highly technical work. Apprentices in the school's electrical department learned how to splice cable, solder, and drill and tap cable hangers. Beginning plumbers were taught to measure for pipe lengths, to cut, bend, and thread pipe, to make up joints and insert valves.

Like every shipyard in the country, Via's school had to submit, to the Maritime Commission and Jack Wolff, monthly reports that laid out their training methods, how many hours it involved per worker, how many trainees were going through their system, and locations of its training centers. Via grasped the urgency the country faced, as he shared in a speech he delivered about the role Newport News Shipbuilding was playing in the war.

"Time is indeed short," he said. "Years must be shortened to months, months to weeks, weeks to days, days to hours, hours to minutes. There is not a moment to be lost in building ships, nor a moment to be squandered in training the men whose labor now means so much to our survival as a free nation."[6]

Everything in Guy Via's speech was true—except for the part where he said the nation's survival would depend on "training the men." On that point, he could not have been more wrong.

CHAPTER THIRTY

Wendy the Welder

THE WESTBOUND TRAIN CHUGGED ACROSS THE FLATLANDS
of Mississippi and through the southern tip of the Texas panhandle. It was the
spring of 1942, the world was at war, and help was on the way. Unfortunately
the help in this case was stuck inside a sweltering, slow-moving train where
every seat was filled and people were forced to stand shoulder to shoulder in the
aisles. Cillie Preston—nobody called her Lucille—was among those standing,
and she desperately needed to sit.

Preston was twenty-seven years old and eight months pregnant. She already
had five children—four of them leaned on her legs or clung to her dress, as
the fifth squirmed in her arms. These were Willie, Marie, Ophelia, John, and
Jim. Preston was sure she would never manage to get off the train at the right
station and find her way to the next train to take her northbound. But then
she felt a hand, and when she heard the polite voice, in that moment she knew
everything would work out just fine.

"Where are you trying to go, ma'am?"

She looked up at the conductor. Then she looked down at the little people
at her feet, and she paused for a moment to collect herself. Jim, the one she was

holding, had just started walking, but he was too little to stand on a crowded train.

"I'm trying to get to Richmond, California," she told him.[1]

A FEW MONTHS earlier, Preston's husband, Willie, had come home one evening with some news about wartime jobs and government housing they were building in Richmond.

"They're going to open up the Kaiser shipyard and I would like to go," he told her. "When I'm able to get a house for you, I'll send for you."

"Why, sure," she said.

Willie drove to Richmond, found a place to live with a preacher and his wife, and put in a request for housing. When he started his job as a union metal-worker, he saw that women were working in Kaiser's shipyard right alongside the men. As soon as he got an apartment and bought all the furniture so that everyone could sleep, he called Cillie and told her to pack up the family and head west. She didn't waste a day.

In 1941 when the United States entered the war, one-quarter of American women were already earning wages outside their homes. And it was closer to 40 percent for Black women. But wartime defense work opened new opportunities, and between 1940 and 1945, the number of employed women grew from 12 million to 19 million.

By the summer of 1942, women were holding 200 different jobs in Navy and commercial shipyards, from painting to minding the tool sheds to helping shipfitters to bookkeeping to operating acetylene burners. Some said, with not a hint of cynicism, that the reason women so easily transitioned from minding their household to building a Liberty ship was that their tasks were actually not much different. A woman who was used to operating a clothes wringer could find that operating a crane was no different, just a lot bigger. Women who loved to crochet discovered that winding large electrical wires around giant spools was the same motion. Using an eggbeater was equivalent to running a drill press. A propaganda film called *Glamour Girls of 1943* took the metaphor to embarrassing heights. "Instead of cutting the lines of a dress, this woman cuts the pattern of aircraft parts," the newsreel said. "Instead of baking a cake, this woman is cooking gears to reduce the tension in the gears after use. . . . They are taking to welding as if the rod were a needle and the metal a length of cloth to be sewn."[2]

Despite the propaganda painting a picture of middle-class housewives dropping their aprons on their kitchen floor and leaving their children with grandparents, the vast majority of the women who took up wartime defense work were mostly low-income migrants and working-class women like Cillie Preston who needed the money and had no choice but to bring their kids along with them in order to collect that paycheck.

What nobody had anticipated was that the single most important job that emerged in building Liberty ships—welding—also turned out to be a job that was best handled by the nimble fingers and slimmer frames of women. Women and men could be trained just as speedily in the techniques of welding. But when it came to crawling into narrow, claustrophobic spaces and pointing a welding rod into hard-to-reach corners, women had a distinct advantage over their male coworkers. In the tight confines of a Liberty ship under construction, they could reach tricky places that men could not.

As welding jobs emerged as the highest-paying jobs in shipyards, most managers did not care if hiring more women welders caused some consternation among the men. What they did care about was why so many women were signing up to be welders, only to leave the shipyards a few weeks later. With men being pulled into the war, the women were too important to lose, and the turnover rate was unsustainable.

When Redd Evans and John Jacob Loeb wrote a ditty in 1942 called "Rosie the Riveter," singing "She's making history, working for victory," it elevated the women working at aircraft factories around the country to a national phenomenon, celebrated as wartime heroes.

Norman Rockwell's portrait of a pretty, fair-skinned, red-cheeked Rosie, wearing goggles on her forehead, eating a sandwich and flexing her muscular arm while holding a rivet gun, was a cover of the *Saturday Evening Post*—and a symbol of the contributions women were making to the war. Magazines convinced women that wartime work could even be glamorous, while companies like Lockheed Aircraft held Victory Fashion Shows at lunchtime where women modeled two-piece work outfits.[3] They were told they could stomp out fascism and help crush the Nazis in their denim overalls while still being feminine and preparing a home-cooked meal at the end of the day. *Women's Home Companion* reported that women "are learning how to put planes and tanks together, how to read blueprints, how to weld and rivet and make the great machinery of war production hum under skillful hands and eyes." But in the same article, it glowed about women who are "also learning how to look smart in overalls and how to be glamorous after work. They are learning to fulfill both the useful and the beautiful ideal."[4]

Kaiser's company didn't go so far as to design uniforms for women employees and instead asked women to share their ideas with a fashion designer, who would take their suggestions and create a line of work clothes suitable for their bodies and sold in local stores. A local magazine called *Charm* even ran sketches of the work clothes for women to see.[5]

But while Rosie the Riveter was being hailed, a cousin of Rosie was struggling to gain the same appreciation. Wendy the Welder, representing the women working in the shipyards in posters that more typically showed Black women, never quite caught fire in the national consciousness—even if Wendy's contributions were no less heroic.[6]

What had started in the winter of 1942 as a trickle of new workers arriving to work in shipyards across the country had become a roaring river by the summer. The newer West Coast shipyards, heavily concentrated in the Pacific Northwest, showed more interest in hiring women than the older, traditional East Coast yards. More than half the new shipyard workers on the West Coast were women, while on the East Coast not even one-quarter were.

For Jerry Land, his responsibilities went to a whole new level. No longer in charge of a workforce of 100,000, he was preparing himself for 700,000 workers. And instead of building 200 ships, his new target was a staggering 2,900 as fast as possible. A nationwide shipbuilding program that used to have 46 shipways to construct new vessels was on its way to having 300. Most important of all, the days were long past when one new ship a month or even a ship a week was considered impressive. Anything less than one new ship finished and launched per day was unacceptable for Land. He needed two ships a day right now, and ultimately if he was going to achieve Roosevelt's goal of almost 3,000 ships, he would soon need five ships launching every day.

Although the numbers of Liberty ships produced in the first six months of 1942 had climbed steadily, from 3 in January to 16 in March to 43 in May and 51 in June, that total of 151 ships in six months was not nearly enough to satisfy Roosevelt and Land. The progress was extraordinary, but it worked out to an average of 26 ships per month, or not quite one per day.

"This is a superman's task," *Fortune* magazine wrote in the summer of 1942. And Jerry Land, it said, is sitting at one of "the hottest desks in Washington."

HENRY KAISER, THE father of two boys, took an almost paternalistic approach to hiring women. And it paid off for him. He demanded his yards provide not only the best pay for women, but also the best health care and even childcare centers for them on site at the shipyards. The more he urged for greater comfort for women, the more controversy Kaiser courted, especially when studies began to show that women suffered more strains, sprains, and eye injuries than men and requested more time off to heal. Not surprisingly, men began raising the question of whether women deserved equal pay if they were getting special facilities and rest periods.

Nowhere did the tension between men and women play out more than around workplace safety. Women, who were confident in their ability to watch over and protect their family all day, saw men as messy housekeepers who let piles of tools and nails and cords pile up until an accident occurred. But men saw things differently. Marvin Geister, a control engineer at the Marinship yard, said women were dangerous without proper training.

Left: Emory Scott Land, known as Jerry, led American's World War II shipbuilding program as the chairman of the United States Maritime Commission.
National Archives photo no. 19-N-16422

Right: Robert Cyril Thompson, the British shipbuilder whose design the Liberty ship was based upon.
"One Hundred Years of Shipbuilding: 1846–1946, Joseph L. Thompson & Sons Ltd."

Left: Howard Vickery, vice chairman of the Maritime Commission, was instrumental in finding the shipyards to build the Liberty fleet.
Naval History and Heritage Command

Left: A young Henry Kaiser growing up in upstate New York.

Henry J. Kaiser Papers, University of California, Berkeley

Right: Kaiser with his wife Bess in front of workers at the Richmond, California, shipyard.

Courtesy of Kaiser Permanente Heritage Resources

Below: Aerial view of Kaiser's Richmond shipyard under construction in July 1941.

Courtesy of Kaiser Permanente Heritage Resources

AIRVIEW OF RICHMOND YARD LOOKING SOUTH   JULY 31, 1941
RICHMOND SHIPBUILDING CORPORATION

Top: Worker shift change at Kaiser's Richmond shipyard.
Courtesy of Kaiser Permanente Heritage Resources

Middle: President Franklin D. Roosevelt at the opening of the Boulder Dam, built by Kaiser and his Six Companies operation in 1935.
Courtesy of the Franklin D. Roosevelt Presidential Library and Museum website

Left: President Roosevelt and Kaiser at a celebration for a Liberty ship launching.
Courtesy of Kaiser Permanente Heritage Resources

Above: President Roosevelt attends the launching of the SS *Joseph Teal* with Kaiser.
Courtesy of Kaiser Permanente Heritage Resources

Left: Clay Bedford, one of Kaiser's most trusted leaders, ran the Richmond shipyard operation.
Courtesy of the family of Clay Bedford

Right: One of the earliest steps in building a Liberty ship was laying the steel plates that formed the bottom shell, like this one at the Bethlehem-Fairfield Shipyard in Baltimore.
Prints and Photographs Division, Library of Congress

Above: Sidney Garfield, with Kaiser, helped revolutionize health care in America with the Permanente Hospital they opened for Richmond shipyard workers.
Courtesy of Kaiser Permanente Heritage Resources

Left: Garfield and Kaiser in 1953 studying plans for expanding their hospital network.
Courtesy of Kaiser Permanente Heritage Resources

Right: William Stark Newell was the president of Bath Iron Works in Bath, Maine, and led the East Coast Liberty ship operation.
Photograph by Franklin Grant, William Stark Newell Collection, MIT Museum

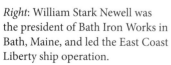

Right: Todd Shipyards in Maine produced reams of promotional materials like this, to boast of its Liberty ship production prowess. This is not an original but a later reproduction.
South Portland Shipyard Society Collection

Below: Aerial view of Richmond shipyard.
Courtesy of Kaiser Permanente Heritage Resources

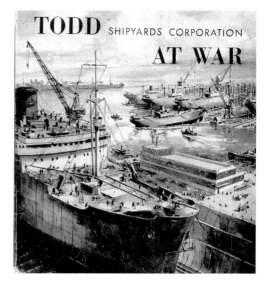

Right: Kaiser was largely beloved by his workers for the way he treated them and provided them with health care.
Courtesy of Kaiser Permanente Heritage Resources

Above: For his address to the nation in February 1942, President Roosevelt asked Americans to have a map of the world in front of them, so they could better understand his explanation of the complexities of the war.

NYWT&S Collection, Prints and Photographs Division, Library of Congress

Left: Kaiser, shown in 1935, atop scaffolding at the nearly completed Boulder Dam project.

Courtesy of Kaiser Permanente Heritage Resources

Right: The sprawling deck of a Liberty ship under construction at Terminal Island in Los Angeles.

Records of the Maritime Administration, National Archives

Right: The towering Whirley cranes were essential to hoisting heavy, prefabricated sections of Liberty ships into place.
Records of the Maritime Administration, National Archives

Left: William Francis Gibbs, the world's preeminent ship designer who took British plans and formatted them for American shipbuilders to build the fleet of Liberty ships.
SS United States Conservancy and BJ Nixon Photography

Right: The laying of a Liberty ship's keel, shown here on the second day of construction at the Bethlehem-Fairfield Shipyard in Baltimore, was the first step in construction.
Farm Security Administration/Office of War Information Black-and-White Negatives, Prints and Photographs Division, Library of Congress

Left: Immense scaffolding surrounded the bays where Liberty ships were constructed, allowing hundreds of workers to perform their tasks at the same time.

Records of Maritime Administration, National Archives

Right: Kaiser with his son, Edgar, who he picked to run his Portland, Oregon, shipyard.

Courtesy of Kaiser Permanente Heritage Resources

Below: August 10, 1941, President Roosevelt and Prime Minister Churchill aboard the HMS *Prince of Wales* during the Atlantic Conference in Placentia Bay, Newfoundland.

From the collection of the Imperial War Museum

Right: Trucks or jeeps were often double stacked on a Liberty ship deck to maximize capacity.

Records of the Maritime Administration, National Archives

BE A HEALTHY SHIPBUILDER

Left: Kaiser used marketing and propaganda posters to recruit workers to sign up for the shipyard's health plan.

Courtesy of Kaiser Permanente Heritage Resources

Below: The launching of the first Liberty ship, SS *Patrick Henry*, in Baltimore on September 27, 1941, as part of the Liberty Fleet Day celebration.

Courtesy of Kaiser Permanente Heritage Resources

Left: Nurses caring for shipbuilders at a hospital opened by Kaiser and Garfield.

Courtesy of Kaiser Permanente Heritage Resources

Left: The August 1941 launching of the SS *Ocean Vanguard* from Kaiser's Richmond shipyard, the first of sixty ships delivered for the British.

Courtesy of Kaiser Permanente Heritage Resources

Right: Recruiting women to join the ship-building workforce was a critical component to the success of the Liberty ship program. *"Soldiers Without Guns" poster, artist Adolph Treidler, Prints and Photographs Division, Library of Congress*

Left: Cora Clonts at Kaiser's Richmond yard was one of the nation's fastest welders, winning competitions and earning a spot on the cover of the shipyard newsletter, *Fore 'n' Aft*.

Author's collection

Right: Gladys Theus, a native of Pueblo, Colorado, and one of the fastest and most efficient welders at Kaiser's shipyards.

Franklin D. Roosevelt Presidential Library and Museum website

Below: Eastine Cowner welding at the Richmond shipyard in 1943 on the Liberty ship SS *George Washington Carver*.

Courtesy of Kaiser Permanente Heritage Resources

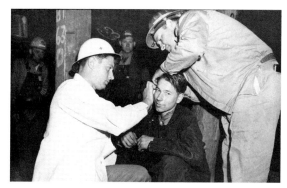

Left: Injuries on the job were common at the shipyards, which is why Kaiser prioritized urgent health care.

Courtesy of Kaiser Permanente Heritage Resources

Right: Workers gather to watch a launching ceremony. The Bethlehem-Fairfield Shipyard on Baltimore Harbor was established in February 1941 and quickly set 27,000 employees to work building these new "Liberty ships."

Photo by Arthur S. Siegel, Farm Security Administration/Office of War Information Black-and-White Negatives, Prints and Photographs Division, Library of Congress

Left: Nighttime Liberty ship work at Oregonship, the yard led by Kaiser's son Edgar.

Courtesy of Kaiser Permanente Heritage Resources

Left: The SS *John W. Brown*, one of only two Liberty ships still floating today, launches from Bethlehem-Fairfield Shipyard on September 7, 1942.
Howard Liberman for the U.S. Office of War Information, Farm Security Administration Collection, Prints and Photographs Division, Library of Congress

Right: Most Liberty ships splashed into the water vertically, but some shipyards had to slide them in horizontally, creating a dramatic moment when it looked like they might almost tip over.
Prints and Photographs Division, Library of Congress

Left: Charles E. Moore, here at right alongside U.S. Senator Harry S. Truman, manufactured the engine that propelled nearly three thousand Liberty ships.
Courtesy of the Moore Family

Left: Shipyard welder Mary Carroll preparing her cutting torch at the Portland, Oregon, shipyard.
Photo by Ray Atkeson, courtesy of Kaiser Permanente Heritage Resources

Below: The 140-ton triple expansion steam engine used to power the Liberty ships could propel a ship at about 11 knots.
United States Maritime Commission

Left: The massive propeller and rudder of a Liberty ship at the Bethlehem-Fairfield Shipyard in Baltimore just before a launching.
Prints and Photographs Division, Library of Congress

Below: James Horton, in the white shirt, aboard a Liberty ship.
Courtesy of John Horton

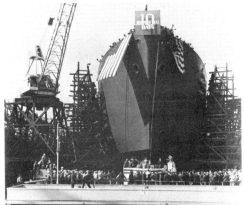

Left: President Roosevelt (left) and Kaiser in the foreground watching the christening of the SS *Joseph Teal* at Oregonship, built in ten days.
Courtesy of Kaiser Permanente Heritage Resources

Right: The Richmond shipyard newsletter, *Fore 'n' Aft*, covered the Liberty ship project for three years and produced a special edition for the record-breaking SS *Robert E. Peary*.
Author's collection

Below: The launching of the SS *Robert E. Peary*, the ship built in a record four days, fifteen hours, twenty-nine minutes, on November 12, 1942, at Kaiser's Richmond shipyard.
Courtesy of Kaiser Permanente Heritage Resources

"Most women may learn how to use a tool," he said, "but they never completely understand it. They are not mechanically inclined—and the accident figures are the proof." He described them as "ornamental," but not "built for safety." Ultimately it was left to shipyard managers to referee the tension, and almost always they concluded that if you wear the proper equipment and follow the safety rules, there should be no difference in job performance between the two sexes.[7]

The summer of 1942 in Richmond saw the greatest surge in the workforce of any time during the war. And women were the driver. In July, Kaiser's Richmond shipyards employed 3,500 women, and of those only 250 worked directly on ships as welders. In the next six months, more than 21,500 women were working in the Richmond yards—almost 5,000 as welders.

Some, like Cillie Preston, came with their children to join their husbands. Others came by themselves for the paycheck and the housing. The question for shipyards was no longer whether they should hire women, but how could they hire as many of them as possible. One report even suggested the traits in women that shipyards should seek out: "She should be broad minded enough to work shoulder to shoulder with men and forget she is a woman; and yet never become masculine in her way of talking or thinking or living. . . . The chosen woman should be a diplomat, an industrialist, a patriot, and should combine the wisdom of the ages with the patience of Job."

With five children and a sixth on the way, Preston certainly showed the patience of Job as she stood on her crowded train from Mississippi. When her train came to a stop in El Paso, she and her babies switched to a Southern Pacific Sunset Route train headed north. She stood again, for two straight days, passing along tiny sandwiches she was able to buy for her children on the train, while she ate nothing. The train moved slowly through southern Arizona, San Diego, Los Angeles, and Santa Barbara, making its way to San Francisco.

"I just don't know how," she reflected years later. "It was God. God helped me get on the train."[8]

It was her husband who helped her get off it. Willie Preston met his family with a huge smile and they all went together to the housing he had arranged, where Cillie immediately washed all her children's clothes. One month later, little Larry was born, and a month after that Willie took Cillie down to the labor office at the Richmond shipyards.

They asked if she could work the graveyard shift and learn to be a welder. She had no idea what a welder did or whether it was an important or menial role. But she jumped at the chance of a job, and in six weeks had completed her training. The way she saw it, she could be home with her kids during the day, cooking, washing their clothes, and ironing, and then while they slept, she could go to work, and still be back home by seven thirty in the morning. She'd find sleep whenever she could.

"I would go to sleep around two o'clock or later, I could sleep until ten o'clock at night, then I would get up and by the time I could get up and get dressed to go to the shipyard, Willie was home," Preston said of her early days.

Getting dressed for work was no easy task for welders. For every shift, Preston would step into her head-to-toe leather outfit, pulling it over her jeans and sweater. Then she would pull on her heavy welding hood, lace up her bulky construction boots, and carry two 50-foot, 35-pound welding lines, one draped over each shoulder, either up a ladder or down into a cargo hold space to get started.

Only a few weeks earlier, Preston had been home in Mississippi, raising her family alone. Now she was two thousand miles away, living by the Pacific Ocean, and walking into a shipyard to help America battle the Nazis by firing up a welding rod and fusing together pieces of giant cargo ships under the light of the moon.

For some, it all happened too fast. As the women welders became increasingly valuable in the summer of 1942, some of the men did not appreciate waiting for work in line behind them. In late August, Richard Halnan, a Richmond shipbuilder, fired off an angry, typo-riddled letter to President Roosevelt so that he could "call your attention to a very important subject." Halnan went on to question the idea of women welders. He insisted that "human nature" would make it near impossible for men to focus on their work alongside them. He said "a lot of fellows . . . take more time all day long gaseing [*sic*] at these good looking ones than doing there [*sic*] own work." He said the women were going to start family troubles if something wasn't done.[9]

NO DECISION ALTERED the course of America's shipbuilding success in World War II more than the one made back in the fall of 1940, when Cyril Thompson's British mission arrived asking Jerry Land for help with riveting together sixty British cargo ships. Land agreed—but with the critical compromise that the British ships would have to be welded, not riveted.

Riveting two pieces of steel together on a ship required a four-person team. One person operated a hot rivet gun, another handled chipping of the metal, a third needed strong muscles to drive a special hammer until the rivet completely filled the hole, and a fourth person caulked to ensure a watertight seal. In riveting, two pieces of steel had to overlap and be connected through rivets, wasting valuable inches of the precious metal. On one ship, more than a million individual rivet holes had to be made, a tedious, time-consuming endeavor. And if one person on the team needed a break or suffered an injury, the entire four-person unit had to shut down their work and wait.

Welding was far more efficient, not just in manpower use but also in the amount of steel required. The technique of welding—creating and controlling a short circuit—was not unlike controlling the flow and pressure of water through a hose or pipe. In welding, there was no waste of metal. Two pieces were laid side by side and joined. A welder used a metallic, slender, 18-inch rod, and an electric current passed through the end of an electrode, heating up the two parts that needed to be joined. The intensity of the heat first melted the end of the electrode and then melted just enough of the two parts that needed to be joined together. The result was that the metal fusion from the electrode, plus the metal of the two parts, came together to form an even stronger metal than they were as three individual pieces. For more delicate or lighter welding tasks, a different form of welding called oxyacetylene was used, but the majority of ship welding was called arc welding, and its greatest advantage was that it created a stronger bond than riveting.

WHAT MADE WELDING so important, and so challenging, in the construction of a ship was there were three different positions in which it had to be done, each one more exhausting and painful than the last, yet each vital to putting together a 250,000-piece puzzle.

The easiest position was down-hand welding, where the two metal pieces could be laid flat on a table or on the ground or a sawhorse, and the welder could comfortably sit or kneel over them and forcibly point the welding rod straight down. It was the best position to ensure that a welder could hold the straightest line, maintain close contact between the tip of the welding rod and the metal surface, and achieve the best welding results. The molten steel would drip down into the space to create a smooth, flat weld.

In vertical welding, all of those skills became harder. It required holding the rod out from the body like a gun and pointing the arc straight across, to fill a corner joint in the deckhouse from floor to ceiling, as one example. The position was tiring to the arms, and even though a ladder or stepstool could help alleviate some of the strain on the forearms, fatigue settled in quickly, shoulders grew sore, and holding a straight line became difficult. Additionally, because the molten metal was being applied horizontally, it did not settle as evenly as in the down-hand weld, and fusing a perfect joint was still possible, though much trickier.

The most challenging position was overhead welding, the equivalent of changing a ceiling lightbulb. It required pointing the welding rod up toward the ceiling of a cargo hold or maybe a bedroom ceiling in the deckhouse and somehow having the strength to keep a straight, continuous line with the electrode. No ladder or stepstool could relieve the intense pressure overhead welding put on the shoulders and arms. Fatigue forced welders to take constant breaks in order to maintain the necessary contact between the rod and the surface. On top of those physical challenges, the downward pull of gravity caused the molten metal to drip away from the surface the second it was applied. That often forced the welder to reapply two or three seams to ensure a solid hold.[10]

Cillie Preston loved welding. Many of the ships she worked on had been finished in the yard and were already floating in the bay, ready to be outfitted with their final touches. But in the early months of the Liberty ship program, not all of the women shared her enthusiasm for the work, and many of them in early 1942 began leaving only a few weeks after starting. Their biggest complaint was that their training deceived them into thinking the work would be far less strenuous than it was. As the news of the high turnover rate of women in shipyards reached Washington, officials decided they needed to find someone to explore what was driving so much turnover—and preferably do it undercover.

CHAPTER THIRTY-ONE

Gus

AUGUSTA CLAWSON HAD THE PERFECT BACKGROUND TO investigate a shipyard.[1] As a thirty-eight-year-old special agent of the United States Office of Education during the war, she was working with employment agencies and private industries to help train women for war-production jobs. Born in Plainfield, New Jersey, she had earned her master's degree in personnel administration from New York University and worked at a vocational and technical school for girls in New Jersey. She decided that the only way she would ever understand why women were leaving shipyard work so abruptly was to join a shipyard herself. If she could experience for herself what they were going through, she assumed she would learn enough to outline necessary changes in the training programs so that women would want to stay in shipyards longer.

But there was a catch. She couldn't just walk into a shipyard and start asking women questions. She had to do it in secret, to make sure that a shipyard did not alter her experience more favorably from what others were going through. With her short, dark hair and wire-rimmed glasses to correct her nearsightedness, she looked more like a school librarian as she headed west to find shipyard employment. By the time she reached the Pacific Northwest, she was no longer Washington bureaucrat Augusta Clawson. She was an undercover government agent, "Gus from Jersey."

On an afternoon in early April, Gus showed up at the welding school for Edgar Kaiser's shipyard in Portland, Oregon, ready to get to work. She walked up to a window that resembled a bank teller under a sign that said "INDUS-TRIAL WOMEN: Shipyard Women" and told the woman behind the partition, "I want to get a job as a welder; or I guess, I mean I want training as a welder. I couldn't very well go in green, could I, until I learn how?"

"Well, you could," the woman said back to her. "But if you're going to be a welder, you might just as well learn to do it right."

Together the two women filled out Clawson's WMC-10 Form, or War Manpower Certificate of Availability, and she brought the slip to another counselor. He told her the training would take about one week, and to go out and buy overalls, boots, and leathers.

She returned the next day and met with her instructor, who told her his name was Mr. Dunn. He looked at her shipyard card.

"So you're a teacher," he said.

"No, I've been one. That's different," she said.

He handed her a welding rod and her welding helmet and started telling her, step by step, what to do, starting with her position—sitting, legs spread, left elbow resting on her left knee. He placed a six-inch square piece of iron in front of her, sat down, pulled down his hood, and reached out with his arm.

"Pull down your helmet now and watch me," he said to his pupil. "Never look at an arc with your bare eyes. If you do, you'll get flash burn, and it's no fun. A burn from an arc is like a very serious sunburn."

She watched in amazement as a tiny pool of molten metal oozed out from his rod onto the piece of iron, and he moved his rod across while the molten pool followed it. His weld looked smooth when they both raised their hoods, but when she tried to copy his work it didn't go so well.

"My finished weld looked as bumpy as the Rocky Mountains," she wrote later in her diary.

She improved each day she returned, suffering a good burn on her final training shift that put a three-inch hole clear through her trousers. And she came to have an appreciation for the work, writing in her diary about developing a "love [of] the smell of hot metal, the frying hiss of the rod, the satisfaction of laying a smooth weld."

She felt ready to put her training to work.

ON A SUNDAY in mid-April, only ten days after her training had begun, Gus from Jersey rode a crowded bus to Oregon Shipyard, met her leadman or supervisor, and followed a shipfitter's helper to the location of her first welding job, hoping it would not require much climbing, considering her fear of heights. As they stepped onto the huge ship, Gus listened to a piece of advice from her helper.

"You'll earn your pay just by dodging being killed," her shipfitter said. "There are so many green workers it's a wonder something doesn't happen to you every day."

They climbed so many stairs it felt like they were reaching the clouds, and when they finally stopped, Gus realized she was on the top deck, in a tiny room, maybe four feet by ten feet, along with two other workers. While one welder splattered sparks from the ceiling, she got down on the ground to weld braces along a baseboard below a door opening. A heavy steel door was going to hang there, so the brace had to be strong to support the door. She welded in every possible position—overhead, flat, horizontal, vertical—and even around curved hinges, a spot where only her slender hands could reach. As she inspected her own work, she saw some horrible welds that frightened her, and others that left her proud. But when the heavy door, four feet by six feet, was brought into the room and hung up by her welds, Gus beamed with excitement and exhaustion. That was her handiwork.

Nothing could have prepared her on her first day for the excruciating noise on the ship while she worked, a cacophony of banging, whining, and hammering that left her ears vibrating. It felt as though the sounds were all around her, and even if she screamed she could not hear her own voice. She couldn't wait for her day to end. Finding her way out of the shipyard, Gus was disheartened to learn she had missed the last bus. She snagged a ride with a young engineer leaving, and by 7 p.m., she was back in her apartment and jotting her thoughts on her first day down in her diary. Her ears were still ringing and her head was buzzing.

"I am back from my first day on the Ways, and I feel as if I had seen some giant phenomenon. It's incredible! It's inhuman! It's horrible! And it's marvelous!"

As days turned to weeks, the entries in her diary filled page after page, first dozens and then hundreds. Her anecdotes were detailed and she was convinced they told a story that Americans wanted to hear. On her last day, she watched an ambulance pull into the yard and take away a worker who'd had an epileptic fit, then she turned in her locker key and shook hands with the man she knew only as Pop, who ran one of the lunchrooms.

"I hate to see anyone leave," he told her.

When she returned her leathers, lunch pail, and helmet to her counselor, she was asked what job she wanted to transfer into.

"Shipfitter," Gus said.

Told there weren't any openings, Gus looked relieved and explained she might have to take a break and return east anyway. Under a bright blue sky with pillowy white clouds, Clawson heard the day's shipyard whistle blow and knew it was time to go. As she walked out, she reflected on her experience building ships to help win a war and put her thoughts into the last pages of her diary. It didn't take Clawson long to see what was pushing women away from the shipyards. The training she had received was easy, comfortable, and relaxing. As she learned on her first day of work, and every day after, the actual act of welding a ship together was unglamorous, tedious, and painstaking. And it could be painful and dangerous. The positions she was forced to weld in aboard the ships were positions she had never learned during her training.

"No one told me that on my first weld at the plant," Clawson wrote in her diary, "I would climb down a ladder into the depths of the ship wearing 30 pounds of equipment, lie flat on my back, hang on a scaffold with one hand and do an overhead tack with the other while ear-splitting noises rang through my unprotected ears."

Her recommendations for change focused on making sure the training that welders received resembled the actual shipyard work as much as possible, reducing the element of surprise for welders who misunderstood just how rigorous the work would be. If they were not surprised about the work, they would be less likely to walk away so quickly without spending enough time forging relationships that might strengthen their bond to the shipbuilding effort.

"I've been one of a group," Clawson wrote of her experience. "We've worked together. We've been afraid together. We've sweated together in the deepest tanks, and in the meanest spots in a tough job."

WHEN HER WORK in Oregon was done, Clawson's entries were published as a pocket-sized book called *Shipyard Diary of a Woman Welder*, which appeared during the war in drugstores around the country. Wendy the Welder, like Rosie the Riveter, had earned her recognition, but with America waging wars in two oceans, Wendy's work was only getting started.

Though the war in the Pacific Ocean was beginning to turn in America's favor, after three U.S. carriers managed to sink four Japanese carriers in the Battle of Midway in early June, the war in the Atlantic was not. German U-boats sank 146 ships in May 1942, including 44 merchant ships in United States waters, by far the most in any month since the United States entered the war and more than double the total from January. In an unusually brazen act, *U-701* snuck into the mouth of the Chesapeake Bay on the warm evening of June 9, laid a string of fifteen mines in the water, and quietly left undetected. Five days later, an inbound convoy of Allied ships, twelve giant oil tankers, and five small naval escorts lined up in single file to enter the bay, within sight of thousands of people frolicking on a nearby beach. When the fifth ship entered the bay, almost close enough for swimmers to reach it, it exploded in a violent burst, its 152,000 barrels of crude oil shooting a towering plume of black smoke.[2]

"The bottom of the ocean appeared to tremble," one witness told the *Virginian-Pilot* newspaper.

Six months into the war, Germany was growing more confident by the day, willing to bring the battle right to America's shoreline in broad daylight. Dönitz, Germany's U-boat commander in chief, had long believed torpedoes were his most effective weapon against the enemy. But as the successful mine operation showed him, other tactics could work equally well. His only goal was to sink enough Allied ships so that Germany could effectively strangle the military buildup and economy in Great Britain and drive the United Kingdom from the war once and for all. Only then would Hitler turn his attention fully toward the United States.

Nobody in America could have imagined that, as terrifying as the Chesapeake Bay explosions were, the fighting was going to take an even darker turn. And Wendy the Welder was about to become the most important employee in the country.

PART VI

Fast, Faster, Fastest

CHAPTER THIRTY-TWO

Lessons from Motor City

A LITTLE LESS THAN TWO YEARS AFTER HENRY KAISER FIRST recalled Clay Bedford from Corpus Christi, Texas, he reached out to his most loyal employee again for another favor. He needed Bedford to take a business trip to the Midwest—far away from any ocean.

Bedford was consumed day and night with running the Richmond shipyard operation, and his workers appreciated his commitment to them. On August 25, his thirty-ninth birthday, he showed up for work to find a group of his employees waiting to surprise him with a birthday celebration and a cake adorned with a single candle. When they handed him a gift, a beautiful deer rifle, he held it aloft, took aim at the sky, and said he looked forward to using it as soon as the war was over. Then he turned serious. He did not want any more time wasted on him. The man he'd been calling "H.J." or "Boss" for more than fifteen years was not known for his patience. "He wouldn't get angry if he found you in error; he would sure correct you," Bedford said of Kaiser. "But if he found you were lying to him, he would really raise hell!"[1]

But Bedford was no pushover.

"If I thought Mr. Henry Kaiser was wrong, I'd tell him!" Bedford said. "And if he thought I was wrong, he'd tell me."

Kaiser trusted Bedford. Kaiser understood his own strengths and weaknesses. He was not an inventor. He was not an entrepreneur. He was certainly not a welder. And he knew that unlike Bedford, he was no engineer either.

WHEN ROOSEVELT'S EMERGENCY shipbuilding program began in January 1941, aspirations were modest. Along with building the sixty ships for the British in Portland, Maine, and Richmond, California, the shipyards were charged with building a few hundred more to bulk up America's sagging merchant fleet. Pearl Harbor changed everything overnight. Merchant ships became the lifeline to troops stationed around the world, and there were not nearly enough of them to carry the unprecedented volume of tanks, jeeps, guns, bullets, and everything else that was coming out of America's factories since the Japanese attack.

In 1941, America made 3,964 tanks. In 1942, that number swelled to 24,754. In 1941, the United States manufactured 97,000 machine guns along with 617,000 small firearms. In 1942, firearms manufacturers produced 663,000 machine guns and 2.3 million small arms.[2] Roosevelt's demand for an arsenal unlike anything the nation had produced was being met, and his country was pumping out more war material than Germany, Italy, and Japan—the three Axis powers—combined. But the president's greatest fear, that his arsenal would be left sitting on America's shores if the cargo fleet wasn't there to carry it overseas, remained.

WITH EACH PASSING month after the Japanese attack, U.S. shipyards increased their production rate. In the fall of 1941, prior to the attack, the average building time for a ship was 250 days, or eight months. That dropped to 150 days, or five months, as 1942 got underway, and their next target became 105 days, or about three and a half months.[3] That was broken down into 60 days to construct the ship and 45 days for it to be outfitted with all of its furnishings and final touches, jobs that could be done in the water while new ships were built on land.

But shipbuilding crews were already working twenty-four hours a day, seven days a week. If the current pace of launching 50 or 60 new Liberty ships per month was not enough, there was only one way it could get any faster. It wasn't about shipbuilders. It was about shipbuilding. The way that these 441-foot long, 250,00-piece puzzles came together had to change.

Constructing an entire Liberty ship from scratch, piece by piece, clogged up a single shipyard basin for far too long. Hundreds of workers—pipefitters, electricians, burners, welders—would swarm around as the hull slowly came together, and then as the ship began to take shape, confusion reigned. Hundreds of workers would sit around and wait for their turn, as a different part of the ship was finished. Then they would jump in to work, literally shouldering other workers out of the way while they got to their task and rendered their coworkers useless. The inefficiency was staggering. And it was the reason why a single ship took so long to build, and why so few Liberty ships were produced in the program's earliest months.

Around the country, the average shipway was seeing 4 ships slide into the water per year. But the Maritime Commission believed 5 and even 6 ships per shipway, per year, was within reach. Kaiser did too. He just needed an edge, and he had an idea.

If automobiles could be built in hours and days, rather than weeks and months, why couldn't Liberty ships? That was the question Kaiser wanted Bedford to go answer for him. He told him to go visit the city that knew the most about the business of mass production.

In sending Bedford to Detroit, Kaiser was not being naive. He understood that comparing the popular Ford coupe to a Liberty ship was like comparing a skiff to an ocean liner. A Coupe stretched 15 feet long, weighed about 3,000 pounds, and contained roughly 5,000 parts. A Liberty ship was 441 feet long, weighed 8,000 tons, and had 250,000 pieces and parts. But Kaiser was not interested in size. He was interested in scale. He told Bedford to study and learn how the Ford Motor Company achieved and maintained a blistering and relentless pace of automobile production.

BY 1942, COMPARING Henry Ford and Henry Kaiser had become a media parlor game. Writers looked for similarities between the two men, and they did find some common ground. In World War I, Ford tried to mass-produce warships called "Eagle Boats" to chase submarines, but the idea faltered in the building process. Kaiser had his own dream that seemed to be going nowhere, to produce massive cargo planes. Otherwise the two men were more different than alike. Ford was twenty years older, a trim and fit man who was born in Michigan and built his empire there. His business fortune was built on his own idea and creative spark. Kaiser was round and bald, born in New York before he settled on the West Coast—the vast middle of the country was foreign land to him. His business was built on the back of public projects and government contracts, not his own ingenuity. He created teams of people and hired managers to oversee them, and then those units built giant things. Kaiser was no Ford. But Ford was no Kaiser either.

"There is a difference between Henry Ford and Henry Kaiser," Clifford Prevost wrote in the *Detroit Free Press* in August 1942. "The former has never sought government business because he has such a financial reserve to permit him to do anything he wants to do. . . . Ford had to sell his product to a skeptical public. Kaiser has to sell his ideas to skeptical career men in the Army and the Navy."

Fortunately for Kaiser, he would not have to sell his idea for mass production very hard. Vickery had wanted the shipyards to do it from the day they broke ground in Richmond back in January 1941. A British engineer named John Tutin had even submitted sketches to the Maritime Commission outlining how an "assembly line shipyard" could work.[4] The idea fizzled because it called for too much material and too many men to all be concentrated in a single shipyard. But that was before Pearl Harbor. No obstacle was too big to overcome now.

"We are not only building ships, as Admiral Vickery says, we are assembling ships," Jerry Land said. "We are more nearly approximating the automobile industry than anything else."[5]

LIKE HENRY KAISER, Henry Ford did not build his empire overnight. It started three decades earlier, in the winter of 1906, back when a young Kaiser was still in the photography business and wooing Bess Fosburgh. Ford, then in his early forties, had created a secret room at his plant on Piquette Avenue in downtown Detroit. It had a door big enough to drive a car through, and a strong lock to ensure privacy. Inside the room, Ford would sometimes sit in his lucky rocking chair and stare for hours at a blackboard, where the design for his Model T had come to life.

"I will build a motorcar for the great multitude," Ford said of his idea. "It will be so low in price that no man making a good salary will be unable to own one."[6]

The legend of Ford suggests he got the idea to produce a car for the masses from watching cow carcasses be dismembered at a slaughterhouse. But he was hardly the founder of the concept of mass production. Examples went back centuries, to Eli Whitney's cotton gin, Connecticut craftsman Eli Terry's clocks, famous blacksmith Paul Revere's bells, Isaac Singer's sewing machines, and Stickney Lamson's trolley baskets that moved high above store shelves through pneumatic tubes. Mass production was an idea more than an invention, an idea that Henry Ford realized could help him achieve his dream of seeing the country's roads lined with Model Ts as far as the eyes could see.

He articulated the idea in descriptive fashion: "The man who places a part does not fasten it. The man who puts in a bolt does not put on the nut; the man who puts on the nut does not tighten it. Every piece of work in the shop moves. It may move on hooks, on overhead chains. . . . It may travel on a moving platform or it may go by gravity."[7]

Ford believed two principles were essential to his company's success in mass-producing automobiles: First, a successful assembly line is one that brings the work to the men, rather than bringing the men to the work. Second, workers were at their best when they became experts at a single task or skill, which they repeated over and over, learning to do it faster and faster until it was something they could almost do blindfolded.

Ford did one other smart thing—he listened to his wife, Clara, a fierce advocate for women's rights. Not only did he welcome women into the Ford manufacturing plants, but he launched a training program for new women hires so they could learn assembly skills, engine testing, inspection, and machine operations.

Ford built almost 700,000 automobiles in 1941, an average of nearly 2,000 vehicles daily. That production would slow down to 160,000 in 1942 as Ford pivoted to manufacturing tanks, jeeps, and other military vehicles.[8] But the Model T, followed by the Model A, followed by the Coupe and others, remained towering symbols of America's machine age of the early twentieth century, a period that saw airplanes take off, elevators rise up, radios turn on, motion pictures entertain audiences, electric railways and subways crisscross the country and modernize cities, and telephones connect households and businesses. But none of those transformed life in America as swiftly as the mass production of safe and affordable automobiles through the use of assembly lines.

New Liberty ships were now rolling out of shipyards around the country in about two months on average, with occasional ships coming together in one month. Since the start of the year through August, 262 Liberty ships had been completed, with Kaiser's yards leading the charge. Bedford's Richmond yard was the model of efficiency. Right behind it was Edgar Kaiser's shipyard in Portland, along with Bethlehem-Fairfield in Baltimore.

After laying the keel in late July for the SS *John W. Brown*, shipbuilders in Baltimore saw their newest Liberty ship slide down into the Patapsco River just forty-two days later, on September 7, 1942, seven months ahead of schedule. Named after a labor leader from Maine who worked at Bath Iron Works and died in 1941 from a rifle accident at home, the ship went into the water along with five other Liberty ships around the country on the same day. But in a sign of how the war was changing American military tactics, the *John W. Brown*, which was to carry both troops and cargo, was no defenseless cargo ship—it was armed with a .50-caliber gun in the bow, a .38-caliber gun and two .50-caliber guns in the stern, four more 20 mm firearms on the bridge, and a pair of 20 mm guns resting on elevated platforms on the starboard and port.

An audience of 20,000 shipyard workers stood and cheered when she slid into the water, but the tone of the day's speeches was somber. J. M. Willis, the general manager of Bethlehem-Fairfield Yard, said there had never been a Labor Day more significant. "This is labor's gravest hour," he said. "This is management's gravest hour. This is the gravest hour for all Americans who are the beneficiaries and heirs of our democratic way of life."[9]

Shipyards were building an average of 33 Liberty ships a month through August 1942, while Ford was churning out an average of 13,000 automobiles per month. Clay Bedford did not need to build 13,000 Liberty ships a month. He just needed to figure out a way to build Liberty ships faster.

During his visit to Ford's factories, Bedford was astonished at how efficient the process was. Each car came together in rapid succession, with the bigger components prefabricated away from the assembly line, like the chassis, the body, and the engine. As one vehicle began to take shape, it slid down an assembly line to waiting workers to handle smaller tasks, like attaching doors and tires and interior components, so that the next one could follow, and another one after that. It was mesmerizing to watch.[10]

Bedford could see that an assembly line for Liberty ships was probably not feasible, since the parts, and the finished product, were simply too big to slide down a conveyor belt. But the idea of constructing the largest components of a ship in separate locations and then somehow bringing them all together at the shipways was too appealing to ignore. Even more amazing to Bedford than the mass production and assembly lines were the training methods. One Ford worker told him that his training took just two days, and that he was watched for another day or two after that to make sure he understood his problem. After that, he was on his own. Bedford thought about how the shipyard workers endured weeks and months of training before they were entrusted to their roles without oversight.

"I thought, these fellows really have something," Bedford said later. "If it were only possible to train the new people that we have in two days, wouldn't that be grand."[11]

Bedford returned to Richmond determined to empower shipyard workers.

He was impressed at how Ford's workers seemed as if they were not merely carrying out instructions like soldiers following orders, but they were genuinely invested in their jobs to a degree that surprised him. He wanted more of that in Richmond.

"The key, in short, to the shipyard work was cutting the work down into small pieces and putting those pieces together in sections," Bedford said. "Because if you built it all on the ways, that would be like building an automobile in one spot. Nobody could work while somebody else was working."

Bedford left Detroit convinced he had seen the future of building Liberty ships. Instead of trying to accomplish a huge number of tasks at once, in the same location, he needed to create a system where tasks were done in sequence, yet in different locations. That way no group of workers was waiting for their turn. All of the groups were working at the same time.

"You could build a ship in a day if you had enough people scattered out, for five miles, working on that ship's parts!" he said. "When the day came you put the assemblies together and voila! You could launch a ship. That meant with twelve ways you could put off a ship every day, you could build a ship every twelve days."[12]

WHEN HENRY FORD set out to perfect the idea of prefabrication, he constructed a towering, four-story factory at the sight of an old horse-racing track in the Detroit neighborhood of Highland Park. It opened on January 1, 1910, a sprawling space with rows of windows that glistened so brightly in the sunlight that it was dubbed by the media as the "Crystal Palace."

Once it opened, one writer who wandered through it described it as "a jungle of wheels and belts and weird iron forms—of men, machinery, and movement," and filled with too many noises to even imagine. "The sound of a million squirrels chirping, a million monkeys quarreling, a million lions roaring, a million pigs dying, a million elephants smashing through a forest of sheet iron," he wrote.[13]

To say that the moving assembly line inside Highland Park succeeded does not give it justice. After manufacturing 10,000 Model Ts in 1909, Ford built 19,000 in 1910, more than 34,000 in 1911, and more than 78,000 in its third year.[14] So stunning was the growth from mass production that it inspired a new term—Fordism.

Bedford knew if he could somehow re-create Ford's magic, perhaps even build his own Crystal Palace where the parts of the ship came to the worker, and where the workers learned their skills in only a few short days, there was no telling how fast America's shipyards could one day pump out new cargo ships.

"I went away from there quite amazed," Bedford said.[15]

He began to imagine a future when the amount of time it took to build Liberty ships was no longer measured in weeks or months, but in days, hours, even minutes.

CHAPTER THIRTY-THREE

Darkness, Disgrace, Defeat

AT THE STROKE OF MIDNIGHT ON SUNDAY, MAY 18, 1942, A startling message appeared on the famous news zipper that wrapped around the Times Tower in New York City: THE NEW YORK TIMES BIDS YOU GOODNIGHT.[1]

And with that, all 14,800 bulbs turned off and the zipper went black for the first time since it captured the attention of passersby with streaming headlines on November 6, 1928. It had lit up with news of the election of Roosevelt and the rise of Hitler. Turning it off was not some cost-cutting business decision by the newspaper. It was a desperate, strategic act from Washington. German U-boats were lurking in the waters off America's East Coast and Japanese subs were off the West Coast and in the Gulf of Mexico, and they were using big-city lights as backdrops to see the silhouettes of departing or arriving cargo and military ships.

That knowledge, along with Hitler's unpredictability, put America's military leaders on edge. Hitler visualized skyscrapers as "gigantic towers of flame" and "blazing bundles of firewood," it was reported, and he grew determined to turn Manhattan into a "bursting city." The message to American citizens was simple: the enemy can't shoot what it can't see.

Neon lights, theater marquees, and skyscrapers all across the country were going dark, especially in coastal cities like New York and New Orleans, Seattle and San Francisco, Los Angeles and Anchorage. People covered over the top half of their car lights and they were discouraged from driving at night. The Empire State Building turned off its beacon light, and the skylights atop Grand Central Terminal were blacked out. Trains pulling into Pennsylvania Station were instructed to pull down their shades and keep their windows hidden. The Statue of Liberty's torch was extinguished.

Millions of Americans who were not eligible for military duty volunteered to defend their homeland from invasion, training in first aid, learning how to spot aircraft, leading air raid drills, and monitoring blackouts. In Charleston, South Carolina, teenagers wearing civil defense armbands with a lightning bolt served as bike messengers at nighttime during air raids. Seattle was one of the first cities to experiment with a blackout. When a fighter pilot there named Samuel Hynes left his apartment one evening, he walked out into an overcast night, no moon or stars visible. Without any warning, sirens began to wail and the streetlights in his neighborhood went out. "The night was entirely dark and featureless, cloud and earth one black emptiness," he recounted.[2]

When the Army Air Corps staged an air raid test in Anchorage one afternoon with no warning, it did not go well. As sirens wailed and airplanes roared just over the city streets, imitating a dive-bomb attack, residents, teachers, and their students, instead of seeking shelter, casually walked outside to investigate all the commotion and noise. They lined the streets and even scrambled onto rooftops to get a closer look at the planes.

"Almost every man, woman, and child in the city would have been shot down had it been a real raid," the Anchorage newspaper reported.[3]

ON JUNE 13, 1942, on a beach near Amagansett, New York, in eastern Long Island, four men wearing German uniforms stepped from an inflatable rubber boat onto the shore and slipped away in the night. U-boats had already attacked Allied ships just a few miles off the U.S. coast, even visible from beaches, but Hitler wanted to get even closer. He demanded to see Nazis standing on American soil. Their hatched plan was called Operation Pastorius, named for the German-born educator Francis Pastorius, who founded Germantown, Pennsylvania, regarded as the first German American settlement. The Germans carried enough explosive devices to spend the next two years sabotaging and destroying tank factories, aircraft, and especially shipyards. The shipyards were seen as the lifeline for the mighty American military, as they were producing the vessels that carried the supplies, weapons, and equipment to U.S. troops on the front lines in Europe. And because shipyards were not military bases, they were vulnerable. The four men buried their explosives and changed into civilian clothes.[4]

Four days later, another group, similarly armed, came ashore at Ponte Vedra Beach in northern Florida. They also buried their explosives, changed, and took a bus to Jacksonville. Eight Nazis, disguised, carrying a total of $154,000 in American money, and intent on destroying America's defense operation, were now on American soil hungry to bring the war to President Roosevelt's doorstep.

The New York interlopers were not exactly discreet. They visited Times Square, ate in a deli, shopped at Macy's, and played in a late-night game of pinochle. One of them could not resist buying a sharkskin suit. Their invasion was planned with meticulous detail, and then blown by their clumsiness. When two of the Germans knew they were being tracked, they called the FBI and surrendered. The FBI used information from the two in custody to round up the other six, including the ones in Florida, and within two weeks all eight Germans were arrested.

The White House wondered if the arrests of eight Nazis who had walked out of the Atlantic Ocean and onto New York and Florida beaches, and then made their way to Chicago, Cincinnati, and New York City, might be the turning point for Americans. Headlines screamed "Nazi Saboteurs" and newspapers weaved dramatic stories of the secret plot to destroy the nation.[5] Roosevelt, embarrassed that Nazis had visited his shores, wanted to make sure their trials and convictions were public so that there was no more lingering doubt about the threat Hitler posed. All eight Germans were quickly tried in a military court in Washington, found guilty of espionage, and sentenced to death. Roosevelt commuted two of their sentences. But executions for the remaining six were scheduled at the District of Columbia Jail.

ONE RESULT OF America being pulled into the war was that it solidified the friendship between Roosevelt and Churchill. Churchill's visits to Washington had become a regular occurrence, as the leaders discussed strategy and policy in their front against Hitler.

"There was something so intimate in their friendship," Lord Ismay, Churchill's aide, said. "They used to stroll in and out of each other's rooms in the White House, as two subalterns occupying adjacent quarters might have done."[6]

On June 22, the two world leaders were enjoying each other's company at the White House. After breakfast and their morning briefings, Churchill met up with Roosevelt in the president's study. No sooner had they sat down than a secretary walked in and gave the president a telegram, relaying the news that 25,000 British soldiers protecting the small town and military base of Tobruk in Libya had been taken prisoner after surrendering to a German platoon that was maybe half that size. A somber Roosevelt silently handed the paper to Churchill, knowing it was devastating news. Fighting at Tobruk had gone on for eight months, with British soldiers helping hold Germany at bay. Now Tobruk belonged to Hitler.

"It was a bitter moment," Churchill recalled. "Defeat is one thing. Disgrace is another." He later called the fall of Tobruk "one of the heaviest blows" of the war because he believed the surrender embarrassed the British army, not to mention his own leadership. After letting Churchill absorb the news, Roosevelt turned to him.

"What can we do to help?"[7]

"Give us as many Sherman tanks as you can spare and ship them to the Middle East as quickly as possible," Churchill replied.

Later in the evening, a Churchill aide found the prime minister pacing in his bedroom, clearly anguished. "I am ashamed," he said. "I cannot understand why Tobruk gave in. More than 30,000 of our men put their hands up. If they won't fight . . ." He cut himself off and collapsed into a chair, humiliated and disgusted.

Roosevelt wasted no time securing Churchill's request. Within days, three hundred just-manufactured Sherman tanks, despite having no engines installed, were on a cargo ship headed for the Suez Canal, along with one hundred self-propelled howitzers. A separate ship containing the engines was also put to sea. And when the ship carrying the engines was sunk by a German torpedo, Roosevelt ordered a replacement vessel to bring a second batch of engines.

"A friend in need is a friend indeed," Churchill wrote of the moment in his memoirs.

WITH THE WAR in its third year for Great Britain and just its sixth month for the United States, both Churchill and Roosevelt came to realize that their countries were not the ones suffering the most losses to Germany. Ever since Germany's invasion of the Soviet Union in June 1941, Russia had become—geographically, militarily, and politically—their most important ally in fighting Germany.

Roosevelt and Churchill understood that the longer the Soviet Union remained engaged in the war, the harder it would be for Germany to win. But they also knew that with Germany already occupying Russia's neighbors, Denmark and Norway, if Hitler were to gain the upper hand against Russia, his momentum could become unstoppable. Their only way to keep Russia strong was to keep loading up as many of their enormous Ocean and Liberty ships as possible with whatever Russia needed and sending the ships through treacherous arctic waters teeming with German U-boats to reach Russian port cities.

Through 1941 and early 1942, the Germans had mostly ignored the Russian convoys and allowed supplies to reach the country unimpeded. Each new ship brought tanks, jeeps, planes, weapons, and munitions to Russian troops. The

Allied convoys varied in size but were generally between 15 and 30 ships, a blend of tankers, troopships, and Liberty ships. Each convoy had specific designations based on their route, departure point, and their speed, either "fast" or "slow," depending on the capabilities of the ships. If a convoy was filled with Liberty ships, it almost always got the "slow" designation, but slow hardly meant ineffective. Convoys had 30 to 100 ships typically, crisscrossing the ocean in a dozen columns and accompanied by heavily armed destroyers, frigates, and smaller sloops to protect the merchant ships' valuable cargo and troops.

By February, Hitler had seen enough. He had a slew of new surface ships at his disposal—*Tirpitz, Lutzlow, Hipper,* and *Scheer.* And he was growing paranoid that the Allies were planning to invade Nazi-occupied Norway and reclaim it. Hitler declared that Russia needed to be cut off from American and British merchant vessels, and he instructed his U-boat and Luftwaffe commanders to put all of their strategic resources into that effort.

FOUR MONTHS LATER, on the morning of June 27, under the command of a British naval officer, one of the largest Allied convoys of the war left port in Hvalfjorour, Iceland, bound for the Soviet port of Arkhangelsk. So important was the convoy it was the first one to sail protected by both the Royal Navy and the U.S. Navy. Twenty-three of the thirty-seven ships were American, eight were British, two were Russian, two were Panamanian, and one was Dutch. Six of the American vessels were shiny new East Coast Liberty ships: the SS *William Hooper* and SS *Benjamin Harrison,* both built by North Carolina Shipbuilding, and the SS *John Witherspoon,* SS *Christopher Newport,* SS *Samuel Chase,* and SS *Daniel Morgan,* all built by Bethlehem-Fairfield Shipbuilding in Baltimore.

Along with the cargo ships, the convoy called PQ-17 consisted of more than 40 escort ships for protection. The cargo ships were loaded with supplies for Russian troops, including 594 tanks, 297 aircraft, and 4,246 motor vehicles. But just as important was the armor plate, the steel, the flour, the nickel, oil stills, canned goods, aluminum, and TNT. Surrounded by destroyers and smaller armed crafts, the convoy started out slowly at 6 knots, and on its second day, heavy fog and ice floes caused one merchant ship to run aground and an oiler to suffer enough damage that it had to return. The remaining ships stayed the course.[8]

On July 1, German U-boats spotted the convoy 250 nautical miles northeast of the Norwegian volcanic island Jan Mayen, but heavy fog prevented an attack. Forty-eight hours later, the fog was gone and a barrage of bullets rained down on the convoy from twenty-four, low-flying, twin-engine German attack planes. A British freighter went down and the Liberty ship *Hooper* was also sunk. But the convoy remained intact, for the moment, and sailed on.

The following day, as the convoy cruised at 8 knots through the Barents Sea, British officials intercepted intelligence suggesting that the powerful German surface ship *Tirpitz* had sailed the day before and was en route for the convoy to go on the attack. The intelligence was wrong, but Admiral Sir Dudley Pound flinched, panicked at the thought of losing the entire convoy in a single, devastating sea battle.

In the span of just twenty-five minutes beginning at 9:11 p.m., the Admiralty sent three messages to Rear Admiral Lewis Hamilton, the convoy's commander. The first read: "Cruiser Force withdraw to the westward at high speed." Twelve minutes later: "Owing to threat from surface ships, convoy is to disperse and proceed to Russian ports." The final message came at 9:36, carrying three ominous words: "Convoy is to scatter."[9]

Instructing a convoy of ships to "scatter" was the equivalent of watching children begin a game of hide-and-seek when all participants run off in different directions hoping to become invisible. The Admiralty hoped that by spreading the ships out, the odds of the majority of the convoy reaching Russian ports would improve and make Germany's work harder, since it could not take out the entire convoy in one swoop. It was a deadly miscalculation. It was also an act of sacrificing less critical and less costly merchant ships for the more valuable and expensive battleships and cruisers. Not only was Pound instructing the convoy's lightly armed merchant ships to separate from their heavily armed, battle-tested escorts, but in the vastness of the Barents Sea there was no hiding for 441-foot Liberty ships, the largest of the vessels in the convoy.

When Pound's order first reached the Allied ships, their captains could not believe it. Some of them even requested the message be repeated. It was no mistake. As the word spread, some crew members sensed their mortality and turned to their diaries to vent their frustration.

"The convoy was to split up, every man for himself," one British petty officer, John "Jack" Bowman, wrote while on board the HMS *La Malouine*. "We seemed to be in a very hopeless situation."

Similar words were written by an officer aboard the Liberty ship SS *John Witherspoon*: "It is unbelievable that we are being put on our own without protection—some ships with no guns at all."[10]

On board the American cruiser USS *Wichita*, an angry Lieutenant Douglas Fairbanks Jr., a member of the U.S. Naval Reserves serving as the flag lieutenant, wrote in his diary: "What kind of High Command have we that with such great force in operation we cannot fight it out?"

As the convoy began to break up, Hamilton messaged the captains of the entire convoy in an apologetic tone. "I know you will all be feeling as distressed as I am at having to leave that fine collection of ships to find their own way to harbor. The enemy under the cover of his shore-based aircraft has succeeded in concentrating a far superior force in this area. We were therefore ordered to withdraw. We are all sorry that the good work of the close escort could not be completed. I hope we shall all have a chance of settling this score with them soon."[11]

Once Hitler authorized attacks from the air and the sea, the results were swift. Given the green light from Berlin, some of Hitler's most decorated U-boat commanders recognized the scatter, and with help from Luftwaffe pilots flying overhead, they set out to pick off the unescorted merchant ships, knowing they were easy prey. Heinz Bielfield, commanding Germany's *U-703*, sank the 6,600-ton British freighter *Empire Byron* after the Luftwaffe had already damaged it, and the 5,500 ton-British freighter *River Afton*. Hilmar Siemon, commanding *U-334*, torpedoed the 7,200-ton British freighter *Earlston* and captured her captain. Max-Martin Teichert in *U-456* sank the 7,000-ton American freighter *Honomu* and took her captain. But it was the *U-88*, under Heino Bohmann, that took down perhaps the most valuable piece of the convoy.

On July 5, German planes attacked the Liberty ship *Daniel Morgan* from above while the German sub torpedoed it from below. Nine bombs splashed into the waters around the *Morgan* but she did not go down easily. The ship, with a crew of forty-eight Merchant Marines and twenty-eight Navy Armed Guards, was carrying steel, food, explosives, tanks, and cars. The crew battled for more than twenty-four hours straight before they finally had to abandon ship, and they managed to shoot down two German dive bombers. The *Morgan* finally took on too much water after one final torpedo blow. One seaman died from a concussion and three crew members drowned when their lifeboat capsized. The *Morgan*'s final panicked minutes were captured in a series of transmissions logged by the radio operator of the *Samuel Chase* on the afternoon of July 5.

Unknown ship: "Two subs attacking!"
SS *Washington*: "Being dive bombed."
Unknown ship: "Have just been torpedoed."
Unknown ship: "Attacked by seven planes."
SS *Daniel Morgan*: "Under heavy attack."[12]

Over the course of less than a week, Germany left the PQ-17 convoy in tatters. Twenty-two merchant ships, 14 of them American, were sunk, taking to the bottom of the Barents Sea 430 tanks, 210 aircraft, and 3,350 motor vehicles, along with nearly 100,000 tons of additional cargo. Only two Liberty ships, the *Samuel Chase* and *Benjamin Harrison*, managed to reach Russia. The ships that made it carried only one-third of the original cargo that had left Iceland. Germany's only losses were five aircraft.

The tangible losses were nothing compared to the psychological toll wrought by the slaughter of PQ-17. One hundred and fifty-three merchant seamen perished while drifting in the frigid arctic waters in their rafts and lifeboats. In America, Admiral Ernest J. King, the famously hot-tempered chief of naval operations, was furious when he learned that the German ship *Tirpitz* had not in fact been sailing toward the convoy when the scatter order was given. The convoy had essentially left itself vulnerable for no good reason. From that day forward, King carried a healthy skepticism toward any proposal for a joint operation with the British.

Churchill, already embarrassed by his country's surrender at Tobruk, faced even worse criticism. On July 17, 1942, he telegrammed Stalin the difficult news that future convoys to Russia were being postponed indefinitely. "Believe me there is nothing that is useful and sensible that we and the Americans will not do to help you in your grand struggle," he wrote.[13]

Stalin was livid. He replied to Churchill that he "never expected the British Government would stop the dispatch of war materials" at the precise moment when Russia "requires these materials more than ever." He even wondered, with no evidence, whether Churchill had ulterior motives and might be contemplating a peace deal with Hitler.

"This was one of the most melancholy naval episodes in the whole of the war," Churchill recalled later of PQ-17.[14]

NOT SO IN Berlin. A joyous Hitler was celebrating after seeing the final sinking-reports that showed almost an entire convoy of Allied ships had been erased. Throughout the war, Hitler refused to cower to the United States. In one speech referencing Liberty ships, he said, "an American intervention by mass deliveries of planes and war materials will not change the outcome of the war."[15] He could not believe Roosevelt would allow his own ships to be blown up so close to America's shore that the bodies of dead sailors would wash up on beaches to the horror of his citizens. One of his most loyal aides, Joseph Goebbels, his minister of propaganda, called Roosevelt a "mentally ill cripple."[16] When it came to war, Hitler said Roosevelt had sadly underestimated the power of Germany's submarines. "This Mr. Roosevelt has also not counted on our U-boats. . . . Our U-boat weapon is one of the most decisive weapons in this war."

Hitler's bluster was pure propaganda, of course, aimed at reassuring Germans they had nothing to fear from the Americans. The truth was that Henry Ford and Henry Kaiser, both masters of production, were making Hitler nervous.

Hitler revered Ford so much that in his autobiography, *Mein Kampf*, he called him a "single great man," and he told a reporter, "I regard Henry Ford as my inspiration."[17]

AS JULY CAME to an end, American shipyards produced a record 52 Liberty ships in that month alone, and one of those ships was the 200th Liberty ship to be launched. Each month in 1942 saw an increase in production output, and in production speed, yet it still wasn't enough. By June, German U-boats had successfully torpedoed and sunk 397 total Allied ships.

The only downside to the rapid production of so many new Liberty ships was that they gave Karl Dönitz's U-boats a whole new slew of easy, slow-moving targets to hunt down and destroy. In a briefing he made at Hitler's headquarters, Dönitz presented the intelligence he'd gathered and he called the Americans the largest enemy shipbuilder. He didn't just have the volume of ships being manufactured. He had drawings of ships, specifications of the Liberty model, and shipyard maps. The depth of his presentation showed how obsessed Germany had become with American shipbuilding. And for good reason. Those shipyards posed the greatest threat to Germany, just as Germany's U-boats posed the greatest threat to America.

Writing in *Newsweek* magazine in June 1942 under the headline "Why Shipbuilding Is Our No. 1 Bottleneck," the economist and author Ralph Robey listed what he saw as the five most likely reasons behind what had become a crisis for the president. "Shipbuilding," he wrote, "is still the most serious production problem in our war effort."[18]

Reason number one, he wrote: "Shortsighted planning by Washington authorities." Number two was the War Production Board's poor allocation of critical materials, especially steel plates. Ship sinkings by German U-boats was his third reason. Inefficient production from the shipyards, with their "business as usual" attitude, came fourth. And last, a shortage of steel plates due to the nation's steel shortage. Robey hailed the shipbuilding program as a "brilliant, almost unbelievable achievement." But in the end, he could only blame the construction bottleneck on one of his five reasons. "It is being wrecked, insofar as results are concerned, by the submarine menace. Stop the sinkings, and shipping will no longer be our No. 1 bottleneck."

It was time for the lessons in mass production that Clay Bedford had absorbed from Henry Ford in Detroit to start yielding results with Liberty ships.

CHAPTER THIRTY-FOUR

Perfecting Prefab

IN STUDYING A FINISHED LIBERTY SHIP, BEDFORD KNEW that if he was going to try to revolutionize shipbuilding the way Ford revolutionized automobile manufacturing, he needed to think big. As in, the big parts of a ship. In a Model T, the chassis stood out as a large and complex piece, with hundreds of small parts, that was assembled separately from the body of the vehicle and then attached as one giant component when it was finished. The automobile's body, essentially a shell with an open bottom, was laid on top of the built chassis to create an almost finished product.

That worked when building cars. But Liberty ships were sealed at the bottom with their massive, watertight hull. There was no chassis equivalent. Instead there was something else that sat on top of every Liberty ship, that no ship could sail without: the deckhouse where the crew and officers lived while at sea.

Those deckhouses were being constructed in two, time-consuming phases. About half of a deck house would be built away from the shipways, and then brought in pieces over to a hull, where they were lifted up onto the deck so that they could be put together on the ship. That was where problems emerged. Cranes were asked to perform hundreds of lifts, each one slow, methodical, and dangerous. Once the deckhouse crews and the other workers were forced to work side by side, the deck of a Liberty ship looked like a frantic kitchen with too many cooks bumping hips and rubbing shoulders.

Bedford saw this chaos every day at his shipyard. And he knew that if one crew could construct the hull of a Liberty ship on the shipway, while at the same time a separate crew was building the complicated deck houses in a different location, it would dramatically cut the number of individual lifts required by cranes. In turn, the amount of time that would be saved when an already finished deckhouse was welded onto a nearly finished ship could be the game-changing move that everyone from President Roosevelt to Jerry Land to Howard Vickery to Henry Kaiser was looking for.

The midship deckhouse weighed 265 tons by itself, the equivalent of eight Sherman tanks. The deckhouse held the captain's stateroom and office, radio operators, the quarters for the engineers, deck officers, and the crew, with the cramped cabins housing two bunk beds to sleep four men. A small lounge to play cards and games and the messrooms were at the forward end of the deckhouse. The kitchen galley, with its two-oven, coal-burning range and 25-gallon steam stock kettle, sat midship, between the engine casings and the boiler. There was also spaced carved out for the ship's hospital, medical supply rooms, showers, and toilets. The midship deckhouse was almost the size of a three-story building, measuring 24 feet high, 60 feet wide, and 75 feet long.

Just as Kaiser entrusted Bedford with investigating Ford's production methods, Bedford worked with his own top man in Richmond, Norman Gindrat, a facilities design engineer. Bedford charged Gindrat with figuring out where and how crews could build the deckhouses away from the shipway where the hulls were being assembled. Meanwhile, Bedford would devise a way to move preassembled deck-houses and hoist them up onto the ships. That wouldn't be easy since the heaviest section of steel used to build the deckhouses weighed 75 tons and the lightest piece 45 tons. But Bedford was confident in the heavy-lifting machinery at his disposal.

Kaiser first used the huge Whirley cranes on the Grand Coulee Dam. The cranes derived their name from their ability to whirl around a full 360 degrees. The job of Whirley crane operator quickly became one of the most envied roles at a shipyard, as he sat up high in the cab and teamed up with the riggers below on the ground to safely guide heavy loads on to the ship with chains, cables, and ropes.[1] That relationship was critical, because a Whirley crane's hoisting capacity was much greater when the arm was not fully extended outward. The operator had to know precisely how heavy the load was he was about to lift so that he knew how far out he could extend the crane's arm. Loads didn't get much heavier than a deckhouse, which weighed about the same as America's symbol of freedom, the Statue of Liberty.

"One of the striking characteristics of the Richmond shipyards during their operation was the array of Whirley cranes that helped define their skylines," announced an article in Fore 'n' Aft. "Whirley cranes were also an essential component of the pre-assembly system that allowed Richmond and other emergency yards to produce merchant ships with such speed."

With Bedford's support, Gindrat designed his own version of Henry Ford's Crystal Palace right on the sprawling Richmond shipyard property, between yards No. 1 and No. 2. It cost $1.5 million. A warehouse-sized steel-framed shed, it measured 200 feet wide and 480 feet long, 40 feet longer than a Liberty ship. Ford had the luxury of making his prefabrication building taller because the automobile parts were smaller and lighter and could easily be moved up and down. Gindrat's design kept the operation on one floor, because of how big the parts would become. Bedford assigned 2,500 workers to the prefabrication shed, many of them women trained as burners and welders.[2]

Inside the shed were two bays, each 90 feet wide, with three mammoth bridge cranes in each bay. There was a 150-foot platform extending from the building on which to put the enormous steel slabs. Alongside the wide working areas, Gindrat laid out space for pipefitting, joining, electrical, and sheet metal work.

The most important element of the prefabrication shed was a conveyor line in each of the two bays. Each conveyor line was big enough to carry three enormous deckhouses at one time, or six in total. It was nothing like Ford's smooth conveyor belt, which briskly moved mostly smaller parts down a line to waiting workers. But Gindrat's system was just as effective. The conveyor lines were concrete foundations, three feet high, with trolley wheels mounted every two feet. Jigs were set up on the wheels to carry the deckhouses. When a finished deckhouse reached the end of a conveyor line at the west end of the prefabrication plant, it slid onto tracks 80 feet long. The tracks included 40 feet of a retractable conveyor section that could slide into the prefabrication shed to make an easy transfer of the deckhouse. A pair of hoists powered by 10-horsepower motors worked at the opposite end to pull the deckhouse along the tracks.[3]

EDYTHE ESSER, OR Edie as she was called as a little girl growing up in San Pablo, California, married after high school; then at the age of nineteen, after Pearl Harbor, joined her husband at the Richmond shipyard. Her first job in the man-hours department required a lot of typing of numbers, at which she failed miserably. She assumed she'd be out of work.

"You know, Edie," her boss told her one day, "I don't think you're going to make it."

"No," she replied, "I'm not."

He told her they were hiring women out of the main yards, in something called "the fields," in what was the beginning of the prefabrication yard.

"How does that sound?" he asked her. He knew she wanted the work, and she landed a job in prefab, where her team began work on the deckhouses and then watched them disappear on the giant flatbed trailers.

"They would take the pieces of these deckhouses to Yard 1, or Yard 2, wherever," she recalled. "I never did go to see where these bulkheads went."[4]

Only when she went outside on her lunch break, to quickly down a sandwich or half an avocado with a hard-boiled egg that she'd brought, did she see what was happening outside the prefab shed and begin to appreciate the work she was doing back inside.

AT STATION ONE, a team of workers constructed the main deck in four parts in an upright position. Butt straps, plates that overlapped and fastened two pieces together, were used to create rigidity and hold the parts in place throughout the assembly line. Crews also put in the equipment for the galley kitchen, and pipe penetrations through the deck were installed here. Building the deckhouses began with laying out thirty-six steel plates, each one about three-quarter inches thick, and marking each one clearly so they could be pieced together like a puzzle. The plates, which were about 7 feet long and 15 feet wide on average, were moved on to a jig in an upside-down position on the conveyor belt so the welders and welding machines could begin their work. While the biggest pieces were being connected, the stiffeners, beams, and smaller miscellaneous pieces were cut and shaped ahead of time. The four main pieces of the deckhouses were not permanently connected in the shed, but were instead held together with temporary tack welds, allowing them to be separated and moved more easily onto the ship.

A critical move came next when a bridge crane raised each deckhouse off the conveyor line and flipped it right side up and back onto the jigs, allowing it to continue moving while bridge decks, bulkheads, doors, and the "house tops"—pieces that had all been precut and shaped and stored ahead of time— could be welded to the steel frame. As it continued down the line, wiring for heating and electricity was added, along with piping and plumbing, each element taking place at a new station along the belt so that workers never got in the way of each other.

Piping in particular became one of the great time-saving innovations during construction.

Richmond shipbuilders built a mock-up of a Liberty ship engine room, even creating a dummy engine made of wood. Pipefitters would bring in various pipe lengths to the mock engine and cut them precisely to fit by measuring them against the dummy pipes. Most of the time their cuts were perfect and could be welded into place perfectly, but sometimes spot welding was needed to make small tweaks so there were no leaks during the connections.

One final step came as sections approached the end of the runway, when workers attached cable hooks to the sides so that the deckhouse could be hoisted. By the time a deckhouse reached station five in the conveyor line, all that was left was the painting and outfitting, including the fastening of light fixtures, davits for the lifeboats, and insulation.[5]

When a completed deckhouse came to the end, it marked the transition from prefabrication to ship assembly. But one last step came first.

"We prefabricated the whole deckhouse," Bedford explained. "We put the linen and the knives, forks, and spoons all in it, you know. Bedding, and the whole kitchen equipment, and we just set the whole deckhouse on board on top of the deck."[6]

Two Whirley cranes lifted the four enormous pieces of a deckhouse while a specially designed trailer backed in underneath it. The Trailermobile, at 21 feet wide and 60 feet long, had to be large enough and strong enough to carry and move a 72-foot deckhouse, which was why it had thirty-two tires on it. A Caterpillar tractor hooked on to the Trailermobile and pulled it to the shipways for the final step. Four high gantry cranes carefully hoisted the four deckhouse pieces up onto the ship—a deft act that required perfect harmony from all four crane operators so that the deckhouse never tilted too far in one direction—and set each piece in place. The cranes all had a gauge in the cab so that the operator could see precisely what angle his boom was at, to maximize the lifting capacity. That's when the final welds took place, connecting all four sides together with the roof, and tightly welding the bottom to the ship's deck.

With Henry Kaiser's vision, Clay Bedford's planning, and Norman Gindrat's execution, prefabrication and assembly line production were on the way to revolutionizing America's shipbuilding. No longer was a deckhouse being half-built, then carried in pieces to a ship, and then finished up on the deck. Now 95 percent of a deckhouse could be built away from the shipways, so that only a few final touches were necessary once it was in place. The achievement of setting in place a finished 75-foot-long deckhouse and welding it to the deck of a nearly completed Liberty ship showed the world that America's shipyards had mastered assembly line production.

The editors of Richmond's *Fore 'n' Aft* never missed an opportunity to boost the morale of the workers. As the modern shipbuilding method took hold in the shipyard over the summer of 1942, an article titled "Welders Go to Town!" about the increased speed at which ships were coming together ended with three telling words:

"Look out, Hitler."

CHAPTER THIRTY-FIVE

Pistol-Packin' Mamas

BASEBALL FANS WERE NOT SURE WHAT TO EXPECT DURING the summer of 1942. They were just glad to have any games at all to attend and a heart-wrenching new movie about Lou Gehrig, *The Pride of the Yankees*, starring Gary Cooper, to go see. Following Pearl Harbor, a poll in the spring by the American Institute of Public Opinion asked if sports should be stopped or should continue for the war's duration, and more than two-thirds of people wanted to see the games go on. Only a quarter supported a pause. Some traditions did deviate, however. After eight straight years of throwing out the baseball season's first pitch, President Roosevelt was otherwise occupied on April 14, as British and American destroyers sank two German U-boats that day and he was dealing with the aftershocks from the surrender of U.S. forces at Bataan in the Philippines after a three-month siege by the Japanese. But the games still had his full support, as he made clear to Major League Baseball commissioner Kenesaw Mountain Landis.

On January 14, as Landis began to see more and more of his players swapping their cleats for combat boots, he sent off a handwritten note to Roosevelt. Landis had decided enlisted players home on furlough were not permitted to play for their teams, but he wasn't sure if that was a strong enough move and so he wanted some reassurance from the White House about the upcoming season.

"The time is approaching when, in ordinary conditions, our teams would be heading for Spring training camps," Landis wrote. "However, inasmuch as these are not ordinary times, I venture to ask what you have in mind as to whether professional baseball should continue to operate."[1]

Roosevelt, a keen fan of the game since he was a young boy, wasted no time in replying with a heartfelt letter three days later. His own military in fact had specifically designed a new hand grenade, the BEANO T-13, to be the same weight, size, and shape as a baseball, figuring that all the young men who might one day be throwing them at the enemy would find the feel of it in their hands to be like a baseball they threw growing up.

"My dear Judge," Roosevelt began, immediately assuring Landis that the president's opinion was "solely a personal and not an official" point of view.

"I honestly feel that it would be best for the country to keep baseball going," he wrote to Landis in what became known as "the green light letter."[2] Roosevelt said the game was good for the economy, it created jobs, and it helped people take their minds off work and the war. He suggested an increase in night games so that wartime workers on daytime shifts could attend more frequently, but the president acknowledged that the quality of play on the field would suffer with players entering into service.

Instead of another epic season of batting records being smashed as they were in 1941, fans had to follow along as some of their favorite players disappeared from the diamond and a number of young players in the minor leagues were killed in battle. Buddy Lewis of the Washington Senators went to Fort Knox, Kentucky, to lead a platoon squad. Red Sox pitcher Earl Johnson joined the Army, as did Yankees pitcher Steve Peek. Minor-league pitcher Ed Tuttle died in a plane collision during pilot training in Florida. Walter "Rabbit" Maranville went into the Navy. Dodgers star Cookie Lavagetto enlisted in the Naval Aviation Reserve. As for baseball's best-known faces and rivals, gangly Ted Williams and dashing young Italian Joe DiMaggio, they passed their physical exams for the military while still competing on the field in 1942, awaiting the inevitable call to serve their country.

———

IF COMPETITION EVEN during wartime could drive baseball players to perform their best with the president's blessing, Howard Vickery wondered if maybe some competition could also drive shipbuilders. Inside each shipyard, it was already happening.

"Welders of all shifts in Richmond Shipyard Number One are staging a spirited competition and rivalry is increasing rapidly as a result of the big sign erected over the Field Personnel building which shows daily production of each weld leaderman's crew," *Fore 'n' Aft* reported on September 3, 1942.

Welding was a skill just like hitting a baseball, and welding competitions began to crop up at shipyards around the country. For female welders, who were adept at sewing a precise and straight seam, welding contests allowed them to show off their speed and precision in this new arena, and to earn the respect and workplace equality they sought. The first contests pitted male shipbuilders against each other, and one in Portland drew a crowd of six thousand people. But when women were pitted against one another the competitions heated up, covered by a fascinated media like championship boxing matches. Some articles even started off with "In this corner . . ."

Headline writers could not resist the puns, especially when it came to one of the best welders in the country, male or female, Cora Lea Clonts, a young typist in an Arizona real estate office who got her driver's license at the age of fourteen, and her pilot's license at twenty-one. When she came out to California on a vacation, she saw the bright lights from Richmond in the night sky, and the next thing she knew, she was hired as a welder to work in Richmond Yard No. 3. Always a daredevil, she took to the skill of welding quickly, showing none of the fear of injury that often slowed both men and women. She entered local, regional, and national welding contests, almost always coming out on top. In one of the many contests she entered and shined, Clonts welded her two plates together in a speedy thirty-six minutes.

"Joan of Arc-Welding," read one headline about Clonts. "Pretty Ex-Stenographer Wins Shipyards Welding Contest," read another, with a big smiling picture of her atop the front page. Her skills made her a shipyard celebrity and landed her lunches with the Richmond mayor, the California governor, and the president's daughter in Washington. When she appeared on a cover of *Fore 'n' Aft* with her welding helmet flipped up on her head and a big smile on her face as she squatted with her welding gun, she was described as a "Pistol Packin' Mama."[3]

Asked one day what makes a good welder, in one of the dozens of interviews she gave after winning another contest, she said she simply preferred eight hours of welding over eight hours of housework. "It's a job done primarily with the hands," she explained. "If they're sensitive and sure, it doesn't take you long to catch on."

ONE OF THE war's most hyped welding contests took place in Pascagoula, Mississippi, when Oregon Shipbuilding sent its best welder, a thirty-five-year-old, 118-pound, blond-haired, blue-eyed woman named Hermina "Billy" Strmiska south to go up against the ninety-pound Vera Anderson, all of nineteen years old, from Ingalls Shipyard. Anderson's path to the war started when her father died when she was eleven and her family, with six girls, moved to Gulfport, Mississippi. She worked at a local shoe store during the war's early days and graduated from high school in 1941. She and one of her sisters entered a training program for welders, where her skill was immediately apparent to the trainers, and she was assigned to weld Liberty ships at Ingalls. Ingalls staged an internal welding competition, and when Anderson emerged as their best, the shipyard challenged any and all yards from around the country to see if they had someone better. It offered a large silver cup as the winner's trophy, along with $350 in war bonds, and promised that the competition would be broadcast nationally over the radio.

Both Anderson and Strmiska wore khaki overalls for the contest as they stepped into a roped-off square at the Ingalls Shipyard on a steamy hot Saturday. Their competition was divided into two periods, and judges would base their decision on speed and the quality of the welding. Their contest called for welding two steel plates together without bumping them out of alignment, using vertical and flat welding positions. When they finished, their individual numbers were meaningless to the observers, but Anderson's time of 24 minutes, 46 seconds and her quality weld score of 95.55 percent easily bested Strmiska's numbers. She was crowned Champion Woman Welder of the World.

"I've never been so proud of anything in my life as the championship," Anderson told reporters afterward. She said she only wished her father had been there to see her win.[4]

Both women were rewarded a few days later with a trip to Washington, to share tea with the first lady. When Anderson was asked what she would do after the war, she said that she loved her work and the good pay, and saw no reason to quit just because the fighting was over. "I'll still be a welder, I guess," she said.

The answer surprised Eleanor Roosevelt, who said she had a different hope for the women of the shipyards. "Many of these women welders should return to their homes as soon as the war is over," she said.[5]

The publicity surrounding the female welding contests spun gold for the Maritime Commission. The competitions highlighted the role of women in the war effort while at the same time intensifying competition among the shipyards to build ships faster.

"Stage welding contests, ball games, dances, and other yard activities," the Maritime Commission encouraged in a memo to all shipyards, "so long as they do not interfere with production."[6]

EIGHTEEN SHIPYARDS WERE building Liberty ships across the country. The shipyards had a combined 171 slipways where they could build and launch ships. Vickery knew the specifications, labor forces, and shipbuilding output of each yard, like a baseball manager knew the batting averages and hitting tendencies of all of his players. His incessant pushing for the shipyards to go faster and faster became the stuff of legend. He filled a glass-covered case in his office with small medicine bottles, all labeled with words he'd become famous for uttering. "Heckling." "Jeering." "Belittling." "Sarcasm." "Fury." "Nagging."

"Profanity." And on the very tiniest of bottles, "Compliments." If you needed to be complimented to want to defeat the Nazis, you were in the wrong line of work, Vickery believed.

U.S. shipyards all employed hundreds, often thousands, of individual welders. Shipyard managers, meanwhile, were obsessively keeping track of how many ships were rolling out of each competing shipyard, the same way that baseball fans were tracking the home runs hit by Williams and DiMaggio.

With the welding contests proving successful, Vickery decided to go one step further by pitting shipyard against shipyard and turning the business of shipbuilding into a competition—a race.

BY LATE SUMMER of 1942, as workers became more skilled and prefabrication of ships took hold, the average time to build and launch a single Liberty had already been down from more than 200 days to 120 days to 60 days. Never satisfied, Kaiser set out to organize and motivate his workers to do things none of them thought possible.

He put in place a little trick he had experimented with a few years earlier in building the Grand Coulee Dam along the Columbia River in Washington, a project that was now providing cheap power across the entire Pacific Northwest. It was a massive job begun in 1938, creating a 151-mile-long reservoir called Lake Roosevelt that was 375 feet deep and 4,000 feet wide. The dam required a concrete base 500 feet thick and 550 feet tall. As impressive as the Boulder Dam had been, the Grand Coulee needed three times as much concrete, and the engineers who looked at the plans said that it dwarfed Hoover as far as complexities. (So proud was Kaiser of the Coulee Dam that the candy machines at his Richmond shipyard began carrying a new candy bar, the Dam bar, wrapped up in paper with a description of the Coulee project.)

When construction began, Kaiser decided to create some sort of incentive for the workers to avoid falling behind schedule. So he turned dam building into an athletic competition.[7] He divided the project into two separate but equal-sized chunks, assigning one half to his son Edgar and the other half to Clay Bedford, and he gave each man a separate team of workers. Then Kaiser erected a billboard near the middle, just like a giant scoreboard, and made sure it was updated daily with progress reports. This ensured that both managers and both sets of workers could see at all times which side was moving faster and winning. It worked. The project finished eighteen months ahead of schedule, allowing it to earn $7.2 million in profit.[8]

If creating competition could work on the Grand Coulee Dam, Kaiser saw no reason it would not work just as effectively to speed the production of Liberty ships.

Clay Bedford and Edgar Kaiser knew that intense competition could bring out the best in workers. But as impressive as their feat was on the Columbia River, the fate of America's democracy did not hinge on how fast a single hydroelectric dam in central Washington State could be built. Four years later, with the country at war, and with the young Kaiser in charge of Oregon Shipbuilding and Bedford leading the shipyard that he'd built in Richmond, California, the two longtime friends and coworkers embarked on a new contest with each other. Only this time the stakes were a lot higher.

CHAPTER THIRTY-SIX

Shipyard vs. Shipyard

IN MID-JULY, ADMIRAL HOWARD VICKERY SET OUT FROM Washington for the West Coast. His first stop on Sunday, July 19, was Portland, Oregon, and the shipyard run by Henry Kaiser's son Edgar. The official purpose of the visit was to help celebrate the launching of the Liberty ship SS *Harvey W. Scott*. But the day did not go as Vickery planned.[1]

In his formal dark Navy uniform and white cap with its dark bill, Vickery stood behind Kaiser expecting him to boast about his company's shipbuilding achievements. Instead, Kaiser blindsided the maritime official. Kaiser had been angered by Vickery a few weeks earlier when some materials he expected to be delivered to his shipyards were diverted at the last minute to another yard. Knowing that Vickery was coming to visit, Kaiser worked with the publisher of the *Oregonian*, Palmer Hoyt, a backer of the airplane industry in Portland, and the two men wrote up a fast speech announcing plans to build cargo planes in Kaiser's shipyards.

Vickery listened in stunned silence as the nation's preeminent shipbuilder announced to the crowd of thousands that he was prepared to convert nine major shipyards and begin mass-producing 70-ton cargo-carrying airplanes instead. Kaiser said that an entire fleet of 5,000 "Mars" planes could drop

500,000 armed soldiers in England in a single day, along with "fresh milk, beefsteaks, sugar—and bombs," without fear of being attacked by the swarming U-boats below.

"No submarines could shoot them down," Kaiser said.[2]

This was true, submarines could not shoot down airplanes. And the plane Kaiser wanted was already being test-built by Glenn L. Martin Company. Roosevelt and his War Production Board expressed enthusiasm for the idea. Kaiser, who was being called "Miracle Man" by the press for his Liberty ship exploits, hoped to capitalize on his popularity with a follow-up idea and to him, aviation made the most sense.

"Our studies indicated what I believe most of the people of America now believe—that the answer lies in the aerial freighter," Kaiser said.[3]

But he was premature in announcing his intentions. He had hoped that his announcement would pressure Congress and Roosevelt to approve his air freighters, but he allowed his business dreams to overshadow the larger military picture. The Mars project required a dramatic shift in the government's priorities and spending, and this was an extremely delicate time in the war.

The aftershocks from the PQ-17 convoy disaster a few weeks earlier were still reverberating across the country, and in the Oval Office. German saboteurs had just been arrested only days earlier on American soil, and their cases were still being judged. In early July, a disaster had been narrowly averted when the Liberty ship SS *Rufus King* ran aground on a barrier reef near Brisbane Harbor in Australia and cracked in half. Her payload was different from most Liberty ships, as she was loaded with medical supplies to assemble twelve hospitals with 4,000 beds for injured Allied troops. Each half of the ship remained afloat just long enough for a salvage crew of two hundred men from the U.S. Army Medical Department to make a daring rescue attempt. While they were able to recover approximately three-quarters of the materials on board, had they failed it would have been a catastrophic loss that would have taken months to replace and left thousands of wounded troops in peril.[4]

Vickery knew all of this background. As he listened to Kaiser's speech in Portland he couldn't help feeling slightly annoyed. When it was his turn at the podium, he called Oregonship "a yard of firsts." Afterward, despite repeated requests, Vickery offered no comment on Kaiser's proposal other than saying he considered himself to be in the ship business, not the airplane business. This was not the reason he had come all this way.

A FEW WEEKS earlier, Vickery had sent out a memo to all seventeen shipyards building Liberty ships. His goal was to get even more speed out of the yards and the only way he thought he could do that was to turn shipbuilding into a nationwide competition. He wrote that in order to earn one of his "M" awards, a shipyard had to "consecutively deliver EC-2 vessels [Liberty ships] into service within 105 days or less from keel laying to delivery from all their shipways."

The Navy had its own program called the "E" awards for "Excellence," which were given out generously to its most outstanding private contractors. Kaiser's shipyards in Richmond, Portland, and Vancouver were setting the pace for the rest of the country and winning their share of E awards, along with a "Golden Eagle Merit Award" and a "Gold Wreath Award" for outstanding performances.

"The ace shipbuilding plant in the country is the Portland, Oregon shipyard managed by Kaiser's son Edgar," the noted political columnist Drew Pearson wrote.[5]

Vickery planned to be more stingy with his awards than the Navy. He ran the program like a dictator—all decisions were his and they were final, though he would take recommendations. He had lapel pins designed for valuable shipyard workers to wear and special pennants embroidered with a large, gold *M* that shipyards could hoist up a flagpole for all to see as a symbol of success. Some believed the letter stood for *maritime* while others assumed *merit*. No matter—Vickery was determined to make sure the M awards were not some public relations stunt. Shipyards would have to earn Vickery's praise. He had no intention of gallivanting around the country handing out M awards like candy bars merely to boost morale. In his words, receiving an M would be based on a "tangible" accomplishment and should serve as "an incentive to even greater achievement."

During the worst years of the Great Depression, workers used their union pins as a way to tout the importance of Roosevelt's New Deal programs. In the same way, Vickery hoped the M would become more than a symbolic letter during the war. He wanted workers to proudly wear their M lapel pins to show off their collective effort and achievements—proof of the work they were doing. He also hoped that by creating a little tension and conflict through competition, it might unify teams of builders at the shipyards to work faster.

The awards would not be limited to shipbuilding. They were open to other businesses in the government's wartime manufacturing industries. Even Vickery would be surprised at how quickly the M awards made an impact.

TWO DAYS AFTER Portland, Oregon, launched the SS *Harvey W. Scott,* the SS *Joaquin Miller,* named for a famous Oakland poet, was ready to be launched. Built by Richmond shipbuilders in just sixty-one days, it was a feat that Vickery wanted to honor with an M award. A special program had been printed for the day's celebration: *On to Victory: Award of Merit by the United States Maritime Commission Honoring Each Workman of Richmond Shipyard Number One of the Permanente Metals Corporation.*

But another special guest was on hand for a different vessel. F. C. Cocks, the local representative of the British Purchasing Commission, had come to Richmond to take possession of the *Ocean Victory.*[6] It was the thirtieth and final ship in Richmond's British shipbuilding program. Kaiser's Richmond Yard No. 1 had not only completed its thirty Ocean-class freighters for Great Britain ahead of schedule, but they were also much faster than their competitor across the country in South Portland, Maine, which was still four months away from finishing its thirtieth ship for the British.

As the festivities got underway, Kaiser repeated much of his Oregon speech about building air freighters, and again Vickery cringed without wanting to appear disrespectful.

"My business at present is ocean ships," Vickery said, "but we could use airships, too."[7]

When it was Vickery's turn to speak, he told the crowd that every employee would receive an M pin and the shipyard would get a burgee that it could hoist up and fly over the grounds as a proud marker of its work. He reminded everyone that when Richmond was first suggested as a home for the emergency shipbuilding program, it was a barren mudflat and nobody believed a single ship would emerge for at least a year. Not only had Richmond built 30 ships for the British in a year, Vickery said, but it was setting the standard for Liberty ship construction now.

Bedford stepped forward to formally present the *Ocean Victory* to Cocks. Then the two men traded papers. Bedford handed over the detailed documents about the ship, and Cocks gave to Bedford formal records accepting the ship and papers that acknowledged completion of the contract. As soon as the *Joaquin Miller* glided down the shipway into the bay, the crew at Yard No. 1 wasted not a minute. Tugboats were still tying up the finished ship when workers began to lay the keel for the next Liberty ship to be built.

BEFORE HE RETURNED east, Vickery had one more M award to hand out, sixty miles away in Sunnyvale, California, at the southern tip of San Francisco Bay. Each Liberty ship required 250,000 individual pieces, or about 7,000 items. Bolts and screws were the most numerous, and then there were the quirky items like life jackets and window curtains, toilets and toilet paper, forks and spoons, pots and pans. But one item outranked all others in importance because it rendered everything else irrelevant—the 135-ton, 21-foot-tall, dark gray steel reciprocating engine. The Maritime Commission needed its engines produced at the same speed its ships were being built; otherwise the entire shipbuilding program would fall behind schedule with finished ships sitting idly in waters waiting for their final, most important, part.

The 2,500-horsepower Liberty ship engines were being built by more than a dozen manufacturers around the country, including the Ford Motor Company and the pioneer of the engine type, General Machinery Corporation. The Maritime Commission needed more than a thousand engines in a year, and its original contractor, Joshua Hendy Iron Works, remained the largest and most important.

On July 23, Vickery stood at a podium on a sunny Thursday morning in front of more than a thousand Hendy employees. California governor Colbert Olson, standing beside him, praised the factory for setting "an example to the rest of the country in the manufacture of wartime equipment."[8] Vickery went further, calling their effort one of the most amazing examples of industrial organization and expansion in the country.

He announced that all two thousand Hendy employees would receive an M lapel pin. When he finished his speech, he called three men to the stage to join him. A pair of longtime employees accepted Maritime Commission merit insignia badges, and then Charles Moore, the president of Hendy Iron Works, came up to accept the pennant that would fly over his factory. At six feet six and nearly three hundred pounds, Moore towered over the admiral. Vickery said the government put its trust in Moore and his company because it knew, "When we put a Hendy engine in a ship, it would get to its destination and back."

Eighteen months after President Roosevelt announced his emergency shipbuilding program in January 1941, it seemed to be clicking in every possible way by August 1942. Vickery's M awards program began to pay off almost immediately, as shipyards fought to win his attention and be honored with a visit and hopefully receive a pennant to fly. The idea of prefabricated ships was no longer an experiment isolated to a couple of West Coast shipyards. Shipyards around the country were adopting the concept, and the average time to build a Liberty ship in the country continued to drop. The *Patrick Henry* had needed five months of construction, from keel laying to launching on Liberty Fleet Day in September 1941, but then it still needed another four months to outfit it for duty—a total time of more than eight months. A year and a half later, the *Joaquin Miller* went into the water after just sixty-one days, barely two months, a speed that once seemed unimaginable. Henry Kaiser, with his

Liberty ship operation, and the California steel plant he was about to build, was being hailed as a miracle worker, and whispers were even beginning that he might be worthy of the vice presidency.

TO KAISER, ADMIRAL Vickery's idea to promote competition among shipyards was old news. Kaiser had been using that strategy for years with Clay Bedford and his son Edgar. Albert Heiner, Kaiser's longtime public relations official, saw up close how his boss's construction experience drove his thinking, and drove results. "When workers are given high goals, when they compete with another group, and when they get recognition for their achievements, they are sure to break one record after another," Heiner said.[9]

Separated by six hundred miles, the Richmond and Oregon shipyards had become more than Kaiser's pride and joy and models of shipbuilding for the rest of the country to follow. They were rivals. And just as he had hoped, as the first summer at war for America wound down, the two men Kaiser had put in charge were no longer satisfied with merely pumping out one ship after another. This had become a game to them, where there was a winner and a loser. The thirty-four-year-old Edgar and the thirty-nine-year-old Bedford entered into a heated competition to see whose crews could build the fastest Liberty ship.

And why not? Prefabrication simplified shipbuilding beyond anyone's imagination. There was no more standing around and waiting for hundreds of workers to finish one task so that another group could jump in. Every inch of the shipyards that practiced prefab was being used, and every second of every day was filled with activity. Prefab had sliced the average construction time of Liberty ships across the country from an average of 227.8 days in March down to 64.4 days by September. *Time* magazine glowed about the man responsible. "Kaiser is to shipbuilding," it wrote, "what the late Knute Rockne was to football: both introduced a revolutionary shift."

CHAPTER THIRTY-SEVEN

A Liberty Carries a Legacy

ON AUGUST 20, 1942, AT THE NORFOLK NAVY YARD IN VIR-
ginia, a towering crane hoisted three charcoal-gray, 80-foot, 40-ton patrol boats
up onto the deck of the Liberty ship SS *Joseph Stanton*.[1] Every inch on board a
Liberty ship was considered storage space. When a deck was covered from side
to side and end to end, temporary walkways erected overhead allowed crews
to make their way around the vessel. The patrol boats, three of hundreds built
by Elco in Bayonne, New Jersey, between 1942 and 1945, were headed for the
Panama Canal Zone.

A standard PT boat had a range of five hundred miles, not enough to reach
a faraway destination without making frequent stops to refuel. But for a Liberty
ship, hoisting three patrol boats onto its deck was like an elephant carrying
around a grown man on its back. The challenge was making sure the boats
were secure. They could not rest directly on the deck because their rounded
mahogany hulls would not sit flat. So crews in Norfolk erected a strong scaffold
and the three PTs were strapped down with heavy braces to avoid swaying.

Two of the boats on board the *Stanton*, the *PT-107* and *PT-108*, were placed
side by side on the rear deck. The third boat sat by herself on the forward deck.
The *Joseph Stanton* sailed from Virginia south around the tip of Florida and

through the Panama Canal. At Balboa Naval Base, the patrol boats were taken off and stationed at a motor torpedo boat base on Taboga, an island ten miles west of the canal. Before they were allowed into combat, the crews of the PT boats received several more months of training at the Navy's Motor Torpedo Boat Squadron Training Center in Newport, Rhode Island.[2]

One of the trainees so impressed his officers they asked him to stay a little longer as an instructor. The skinny, brown-haired, twenty-five-year-old junior-grade lieutenant with a chronically bad back, asthma, and ulcers seemed like a surprising candidate to lead anyone. But his commanding officers saw something in him besides his 1940 degree from Harvard and family pedigree. His father had briefly served as the chairman of the Maritime Commission under Roosevelt and later as ambassador to Great Britain. When John Fitzgerald Kennedy finally caught up with his squadron to man one of the boats carried by the Liberty ship that would patrol the Panama Canal Zone, he was assigned to command *PT-109*.

CHAPTER THIRTY-EIGHT

Stunt Ships

IT WAS ALMOST NINE O'CLOCK, AND DARKNESS WAS SET-
tling over Portland, Oregon, on Thursday evening, August 27, 1942, when the
celebration finally got underway. It was later than scheduled. But noon had
proved too ambitious for the yard's 3,000 workers. They needed a little more
time. As a crowd gathered at the St. Johns Plant of Oregon Shipbuilding, sparks
flew from the tip of an acetylene welding torch. It quickly cut the plates that
were holding in place the Liberty ship SS *Pierre S. DuPont*, and in less than a
minute the vessel was sliding down with a splash into the Willamette River.[1]

The reason for the party was the date. The keel for the *DuPont* had been laid
only twenty-six days earlier, on August 1, making it the first Liberty ship to have
its keel laid and its launch party held in the same month. The first Liberty ship
to come out of the shipyard, the SS *Star of Oregon*, had taken 131 days to build
from the keel to launch—and then it still needed another 95 days of outfitting
before it was ready to be delivered, a total of 226 days, or more than seven
months. With the *DuPont* safely away, the youthful Edgar Kaiser crowed that
his shipyard and all of his father's entire West Coast shipbuilding operation had
taken a giant leap forward in a little more than a year—and they were not done.

"In the future, average time on the ways should be 25 to 30 days," he said, adding that the extra time outfitting ships in the water should only require another ten to twelve days. "The experimental period is over. From now it will be a steady grind in this yard. There will undoubtedly be records, because we need ships more than anything else."[2]

This wasn't the first time American shipbuilders were using speed as motivation. In 1861, in the early days of the Civil War amid rumors of the Confederate Navy building an ironclad, impenetrable vessel, President Abraham Lincoln demanded that his Navy build him his own impenetrable vessel, and 101 days later the USS *Monitor*, a bizarre-looking ironclad ship that resembled a "cheesebox on a raft," splashed into the East River.[3] Henry Ford gave speed building a whirl too, but his World War I antisubmarine ships took too long to come together in time for battle.

For Henry Kaiser's shipbuilders, competitions became an outlet for them to stave off boredom. Their jobs were getting monotonous, as the results of their tedious work always created the exact same ship with precisely identical dimensions. Turning jobs into races gave shipyard managers, workers, the Maritime Commission, and even the public something to pay close attention to in the late summer and early fall of 1942. The ships became marketing gimmicks, stunts that allowed shipyards to experiment, to tweak some production techniques, to try anything that might shave a half an hour here, two hours there, or maybe an entire day from the construction timeline.

Not everyone was convinced. Critics of the stunt ships accused Kaiser's men of using techniques that could not be replicated easily and spending wildly on man-hours to just reap some cheap publicity. Jerry Land and Howard Vickery were not fans of the stunt ships. They worried that by pouring so many man-hours and resources into a single vessel, it actually hurt overall production by pulling men off one ship to work on another.

But shipyard managers insisted they were not cutting corners or putting workers at risk just for a front-page headline. They said the faster they built, the more they learned about what was achievable during emergency wartime conditions. They considered their yards to be laboratories and their ships to be their experiments—as long as a ship built in three weeks was no less safe than a ship built in three months. The only difference was that a record ship had more men working on it, following a faster schedule. They were intentionally built fast because the workers wanted to see if they could do it.

"We simply program the erection on a faster schedule," Edgar Kaiser explained. "More men and equipment are swung into the job and the groups work on a rapid schedule. The record ships get every inspection the regular vessels get."[4]

WHEN PRESIDENT ROOSEVELT upped his tonnage demand for construction of Liberty ships to 24 million for 1942, most dismissed it as bluster and propaganda. His insistence that the only way the war could be won was if America built more cargo ships than it lost made sense, even if it seemed impossible. But as summer gave way to fall, to almost everyone's astonishment the goal was being met, and even surpassed, as shipbuilders were on their way toward building 27 million tons for the year. In the race between American shipyards building new ships and German U-boats sinking existing ones, it appeared the Americans were winning. And then, unexpectedly, more reason for hope emerged from Russia—at the Battle of Stalingrad.

After months of seeing Nazi dive bombers and the German Sixth Army level much of their beloved city, Russian forces had stunned their enemy with a fierce counterpunch that divided the German army in half, rendering it far less powerful and ultimately starving almost 100,000 Nazi soldiers to death. When word reached Roosevelt and Churchill after all had seemed lost there, both men knew this could be the turning point they'd been hoping for. American supplies, much of them carried on board Liberty ships, including 60,000 trucks, 2 million pairs of boots, and 250,000 tons of gas to fuel airplanes, had been vital to support the Russian forces as they defended Stalingrad. "After nearly three and one-half years of victories, conquests, advances and the exhilaration of creating fear and uncertainty, the Germans appeared vulnerable," Martin Gilbert, the British historian, wrote of the battle. "The inevitability of triumph was gone."[5]

Energized by the news that the war's momentum was shifting, shipbuilders saw new records as achievable goals with each new keel that was laid. As they perfected the standardized design, and the manufacturers of the various parts for the ships got their work down to a science, building a 441-foot Liberty ship in a matter of a few weeks was becoming almost routine.

At Bethlehem Steel Company, workers installed a special system so it could crank out 120 rudders a month for Liberty ships. The windows for a Liberty ship's wheelhouse were being cut in a prefabrication shop to precise measurements and then marked as to which window went where, so they could be speedily set into the frame as soon as they were lifted on board. Even though the mammoth reciprocating engines were being made by fourteen different companies, they were all using identical and interchangeable parts, so if one manufacturer fell behind, it didn't matter. An engine from another one worked just the same. Fully loaded and prefabricated deckhouses were being hoisted up onto ships and welded to decks like car doors being snapped and bolted into place on a Ford coupe. The newest Liberty ships were launching twice as fast as the first round of ships a year earlier. Finishing a Liberty ship faster than any shipyard had finished one before became the new game, an athletic competition.

THE SHIPBUILDING RACE lifted Henry Kaiser to new heights, as it put everything his operation had accomplished on full display for the country to witness, from the workforces he hired to the welders he trained to the prefabrication methods his shipyards perfected. The race stayed on the West Coast. The more historic, traditional shipyards on the East Coast, from Portland, Maine, to Baltimore, to North Carolina, which had been around long before World War II started, were content with their programs and showed little interest in modifying their ways just to compete in some construction gamesmanship.

Not twenty-four hours after the *Pierre Dupont* launched in Portland, on a warm and sunny Friday afternoon under clear skies in Richmond, Kaiser stepped up to a podium. It was a proud moment for him as he stood alongside his wife and his son Henry J. Kaiser Jr. A Liberty ship draped in flags towered behind them, the SS *John Fitch*, named for the man credited with building the first steamboat in 1787. It was a merchant ship built by men who had never set foot on a ship before, under the leadership of a man, Clay Bedford, with absolutely no maritime experience, and by a company headed by a man who only a few years ago did not know the difference between a bow and a stern.

Kaiser looked out at the sea of faces with pride, thousands of his workers wearing red shipyard helmets, their sleeves rolled up, their grease-covered muscled forearms on display. As the crowd fell silent, the shipyard band struck up "Columbia, Gem of the Ocean."

Edgar Kaiser up in Portland had just knocked 9 days off the speed record for building a Liberty ship, from 35 days to 26. And now one day later, Bedford's Richmond shipyard was ready to launch the *John Fitch* only 24 days after laying her keel. Rather than feeling jealous of losing the record so quickly, Edgar Kaiser wrote a touching telegram to his mother, who had been asked to officially christen the *John Fitch*.

> Dear Mother, today really is a history making day. The ship is not only a world's record ship, but is a forerunner of the tremendous drive, energy, and effort dad and you have given to all we boys. I should like to be there today to see you crack her over the bow. But you know while I cannot be there, I am there in heart and spirit. Good luck mother to you and dad . . . With all my love, Edgar.

As for his father, Henry Kaiser never much liked public speaking, but he had come to accept that he needed to be his own best lobbyist. Some ideas flopped, like his giant cargo plane, and others, like his steel plant, soared. But Kaiser lived for the successes and the failures, as long he wasn't sitting still. And he had grown more comfortable with turns of phrases that fired up a crowd like only the best politicians could do.

"To me," he began, "this day is full of sentiment and romance."

He was in a good mood. Only a few days earlier, he had learned that the housing crisis in Portland finally could be addressed. His shipyards there had flooded the city with so many workers that the vacancy rate for housing was less than 1 percent and workers were so frustrated with their living conditions they were leaving their shipyard jobs. In early August the Portland Housing Authority gave Kaiser permission to build 6,000 units that the government would pay for, and within days tractors broke ground and crews were erecting 700 new buildings.

He told the crowd of the record achievement in Portland a day earlier. Then he told them what they had all come to hear.

"Today you have broken that record and have established a new one of twenty-four days!" he shouted.[6] He said that, even more remarkably, the ship's engine had been completely assembled in Sunnyvale in thirty hours.

To his workers, he was a hero.

"What this country needs right now is more Henry J. Kaisers," one of them said in an interview for *Fore 'n' Aft*. "If he says for us to build a ship in 18 days, we'll build her in 18 days," another said. The newspaper said it lost them in the excitement of the crowd before catching their names. "Mr. Kaiser gave all credit to the men in the yard," the paper reported. "The men give Kaiser his due credit."[7]

For Kaiser, it was an opportunity to bask in a moment that reflected his remarkable rise in such a short time period. As much as the Boulder Dam had established him as one of America's most successful public works contractors, building a hydroelectric dam of concrete and steel in the middle of a western desert was never going to elevate his profile from coast to coast. But it did put him on the radar of the people who doled out the contracts that could ultimately lead to his name being spoken in the same breath as Edison or Ford. And not only did he win those contracts, but the speed with which he built the shipyards and started building ships surprised almost everyone. In just two years, Kaiser went from being known as a smart businessman and a regional builder of highways, dams, and bridges to a miracle worker, described by one peer as "a rolling mountain of a man just full of ideas," and someone whom

Roosevelt considered worthy of consideration as his vice president and maybe even his successor in the White House one day.[8]

One year into the war for America, Roosevelt was beginning to understand the fascination with Kaiser. His Richmond and Oregon shipyards were setting the pace for the nation's shipbuilders. Jerry Land told the president that between March and November of 1942, shipbuilders had reduced the average time to build a Liberty ship from approximately 228 days to 64 days, a breathtaking 72 percent improvement. Land emphasized that while the stunt ships might be exciting efforts to energize Americans, and useful to discover new building techniques, they were exceptions. The only figure that mattered was the average rate of construction.

When *Time* announced its annual Man of the Year it honored Joseph Stalin while naming the Archbishop of Canterbury as runner-up. Roosevelt was missing. But "bald, tight-lipped" Henry Kaiser finished third, evidence of his remarkable rise to prominence in such a short time.[9] Roosevelt's aides began to wonder if perhaps a partnership between the two men should be in their future. Rumors began that Kaiser would make a strong running mate in Roosevelt's pursuit of a fourth term, or that he could replace Roosevelt on the ticket if he chose to not run again in 1944. Even Roosevelt whispered it to a confidant, saying, "There would be such a gasp when his name was suggested," but the nation would have to be convinced of his worthiness. Roosevelt believed Kaiser the businessman was more like Stalin and Churchill than people realized.

"I believe he would have a good chance if he were 'sold' to the country in the right way!" Roosevelt told his friend.[10] (In the end, any aspiration Kaiser might or might not have had for the White House died when an old speech of his was dug up in which he advocated for a sales tax.)

AS HE TOOK the podium, Kaiser allowed himself to bask in the moment. "Isn't this a remarkable day for America, too, when she can proclaim to the world that her sons, literally 100,000 men, in the shipyards of Richmond and

Oregon have helped to perform that which only yesterday seemed a miracle and which today is a message and challenge to the axis that America has just begun to fight," Kaiser said.

He praised the duo of Jerry Land and Howard Vickery for their leadership of the Maritime Commission, for demonstrating "unbelievable courage which enabled them to draw from the resources of America, men and women who could produce an amazing amount of tonnage." He acknowledged that only the ongoing steel shortage stood in their way, and he said, "We are fighting shoulder to shoulder, bolder and bolder, to get every ounce of steel."

His enthusiasm was echoed by the Maritime Commission's representative at the celebration, Carl Flesher, who told the workers that the faster they went, the more it boosted the spirits of the men in battle.

"It will cheer our fighting men and help them to victory," he shouted. "For they will know that you men on the production front are on the offensive and out to win the war! They will know that supplies are on the way!"

When the speeches were finished, and with workers screeching and whistling in delight, the ship began to slowly inch down before Bess Kaiser was ready with the celebratory champagne bottle. She swung to smash it on the hull, but missed, leaving the bottle dangling at the end of its red, white, and blue ribbons. Henry Kaiser Jr., who had been the football manager at nearby Stanford University, grabbed the bottle and hurled it at the moving ship with perfect accuracy, causing it to smash and splatter over the prow, eliciting great cheers. The ship continued its slide into the water with a giant splash, as tugboats surrounded it and towed it away for its final few days of outfitting. Speaking to his shipbuilders, Kaiser told them to enjoy the moment, because it would not last.

"Today's record, too, will be short lived," he promised, "for I am told by our boys that tomorrow's record of less than 18 days will be established within the next few months."

Kaiser's wife, embarrassed at her failure to successfully smash the bottle, leaned into her husband as he put a comforting arm around her shoulder.[11] Then, in a blink, the celebration was over. With the shipway clear and the water still rippling from the splash of the *John Fitch*, a giant crane lifted a new keel plate into place. The helmeted workers stared at the fresh keel like pigs eyeing a trough. They spat on their hands, eager to grab hold and start anew.

The *John Fitch* had barely splashed into the bay and six hundred miles to the north, Kaiser's son Edgar was already aiming to build one faster than 24 days and to reclaim the title of fastest shipbuilder.

ON TUESDAY, SEPTEMBER 22, 1942, Clay Bedford got a surprising call from his friendly rival. In the last month, the two men had built Liberty ships in 37 days, then 35 days, followed by 26 days, and finally the *John Fitch* came together in 24 days. Given that when the program began eighteen months earlier, it took more than 250 days to complete one ship, and most Liberty ships still required one to two months to build and launch, their latest achievements were even more remarkable. But Edgar Kaiser still had one more magic number in his head: 10.

He invited Bedford to come to Portland to witness a launch. But because Kaiser did not explain when the keel for the ship had been laid, Bedford had no interest in traveling to see a routine ship-launching.

"Gee whiz, I'm right up to my eyebrows in Richmond," Bedford told Edgar. "Is it important?"[12]

Yes, Edgar said. It was important.

"I can't tell you why. Do you want me to call my father and have him order you to be here?" he said, only slightly teasing.

"Okay, okay," Bedford replied with a huff. Truthfully, he didn't understand what the big deal was about this launching after so many others. He took a night train from Richmond that got him to Portland first thing the following day. It was only when he arrived and was met by Edgar Kaiser's men at the train station that Bedford began to grasp what was happening. He saw President Roosevelt and his daughter, Anna.

FDR had just arrived himself after touring the Boeing plant in Seattle and the Navy Yard in Bremerton, Washington, where he spoke from his open car to 5,000 ship workers. Henry Kaiser greeted the president and introduced him to his son Edgar, then led him on a tour of the yard.

For Edgar, it was a huge moment. It was the 75th Liberty ship his yard built, and in the span it took to finish the latest Liberty, his Portland yard had laid three other keels, launched three other hulls, and delivered four fully completed ships. What he didn't tell anyone was that the ship he was about to launch had actually been completed two days earlier. He only held it up so that Roosevelt could attend the ceremony, which he knew would bring along a gaggle of national news reporters.

Roosevelt was eager to see what all the fuss was about with the western shipyards that were building him so many Liberty ships. Henry Kaiser, who had hurried back from New York to attend the launch, beamed as he stood beside the president.

"Just look at those assembly lines," Kaiser said.[13]

When Roosevelt, wearing a light gray suit and black tie, saw Bedford, he immediately approached him, despite a growing crowd of almost 15,000 people. By this time, Roosevelt had almost no use of his legs. When his train would come to a stop, a ramp with railings was set in place for him to gently step down on his own, using his metal braces to support him before he might sit down in a wheelchair. It required real effort on his part, which showed on his face, but it was important to the president, and photographers in the day never photographed him straining to take his steps.[14]

"I remember you from Grand Coulee, when you were one of the men who showed me around there," Roosevelt said. Bedford couldn't believe the president recognized him.[15]

To get into his specially outfitted Lincoln limousine required a different sort of effort for Roosevelt, as a burly guard would hoist him up and into the back seat. Roosevelt, with Kaiser sitting alongside, watched from his open car, which was parked on a high ramp that afforded him a terrific view of the workers burning away the steel plates that were holding the SS *Joseph Teal* in place.

A voice boomed over the loudspeaker as workers freed the ship for launching.

"The first rivet is out! The second rivet is out!"

Finally, with all the rivets removed, Anna, standing next to the towering ship, reared back with the champagne bottle, remembering how her father had taught her to swing a baseball bat, and she smashed it against the hull. *Thud.* She smashed it again. *Thud.* Laughing at her failed attempts, Anna on her third try at last exploded the bottle against the hull, sending so much glass and bubbly flying everywhere that she was "dripping from head to skirt," one onlooker recalled.[16]

"I am very much inspired by what I have seen," Roosevelt said to the throng from his car up on the ramp, "and I wish that every man, woman, and child in these United States could have been here to see the launching and realize its importance in winning the war."[17]

Sitting next to the president in his vehicle, Kaiser spoke next. His boundless energy impressed Roosevelt, who called him a "dynamo" in a moment of privacy.[18] Roosevelt was well aware that his seemingly unachievable shipbuilding goals for 1942 and 1943 were being achieved because of Kaiser.

As Kaiser began to speak, he refused to show even a hint of favoritism in the shipyard competition between Portland and Richmond, even though one of them was run by his flesh-and-blood son.

"Our original contract called for the delivery of ships in about 150 days," he said. "The average in the first World War had been more than 200. Many experts shook their heads and said we could not do it. Yet, here beside us is this great craft—only ten days from keel laying to launching; and in a few days she will be on the ocean bearing cargo to our allies and to our soldiers. It is a miracle no less—a miracle of God and of the genius of free American workmen."

When he finished, a reporter shouted a question at him.

"How long will the ten-day record stand?"

It was an absurd question. Shipbuilders in Portland, Oregon, had just constructed a cargo ship longer than a football field and taller than a ten-story building. Its assembly required 250,000 pieces to come together like a Beethoven masterpiece, with not a second to waste and every shift of new workers rotating in and out for twenty-four hours a day, for ten straight days. And if that was not historic enough, it happened under the pressure of a world war with a president demanding that shipyards go faster, faster, faster!

And yet, Henry Kaiser answered the absurd question as if he knew a secret. "Nothing is impossible!" he shouted. "Absolutely. I expect that record to go by the boards in the very near future. Never in my long experience have I seen men so imbued with the joy of achievement as these shipyard workers."[19]

IF THE STUNT-SHIP exercise was proving one thing, it was that even more men and women were needed in the shipyards. Across the country, one day after the historic launching, several thousand workers spilled into the streets around a midtown Manhattan office building.

There were almost 400,000 registered workers in New York City qualified and available for defense jobs, equivalent to half the population of Boston. But where to put them? That question fell to Anna Rosenberg, a White House adviser whom Roosevelt entrusted so much that some questioned whether she was stepping into the duties of the secretary of labor. *Collier's* even ran a piece about Rosenberg headlined "The Woman Nobody Knows." But the president ignored the barbs. When she suggested assigning those unemployed workers to West Coast shipyards, where they were needed the most, that's exactly what happened.

Word quickly got out that Henry Kaiser was recruiting 20,000 workers for his West Coast yards, and he had opened a recruiting office in a vacant store at 381 Fourth Avenue. By four in the afternoon on September 23, more than a thousand workers, from teenagers to middle-aged men to retirees, had been hired, each one advanced $75 by Kaiser that would be deducted from their first paycheck in Portland, Oregon. Sixty-seven-year-old electrician Luigi Lupo was an ideal hire, too old to be drafted, but healthy and an expert in a valuable skill. Martin Weiner was a forty-one-year-old executive from Perth Amboy, New Jersey, who was told his management experience could be useful.[20]

The men were told the pay scale would start at 95 cents an hour and go up based on their background and experience level. (Weiner was promised $1.65 an hour.) They would be paid for fifty-two hours a week, which included twelve hours of time-and-a-half pay. There was just one catch: they had to travel alone and leave behind their families for the time being. The only ones rejected for jobs were those likely to be drafted soon or were already working in a vital wartime industry.

THERE WAS NO denying his envy. When Clay Bedford returned to Richmond after seeing the *Teal* launch, especially after it seemed like Edgar had invited him just to rub the ceremony in his face with the president in attendance, he wondered if 10 days could be broken. One morning, he gathered his shipbuilders around and shouted a message to them.

"What has Oregon got that we haven't? Have we got what it takes to beat this record? Can we cut down our average time? Can we produce still more ships per month?"[21]

He knew the answer because he had the numbers. Of sixteen Liberty ships that were launched prior to Hull No. 72 in August, the average length of time from keel laying to launching was 57 days per ship. Of the sixteen ships that followed Hull No. 72, the average building time dropped to 42 days. They were getting faster and faster, as they got better and better.

In late September, Bedford bumped into his chief superintendent, J. C. McFarland. He saw something McFarland was working on, but it didn't look quite right.

"Mac, that is not to drawing," Bedford told him. "That is not the way we build that ship."

McFarland, of course, knew what he was doing. He leaned in to whisper to Bedford.

"I know it," he said. "But we're going to build a ship in half of their time."

"Oh, oh," Bedford exclaimed with some nervousness. "Remember this is President Roosevelt's daughter that sponsored that ship. We're on risky ground. We'd better check out with the boss."[22]

As much as Bedford also wanted to reclaim the record from Edgar Kaiser, he had a big concern. He explained to McFarland that Roosevelt had just finished a visit to the West Coast. He even gave a speech in Oregon saying how "inspired" he was by the shipbuilders that was quoted in newspapers across the country. Roosevelt's daughter had smashed the bottle that sent the record-setting *Teal* careering into the water. If Bedford's Richmond shipyard was able to construct a Liberty ship even faster than the *Teal*'s 10 days, it would instantly render everything Roosevelt had just done as pointless, especially since there was no chance the president would come back across the country to witness another record launching. Bedford told McFarland to wait on his plans, and he called up his boss to explain the situation.

"You know," Bedford said to Kaiser, "these guys out here want to build a ship in half the time that Portland did. They've got it on the way, and I think we're going to be able to do it. And I thought since the president's daughter sponsored that ship, maybe we better clear with you first."[23]

Kaiser understood politics. He certainly understood competition. All of his stunt ships being built out west—the 26-day *Dupont,* the 24-day *Fitch*, the 10-day *Teal*—were a direct result of his idea to give one shipyard to Bedford, another shipyard to his son, and to step away. When Kaiser heard that Richmond now wanted to build a ship in "half the time that Portland did," he knew exactly why Bedford was telling him first, rather than just rushing to build it. Neither Bedford nor Kaiser wanted to do anything that might embarrass or undercut the president, whose picture had just appeared in *Life* magazine beaming at the launching ceremony of the *Teal*. Kaiser reached out to James F. Byrnes, a former senator and Supreme Court justice who had left the court to head Roosevelt's Office of Economic Stabilization, to ask him to take the president's temperature before Richmond moved forward.

The president was in no mood to worry about wounded egos and hurt feelings. Only a few weeks earlier, six of the eight Nazi saboteurs who had stepped on American soil intent on blowing up merchant shipyards and other American defense efforts were put to death by electric chair in Washington. On the same day as the executions, one of Roosevelt's most senior officials had painted a dark picture of the war at sea. Admiral Chester W. Nimitz, commander of the

Navy's Pacific Fleet, warned the nation that victory "will be a long and bloody task" and asked Americans to "work, work hard, and keep on working."

There were plenty of reasons for his harsh outlook. In one ten-day stretch as summer came to an end, German U-boats destroyed twelve Allied merchant ships, killing more than sixty seamen and leaving another fifty missing. And on September 13, an emotional and symbolic blow to the shipbuilding program moved across the news wires: the British cargo ship *Ocean Vanguard*, the model upon which every Liberty ship sailing the world had been built, was gone. The very first of the merchant ships launched in Richmond in the summer of 1941 following the original design of Cyril Thompson and the improved version of William Francis Gibbs, it was torpedoed by a German U-boat and sunk near Trinidad, off the northern edge of South America. Eleven crew members were killed.

None of this news put Roosevelt at ease. Since Pearl Harbor, the president felt as if the war had been a battering ram of bad news. His speechwriter described the early days of fighting as "the winter of disaster," and Donald Nelson, the head of the War Production Board, had said that "America was losing a war, the greatest in history, one upon which our national existence depended." Roosevelt accepted that Germany and Japan would not go down quickly and that there would be more bad news before any good news began. But he refused to sit quietly. While his emergency shipbuilding program under Kaiser seemed to be picking up momentum, from building 12 Liberty ships in February to 67 in September, a fivefold increase, airplane production under Henry Ford was a disaster. A *Life* cover story shouted, "Detroit Is Dynamite." It wasn't a compliment.

When Byrnes asked the president whether he cared about another West Coast Liberty ship being built even faster than the one he had just helped launch in Oregon, Roosevelt snapped back his answer.

"Build it," he said to Byrnes. "Tell H.J. if he can build it in *one* day, go ahead!"[24]

Byrnes got Kaiser back on the phone.

"Go ahead," he said. "You're in the clear."

CHAPTER THIRTY-NINE

A Liberty's Victory

THE UNMISTAKABLE OUTLINE OF A LIBERTY SHIP ON THE
ocean's horizon was usually cause for celebration on board a German U-boat or
warship. They may have been ugly ducklings back home, but they were sitting
ducks on the ocean—slow, lightly armed, and filled with valuable goods for
American and Allied troops. Sinking any American vessel, especially one from
the American president's proud fleet of new cargo ships, was the golden ticket
for German commanders, a chance to earn Hitler's highest praise by sending
tanks, guns, ammunition, boxed-up airplanes, or maybe millions of rations
for soldiers to the bottom of the sea. That's why excitement filled the German
auxiliary cruiser *Stier*, a heavily armed gray freighter, when it spotted the Liberty
ship SS *Stephen Hopkins* through thick fog around 9:30 a.m. on September 27,
1942, exactly one year to the day after America had celebrated Liberty Fleet Day.

For the *Hopkins* crew and Captain Paul Buck, whose ship was only the
seventh Liberty to come out of Richmond Shipyard No. 1 four months earlier,
the moment the *Stier* came into sight, they knew they faced two choices, both
of them fraught. Their ship was named for a colonial governor of Rhode Island
and one of the signers of the Declaration of Independence, a point of pride for
Buck and his crew. They could surrender and give themselves up to the Nazis

while their ship was likely scuttled, or stand their ground and fight despite being grossly overmatched in firepower.[1]

The thirty-nine-year-old Buck, a career sailor with a wife back in Massachusetts, didn't hesitate. After first ordering the American flag be raised, only to see the German ship raise its swastika-emblazoned flag, he sounded his general alarm and ordered his crew to their action stations. Then he ordered his clunky Liberty ship to turn hard left rudder, leaving only its stern visible to the *Stier*, the narrowest possible target. There would be no surrendering.

The *Stier* accelerated up to 14 knots and made up ground on the *Hopkins* quickly. Even though the *Hopkins* carried fifteen Navy Armed Guards, along with its Merchant Marine crew, she was hardly primed for battle, with only one main 4-inch gun, dual 37 mm guns perched on her bow, and four .50-caliber machine guns scattered on board. That was it. A Liberty ship's weapons were never meant to save her from sinking, or to defeat an enemy ship. Their purpose was to give the crew something to shoot back with, to stave off the inevitable for as long as possible while the crew used their lifeboats to flee and hoped to be rescued.

The heavily armed *Stier*, with its 5.9-inch guns trained on the *Hopkins*, closed its gap in minutes and whistled a relentless stream of shells into its enemy's hull, slicing open holes in the bulkheads and sparking fires. Up on deck of the *Hopkins*, Ensign Kenneth Willett, the commander of the naval armed guard, was sprinting to a stern gun when he felt a sharp pain in his stomach and gasped for breath, bleeding from shrapnel. He still managed to take hold of the after gun and with dead aim riddle the *Stier* with more than thirty shots, including a penetrating blow to its engine room and another that crippled its torpedo tubes.[2]

But the Nazis had tremendous firepower and her machine guns rained down on the deck of the *Hopkins*, slicing through flesh and shattering anything in sight. The radio operator was killed when a German shell landed square in his room, and Second Mate Joseph Layman was killed while firing the Liberty's 37 mm gun.

The chief steward on board, Ford Stilson, was still in his stateroom when the fighting began.³ Word reached him of injuries up on deck. He grabbed bandages and antiseptics along with his life jacket and rushed up to find the chief mate reclining with a gaping wound to his thigh and left forearm while still barking orders to the crewmen. With shrapnel flying all around him and shells exploding on the bridge deck, Stilson knelt down.

"I applied a tourniquet and bandaged both wounds," he recalled. "I started below to get more material ready for the next casualty, but returned up the ladder at the sound of severe groans."⁴

Meanwhile, as the *Stier* continued its assault, and Buck, from the wheelhouse, tried to keep his ship's stern to the enemy, he was confused why his crew did not seem to be firing back with the same fury. With Layman gone, nobody was manning the bow's 37 mm guns. Despite the confusion, there was no panic on board the Liberty ship, and as soon as Buck's shouts were heard, all of the guns were quickly firing again. Even one of the loose machine guns joined the fray, causing surprise on board the *Stier*, which had expected a quick and easy sinking rather than a spirited firefight.

The *Hopkins* crew was not only fighting, they were winning. Their relentless pounding of shells caused white smoke to pour from holes in the *Stier's* hull. With each new blast, shouts of encouragement rang out on the Liberty ship, as the crew saw the effects of their accurate shooting and watched in amazement as the enemy ship started to settle by her stern and burn at her bow. When an explosion sent one *Hopkins* crew member flying from his gun perch, the youngest seaman on board, eighteen-year-old Edwin J. O'Hara, an engineering cadet midshipman, gently moved his wounded mate and returned to the gun. It was undamaged and O'Hara's instincts took over. He ran to a nearby ammunition locker, found five shells, loaded the gun, and pumped all five into the *Stier*. O'Hara was never to be seen again.

Both ships had taken a pounding in twenty minutes of fighting. From the bridge, Buck looked out at the bodies scattered, the fires on board, and the shattered deckhouse and engine room. A shell that struck that boiler room proved devastating, shutting down the engines. As more and more of the *Hopkins's* guns fell silent, Buck saw how much his ship had settled and so ordered what was left of his crew, nineteen men, to abandon ship. Seconds after giving his order, his crew watched as a shell exploded on the deck where Buck had been standing. One of his last acts was throwing the ship's codebooks over the side. Even as the lifeboats were lowered, the shooting continued and those in one raft watched as machine gun fire cut down more of their mates in another lifeboat.

The *Stier's* captain, Horst Gerlach, ordered his crew to cease fire. The entire battle had lasted only twenty-two minutes. But while Gerlach was satisfied with the destruction they had caused, his own ship was on fire and had lost its steering. One fire was creeping dangerously close to the ship's torpedo store, which would be catastrophic. Three of his crewmen were dead and another twenty-eight injured. It became clear to Gerlach that while the Liberty ship was indeed going down, it would not go to the bottom of the ocean alone. The German cruiser had sustained a relentless pounding of more than thirty rounds near its waterline, and smoke and flames were starting to appear from her stern up to her bow. On Gerlach's bridge, the hope of a quick, easy victory had vanished. The *Stier's* torpedo tubes were disabled, and below deck, men struggled in waist-deep water to plug holes and keep her afloat.

Finally, with the fires raging on deck, he began evacuating the *Stier* and took the final step that every vessel commander dreaded—he set demolition charges to explode. His surviving crewmen were picked up by a nearby German supply vessel, the *Tannefels*, which had been escorting the *Stier.*

As the lifeboats for the Liberty ship drifted away from the enemy, carrying nineteen survivors, they heard a faint but unmistakable explosion off their stern. They could not see far through the mist and rain, but they knew what it meant. In a rare and astonishing victory, the undermanned, lightly armed, battered, and beaten SS *Stephen Hopkins* had managed to sink a fierce German raider, the first known incidence of a Liberty ship victory. Four of the men who had been injured in the battle died aboard the lifeboats. Thirty-one days after their ship sank, the fifteen survivors reached a small town on Brazil's coast.

Lieutenant Joseph Rich from the U.S. Navy Reserve was dispatched to bring them home from Rio de Janeiro, and when he met with them he was astonished at their good spirits.[5]

"The survivors were in wonderful conditions, considering what they'd been through," he wrote later. "One could not help but feel the deepest admiration for these men who had faced such odds and were never for one moment beaten."

Because America's ship losses were still being closely guarded by the White House, it would take months before news of the David-and-Goliath battle reached the public. The crew, both the survivors and those who perished, were all hailed for their heroism, and some received Distinguished Service Medals. Two of the sailors, eighteen-year-old Moses Barker, who looked like he had never shaved a day in his life, and twenty-four-year-old Virgil Bullock went back to the Richmond shipyard where their Liberty was built and shared their harrowing tale with the shipbuilders, including their landing in a fishing village on the coast of Brazil. They told their story over the radio in a lunchtime broadcast played over loudspeakers. Months later, in a special honor, a hall at the Merchant Marine Academy was named for Cadet Edwin Joseph O'Hara. The *Stephen Hopkins* received the U.S. Maritime Administration's Gallant Ship Award. A future Liberty ship would be named the SS *Paul Buck*.

PART VII

"There She Goes"

CHAPTER FORTY

Setting the Table

A BRISK WIND BLOWING OFF SAN FRANCISCO BAY WAS starting to rip through the shipyards in early November. No longer were the workers enjoying commutes in short sleeves and trudging to the shipyard bathed in 75-degree California sunshine. The days were starting in the high 40s and barely reaching 60. Once on-site, welders who looked like Martians in their heavy leathers and protective masks walked purposefully through the grounds, their gloved hands holding piping-hot rods. New ships were sliding into the bay every day, droplets of champagne dripping from their hulls, and before one ship was gone, the hull of a new one slid into its place and the work began all over again.

Small cards greeted workers on their ferries and buses or when they arrived at the shipyard, with a short, simple message: "What has Oregon got that we haven't?"[1]

The cards were slipped inside their latest edition of *Fore 'n' Aft,* a message from Clay Bedford. Of course it was a rhetorical question, meant to stir them up and remind them that they had held the record for the fastest-built Liberty ship for only a few days before Oregonship took it away. If there was any question about whether there would be another attempt to build one even faster than the *Teal,* Bedford erased it with his cards.

THE IDEA IN Richmond to reclaim the title of the fastest-built Liberty ship was never just about breaking a record. Or capturing more favorable headlines. Or racing just for the sake of racing. It wasn't even about sending some sort of warning shot to Hitler about what America was capable of. And even though the rivalry between Edgar Kaiser and Clay Bedford was real, and it was motivating, it was not the driving factor. The idea was always about using the most advanced building methods, the most creative new ideas, the most surprising inventions, and the ideal tools, all to prefabricate and build one ship faster than anyone could possibly imagine—the perfect Liberty ship. It would never be replicated. And that was the whole point.

One shipfitter who was overheard describing in detail what it would mean to build a ship almost entirely preassembled made it sound like a joke.

"It would mean building the dining room, kitchen, and bathroom in one piece, the bedrooms and the parlor in another," she said. "You put in the piping and wiring, hang up the curtains, cover the floor with hardwood and a carpet, build in the furniture, paint and varnish the doors, paper the walls, hang pictures on them, place the refrigerator and the stove in your kitchen and the telephone next to your bed. Then you load the whole piece on a trailer and take it a mile downtown where the foundation of your house was laid. You drop it in place, join it with the other pieces preassembled somewhere else, put on a ready-made roof with a chimney on it, and the next day you can move in!"[2]

Except it wasn't a joke. It was precisely what Clay Bedford had in mind.

SHIPBUILDING REQUIRED A team to work in perfect harmony; no one man, or woman, or unit, could do it alone, from the very first screw to the very last weld. The shipbuilders had real pride. Every worker believed their job was the most important step to launching a floating Liberty ship. Painters thought the paint was critical. Installers of the steel doors were sure their job was the most essential. Even the workers who did things as trivial as stocking the deckhouse and pantry believed their role was vital to making a ship seaworthy.

So when Bedford asked his shipbuilders, "What has Oregon got that we haven't?" the answers came back in the form of more than 250 new ideas, from welders, pipefitters, shipfitters, draftsmen, boilermakers, and machinists, from the most senior managers down to the greenest trainees, from men and from women. Drawings and three-page letters poured in, enough to fill a book. Instead of building a ship's deck in twenty-three separate pieces that all had to be hoisted up into place then welded together, could that be done in fifteen pieces? Or ten? Or, as some believed, as few as seven? One letter left no doubt that "a 10-day record could be easily surpassed."

The way they were going to do it was to build the ship almost entirely on land. To prefabricate and prefabricate and prefabricate until the pieces grew so big that they could be moved only by trucks and by cranes to the shipway, where only then would they finally come together in the actual construction of a Liberty ship.

They were going to take Henry Ford's model of assembly-line automobile production and apply it to shipbuilding. A 15-foot Model A could easily slide down an assembly line for waiting workers to attach a door, a wheel, a windshield, a hood, or a fender. But a 441-foot Liberty ship was far too massive for that operation to work. So instead, smaller components would all be constructed away from the shipway, with individual teams assigned tasks, and their finished work would then be sent to a subassembly team, where smaller parts were added to other smaller parts, thereby growing the prefabricated components bigger and bigger. It was as if four teams were building one puzzle, and each team had one quarter of it to finish on their own, and when all four teams finished their work, those four quarters all came together with a few snaps and the entire puzzle was completed in record time.

Another advantage of prefabrication for the shipyards that used it most was that it created a deceptive measure for how long it actually took to build a single ship. Shipbuilding speed was measured from keel-laying until delivery of the ship, which did not take into account the days spent on prefabrication prior to a keel being laid. But that was marketing.

JULIAN MESIC, A curly-haired, middle-aged woman whom some liked to call the "first lady" of the shipyards, had one of the more ingenious ideas that she was already putting into practice. She used her background in architecture to play around with building a model Liberty ship at her desk, and when word got around, she realized that building miniature versions of all the ships Richmond was constructing could actually be useful to the shipbuilders. At Richmond's Yard No. 3, eleven artists and craftsmen began making scale models of ships in block form, using tagboard, glue, and wire, taking particular care on how the bows and sterns were constructed. A few of the models deemed especially important were built with galvanized iron instead. The models were on a scale of one-half inch equaling one foot, and every part was designed according to the actual blueprints. Liberty ships and frigates were all built to scale, down to the details in the engine rooms and deckhouses.[3]

"As the design progresses in the model from the ship's drawings, shipfitters learn how the parts fit together—which way the toes of stiffeners and frames turn, how beams and headers face, where ladders are placed and connected," *Fore 'n' Aft* wrote of their work. By building the models in sections, they were easily carried to various yard offices where they could be studied for little improvements that could be translated to the actual ship construction.

BEDFORD SAID THE flood of time-saving suggestions inspired the shipyard managers to try them all out at once, on a single hull. The ultimate lab experiment, the stunt ship to end the race, once and for all.

In the waning days of October and first few days of November, Richmond workers began piecing together prefabricated pieces of one Liberty ship, away from the shipway, all of their work taking place on land. When those prefabricated pieces were finished, they were snapped and welded together to their neighboring parts, so that two smaller prefabricated pieces became one larger prefabricated piece, and then that larger piece was attached again to its neighbor, with each step ultimately creating far fewer necessary steps to put the ship together.

"Our workmen told us, 'You order the parts, prefabricate the sections, call for volunteers, give us the tools, and we'll do the job.'"[4]

When the Richmond managers finally announced plans to build and launch a ship in exactly one week's time, breaking the unthinkable *Teal* record by three days, the workers protested. They believed it could be done even faster by prefabricating it, building an entire ship almost completely in advance and then piecing it together with lightning efficiency.

"Nuts to seven days! We're gonna do this baby in five!" they shouted.

Every single one of them received a red tag to give them clearance to move about the shipway and the ship once it came together. As the day grew closer, shipbuilding inspectors arrived in Richmond too. Bedford invited them because he wanted to make sure there was never a question of any safety corners being cut for the sake of speed. After Oregonship launched the ten-day *Teal*, rumors started circulating within days that the ship disintegrated like soggy paper at sea, which were all untrue. He prepared himself for the same attacks.

"We are proving the worth of our prefabrication methods, some of which have never been tested in actual operations before," Bedford said. "Throughout the ship, every advance step which could be taken has been taken. The workmen themselves have submitted many time and labor-saving suggestions which we are using."

With each passing day, crowds started to gather outside the shipyard and idle workers began hanging around inside it, even though they were off the clock and had nothing to do with the construction. They showed up to shifts early and they stayed late. The shipyard became so congested that voices boomed over the loudspeaker system throughout the days in early November, instructing anyone not assigned to work on the prefabricated ship to stay out of the way and avoid interfering once building began.

The word was out. Henry Kaiser was going to build a Liberty ship in a new record time. Everyone associated with the Richmond shipyards, it seemed, wanted to be there to witness the record, or they were on their way there, like Maude Byrnes. The wife of James F. Byrnes had been picked to christen the ship once it was finished and she was on a train headed west. That was more than could be said for Henry Kaiser. He was content bouncing between Washington, D.C., and New York City on business even as his California shipyard prepared to make history.

THREE THOUSAND MILES away from Richmond, the president was sitting and waiting for some of the most important news of his ten years in office. He'd come to Shangri-la, the presidential retreat in the woods of Maryland now known as Camp David, for the weekend of November 7, after giving the go-ahead for American troops to join British troops in invading North Africa. His heavy dinner of musk-ox steak was making him tired, but there could be no sleeping until he received a phone call.[5]

This was to be the war's first large-scale amphibious landing by Allied forces. Operation Torch was an invasion that Roosevelt and Churchill had been planning secretly since the summer, to open a second front aimed at preventing Hitler from gaining control of territories occupied by the French. If it succeeded, it could turn the war in their favor. But if it failed, there was no telling of the consequences, which is why one observer said Roosevelt's face showed an unusual amount of tension.

"He knew that it was largely because of his insistence that this invasion was taking place," Samuel Rosenman, the White House special counsel, said, "that on the next day many American lives might be lost."[6]

The president told his close friend Margaret "Daisy" Suckley, whom he'd invited for the weekend, that their weekend could go in one of two directions. He explained in not very subtle code that an "egg" was going to be either "hatched" or "laid" while they were away. If it "hatched," they could enjoy the weekend, but if it was "laid" he would be rushing back to Washington. Every phone call that came in was answered with nervous anticipation, until finally the phone rang and Roosevelt put the receiver to his ear and listened as a War Department official explained what was happening.

"Thank God! Thank God!" he burst out after a long delay. "That sounds grand. Congratulations. Casualties are comparatively light, much below your predictions. Thank God!"[7]

He placed the phone back in the cradle. The egg had hatched.

"We have landed in North Africa," he told those in the room. "Casualties are below expectations. We are striking back."

It did not take long for news of the invasion to reach the news wires. In Richmond, as the clock ticked toward midnight, huge crowds began gathering both inside the shipyard and surrounding it, creating a stir in the darkness when most of Richmond was asleep. Without any warning, the nervous tension that had settled over the shipyard was replaced by a sudden burst of electricity. A bulletin on the radio carried the news from Washington. Shouts rang out that a crush of British and American troops had landed in North Africa and were pushing forward. A surge of adrenaline could almost be sensed in the air.[8]

"*This is it.* Those were the words that raced through the mind of the nation at nine o'clock on the night of Saturday, November 7th," *Newsweek* trumpeted only minutes after news of Operation Torch broke. "The U.S. had at last taken the offensive on a major scale. In a nation where the sting of defeat had gone deeper than most citizens would admit, this was the best of all possible news. From one end of the country to the other there spread a feeling that now the United States was going to show the world—as it had always done before."

Eleanor Roosevelt could not resist celebrating in her near-daily newspaper column. "Sunday morning the church bells all over Great Britain pealed to celebrate the victory in Africa," she wrote.[9]

The news across the Atlantic was just as exuberant. British forces in Egypt, supported by three hundred Sherman tanks that arrived mostly on board Liberty ships, had gained momentum in El Alamein. They had captured 30,000 German soldiers, prompting Churchill to sound some of his first cautious words of enthusiasm in months.

"Now, this is not the end," he told the British citizenry. "It is not even the beginning of the end. But it is, perhaps, the end of the beginning."[10]

In Richmond, the clock struck midnight. Instead of 250,000 individual parts and pieces needed to build the record ship, the work inside the prefabrication buildings had been remarkable, and only ninety-seven massive sections needed to be lifted by cranes to the shipway. As for the mammoth main deck, normally hoisted in twenty-three separate pieces, it was instead only seven larger ones. Everything was in place for history to be made.

CHAPTER FORTY-ONE

Hull No. 440

SIXTY SECONDS INTO SUNDAY MORNING, THE KEEL FOR HULL No. 440 began to swing down into place. The silence in the shipway evaporated, replaced by so much banging, clanging, hissing, and hammering that workers had to shout to be heard. Six completed sections, the heaviest weighing more than 100 tons, were gently placed into the shipway by cranes like the biggest puzzle pieces anyone had ever seen. Within minutes, welders pounced and in the black of the night, sparks flying off the metal looked like thousands of fireflies.[1]

Every worker had been handpicked by the shipyard managers to be there. There were 509 electricians chosen, 495 drillers, 2,803 flangers or plumbers, 899 machinists, 575 painters, 289 riveters, 1,781 shipfitters, 571 sheet metal workers, 2,258 steamfitters, and the largest number of welders—7,445. Hard hats covered every head, most of them brown, but some were white, others black, and still more were silver. The riggers handling the cranes had every lift they would be making written on a master list and timed down to the second. They also had a strategy. Any time a completed unit was finished, a rigger was ready to carry it next to the shipway rather than leaving it back on its assembly table to wait for its turn to be moved closer. The second that one finished unit was lifted up onto the ship, an assembled section slid into its vacated space, ready to be hoisted on board.

If a worker walked away for a trip to the bathroom, or a fifteen-minute smoke break, they returned to find entire new sections in place and the ship resembling nothing like what they had just left minutes earlier. One year earlier, when Liberty ships were being built almost entirely in the shipways from the bottom to the top, there was enough room for 800–900 workers at most inside and around the cramped hull. Prefabrication allowed more than 2,000 shipbuilders to be working at the same time. One welder described the swarm of shipbuilders as "like maggots on a dead fish."

Bernard Taper, who was raised in London in an Orthodox Jewish household and came to America by himself on a freighter in 1929 when he was eleven, was among the volunteers chosen to build Hull No. 440. He was twenty-four years old, a recent college student who left the University of California, Berkeley before graduating who would go on to fight in the war and later become a prolific journalist and author. His first job as a shipbuilder was putting up temporary wooden supports for the bulkhead sections before they were welded together, and he later moved to installing the steel doors. In reflecting on the moments leading up to building Hull No. 440, he recalled how prefabrication had changed the mindset of the shipbuilders.

"For the laying of the keel is no longer a beginning, or even the end of a beginning, to use Churchill's phrase," Taper wrote. "For us workmen, who spend about a month putting together deckhouses, double bottoms, forepeaks, and the numerous other gigantic sections—some weighing over a hundred tons, which are ultimately hoisted on to the ship, the laying of the keel represents, in fact, the beginning of the end."[2]

Welders swarmed all over the first sections, and within two hours, the bottom shell was finished, along with the engine assembly, and four enormous bulkheads were in place. It was work that normally might have taken a week or more, and that a year earlier would have taken months. Welders, burners, riveters, painters, flangers, riggers, hangers, shipwrights, crane operators, laborers, electricians, plumbers—all surrounded the shipway, bumping into each other, rubbing shoulders, stepping around and over each other, climbing ladders to reach the top of the keel, or watching carefully as the cranes continued to lift and lower pieces into place.

Welding had replaced riveting as the most important skill in shipbuilding, but riveters did not disappear. The riveter's rat-a-tat-tat machine gun bullets were still essential and each Liberty ship had 23,095 rivets driven into it.[3] For Hull No. 440, 80 percent of those rivets were driven home on assembly tables away from the shipway.

"Didn't need a shipway for that hull," one burner working on the ship said with a grin. "Easier to have dug a ditch from assembly and floated her out."[4]

He was probably right. By eight o'clock Sunday morning, when the day shift crew took over, Hull No. 440 looked like it had been under construction for eight days, not eight hours. What had been an empty shipway twenty-four hours earlier was now the bottom half of a fully formed ship. The alley that would contain the long propeller shaft, running almost the entire length of the vessel, was also finished. Already half of the hull's 2,899 tons of steel were in place and more than 18,000 feet of welding was finished.[5]

TWO YEARS HAD passed since Cyril Thompson first carried the blueprints for his never-before-seen cargo ship across the Atlantic. Now everything that had started with the British Merchant Shipping Mission's barnstorming trip across the country was clicking in one, defining, signature boat. The preassembly of parts and prefabrication of bigger components. The benefits of welding over riveting. The highly trained and organized workforce. The mountains of necessary steel. Liberty ships at the most productive shipyards were now being built mostly on land and then assembled on the shipways. And all of that prefabrication was paying off. The only limitation was how much the cranes could lift. It made no sense to put together a 40-ton component if the nearest Whirley crane could only hoist 10.

Even the layout of the shipyards was contributing to the progress. During

World War I, the cranes were smaller and positioned away from the ways and nearer to the docks, where the ships got their final fittings and cargo. But now the cranes were stronger and working right next to the ships as they were being built, since they were capable of lifting much heavier sections. The World War I shipyards were mostly horizontal along the water. But new shipyards were more vertical and narrow, making it easier to bring giant sections of steel, many weighing 10–20 tons, alongside so they could be lifted up onto the hull from either side. The cranes on each side of the hull ran the length of the ship and moved along tracks.

When the first Liberty ships were under construction in the spring of 1941, it was estimated that 640,000 man-hours would be needed to complete one ship. Some shipyards had managed to almost cut that in half in eighteen months. The average time to build a Liberty was also dropping, from 180 days back in April to 70 days in September to 60 days in October and down to 56 days by November, less than two months per ship. Sixty-five Liberty ships were built in October, and November was already on pace to surpass that. A total of 394 Liberty ships had been built by the time Hull No. 440 began coming together, making it all but certain that by the end of 1942, American shipyards would launch more than 500 Liberty ships in one year, an astonishing tally.

WITH THE KEEL for Hull No. 440 laid, and the pace of work so fast, Bedford sent a series of telegrams to Kaiser on the East Coast. Bedford explained they were building another new ship in record speed, and that the launching would take place later that week: Wednesday, Thursday, or Friday.

"For technical reasons," Bedford wrote, "the actual launching date cannot be selected until Tuesday, November tenth at noon. And we will then advise you of the exact date and time by wire."[6]

He invited Kaiser and his wife to Richmond to celebrate the launching and to attend a dinner afterward. But he implored his boss to please maintain the secret, knowing how much Kaiser liked to boast about his shipyards to the press.

"Information concerning this launching is extremely confidential and we would appreciate no information concerning it being released to the press or public," Bedford wrote. "Thank you for your cooperation."

In a separate telegram, Bedford told Kaiser the idea for the ship was born after the "launching of the 10-day boat at Oregon Shipbuilding Corporation," and he said he had received more than 250 letters with suggestions to improve prefabrication and production methods. He said the ship's keel had already been laid in a short time and that workers were arriving at the shipyard one or two hours ahead of their schedule "in order to watch the operation."

Because all of the stunt ships had been West Coast projects directly credited to Kaiser's shipyards, Bedford told Kaiser that if the work continued on schedule, he preferred to tip off the Bay Area newspapers first.

IT WAS OUR THOUGHT THAT SINCE THE NEWSPAPERS HERE HAVE COOPERATED BY NOT RELEASING THE INFORMATION AND SINCE THEY ARE ON THE GROUND THAT THE STORY SHOULD BE RELEASED THROUGH THEM AND NOT IN THE EAST FIRST.[7]

One of the most time-consuming tasks in building an ordinary Liberty ship was the backbreaking work of attaching the steam fittings, pumps, freshwater tanks for drinking and showering, and machinery to the ship's floor. It required workers to crawl around on the hard metal, reach into tight corners, and secure the foundations so that nothing moved when the ship was out on the ocean. But for Hull No. 440, all of that work had been done days ago, on dry land, and then built into the bottom pieces so that when the hull came together, the guts were already attached inside. In total, six miles of pipes were fitted together in prefabrication before building even began, leaving only the job of joining the various systems together and testing them.

One worker said that the hull construction went so smoothly at the start, their biggest obstacle on the first day was persuading anyone who was not working on the ship to stay out of the way of those who were.

"No wonder," he admitted. "It was something to see—just one big seething mass of shipfitters, welders, shippers. Ten chippers hacking away on a transverse seam, hose, and cable a foot deep. I'll be blind and deaf by next week, but it's worth it, I guess."[8]

The Sunday night crew arrived with the responsibility of attaching the 135-ton, 21-foot-tall Hendy engine. By the time they arrived more than 1,300 tons of steel had already been erected, five or six times the usual amount for a single day, and they had completed 16,000 feet of welding, twice the usual amount. The boilers were in place too. Ordinarily the engine was put together away from the ship over three weeks by twenty-five marine machinists. The engine was preassembled in five days and then lifted into place in three separate parts—base, cylinders, condenser—in one hour. After that, it was ready to whirr in two days.

Several more 50-ton bulkheads were placed in the hull, creating the finished compartments that would divide the ship's different sections and cargo holds. With the guts of the ship in place by the end of day two, it was time to attach the main deck.

The main deck of the Liberty ship arrived early on Tuesday morning on trailers in seven huge sections. Each one was carefully hoisted by two cranes and laid flat into place, where welders quickly pounced and secured them. As the cranes moved in, McFarland constantly had to clear a path for prefabricated parts to reach the ship through the throng of onlookers who couldn't stay away. When the main deck was attached, it allowed a thousand workers at once to move about freely on a wide surface. But it also created a more dangerous workspace, since the deck was instantly blanketed with miles and miles of twisted cables from the tools of the welders and burners. One false step was a surefire way to trip and fall. As builders walked around the square holes of the gigantic cargo holds, they looked like ants on an airport tarmac.

After forty-eight hours of construction, Hull No. 440 began to look like a fully formed 441-foot Liberty ship from the bottom of the keel up to the deck. It was time to bring in the most important, largest, and heaviest prefabricated component of all.

A LIBERTY SHIP was not a Liberty ship without its deckhouse, where much of the crew would sleep and eat and shower, where the captain could navigate from, and from where the radio operators communicated with the shore. As day two of construction wound down, excitement began to build. If Hull No. 440's deckhouse could be completed and installed early on Tuesday, day three, that would leave only decorative touches like painting, along with the electrical wiring and some final welding for the next day.

When it came time to prepare Hull 440's deckhouse for installation, extra precautions were taken. An accident on a rainy afternoon three weeks earlier in Vancouver, Washington, had to be weighing on the Richmond shipbuilders. All of the newspapers had covered it. The last thing they wanted to happen in their pursuit of a speed record was to repeat the embarrassing and almost fatal mistakes at Henry Kaiser's shipyard in Vancouver.

The rush to prefabricate more and more of each individual Liberty ship, combined with the West Coast shipbuilders' race to build their ships faster and faster, heightened the dangers inside the yards. It's why McFarland had reminded his workers in Richmond that SAFETY PAYS! Prefabrication required lifting heavier sections, with multiple cranes working in tandem, a delicate skill that could have disastrous consequences. And workers picking up their pace at welding or cutting steel or fastening bolts increased the possibility of steps being missed, bolts being left loose, and welding seals not being watertight, any of which could have disastrous consequences at sea.

A month earlier, on October 14 in Vancouver, four cranes were hoisting a completed deckhouse up onto the main deck of the SS *Samuel Colt*. The ship had come together in less than a month, and it was launched in Portland, Oregon, one day earlier before being towed ten miles north up the Willamette River, where it was to be finished at the Vancouver yard. In order to make sure the deckhouse could be lifted high enough to get over the lip of the ship's deck, water had to be pumped into the cargo holds to simulate heavy cargo and lower it in the water.

Lifting a three-story deckhouse required delicate skill. Crane operators had to make sure it stayed perfectly balanced and did not tilt in midair, putting more strain on one crane than the others. Usually a few workers rode in the deckhouse as it was being lifted so they could be the first ones to help attach it to the deck as soon as it touched down. In Vancouver, that task fell to a pair of men, George Walker, a shipyard guard, and Stanley Bergman, a rigging superintendent.

A finished Liberty ship deckhouse was a structure the size of a small house, with forty-seven individual fully outfitted cabins, lighting and plumbing fixtures installed, and seats, storage lockers, and file cabinets all in place. One workman with a flair for interior design had even placed a vase of flowers on one of the stateroom's tables as the *Samuel Colt* deckhouse was being lifted. An optimistic gesture, to say the least.

But just as the four crane operators, all working as one, managed to get the deckhouse up and over the *Samuel Colt's* main deck, one corner of it began to tilt, causing a giant screech, and the cables and I-beams on two of the cranes gave way and snapped. The deckhouse crashed to the deck floor from twenty-five feet overhead. The Liberty ship rocked precariously for a few seconds before righting itself, and for several panicked moments it was feared, incorrectly, that the deckhouse had pinned or crushed a number of workers on the ship's deck.[9]

Walker suffered a fractured foot and badly injured knee, and when he was asked later at the hospital to describe what happened, he was still in shock and had no memory of the accident. Bergman somehow escaped unscathed. As for the deckhouse and the *Samuel Colt*, both suffered minor damages. The scattered wreckage on the deck served as a terrifying reminder to shipbuilders across the country that they could never relax their safety standards, and that one misstep could have deadly consequences.

DESPITE A STEADY rain that fell most of Monday into the nighttime, nothing slowed the progress, and each new component became a reminder that Liberty ships were United States vessels. The ship's boilers from Los Angeles were installed. Ventilators built in Chicago went in. A giant compass all the way from Boston was placed into the hull so the workers below deck would know which way is north, south, east, or west when they got directions from the helm. The main anchor was installed, labeled from New York City, and so was a propeller from Eddystone, Pennsylvania.

Special attention was paid to the installation of the lifeboats since it was so likely that the plodding, 12-knot Liberty ship would come under attack from a German U-boat, in which case the lifeboats could be the crew's only chance at survival. Each Liberty got four lifeboats, with seating for thirty-one people apiece, all of them equipped with oars, red sails, food, water, first-aid equipment, and signals for passing ships (one of them was also equipped with a motor). The lifeboats were being built in a converted stove factory in land-locked Kokomo, Indiana, more than a thousand miles from either coast. That's where Globe American Corporation was building lifeboats for the United States Merchant Marine, cranking out one 3,500-pound boat every two hours.

Daybreak on Tuesday, day three, saw the rain stop, and a cold fog took its place. One worker, worried that progress has slowed, shouted out, "We're five hours behind. We have to make up for it."

It was a frenzy of activity. Workers sitting atop bulkheads attached clips into place, a rigger saved precious minutes by grabbing a rope and swinging down to the hull like Tarzan, another crewman lugged a hundred-pound fan up a twenty-foot-tall ladder. Then warning bells rang out louder than any other noise emanating from the ship. Four cranes emerged from the fog, moving in slow motion. It was 4:59 in the afternoon.

"Heads up!" a rigger yelled to anyone within earshot.[10]

When Joe Fabry saw it coming, he couldn't believe something so big had been prebuilt down to the last detail and was now just going to be plopped onto the deck of the record ship he'd been building. He'd been working on Richmond Liberty ships for months, mostly as a flanger connecting pipes and valves, and when he first saw the towering deckhouse approach Hull No. 440 in four parts, he was dumbfounded.

"It has three floors and you see rooms and stairs, looking like a house with the front wall ripped off by a bomb but the interior untouched," he said of that moment. "The galley is so fully equipped you could go right in and cook a meal for the whole gang. The captain's room is complete up to the inkpot on the desk."[11] From his ground-level view, he saw the officers' quarters, showers, and toilets, and he looked straight into the wheelhouse, where he could see an array of switchboards and dials.

Bernard Taper was watching as well, but he had a different thought. "As the deckhouse was hoisted through the air we half expected to see a captain—prefabricated, too, perhaps—already pacing the bridge, nervously keeping a sharp eye out for submarines."[12]

Another observer described the moment as watching a "finished bungalow" be moved "from one lot to another without cracking a single vase." In fact, the deckhouse was so polished that an electric fan was already plugged into its socket. Electric clocks, desks, inkwells, and coat hangers were all inside, and there were signs above the toilets that read WATER UNFIT FOR DRINKING.

Fabry stood and watched as the first section was lifted by the Whirley cranes, all working together, and dropped as soft as a pillow onto the deck. The first section was in place by 5:27 p.m., less than half an hour from lift to placement. The second section was in place at 6:49 p.m., the third section at 7:31 p.m., and the last one at 9:05 p.m. Four lifts completed without a glitch and without any mishap like what occurred in Vancouver.

"Victory is within reach," Fabry thought at the moment. "We've caught up with those five hours lost through rain and fog, and on the fourth day we are ahead of schedule."

THE PLACEMENT OF the deckhouse meant that 90 percent of the Liberty ship was built by the end of day three and heading into Wednesday. Hull No. 440 was on pace to be finished not in seven days like McFarland first suggested, and not in five days like his workers had countered. McFarland and Bedford agreed that four days was within reach.

Tuesday night into early Wednesday morning, the orange glow from hundreds of welding torches lit up the nearly completed ship. The ship's propeller was slid into place and required careful adjusting before it could be secured. The cranes returned just before midnight carrying the forward gun platform, and Fabry noticed how it was pointed to the west.

"In the west, there's Japan," he thought.

At 3 a.m., Fabry and a group of workers paused for a nighttime lunch and some coffee. When they came back outside just as the sun was coming up, they saw it. The piece with the ship's name that had been lying on the ground only a few days earlier was in place. On its fourth day of construction, Hull No. 440 was now the SS *Robert E. Peary*. But it was hardly time to rest.

Wednesday morning, the *Oakland Tribune* shouted across its front-page news of the "Richmond 'Wonder Ship.'"

"Worldwide attention is focused on Richmond Shipyard No. 2 today as work progresses rapidly on what is hoped to be the quickest job of shipbuilding in history," the story began. It hinted at questions of safety, and whether the rushed ship would be as seaworthy as every other Liberty ship. Tim Bedford, the younger brother of Clay and the assistant manager of the shipyard, tried to put that to rest.

"Those not in touch with the picture here can't realize that it is just as possible to turn out a workmanlike job in a hurry as it was for Ford to build millions of his cars," he said. "The secret, of course, is prefabrication."[13]

With the ship 90 percent finished, a new urgency took over. Clay Bedford knew the rules—a shipyard was not able to add a new ship to its totals until after a launch took place.

"We are not primarily trying to break any records," he declared, when asked what was so important about this particular Liberty ship. "Our primary purpose has been the experimenting in new prefabrication methods. After receiving hundreds of valuable suggestions and time-saving inventions from our workers, we all decided to try them and see what would happen."

Ever since Edgar Kaiser implored him to come to Portland, Oregon, to witness the launching of the 10-day SS *Joseph Teal* in the presence of the president of the United States, Bedford knew that it was a beatable number. But even he did not expect his team to cut an astonishing record in half.

CHAPTER FORTY-TWO

"Nuts to Seven Days"

THE BAY AREA WEATHER ON THURSDAY MORNING, NOVEM-
ber 12, was perfect, mid-60s with a slight breeze. The late-night rain that had
drenched some of the workers earlier in the week was gone, replaced by intermit-
tent fog. The sun was coming up and already the grounds inside the Richmond
shipyard were overrun. Estimates were that 25,000 people showed up, and it
looked like half of them were wearing silver, black, brown, or white hard hats.
For three full days, thousands of off-duty shipbuilders had been coming out since
12:01 a.m. on Sunday to watch Hull No. 440 come together, and thousands more
showed up for their shifts early or stayed after their shift ended. They all understood it was going to be a phony record, because the amount of prefabrication put
into this one ship could not be replicated over and over. But they had accepted
that. It would be *their* phony record, which is why nobody wanted to leave.

Now on day four, thousands of shipbuilders were joined by curious businessmen in their three-piece suits and fedoras, with cigarettes hanging from their
lips, along with mothers who came out with their young children. Richmond
families who had been taking in shipbuilders for almost two years, moving
out of their own bedrooms to earn some extra money and do their small part
in the war effort, were not going to miss this moment.

THE EUPHORIA FILLING the air in Richmond, however, was absent across the country in Washington. Despite the military success of Operation Torch, the politics of it turned ugly almost overnight. Even though Roosevelt had assured the French people in North Africa that American troops were not there to invade them, but rather had come to help liberate them, his message failed to resonate. The French government proclaimed, "We are attacked! We shall defend ourselves."

Days after he had rejoiced over news of the successful invasion, Roosevelt now felt betrayed. He obsessed throughout the week about his fiercest critics and he read every word by the newspaper columnists who were attacking him. He used leisurely drives in the countryside and relaxing dinners to calm his nerves. The long-planned invasion had succeeded in pushing back German forces, yet somehow it felt like a failure. He needed to escape the Washington bubble and on Thursday he planned a trip to his home in Hyde Park for the weekend to clear his head. His public approval rating, which had soared past 80 percent at the start of 1942 after Pearl Harbor, had dropped down to 72 percent by November.[1]

UP ON BOARD the record ship, the deck of Hull No. 440 was hosed down of debris, the hoses quickly rolled up, welding machines were carried off, and the hull was separated from the enormous scaffolding surrounding it. Speed, not neatness, was the priority just this one time. The freshly painted gray Liberty ship got a dash of color when the string of flags went up, stretching from bow to stern. A launching platform was set up in the hull's enormous shadow.

A sign went up on the side of the deckhouse: COMPLIMENTS OF MEN AT PREFAB PLANT. LOTS OF LUCK![2]

On the bow, workers draped two American flags over each side of the ship, sandwiching a white board with black type that was hoisted high enough for anyone to see. An oversize number 4 was smack in the middle of it to leave no doubt about the record.

ROBERT E. PEARY
KEEL LAID NOV 8, '42. 12:01 A.M.
LAUNCHED NOV 12, '42. 3:30 P.M.
4 DAYS. 15 HOURS. 29 MINUTES

When Robert E. Peary was chosen to be honored with a Liberty ship, there was no way to anticipate that it would be painted on a record-breaking, four-day ship built in America's newest shipbuilding capital, Richmond, California. But now that it was there, high up on the ship's stern, the name seemed more appropriate than anyone could have imagined. Born in 1856, Robert Edwin Peary grew up to become a civil engineer for the United States Navy and later one of America's great explorers. He made his first expedition to the Arctic in 1886 and continued exploring the region for years, until he made history on April 6, 1909. After marching across the frozen Arctic Ocean for thirty-seven days, Peary's observations showed him to be precisely at 90 degrees latitude north, the North Pole. He staked an American flag in the ground. A civil engineer, an explorer, a discoverer—everything that defined Peary defined the Liberty ship experiment. The *San Francisco Chronicle* went one step further, connecting Peary, who died in 1920, with the shipbuilding king, describing Peary as the "man who could not fail," words that just as easily fit Henry Kaiser.

By noon, Shipyard No. 2 was wall-to-wall people and the podium next to the ship began to fill up with dignitaries. The most important one, however, was nowhere to be seen. Despite the personal invitation from Bedford delivered by telegram, giving him advance notice of the record-breaking ship, Kaiser stayed on the East Coast, in New York City. He sent a telegram of congratulations to be read to his workers.

"You have proved you are capable of meeting any challenge," Kaiser wrote. "This is your gift to the world. And above all you have proved the value of the fifth freedom—the right to produce."[3]

With Kaiser absent, Monroe Deutsch, the president of the University of California, was asked to be the event's featured speaker. A little before two o'clock in the afternoon, the ceremony got underway, with music, the hoisting of an American flag up a flagpole, and the unveiling of photos of the ship under construction. When Deutsch took the stand, he told the shipbuilders to never underestimate their role in the war.

"You are building bridges to freedom and to victory!" he shouted. "You builders of ships are making the links, the cables that bind us to our sister nations—ships that carry men, ships that carry food, ships that carry planes, ships that carry tanks, ships that carry munitions. Without ships we could not fight; we could not win."[4]

He finished his stirring speech by waving his hat in the air, prompting the sea of shipbuilders looking up at him to wave theirs back.

A FEW MINUTES after three, the podium buzzed with new activity. The sponsor of the ship, Maude B. Byrnes, made her way up the steps, wearing a blue coat with plump white flowers on the front, and a pink flowered hat atop her silver hair. She was joined on the podium by a younger, dark-haired woman, Mrs. S. Otis Bland, the wife of a Virginia congressman who had accompanied Mrs. Byrnes from Washington. As the two women stood waiting, Mrs. Bland smiled as she was handed a bouquet of flowers, while Mrs. Byrnes took hold of a champagne bottle wrapped up in an American flag. Photographers positioned themselves a few feet away, their flashbulbs ready for the moment. At 3:26 p.m., she stepped forward and with no hesitation she slammed the bottle against the ship's hull. It exploded in a burst of bubbly, drenching the hull along with her coat. The ship instantly began its brisk slide down the way into the bay, taking less than ten seconds to splash into the water. As it drifted away, the crowd stood and watched, almost as if they needed to see with their own eyes that it wasn't sinking, and that after just four days, fifteen hours, and twenty-nine minutes of construction, the SS *Robert E. Peary* was a genuine, floating Liberty ship.

"There she goes!" some of the shipbuilders shouted as they pointed toward their miracle ship, a cry that had become a part of every launching.

Bernard Taper was standing only a few feet from where the champagne bottle had been smashed against the hull, and he experienced an odd sensation watching the *Peary* drift away.

"From where I was standing beside the launching platform," he said, "it seemed to grow larger as it slid away, a strange reversal of the laws of perspective due probably to the fact that its sweeping outlines had become perceptible for the first time."[5]

Reporters who were there covered the moment gleefully. "She went down the ways as a challenge to the Axis dictators and all their claims of America's softness and slowness," the *San Francisco Chronicle* wrote the next day. "By this time next week, she may be on her way to Iceland, to Algiers or Madagascar, loaded with wheat or dive bombers or bullets, no longer a wondership, but just another gray, brine-drenched unit in the bridge of ships to victory."

It was a personal moment for many of the workers too. The project's welding supervisor, Tony Vinelli, managed to collect a clip off of the red, white, and blue ribbon from the bottle of champagne used to christen the *Peary*. He put it into his pocket and would hold on to it for more than fifty years.[6]

Even Edgar Kaiser's shipbuilders in Oregon admitted to being impressed, sending a congratulatory note along with a halfhearted tease. "That was a great job, but if we did cut your time in half what in hell would you do then?"[7]

A REAL-TIME LOG that was kept of the construction effort tallied up 12,000 workers who contributed to the construction. "Most had never worked in a shipyard before but all learned quickly," the log said.

But no log could reflect what Joseph Fabry realized as the *Peary* was in its final hours of work. It wasn't about the number of workers who pulled off the four-day ship, it was about who those shipbuilders represented. The idea that white Okies and Arkies and Texies from middle-America farmland could work so easily alongside African, Hispanic, and Asian Americans was an unimaginable thought before the war. So was the idea of men welding together a cargo ship alongside women, sometimes even alongside their wives.

"We forgot about our squabbles and joined forces for the wonderboat," Fabry reflected.

As they had promised, Kaiser's shipbuilders learned valuable lessons in the construction of Hull No. 440.

For the first time in Liberty ship history, laying the keel involved dropping just six main sections into place and welding them together, creating the entire bottom shell in minutes and saving hundreds of man-hours for future Liberty ships. An equal amount of time was saved by having all of the steam and pipe fittings, and pump and machinery foundations, built into the ship's bottom on the assembly tables and away from the shipway. And when it came time to move the ship's enormous bottom units, they were pieced together as five pieces, the largest one weighing more than 100 tons, instead of a dozen smaller sections. That change meant the slow-moving cranes had to make half the number of heavy lifts, an enormous time-saver. The bulkheads that divided compartments were all cut in advance, away from the shipway, and fitted to sections before being brought out. The biggest time-saving maneuver by far was pre-building the entire deckhouse and lifting it up on the deck in only four sections, eliminating thousands of man hours.

As Fabry and his friends watched her slide into the water, he knew what they were all thinking: "There she goes—MY wonderboat!"[8]

Thirty seconds after the *Peary* splashed into San Francisco Bay and tugboats pulled up alongside her to bring her to the outfitting dock, new keel blocks were in place at Richmond Yard No. 2. A new keel was laid in minutes.

When the crewmen responsible for the final touches on board the *Robert E. Peary* were finally permitted to climb on board later that afternoon, they stumbled into a brief note that was scribbled beside a small and insignificant weld on the bridge deck:

"She is O.K. Put her on the pond now. She will float."[9]

CHAPTER FORTY-THREE

Aboard the *Peary*

WEARING HIS DRESS BLUES, EIGHTEEN-YEAR-OLD JAMES Horton sat in the passenger seat of the pickup truck as it crossed the San Francisco Bay Bridge just after noon.[1] As he looked up and down the bay, all he saw were ships and more ships. "Staggering" was the word that came to his mind. A signalman with the Navy Armed Guard, he was on day seven of his ship leave after serving seven months aboard the cargo steamer SS *Jane Christenson*. He still had a few days left of freedom when a petty officer asked him if he wanted to be assigned to a new ship right away. Without even thinking, he blurted out, "Yes!" The next thing he knew, he was catching a ride across the bay while feeling butterflies in his stomach, wondering if he should have waited and spent more time with his friends and family. He remembered he was supposed to be home for dinner that night at six o'clock.

"What kind of ship am I going aboard?" he asked the driver.

"A new Liberty," his driver answered. It was already fully loaded and ready to sail.

After driving along the Embarcadero, they pulled up to a pier and there it was, its name inscribed in white at the very top of the hull: SS *Robert E. Peary*. As he looked up at the ship, his bag started to dig into his shoulder. He climbed up the gangway and was told to go claim one of the last few empty bunks. It was his first time on a Liberty ship, but the eighteen-year-old was already a veteran of the seas.

He'd first joined the Navy at sixteen, only to get dismissed out for lying on his application—a common violation as teenage boys looked to join the fight after Pearl Harbor. When he turned seventeen, his mother took him back to the recruiting office so he could sign up legally. His parents had divorced when he was five and he was raised by his single mother along with his three sisters. He was again assigned to the Navy Armed Guard and spent more than half a year at sea aboard six different merchant ships. When he learned that after six months aboard a ship or stationed at a base, he was entitled to a seven-day leave, he grabbed it. "We never knew when this might be the last leave for a very a long time," he thought. After his seven days were up, he reported back to his base, which is when he learned his new assignment.

After grabbing a top bunk on the *Peary*, he noticed how everything looked and smelled new—the paint, the wood panels, the leather chairs. Even the stainless-steel sinks glistened. While he was unpacking, he heard a voice from behind. A tall, lanky teenager introduced himself as Al Sayers, a signalman from Seattle. He said this was going to be his first trip to sea, and the excitement was visible on his face. The two decided to go explore their new ship together. As they walked around, it felt like it was still a work in progress, with painters busy spraying and dabbing with brushes.

"Did you know this ship had been built in four days?" Sayers said to Horton.

Horton thought he misheard him. "You mean forty days or four months, maybe?"

"No. You heard me right the first time. Four days, fifteen hours, and twenty-nine minutes and right now they are trying for a record loading time, as well."

Sayers led them to a plaque posted near Cargo Hold No. 3 just below the ship's bridge that confirmed his story. Horton asked if there was any idea when they might sail, and Sayers said they hoped to leave that very evening. Horton panicked. He hadn't even said goodbye to anyone. He was expected home for dinner. He ran back to the gangway and off the ship and found a public pay phone. He called home and one of his three sisters answered. Half an hour later, a Marine truck pulled up to the pier and Horton's mother jumped out and ran straight into her son's arms for a hug. When he boasted to her that his ship had been built in only four days, she wasn't so thrilled. He could see the worry of a mother in her eyes.

"I guess for her, it was bad enough having a son so young in the service in time of war," Horton would recall, "and now he was aboard a ship that might very well fall to pieces before it got to its destination."

His mother turned to her son's new friend and gave his arm a gentle squeeze.

"Please, I would appreciate it if you would take care of Jim and keep an eye out for him, thank you," she said to Sayers. He had to stifle a laugh, knowing he would be teasing Horton throughout their journey about being the guardian of his body.

When his mother left the pier, Horton felt a wave of sadness come over him, as the gravity of the moment suddenly hit him. He thought to himself, *Why am I here? This terrible, tragic war. What's ahead for me on this trip? Will I ever return?* His new shipmate and friend tapped his shoulder, and they reboarded their ship.

They watched as two pieces of a Landing Craft, Tank were lowered into a cargo hold, and that's when they learned their destination: New Caledonia. A tugboat's toot startled them, then came a shout from the ship's bridge to raise the string of call letters and the pilot flag. Before they knew it, the lines to the pier were untied and the *Peary* was pulled away, with Captain Harold E. Widmeyer, a veteran seaman from San Pedro, California, at the helm. One last check was needed before they could leave the bay—the ship's mine-detecting equipment had to be confirmed as working. As she picked up steam and headed out, a water taxi pulled up alongside and the painters who had been on board for some final touch-ups were unloaded. A chilly breeze sent Horton and Sayers looking for cover, and they huddled behind the smokestack and listened to the seawater slapping the side of the ship.

"We passed under the Golden Gate Bridge, its huge dark shadow looming above us and into the darkness of the channel," Horton wrote later of the moment.

———

LIKE A MISCHIEVOUS teenager, the SS *Robert E. Peary* slinked out of the bay quietly at seven o'clock in the evening on Saturday, November 21, 1942. She had been in the outfitting docks for only nine days, a sign of how far the shipyards had come from the days when outfitting could take a month or two. By one in the morning, she was in open waters and every light on board was blacked out to help avoid detection from any lurking Japanese subs. Horton recalled later hearing about a telegram the Japanese sent to Washington indicating that the *Peary* had a bull's-eye on it for the enemy. "The Japanese stated that when they spotted it, they would sink it in four minutes," Horton said.

Up on deck rested two commando landing boats, strapped down tight. They were the reason why in addition to the crew of seventy-one on board, thirteen additional naval commando officers and ten ensigns joined them. It had taken four and a half days to build her. Then another four days were needed to load her up with tanks, jeeps, and ammunition, and fill three cargo holds with canned and concentrated food to feed Navy forces preparing for an armed invasion somewhere in the Pacific. Separate from that was all of the meat, fish, fruit, vegetables, and dry goods needed to feed nearly a hundred passengers for months.

When daylight arrived on Sunday, Charles Smith, the chief cook on board, a forty-five-year-old veteran of two decades at sea, noticed something surprising as he looked out at the horizon.

"No convoy—no planes, no destroyers, no battleships," he jotted down in a diary. "We are just sneaking along all alone, hoping and praying we won't be intercepted."[2]

Even though no lights were allowed to be turned on, submarine sightings were inevitable, and when one happened a few days into the *Peary*'s trip, the entire crew became tense. Around noon the chief engineer approached the captain on the bridge, and then walked away, and without any warning, the ship slowed and fell silent. The only sounds were the water lapping against the hull, the slightest movement of the cargo shifting down below in the holds, and a squawking bird off in the distance. To Horton, the ship felt adrift, or DIW, for dead in the water, but nobody questioned why. Then, just as abruptly an hour later the telegraph began to ring, a message was relayed, and the engine's vibrations started up again. The crew applauded their ship coming back to life. "What a great moment of relief," Horton remembered, though at the same time he felt a sense of nervousness. Like everyone on board, he knew that the farther they went into the South Pacific, closer to Japanese-held territory, the greater the risk of torpedoes whistling toward them.

It did not take long for a rhythm of the days to settle in. Breakfast at a quarter to seven every morning. Watchers for the gun crew took four-hour shifts, starting at four in the morning. A coffee break came at ten o'clock for those on watch, and then at eleven thirty lunch began. Another coffee break came around two in the afternoon and dinner started around five o'clock. The day was filled with chores, from washing clothes to writing letters home to maintaining the battle stations and making sure the guns were clean. Fire drills and lifeboat drills were weekly happenings and they were treated with deadly seriousness. During peacetime, a call to abandon ship was a remote possibility, but in wartime, everyone on board understood it was a very real scenario. The biggest challenge was avoiding complacency with nothing but ocean and horizon in every direction.

AS THEIR COURSE took them westward, each day at sea seemed to get warmer and warmer, and some crewmen broke out in a heat rash. When Thanksgiving Day arrived, Smith was eager to serve up a feast and give the crew something to look forward to. He roasted five giant turkeys, filled bowls and bowls of cranberry sauce, and baked too many pumpkin pies to count. "A real dinner," in his words.

One week later, the *Peary* crossed the equator and temperatures on board seemed to climb with every hour after that. Everybody knew they were headed toward Australia, where summer temperatures were regularly in the 90s. Ten days of sailing had passed quietly, too quietly for Smith, who kept hearing chatter about Japanese attacks on Allied ships and figured it was only a matter of time before theirs came.

When the general quarters bell rang at six o'clock in the evening on Wednesday, December 2, he wondered if this was it. Four watchmen spotted what they thought was a Japanese submarine and then a flare in the sky. Smith hustled into his knee-length slicker, pulled on a life preserver, grabbed two cans of his snuff along with a blanket, and sprinted up to the main deck, anticipating an order to abandon ship and start lowering the four lifeboats into the water. But four hours later, nothing had happened. He hadn't seen another ship since leaving San Francisco Bay. With his nerves rattled from the false alarm on deck, Smith took a moment to reflect.

"These waters are full of sharks and you might as well go down with the ship as be eaten up by those bastards," Smith wrote. "Some of them are as large as three men."

JUST ONE MONTH earlier, the *Robert E. Peary* did not exist. It was nothing but blueprints and buckets of bolts for Hull No. 440, an idea born out of a young and ambitious British shipbuilder's idea for a tramp steamer, and then by hundreds of suggestions made by thousands of excited shipbuilders who wanted to see how fast they could build one 441-foot-long, ten-story-tall cargo ship. An enormous collection of parts lay scattered around a former mudflat on the California coast that had been transformed into a revolutionary shipyard that was owned by a dynamic American businessman. And then, like magic, those 250,000 pieces and parts all came together in the shape of a Liberty ship in precisely four days, fifteen hours, and twenty-nine minutes. Some of those pieces even created the galley kitchen in which Smith had just prepared a Thanksgiving meal in the middle of the Pacific Ocean for a hundred starving sailors. When the head chef allowed himself to think about all of this, the collective achievement of the *Robert E. Peary*, he couldn't hide his awe.

"We aren't going to be back in the U.S. for a long time," Smith jotted down. "And they may take us to the east coast to show this wonder in shipbuilding and sailing to the people there, as an example of what the U.S. really can do."

AFTER THREE AND a half weeks, New Caledonia came into sight. It was an overcast and humid day as the *Peary* docked in a small bay where the crew could unload two tanks. The following day they moved to a different pier to refuel and collect fresh water for drinking, cooking, and bathing. Standing on the deck, Horton watched closely as the *Peary* pulled up alongside another Liberty ship that was docked. The two ships were identical in every way, he noticed—until he saw the twisted metal below, and the large, gaping hole in the bridge, clear evidence of some sort of attack and explosion. When Horton asked about what happened, he was told a Japanese aircraft had been hit by antiaircraft fire near New Guinea and seemed to intentionally dive into the Liberty ship.

"This was my first real encounter with anything actually tied with the war itself," he recalled later in a journal entry, "and it made you very aware, suddenly, how close you now were to the real war."

Six months later, the *Peary* cruised up the eastern coast of South America as part of a large convoy of ships, stopping first in Cuba and then sailing past the Florida tip and up to Savannah, Georgia. From Savannah, with the *Peary* loaded up with cotton bales, a slightly lighter load than Sherman tanks, the convoy shrunk to just five ships on its way to New York. For Horton, the East Coast was foreign land, as he'd never left San Francisco except on board his ships. The air was crisper than he was used to and for the first time he slipped on a cloth face mask to protect himself from the wind and cold water splashing up deck. As their ship pulled into New York Harbor, the sight that Horton had anxiously awaited came into view. It was not what he expected.

"I was always under the impression that the Statue of Liberty was made of cement or some kind of stone, but as we got nearer, I could see that it was a pale green color, which startled me." As they all stared at it, one of the merchant crewmen explained that the base was made of cement, and the statue was made of copper. The closer they got, the more enormous it looked. But in fact, at 305 feet tall, from her base to the torch, and weighing 450,000 pounds, Lady Liberty would have rested quite comfortably on the deck of the *Robert E. Peary*, just another piece of oversize cargo.

A FEW DAYS later, Horton found himself standing inside Pennsylvania Station, holding his leave papers, trying to find the train that would take him and a few of his fellow crewmen west, back to their families. A conductor pointed him to his platform and told him it was a five-day trip to California with the first stop in Chicago. When another conductor saw the group of sailors approaching the train, he waved for them to bypass the long line of waiting passengers and go straight to the front. None of the other passengers complained about being passed by the sailors and instead Horton saw nothing but smiles and nods. "Talk about being very grateful," he thought to himself.

The group had paid only for upright bench seats rather than splurging for the more expensive sleeper quarters. They were not worried about being able to fall asleep. They had just spent a year cramped inside a 441-foot-long cargo ship sleeping on flimsy mattresses while rocking back and forth on choppy ocean waters and fending off Nazi submarines. A quiet, cross-country train ride would feel like a baby's soft crib compared to their time inside a steel box at sea. Then, just as the train pulled away from Penn Station, a friendly conductor came by to check on them. He handed over some blankets and pillows so the sailors of the *Robert E. Peary* could be sure and get some comfortable shuteye.

EPILOGUE

From Liberty to Victory

BY THE TIME THE *PEARY* MADE HER FIRST VOYAGE, THE LEG-
acy of the Liberty ship program was secure. "The U.S. today is turning out five
new merchant ships every 24 hours—more than the rest of the world combined,"
Henry Kaiser said.[1] They were not all Liberty ships; there were tankers and more
modern cargo ships, but the speed with which they were all produced was unques-
tionably the result of what shipbuilders learned from the Liberty ship program.

A chart of Liberty ship production from the end of 1941 until the fall of
1945 when Japan surrendered shows two trends, one rising, one falling. The
one going up tracks the volume of new ships launched each month, from 2
in December 1941, to 82 in December 1942, to 118 by December 1943. In total,
American shipyards produced 2,710 Liberty ships in essentially four years,
peaking in the spring and summer of 1943, when almost 800 ships were built in
seven months, a remarkable pace considering that when the program began the
shipbuilders had no idea what a single Liberty ship was supposed to even look
like. They figured it out fast, thanks in large part to Henry Kaiser's shipyards,
which produced more than half of all Liberty ships—1,490. The second trend,
the one going down, shows the impressive decline in the average number of
days it took to complete a Liberty ship. At the start of President Roosevelt's

program, 241 days were needed for one ship, on average, or approximately eight months. Prefabrication changed everything. One year later, the average time had dropped all the way down to 55 days, or less than two months. And a year after that, the average time per ship in December 1943 was down to 42 days, the fastest month recorded.

All that speed was critical if the Allies were to crank out ships faster than Germany could sink them. But with that speed came sacrifice. In the two months after the *Peary* was finished, ten different Liberty ships suffered alarming cracks in their hulls or their decks. But it was a non-Liberty cargo ship that cracked with such a jarring force that the Maritime Commission could no longer ignore the issue and was forced to reevaluate the emergency shipbuilding program.[2]

Two months after the four-day Wonderboat set sail, on the night of January 16, 1943, another Kaiser ship, the enormous 523-foot-long, 15,000-ton tanker SS *Schenectady*, was floating in its outfitting dock at the new Swan Island Yard in Portland, Oregon. The air temperature was freezing at 26 degrees, but there was no ice in the water, which was considerably warmer. The Columbia River showed only slight ripples and the *Schenectady* bobbed gently up and down. Only hours before, she had passed her sea trial, and her maiden voyage was scheduled for the next day. With no warning, there was a loud roar, almost like an explosion; it was heard a mile away. The *Schenectady* split in two. For observers standing on shore, it was a shocking sight as a fracture across the main deck caused each half of the ship to jackknife and stand up almost perpendicular in the water. The bottom plates held, and she didn't sink. It all happened in seconds and in a ship less than one day old.

When the news reached them, Kaiser and Howard Vickery immediately understood the potential consequences of the *Schenectady*'s failure, and both men reacted with urgency. Vickery boarded a plane in the middle of a snowstorm in Washington, D.C., and flew west to inspect the damage himself. When he checked into the Multnomah Hotel in downtown Portland, wearing his buttoned-up, dark Navy uniform, he was swarmed by reporters whose questions he patiently answered. "Failures in ship structures are not unknown things," Vickery told them. "There is always some reason for it and the job of the people in shipbuilding is to find out what's wrong and cure it."[3]

Kaiser wanted answers too. Swan Island had opened in March 1942 and quickly become one of his elite shipyards, pumping out Liberty ships, tankers, and other wartime vessels. Kaiser was widely viewed as the linchpin to the Maritime Commission's emergency shipbuilding program, and he knew that if his ships, especially any of his celebrated Liberty ships, started to crack in big numbers, it would be a catastrophe for the country at the worst possible moment (and a public relations disaster for his companies).

Just two days before the *Schenectady* split, Churchill and Roosevelt met in Casablanca, French Morocco, where they agreed it was time to increase American bombing of Germany. The Soviet Union was finally beginning to push back German forces and claim momentum in the fighting. The pressure on America's shipbuilding industry was only growing as the Allies grew and took the offensive around the globe. Kaiser flew east to Washington to begin damage control while trying to ignore a growing chorus of critics who couldn't resist a bit of gloating that the boastful newcomer to shipbuilding was now getting his comeuppance.

"No one will deny that speed is needed in the construction and delivery of ships," announced an editorial in the *New York Journal of Commerce* after the *Schenectady* incident. "However, no matter how speedily a ship is delivered its worth is practically nil if its plates crack, or if for any other reason that vessel must spend thirty to sixty days in a repair yard after one or two trips." There was no mistaking who was the target of those words: Henry Kaiser's "Speed Kings."

The early days of the investigation initially ruled out the obvious suspects for such a dramatic fracture. The crack did not follow along the welds, so they could not be the sole source of the issue. The steel was quickly tested by metallurgists, who found that it met the government's strength standards, but later tests would prove less convincing. As the investigation into what happened unfolded in Oregon, Kaiser defended his workers and challenged a report from an American Bureau of Shipping committee that blamed defective welding as playing a key part in the mishap. "We do not know of any defective weld that was a contributing cause of the breaking of the *Schenectady*," he said. He spoke too soon.

A Coast Guard report later described the incident.[4] "The deck and sides of the vessel fractured just aft of the bridge superstructure. The fracture extended almost instantaneously to the turn of the bridge port and starboard. The deck side shell, longitudinal bulkhead, and bottom girders fractured. Only the bottom plating held. The vessel jack-knifed and the center portion rose so that no water entered. The bow and stern settled into the silt of the river bottom."

December 1942 had been the most productive month for building Liberty ships, with 82 completed, bringing the total Liberty count to 544 in less than one year. January 1943 was on pace to almost match December. And when all American vessel types, including the *Schenectady*, were added up, the early days of 1943 were shaping up as the peak of productivity for U.S. shipyards. Then, just as the unreachable goals that President Roosevelt had set for shipbuilders started to appear attainable, disaster struck.

The strain caused by the heavy cargo in the five holds of the Liberty ships and on their decks had occasionally proved too much for some of the early ships as they navigated the heavy swells of the ocean, causing some cracking in their steel plates. Eight previous Liberty ships had also suffered serious cracks by the time the *Schenectady* incident occurred. But those instances occurred in quieter settings, out of sight from the public, and most went unreported. Swan Island was in a major port city, and the cracking sound had been heard throughout nearby neighborhoods. There was no hiding it. On other occasions the cracks discovered were manageable and even repairable, but on several ships one crack bled over to another steel plate and caused a domino effect. The decision to weld rather than rivet the ships, which was made purely in the interest of speed, began to raise questions.

The *Schenectady* splitting in half while moored in calm waters, just twenty-four hours after she was finished, became a story of national importance. And she soon had company. A month later, on February 17, 1943, the SS *Henry Wynkoop*, a Liberty launched in New Orleans, was being loaded with cargo in New York when her deck and upper side shell cracked. Then a tanker, the *Esso Manhattan*, split while pulling out of New York Harbor on a clear blue day. Faced with multiple cracked ships, the Maritime Commission formed a Board of Investigation to learn why they had cracked and to identify a solution.

A single cause, as investigators learned, became impossible to pinpoint. Instead they called out half a dozen factors they were certain contributed to ships cracking on completely calm waters and in the roughest open seas. Heavy loads shifting inside of a cargo hold caused the immense weight on the keel and the hull of a ship to be stressed at different marks. The quality of the steel being provided to build ships was inconsistent, which was why some shipyards suffered more cracked ships than others. The quality of welding seams on some ships was also inconsistent, and the official Coast Guard report on the *Schenectady* went so far as to say some welds were "found to be defective."

Ultimately the blame was placed on a range of primary factors: an "abnormal amount of internal stress" on the ship caused by the construction process, along with "defective welding" on the ship's right side near the gunwale, and "steel of sub-standard quality." Another concern cited was the faulty design of hatches, openings, and notches, all of which had sharp corners that caused greater stress on the steel and initiated cracks. When all those factors were then aggravated by colder temperatures, the final report said the *Schenectady* "jack-knifed" in such a way that the two ends settled into the silt, causing the ship's midsection to split and rise with a ten-foot gap.[5]

What caused those defective welds became an entirely separate debate. Some shipyards had begun using automatic welding machines midway through 1942, and the machinery was easy to blame. But when Vickery hired James W. Wilson, a former boiler inspector, to visit a handful of shipyards and issue a report on his findings, the results were more far more alarming than the Maritime Commission anticipated. After visiting thirty-five shipyards, Wilson documented cases of fraud, absent supervision of welders, and poor welding skills. He learned of workers being promised bonus wages for exceedingly fast work that turned out sloppy. Talking to workers at Kaiser's California Shipbuilding in Los Angeles, he heard stories of unskilled welders using friends and relatives to weld test plates for them so they could get hired. And in Brunswick, Georgia's shipyard, he stumbled onto a woman welder working inside a deep tank hatch who was using the wrong welding position and the wrong welding tool. But perhaps the most egregious example Wilson found of flawed shipbuilding came from a statement the American Bureau of Shipping had issued to shipyards.

"It must be recognized, not only by inspectors but also by the building yards, to whom copies of this letter are being furnished, that under the present circumstances early completion of serviceable ships is of greater national importance than the high measure of perfection required for full durability." Speed had always been the priority of the Liberty ship program. And now it was being blamed for flawed and broken ships. Nobody was suggesting abandoning the Liberty program. But it was time for some new innovations.

EVEN AS THE yards building Liberty ships across the country in the spring of 1943 were setting production records, launching 103 in March while cutting the average time to 60 days, and then 120 in May with an average time of 57 days, plans for a new type of faster cargo ship were underway. The new ships would be called Victory ships, and they would be built side by side with their Liberty sisters.

If there had been a way for shipyards to get their hands on a bigger, faster turbine engine to keep up with their record shipbuilding pace, the Liberty ships would have been phased much more rapidly out. The 2,500-horsepower Hendy propulsion engine was chosen for the Ocean class and then the Liberty as it was available and accessible. It worked, but it propelled the ships at only 11 knots. "It was a case of those shops or none at all," Vickery said.[6] But even as shipyards kept pumping out new Liberties, politicians and shipping officials sniped that cargo ships moving at 16 or 17 knots could do twice the work of the plodding Liberty fleet. The final straw came when Vickery learned that even the British had begun building faster cargo vessels, because they required less protection on the oceans and could travel outside of big convoys. It was time, Vickery decided, to replace the Liberty fleet with a Victory fleet.

The changes to the Liberty design were minimal, and most of them were made only to accommodate the shape of a 5,800-horsepower reciprocating engine. The length would be 445 feet, or 54 inches longer than a Liberty, and the beam's widest point was cut from 63 feet to 62. But the Victory ship would have the same five cargo holds and the exact same deadweight. The designed speed was 15 knots, and the crew capacity for a Victory was set at fifty-one instead of a Liberty's forty-four, with both ships having a single, midship deckhouse.

As final tweaks to the shape of the Victory ship hull came together, the question of riveting the ships resurfaced, especially after the *Schenectady* disaster. Weeks of debate ended with a compromise that riveting, which some shipyard managers argued was stronger because it allowed for two steel plates to overlap, would be used on the corners of the deck that absorbed the greatest strain. Greater care would also be taken with the welding. The American Bureau of Shipping did not want to signal to shipyards or the American public that it was giving up on welded ships.

To the average American, a Victory ship and Liberty ship when seen side by side appear to be identical twins. To a seaman or a shipbuilder, they would be more like fraternal twins, sharing many of the same qualities and characteristics and a very strong resemblance, yet having some obvious differences. The shipyards needed time to transition, which is why the first Victory ships did not get delivered to the Maritime Commission until the spring of 1944, more than a year after the *Schenectady* cracked. They came from Edgar Kaiser's shipyard in Portland, Henry Kaiser's CalShip in Los Angeles, Bethlehem-Fairfield in Baltimore, and Clay Bedford's Richmond. By the end of the war, 414 Victory cargo ships were delivered. In that same period, 759 additional Liberty ships were also delivered. Of more than 500 hundred Liberty ships that suffered cracks during the war, either in port or at sea, one ship that never suffered a single crack or displayed any hint of substandard steel, poor welding, or inadequate workmanship was the one built in less than five days, the SS *Robert E. Peary.*

———

FOR CREW MEMBERS assigned to the *Peary*, their time on board was the highlight of their wartime memories. Everybody knew its story as the Wonderboat, and no matter how many other ships they served on, the *Peary* was the one they told stories about. Hobbyists who take delight in building detailed replicas of all kinds of ships have designed intricate *Peary* models.

James Horton served on six merchant ships, but it was his time sailing to the Pacific Theater and the Battle of Guadalcanal aboard the *Peary* that remained so vivid for him half a century later. He wrote that the more he read about Navy servicemen and women, the more he understood how they were considered "unsung heroes." But he never thought of himself as a hero, instead more of a survivor. His sister, Avis, later said what it was like seeing her brother come back from war: "He left as a boy and came back a man!"

After the war, Horton finished high school, settled down in San Francisco, where he met his future wife, and pursued a law enforcement career. The couple had eight boys. As dangerous as his time serving in World War II was, it was a botched burglary that he responded to in 1966 as a police officer that nearly took his life, when he trapped a suspect who shot at him. The bullet just missed his head. In retirement he was able to visit the Pearl Harbor Memorial and appreciate how fortunate he was to return home alive. In one of his last acts, he became an honorary crew member of the Liberty ship SS *Jeremiah O'Brien*. It is docked in San Francisco's Fisherman's Wharf, where it serves as a museum and a window into what life was like on board America's great wartime cargo ships.

Fifty years after he served on the *Peary*, in 1993, James Horton was diagnosed with ALS, or Lou Gehrig's disease. One year later, on September 26, 1994, with his family by his bedside, he died peacefully at the age of seventy.

AS FOR THE businessman behind the Liberty ship program, his postwar life only got bigger. For a man who dropped out of school at age thirteen, and whose first attention-getting, significant building achievement, the Hoover Dam, was not finished until he was in his early fifties, Henry Kaiser's accomplishments were extraordinary. And he never lost sight of the fact that his success hinged on his government's success. "I am proud of my government," he said at a news conference in 1953. "I want to do the work and services that it wants me to do, and I want to relinquish anything which it does not want me to do."

Even as he successfully built an empire of steel, cement, aluminum, and magnesium plants, and moved from ships to automobiles, cargo airplanes, hotels, and even baseball stadiums, he was proudest of his one accomplishment that was rooted not in construction, but in providing care to workers. When Kaiser died in Honolulu on August 24, 1967, at the age of eighty-five, his prepaid health care system that he started in the desert while building a giant dam, and which became the Kaiser Permanente Medical Care Program, covered 1.6 million participants. In the next fifty years it would grow to become one of the nation's largest health care providers and the largest private nonprofit health care organization, with nearly 13 million members participating, and more than 300,000 employees.

He took pride in the services and care his medical program provided, even as he was a notoriously horrible patient himself in his sunset years. His own health was remarkable into his seventies despite his subsisting on three hours' sleep many nights, abusing sleeping pills, eating a steady diet of rich foods, chain-smoking cigars, and growing increasingly fat. Sidney Garfield, the physician and his longtime friend, noted that Kaiser's longevity was perhaps his greatest achievement of all. "He really abused himself," Garfield said. "He had incredible genes. If he took care of himself, he'd have lived even longer."[7]

Kaiser's death after slipping into a coma brought condolences from the highest orders. His dam building, cement production, steel and aluminum manufacturing, and hospitals and health care had all built his storied legacy. But none rivaled the contributions of his wartime shipyards. Combined, Richmond and Portland, two shipyards that did not exist before the war, built 2,980 total ships, a figure that comprised 25 percent of the Maritime Commission's total emergency shipbuilding program from 1941 to 1945.

"Henry J. Kaiser embodied in his own career all that has been best in our country's tradition," President Lyndon B. Johnson said. "His own energy, imagination and determination gave him greatness—and he used that greatness to give unflaggingly for the betterment of his country and his fellow man."[8]

Kaiser, who couldn't even bother to attend the Boulder Dam celebration in 1935 despite the presence of President Roosevelt, would not have cared for such accolades. When he was honored in Washington, D.C., with a prestigious labor award by the AFL-CIO two years before his death, becoming the first industrialist to receive the honor, he skipped that celebration too and asked for his son, Edgar, to read his prepared remarks at the dinner.

"I have often been asked, 'What is it, Mr. Kaiser, in your organization that enables you to make impossible projects become possible?' I appreciate the compliment and answer that our real job is not the building of dams, ships, factories and hospitals; our job is to build and develop people to bring out their courage, their talents, their zeal, and their will to work."[9]

Edgar Kaiser carried on his father's legacy by not only continuing his businesses, but also serving four presidential administrations, including the one led by the same John F. Kennedy whose PT boat was carried by a Liberty ship to war. In 1969 he was awarded the Medal of Freedom in recognition of his efforts to expand low-income housing. He died in 1981.

KAISER'S HEALTH CARE plan would not have been possible without the foresight of Garfield. His death in 1984 passed without any of the acclaim Kaiser received. But he had remained active with Kaiser Permanente throughout his life, serving on its board and building new hospitals and clinics. A doctor who worked with him in the 1970s described him as a man who was always thinking of where the health care field should go next, which is precisely how he first got started with his idea to bring health care to the workers and have them contribute a small amount to their own care. "He had a marvelous ability to visualize the future of medical care delivery and to see clearly the main issues that needed to be approached in solving a problem," Robert Feldman wrote.

"His analyses were remarkably and deceptively simple. It frequently seemed that he was too far ahead of the field."[10]

Edgar Kaiser, who was brought into the world by Garfield's hands, said Garfield's ideas were always daring and controversial. But when there was debate about whether to move forward with one or ignore it, the Kaiser son said, "I usually voted for Sid. He was truly a man of vision."

It was a Garfield biographer who put in the simplest terms the significance of the Garfield and Kaiser health plan:

> The most important single factor in all of our war effort was shipbuilding of which he, Kaiser, was the unquestioned leader and master. The wounds and the sickness of shipyard workers, if they are not cared for, mean guns that will not shoot, planes that will not fly, because ships will not sail—because the men who could have built them are sick, or disabled, or dead. And if the building of the ships was as basic to victory as the actual fighting, then it was just as important for his industrial army to be healthy as it was important for our front-line fighters.[11]

For many of the men and women who worked in the Liberty ship program—whether for Kaiser, for themselves, for the Maritime Commission, or for the White House—it was the defining moment in their careers and lives. Some wrote about it in their journals; others told their stories in intimate detail to librarians and researchers so they could be recorded for the history records. All left a pride-filled record of their days.

Cillie Preston, like dozens of Richmond shipyard workers, told her story to a beloved oral historian in the community, Judith K. Dunning. As the war was coming to an end in 1945, the need for as many shipyard workers dwindled and the inevitable layoffs began. "When they started laying off female welders, they laid them all off and changed a few of them to day shift," she recalled. "I happened to be one of the ones who they put on days. They closed down the graveyard [shift]."[12]

She loved welding, and with her experience she was offered another welding job at Mare Island, America's first West Coast naval station, just twenty miles north of Richmond. But Cillie was dealing with the same issue at the end of the war as when she first came north on the train from Mississippi. She was pregnant—this time with her sixth. She turned down the welding job, and three weeks after giving birth, she started a position in the laundry at Treasure Island. A man-made island opened in 1939 for the Golden Gate International Exposition, it had been taken over by the Navy in 1941 to serve as an administrative hub, a role it played through the Korean, Vietnam, and Gulf wars. From welding ships to ironing clothes, it was a transition Cillie was happy to make if it kept food on the table. She worked at Treasure Island for the next twenty years. "I was a press operator for all the big officers, lieutenants and all the big people who are on Treasure Island. We prepared their beautiful uniforms and shirts that they wear out in public."

Arthur Babineau, the weld inspector in the South Portland, Maine, shipyard, met his future wife on the job. He dated his "Wendy the Welder," Alphena Violette, for two years until he enlisted with the Army and went off to basic training at Fort Devens, Massachusetts. Just before he shipped out to Europe with the 119th Evacuation Hospital, they got married. He served across England, Wales, Belgium, France, and Germany, and came back home in luxury aboard the *Queen Mary*. After one more brief deployment, the war ended and he settled down in Old Orchard Beach, Maine, raising three children and teaching them to love the outdoors as much as he did.[13]

For two of the war's fastest welders, Vera Anderson and Cora Clonts, shipbuilding opened unexpected doors. Clonts met a handsome sailor named Harley Albert Holley on June 6, 1944, in Sparks, Nevada. They married the same day, had three boys after the war, and stayed together fifty-nine years, until Albert's death in 2003. Anderson went from being a nineteen-year-old champion welder to living a long life doing just what Eleanor Roosevelt hoped all Wendy the Welders would do—go home and raise a family. Toward the end of the war, Anderson even said, "I'm just going to be a housekeeper." She died at the age of ninety.

Gus, or "Jersey Gus" as she was also known, returned to being August

Clawson after her undercover experience and went back to the Office of Education, directing changes to wartime training so it more accurately mirrored the actual work experience. Her efforts won her a Superior Performance Award from the Labor Department. Clawson died in 1997 at the age of ninety-three.

The Singing Shipbuilder Lewis Van Hook kept on singing for years after leaving the shipyard in 1945, and he stayed in Richmond too.

But for some, the Liberty ship experience helped inspire them into an entirely alternative career. Bernard Taper, who helped build the *Robert E. Peary*, had come to the States when he was eleven by himself on a freighter from London. He landed a job in Kaiser's shipyard in his early twenties before joining the Army and rising to second lieutenant. But the moment the war ended, his passion for the arts consumed his life. He was tapped with recovering paintings and sculptures that the Nazis had looted in Europe, and he used his skills as a writer to become a prominent American journalist, first for the *San Francisco Chronicle*, later for the *New Yorker*.

Clay Bedford's obituary in 1991 in the *New York Times* was just six paragraphs long and noted that after working in Kaiser's shipyards, he spent the majority of his postwar years working for Kaiser Aerospace & Electronics. Almost as an aside, it said that Bedford had "supervised the assembly of a 10,500-ton cargo vessel in less than five days."

Pete Newell, who rejuvenated the shipbuilding business in Maine, found time after the war for a more leisurely life: golf, music, reading, travel, even playing the harmonica. Colleges throughout Maine bestowed honorary degrees on him for his work. After once saying that he wanted "to live and die in Bath," he fulfilled that dream, dying in 1954 at Bath Memorial Hospital at the age of seventy-six.

For the duo who struck fear in American shipbuilders during the war while overseeing the emergency shipbuilding program, Jerry Land and Howard Vickery, the end of the war led to divergent paths. Vickery died suddenly from a heart attack in 1946. He was fifty-three and had just retired after beginning to suffer from health issues. Land, on the other hand, had a long career in the private sector after the war working for General Dynamics and died in 1971 at the age of ninety-two.

The man who turned Robert Cyril Thompson's British drawings into an American Liberty ship continued doing what he did best—designing ships. The self-taught William Francis Gibbs designed more than 6,000 vessels in a long career. His greatest contribution remained the compartmentalization of a ship's hull with bulkhead doors that could seal out water and keep a wounded ship afloat. Gibbs died in 1967. He was eighty-one. Right up until his death, he remained a grumpy, rumpled, and brilliant businessman who did not care what others thought of him. "Under this dour exterior beats a heart of stone," he said late in life.[14]

As for Thompson, whose papers inside the brown leather briefcase on board the RMS *Scythia* in the fall of 1940 are what led to the birth of the Liberty ship program, and who survived a near-death experience returning home on the *Western Prince*, he charted a new path. Rejected by the Royal Navy, he joined the Royal Air Force and became a flight engineer, a career he continued postwar. He was just fifty-nine when he died in 1967.

WHEN ALLIED TROOPS landed on the beaches of Normandy on June 6, 1944, approximately two hundred Liberty ships were there. The SS *Francis C. Harrington* was one of the first to be hit, while the SS *Jeremiah O'Brien* was one of the only American ships that ferried troops and supplies on D-Day to escape the invasion unscathed. The *Peary* was there too, shuttling troops and equipment between Wales and Omaha Beach. Liberty ships were playing an increasingly vital role as the fighting in Europe intensified, and the D-Day attack had shown Hitler the full force of what an attack from the land, the sea, and the air would look like, with 7,000 ships and landing craft swarming five beachheads.

On August 6, 1944, under the command of Captain Edward S. Barley, the 116th Signal Radio Intelligence Company drove away from their comfortable quarters in Lymington, England, a hundred miles south of London, and pulled up to a crowded dock in Southampton, prepared to head across the English Channel for the beaches in northern France. Their awaiting vessel was the

Robert E. Peary. The crew watched overnight as cranes lifted their vehicles into the cargo holds, and when "Rise and shine" was hollered out the next morning at dawn, hundreds of company men were snoring, talking, or sprawled out in uncomfortable positions all around the *Peary*'s deck.

Their journey across the Channel was calm and they arrived thirty miles southwest of the Normandy beaches. Dropping anchor off Omaha Beach, they could hear guns in the distance. The *Peary* was surrounded by a flotilla of Allied ships of all shapes and sizes—naval, cargo, and long, flat barges called rhino ferries. The crew of the 116th was tired and hungry, a box of soggy frankfurters had been devoured but hardly satisfied them, and a spirited game of craps helped pass the time. A bloated, unrecognizable body floated past her hull. As darkness settled over them, planes roared overhead and the occasional flash could be seen or explosion heard.

On the morning of August 8, with assistance from the powerful booms and winches on board, the crew started unloading the trucks from the *Peary* onto one of the long barges that pulled alongside them. It took most of the day for the barge to be loaded, and men used rope ladders off the side of the ship to scramble down and find spaces with the trucks on the barge. It would take another night and day for the rest of the crew to join them, so they pulled out blankets for a night on the barge, and even made a small fire. Finally, on August 9, the last barge was loaded with the *Peary*'s trucks and pulled away toward shore, which was crowded with a graveyard of abandoned and sunken German ships.

Landing the barges proved to be more challenging than anyone anticipated, as the trucks shifted and slipped on the decks and the tide kept pushing the barges back out. The first two attempts to land failed, but on the third try, the 116th SRI managed to roll onto French soil. Barley and his company spent the next year providing radio intelligence support to the Twelfth Army Group, commanded by General Omar Bradley, as his troops pushed back German forces while advancing through France on the way to the successful liberation of Paris on August 19, 1944. The most famous Liberty ship headed for home a month later, on September 18, bound for New York to undergo routine maintenance.

In her first year alone, she had traveled more than 42,000 miles, from New Caledonia to the Fiji Islands to Chile, South America, to Savannah, Georgia. While in the South Pacific, the crew successfully used her Lyle gun, a short cannon designed to fire a line to aid ships in distress, to aid instead U.S. troops marooned on an island occupied by the Japanese. The line allowed them to send enough food and ammunition ashore to resupply the defenders who eventually defeated their attackers. The *Peary* ferried prisoners of war back from North Africa, managed to make multiple runs through the treacherous waters of the North Atlantic and the South Pacific, and carried trucks and tanks and rations to the shores of France to aid in the liberation of Paris. She served as a role model for every Liberty ship in World War II. And she avoided any of the unexpected and devastating cracks. When she did suffer a crack during a convoy to England, Captain Widmeyer became livid when it was suggested the crack was a structural failure. His wife later said in an interview with *Fore 'n' Aft* that her husband refused to let the *Peary* drop out of the convoy and proved the crack would not slow them down. "He has always been extremely proud of the *Peary*'s performance," she said.[15]

The last Liberty ship, the SS *Albert M. Boe*, named after a merchant marine, was built in Portland, Maine, and delivered to the Maritime Commission on October 30, 1945. "This is the day we always have looked forward to—the war is won and shipbuilding production has been completed," Andrew Sides, president of New England Shipbuilding Corporation, said in his speech to thousands of shipbuilders. As for the most famous Liberty of all, the *Peary*, twenty years after her historic construction and launching, in 1963 she was scrapped for metal in Baltimore.

WHAT HAD STARTED with Cyril Thompson's roughly sketched blueprints and his perilous journey from England across the Atlantic to lead a secret shipbuilding mission in the United States could now be viewed as a turning point in history. When the two countries were struggling to find common ground and a united strategy against Hitler in the war's early days, it was the Liberty ship program that brought their leaders together, helped the friendship between Roosevelt and Churchill bloom amid the desperation and darkness, and defined what it meant to be an ally in a time of need. When Churchill was asked to share words on a fall day in 1942 for the one-year anniversary of the launching of the first Liberty ship, he wanted the world to know that the American shipbuilders could stand proudly alongside the soldiers as heroes in the battle to save democracy.

"The completion of nearly 500 large, ocean-going cargo vessels in the short space of the past twelve months since the launching of the *Patrick Henry*, the first Liberty ship, is almost unparalleled," Churchill said. "It is a record beyond compare. It is an achievement far beyond even the most optimistic hopes and expectations. . . . The faithful effort of everyone engaged in this honorable program will take an honorable place in history and will be read through the years as a master stroke in freedom's cause."[16]

It took that honorable place in history because of how quickly the ships were built. The average time needed to go from keel laying to launching for ten Liberty ships built just prior to Hull No. 440 was 40.6 days. With all the lessons learned from a single, heavily prefabricated vessel, the average time to build ten Liberty ships directly following the launching of the *Peary* dropped ten full days, to 31.9 days. The experiment had been mocked by many as nothing more than a public relations stunt ship. But that ignored what its real purpose was. Liberty ships were being built faster than ever. It did not go unnoticed in Washington.

On March 22, 1943, Admiral Land sent a message to Richmond. As he always did, he addressed it not to the managers or the bosses at the shipyards, but to the workers. He shared with them the story of the Liberty ship *O. Henry*, which had recently sailed in a convoy to the island of Malta off the southern tip of Italy, where British troops were under relentless attack. German planes bombed the convoy, but the ships managed to push through and even shoot down a dive bomber, Land told the workers. Not a single sailor died in the battle, and in addition to delivering its cargo of munitions and food, the captain had managed to fill every inch of the ship's deck with fresh oranges to feed the children of Malta, where the groves of orange and lemon trees had been damaged.

"I know every worker at your yard will take personal pride and satisfaction in knowing that your ship reached Malta," Land wrote to the Richmond shipbuilders, "and gave new courage to its brave people in their heroic fight against the axis."[17]

It was but one small story of thousands that reflected the role Liberty ships were playing in the war, most often carrying armored tanks, jeeps, guns, bullets, and bombs, stacked high in their cargo holds, but then sometimes just using their spacious decks to ferry thousands of juicy oranges to a remote island in the Mediterranean in order to bring smiles, and dreams of liberty, to the faces of children facing uncertain futures.

RESEARCH AND ACKNOWLEDGMENTS

IN WRITING ABOUT WORLD WAR II, YOU DISCOVER QUICKLY the astonishing volume of material that is available. And you also discover that five different books or papers might tell five different versions of a single story. All five versions might very well be accurate too, with the slightest nuances. Such is history. I relied on so many sources of material, from books, newspapers, and magazines to online records to libraries and museums to handwritten letters and published newsletters printed during the war to research papers and dissertations, and lastly, to recorded personal interviews and email correspondences. My hope is that the narrative I have laid out telling the story of the Liberty ships does justice to all those resources, and to the heroic men and women behind the effort.

If something appears between quote marks, that means it was said, reported, or written down somewhere. Nothing in quotes is made up by me. That also holds for a quote where I describe a person as thinking something. I was not in their head, but that means they uttered or put down their thoughts somewhere or allowed someone else to quote them or interview them, thereby allowing me to reshare those thoughts here.

I'd be remiss if I did not acknowledge a few sources of material that, as others before me have noted, are definitive works. The record of World War II would not be the same without them. One is Frederic Lane's *Ships for Victory*, 882 meticulously documented pages by a decorated historian and maritime expert. Maury Klein's *Call to Arms* is as much of a World War II soup-to-nuts book that you will come across. And Doris Kearns Goodwin's *No Ordinary Time* is equally thorough and does a masterful job of taking you inside President Roosevelt's life at such a perilous moment in history. Mark Foster's biography, *Henry J. Kaiser*, tells his underappreciated story from birth to death, a business story for the ages. And Arthur Herman's *Freedom's Forge* is so well reported and captivating I found myself rereading passages of it just because it always made me feel a little bit smarter. Peter Elphick's simply titled *Liberty* is anything but simple. A retired master mariner, he was able to interview critical people in London before they passed away who were essential to my story, and his interviews were invaluable. One of the very first people I contacted in my own research was Christopher J. Tassava. His 2003 dissertation at Northwestern University, "Launching a Thousand Ships," is an incredible piece of research, and the work that he did poring through files and sifting through records is reflected in the resulting paper. One final thought on another valuable piece of writing, *Swing Shift* by Joseph Fabry. His words were first written down in the early 1940s during his time in the Richmond shipyard, but they were not put into book form until forty years later after he rediscovered his stories. It's unfair to assume he did not take some literary license in retelling his own stories, and he acknowledges that. But I choose to grant him the benefit of the doubt and let his words stand as a record of his time, even if it's likely that some of the words he puts between quote marks were not said verbatim four decades earlier.

One of the privileges of writing about World War II was connecting with the families of those who served or worked in the war. Finding shipbuilders from those early days of the war was a challenge, and thankfully some wonderful librarians, like Judith K. Dunning in California, spent years personally interviewing shipyard workers and transcribing their heartfelt conversations, allowing me to bring their stories back to life. But one morning that I spent with 102-year-old Arthur Babineau and his daughter Donna Somma in Maine will stick with me. Over their kitchen table, he shared his memories of working in the Maine shipyards and his recall of details astounded me. He died not long after our interview, but I was honored to meet him. The family of speedy welder Cora Clonts was gracious enough to share with me a Shutterfly photo album they had put together full of pictures and articles from the war, and without it I could never have brought some of her story to life. Toward the end of my research, I stumbled into a model shipbuilding site, where a man had left a comment saying his father sailed on the SS *Robert E. Peary*. John Horton shared with me typed pages of vivid storytelling that his father had written about his time aboard the *Peary* and I am forever grateful for his cooperation in sharing it with me. Sometimes you just get lucky as a researcher. When I eventually connected with the family of Clay Bedford in Connecticut, a basement full of his archived story was a treasure trove and I can't thank them enough for sharing his story with me.

I have to thank the two men who run Wartime Press, as well as the Richmond Museum of History & Culture, for sharing with me copies of the *Fore 'n' Aft* newsletter from various dates. Amy Reytar at the National Archives was a joy to work with in person in Maryland, and via email. Cuong Le, the archivist for Kaiser Permanente, graciously shared wonderful photos for us to use. And because the library with Henry Kaiser's records was located at the Bancroft Library at the University of California, Berkeley, I needed some cross-country assistance, and independent researcher Maria Brandt obliged, making several trips there for me and sending enormous files through Dropbox. The time and effort she saved me cannot be measured. Similarly, researchers at the FDR Presidential Library and Museum in Hyde Park, New York, especially archivist Patrick Fahy, were always quick to respond, as was Kathy DiPhilippo at the South Portland Historical Society. The same was true of my local librarians at the Needham Public Library in Massachusetts when I was tracking down a hard-to-find book to borrow. Dick Sterne, my tour guide aboard the SS *John Brown*, was a pleasure to talk with and shared infinite knowledge.

ON MORE PERSONAL notes, my agent Susan Canavan at Waxman Literary Agency not only fought for this book but found it the perfect home at Simon & Schuster, a giant in the publishing world that cherishes nonfiction, narrative history storytelling. My editor, Robert Messenger, took great care with the story as its editor and we had a terrific partnership that I will forever appreciate. When Robert handed me off to Tzipora Chein at Simon & Schuster, the process of turning a Word document into a beautiful, polished book could not have gone more seamlessly. Kevin Terry of the Shipbuilders Council of America assisted me with a thorough, expert reading of the manuscript. The incredibly talented Brookline artist Joe McKendry was gracious to produce on short notice a beautiful illustration of a Liberty ship.

Two friends require a special note of thanks. Rich Fernandez did something my wife could not do—turned me into a morning person. Our six o'clock runs through Needham's dark streets and our Monday evening basketball games were therapy for me, clearing my head so that I could jump back into the book reenergized. And Joe Vivaldi was always game for a beer, lunch, quick ski trip or bike ride, and game to listen to me babble on about my research. Friendships, like the trivia group that sustained my wife and I through the pandemic's sadness, mean so much to me now.

I feel unusually blessed at this point in my life to have not only a close brother, Jordan Most, to share exciting news with, but also both of my parents, Al and Paula Most, and both of my in-laws, Eric and Judy Braude. This book represents a new chapter in my own life. I began it when the COVID-19 pandemic was winding down but still paralyzing our lives, and I was in the midst of a relatively new job at Boston University after fifteen proud years at the *Boston Globe*.

Finally, my family. My wife, Mimi Braude, is not only a compassionate psychotherapist who lifts up people's lives every day; she is also a voracious reader who just happens to love getting lost in novels more than nonfiction historical narrative. But no matter. She supported me at every step, always offering to read pages when I hit a block and encouraging me when I started to drag. How did I get so lucky? My children, adolescents when my second book, *The Race Underground*, came out, were teenagers for this one, active in basketball, car shows, a cappella, baseball, golf, and college searches. I refused to miss a single game or concert, as their performances, their happiness, always provided the wind at my back. This book is dedicated to them, Mimi, Julia, and Ben. You keep me afloat.

NOTES

Wonderboat

1. Transcript of interview with Clay Bedford, Mimi Stein, May 3, 1982.
2. John Bunker, *Liberty Ships*, 12.
3. Joseph Fabry, *Swing Shift*, 212.

Author's Note

1. Gus Bourneuf Jr., *Workhorse of the Fleet*, 7.
2. Phillips Payson O'Brien, *How the War Was Won*, 253.
3. Frederic Lane, *Ships for Victory*, 9.

1: Zigzagging the Atlantic

1. National Liverpool Museums, "Liverpool to New York: The Only Way to Cross," Merseyside Maritime Museum, January 28, 2005.
2. Peter C. Kohler, "Cunard's Old Reliable: RMS *Scythia*," Wanted on the Voyage, October 24, 2020, https://wantedonthevoyage.blogspot.com/2020/10/cunards-old-reliable-rms-scythia.html.
3. Peter Elphick, *Liberty*, 29.
4. "Two Liners Arrive with 762 Refugees," *New York Times*, April 18, 1940.
5. Winston Churchill, "Our Geographical Position," speech, International Churchill Society, August 20, 1940.
6. "I have seen war," Jon Meacham, *Franklin and Winston*, 7.
7. "Stay Out of War, Is Advice of H.G. Wells to America," *Wilkes Barre Record*, October 4, 1940.

2: "Secret: Merchant Shipbuilding Mission to USA"

1. Elphick, 29.
2. "The Thompsons, Shipbuilders of Sunderland," George H. Graham: The Will of Robert Cyril Thompson: 1907–1967, https://ghgraham.org/text/robertthompson1907_will.html.
3. "Manufacture Weapons of War," America's National Churchill Museum, https://www.nationalchurchillmuseum.org/the-few.html.
4. United States Maritime Commission, Memorandum for the President, December 6, 1940, FDR Presidential Library and Museum.

5. Lewis Johnman and Hugh Murphy, *British Merchant Shipping Mission in the United States and British Merchant Shipbuilding in the Second World War*, https://www.cnrs-scrn.org/northern_mariner/vol12/tnm_12_3_1-15.pdf.
6. Sir R. Norman Thompson, "One Hundred Years of Shipbuilding: 1846–1946, Joseph L. Thompson & Sons Ltd."
7. Herman, *Freedom's Forge*, 13.
8. "Churchill Offers Toil and Tears to FDR," American Heritage, Spring/Summer 2008, https://www.americanheritage.com/churchill-offers-toil-and-tears-fdr.
9. Moe, *Roosevelt's Second Act*, 133–34.
10. Moe, 133–34.
11. "My Last Appeal to Great Britain," Hitler speech to Reichstag, July 19, 1940, https://www.ibiblio.org/pha/policy/1940/1940-07-19b.html.
12. Elphick, *Liberty*, 26.
13. Elphick, 28.
14. Elphick, 31.
15. R. C. Thompson and Harry Hunter, "The British Merchant Shipbuilding Programme in North America," Andrew Laing Lecture before the North East Coast Institution of Engineers and Shipbuilders.
16. Elphick, *Liberty*, 32.
17. Elphick, 33.
18. "Child Refugees Here on Three Ships," *New York Times*, October 4, 1940.
19. "Child Refugees."
20. "Child Refugees."

3: The Legend of Jerry Land

1. "The British Merchant Shipbuilding Programme in North America."
2. Herman, 120.
3. Library of Congress, Emory Scott Land Papers, undated memo, "Life in These United States."
4. Emory S. Land, *Winning the War with Ships*, 71
5. Land.
6. Lane, xvii.
7. Land, 19.
8. Land, 18.
9. Maury Klein, *A Call to Arms*, 319.
10. Klein, 316.
11. Klein.
12. Lane, 31.
13. Thompson and Hunter, "The British Merchant Shipbuilding Programme," 61.
14. Thompson and Hunter.
15. Elphick, 39.
16. Elphick.
17. Papers of Sir James Lithgow, 1883–1952, Shipbuilder & Industrialist, Archive Collection, University of Glasgow.
18. Papers of Sir James Lithgow.
19. Klein, *A Call to Arms*, 182.
20. C. Bradford Mitchell, *Every Kind of Shipwork: A History of Todd Shipyards Corporation*, 125–28.

21. Donald E. Wolf, *Big Dams and Other Dreams*, 66.
22. *Fortune*, July 1941, 123.
23. Papers of Sir James Lithgow, 1883–1952, Shipbuilder & Industrialist, Archive Collection, University of Glasgow.
24. Papers of Sir James Lithgow.
25. Elphick, *Liberty*, 40.

4: 17,000 Miles, Three Weeks

1. Elphick, 41.
2. Papers of Sir James Lithgow.
3. Papers of Sir James Lithgow.
4. Elphick, 43.
5. Elphick.
6. Elphick, 44.
7. Bourneuf, 13.
8. Bourneuf, 48.

5: Torpedoed

1. Bourneuf.
2. Bourneuf, 49.
3. Bourneuf, 50.
4. "The Loss of the Western Prince," *Guardian*, December 18, 1940.
5. Elphick, 50–51.
6. Elphick, 51.
7. Elphick, 52.

6: Henry the Builder

1. Story is recounted in Heiner, 21.
2. Heiner, 22.
3. Heiner, 10.
4. Henry J. Kaiser, *Lessons My Mother Taught Me*, Henry J. Kaiser Papers, Bancroft Library, University of California, Berkeley.
5. Foster, 18.
6. Foster, 22.
7. Heiner, 29.
8. Heiner.
9. Foster, 29.
10. Foster, 42.

7: Hoover

1. Heiner, 55.
2. James Nagle, "A History of Government Contracting," George Washington University, 1992.
3. Stephen B. Adams, *Mr. Kaiser Goes to Washington*, 41.

4. Adams, 39.
5. "Dam Dedicated by President Roosevelt," *Las Vegas Review Journal*, October 1, 1935.
6. The American Presidency Project, Address at the Dedication of Boulder Dam, September 30, 1935.
7. Franklin D. Roosevelt Papers, Franklin D. Roosevelt Library, Hyde Park, NY.
8. Foster, 60.
9. Foster, 66.

8: A History Lesson

1. "US Ships to Lead World," *Philadelphia Inquirer*, August 6, 1918.
2. "Subsidies to Ship Lines Are Asked by Roosevelt," *New York Times*, March 5, 1935.
3. "A Study of American Merchant Marine Legislation," Clarence G. Morse, Duke University, 1960.

9: Henry the Shipbuilder

1. Foster, 68.
2. Foster.
3. Wolf, 66–67.
4. *Fortune*, September 28, 1943.
5. *Fortune*.
6. Wolf, 67.
7. Wolf, 68.
8. Papers of Sir James Lithgow.
9. Albert P. Heiner, *Henry J. Kaiser: Western Colossus*, 117.
10. Elphick, 47.

10: A Clambake Seals the Deal

1. Herbert G. Jones, *Portland Ships Are Good Ships*, 11.
2. Ralph Linwood Snow, *Bath Iron Works: The First Hundred Years*, 315.
3. *Fortune*, July 1941.
4. *Fortune*, 12.
5. *Fortune*.
6. *Fortune*, 13.
7. Snow, 374.
8. Snow, 15.
9. Snow, 13.
10. Lane, 44.
11. Lane.
12. Mitchell, 127.
13. "Ship Deal Is Signed," *New York Times*, December 20, 1940.
14. *Fortune*, July 1941.
15. *Fortune*, July 1941.
16. Stein transcript.
17. Stein transcript.

11: Arsenal of Democracy

1. Herman, 113.
2. Nelson, 133.
3. Nelson.
4. Video of Roosevelt at Selective Service Draft Lottery, Robert H. Jackson Center, https://www.youtube.com/watch?v=19-8TY0LUdo.
5. Wolf, 86.
6. "Tanker Manned by U.S. Crew Sunk on Way to Africa," *New York Times*, December 28, 1940.
7. A. J. Baime, *Arsenal of Democracy*, XV; "Roosevelt Calls for Greater Aid to Britain," *New York Times*, December 30, 1940.
8. Herman, 128.
9. Emory S. Land, *Winning the War with Ships*, 21.
10. Herman, 129.
11. *New York Times*, January 1, 1941.

12: "Ugly Ducklings"

1. Christopher J. Tassava, "Launching a Thousand Ships: Entrepreneurs, War Workers, and the State in American Shipbuilding, 1940–1945" (PhD diss., Northwestern University), 119.
2. Land, 26.
3. Land, 27.
4. Klein, 178.
5. Elphick, 18.
6. *Time*, January 13, 1941.
7. Elphick, 55.
8. Bourneuf, 26–33
9. All quotes from press conference, Transcript of Press Conference #706, FDR Library, http://www.fdrlibrary.marist.edu/_resources/images/pc/pc0112.pdf.
10. "Japan and Germany, 1941–1943 No Common Objective, No Common Plans, No Basis of Trust," *Naval War College Review*, 53.
11. General Facts and Figures: FDR, Franklin D. Roosevelt Presidential Library and Museum.
12. U.S. Maritime Commission press release, January 8, 1941, National Archives, College Park, MD.
13. Klein, 184.

13: A Boy's Dreams

1. Details of launching story, Steven Ujifusa, *A Man and His Ship*, 3–6.
2. Ujifusa, 5.
3. Ujifusa, 6.
4. *New York Times*, August 3, 1919.
5. *New York Times*, 27.
6. Story of the SS *Malolo* in Ujifusa, 106–10.
7. Frank O. Braynard, *By Their Works Ye Shall Know Them: The Life and Ships of William Francis Gibbs, 1886–1967* (1968); "US at War: Technological Revolutionist," *Time*, September 28, 1942.

8. Associated Press, "Admiral Gives Praise to New Hawaiian Ship," October 28, 1927.
9. Ujifusa, 144–45.
10. "William Francis Gibbs Dead," *New York Times*, September 7, 1967.
11. Elphick, 56.
12. Foster, 70.
13. Elphick, 56.
14. "U.S. at War: Technological Revolutionist."
15. Lane, 72–78.
16. Land, 183.
17. Lane, 79.
18. Ujifusa, 172.
19. Lane, 100.
20. Changes in design, Lane, 84; Herman, 136.
21. Lane, 85, 87.
22. Lane, 85.
23. Lane, 87, 410.
24. Peter M. Bowers, *Curtiss Aircraft 1907–1947*, 445.
25. Lane, 89.
26. United States Maritime Commission, "Liberty Ships Built by the United States Maritime Commission in World War II," http://www.usmm.org/libertyships.html.

14: Engines and Guns

1. Wolf, 98; Tassava, 126.
2. Wolf, 99.
3. Bourneuf, 7.
4. O'Brien, 254.
5. American Presidency Project, transcript of Roosevelt message to Congress on the arming of merchant ships, October 9, 1941.

15: Selecting Sites

1. Lane, 51–54.
2. Lane, 52.
3. Lane, 61.

16: Liberty

1. Bourneuf, 165.
2. Copy of memo, United States Maritime Commission, May 2, 1941.
3. FDR and the Four Freedoms Speech, transcript, FDR Library.

17: Upside-Down Forests

1. Foster, 71; Herman, 124.
2. Heiner, 121; Herman, 131.
3. Heiner, 120.

4. Herman, 131.
5. Historic American Engineering Record (HAER), "Kaiser's Richmond Shipyards," historical report prepared for National Park Service, 181.
6. "The People at War: Downeasters Building Ships," *Harper's Magazine*, March 1943.
7. Transcript of interview with Clay Bedford, Mimi Stein, May 3, 1982.
8. Herman, 138.
9. Jones, 36.
10. "More Than 200 Women Now Building Vessels," *Portland Evening Express*, November 20, 1942.
11. Author interview of Arthur Babineau, October 10, 2023.
12. Foster, 70–71.
13. Foster, 32–33.
14. Foster, 64.
15. *Bosn's Whistle*, Oregon Shipyard newsletter, July 29, 1945.
16. Heiner, 121.

18: The Firsts

1. Doris Kearns Goodwin, *No Ordinary Time*, 262–63.
2. Goodwin, 231.
3. Goodwin, 232.
4. Michael Gannon, *Operation Drumbeat*, 85.
5. "Kaiser Plans a Steel Plant," *Time*, April 28, 1941; FDR Museum, Day by Day log; Herman, 210.
6. Horace N. Gilbert, "The Expansion of Shipbuilding," *Harvard Business Review* 20 (Winter 1942).
7. "Inside in Washington," *Portland Press Herald*, April 30, 1942.
8. Land memorandum to Roosevelt, April 11, 1941, Emory Scott Land Papers, Library of Congress.
9. Roosevelt memorandum to Land, April 14, 1941, Emory Scott Land Papers, Library of Congress.
10. Land, 31.
11. Herman, 180; Klein, 186.
12. Klein, 186.
13. Heiner, 122.
14. Mitchell, 128; "Ship for Britain Goes into the Water," *New York Times*, August 17, 1941; Tassava, 90–91.
15. *Production in Shipbuilding Plants: Executive Hearings Before the Committee on the Merchant Marines and Fisheries, House of Representatives, Seventy-eighth Congress, First Session, on H. Res. 52, a Resolution Authorizing Investigation of the National Defense Program as it Relates to the Committee on the Merchant Marine and Fisheries* (Washington, D.C.: U.S. Government Printing Office, 1944), 1015.
16. *New York Times*, August 17, 1941.
17. *New York Times*.
18. *New York Times*.
19. *New York Times*.
20. Goodwin, 263.
21. Goodwin, 267.
22. Goodwin, 255.
23. American Presidency Project, Fireside Chat, September 11, 1941, https://www.presidency.ucsb.edu/documents/fireside-chat-11.
24. FDR Library, Transcript of Press Conference #767, September 5, 1941.

19: Liberty Fleet Day

1. Tassava, 199.
2. Bunker, 48.
3. *San Francisco Chronicle*, September 1, 1941.
4. Lane, 69.
5. Bunker, 49.
6. "Liberty Fleet Hailed by British Transport," *New York Times*, September 28, 1941.
7. Goodwin, 270.
8. FDR Library, Recorded Speeches and Utterances of Franklin D. Roosevelt, 1920–1945.
9. "The Gardener," *New Yorker*, August 24, 2003.
10. "The Gardener."
11. Details of Patrick Henry launching, "First of 312 Liberty Ships Is Launched in Baltimore," *The Sun*, September 28, 1941.
12. "A Blow at Hitler," *New York Times*, September 28, 1941.
13. "Bay Area Launches Three New Vessels," *San Francisco Examiner*, September 28, 1941.
14. White House news release, President Franklin D. Roosevelt's Liberty Fleet Day Address, September, 27, 1941.
15. Gannon, 42.

20: Launching and Loading

1. "Freighter Destroyed in Zone off Iceland Coast," *Ottawa Evening Citizen*, September 23, 1941.
2. Goodwin, 282.
3. "Hitler Shoots First Following US Warning," *Ottawa Citizen*, September 23, 1941.
4. "The No. 1 Bottleneck Now Is a Lack of Ships," *Fortune*, May 1942.
5. Marinship Yard magazine, *Marin-er*, July 24, 1943.
6. HAER, 143.
7. HAER, 144.

21: Neutral No More

1. Story of the Reuben James: *Ottawa Citizen*, November 1, 1941; *St. Petersburg Times*, November 25, 1941; *Business Insider*, October 31, 2018.
2. Gannon, 91.
3. Message to Congress on the Arming of Merchant Ships, American Presidency Project, October 9, 1941.

22: "A War of Transportation"

1. Goodwin, 289.
2. Goodwin.
3. Goodwin, 291.
4. Goodwin, 293.
5. Herman, 157.

6. Lane, 146.
7. Klein, 313.
8. Goodwin, 305.
9. Goodwin, 311.
10. Goodwin, 307.
11. Personal and Official Diary of Lieutenant General Dwight D. Eisenhower, Eisenhower Library, January 4, 1942.
12. Goodwin, 313.
13. "Ship Launched at Richmond," *Oakland Tribune*, January 1, 1942.
14. Franklin Roosevelt, State of the Union address, January 6, 1942.
15. FDR address, 313.

23: Nerves of Steel

1. "Kaiser Plans a Steel Plant," *Time*, April 28, 1941.
2. FDR Presidential Library and Museum, Day by Day.
3. "Shipbuilders to Use Most '43 Steel," *Baltimore Evening Sun*, January 19, 1943.
4. "Kaiser Urges Steel Plants," *Oregon Daily Journal*, April 22, 1941.
5. Heiner, 173.
6. Klein, 165.
7. Herman, 211.

24: "Avalanche of Humanity"

1. "On the Waterfront: Richmond, California Oral Histories"; Bancroft Library, University of California, Berkeley; interview of Stanley Nystrom conducted by Judith K. Dunning, 1985.
2. Herbert R. Northrup, "Negroes in a War Industry: The Case of Shipbuilding," *Journal of Business*, University of Chicago, July 1943.
3. "On the Waterfront."
4. Archibald, 53–54.
5. Oregon Historical Society, Oral History by Karen Beck Skold, "Women Workers and Childcare during World War II," interview with Laura Fortier, February 14, 1976.
6. Lewis Van Hook's story is from "On the Waterfront," interview conducted by Judith K. Dunning.
7. *Fore 'n' Aft*, December 24, 1942.
8. Marilyn Johnson, *The Second Gold Rush*, 37.
9. "An Avalanche Hits Richmond," Report by the City Manager, City of Richmond, July 1944.
10. Charles Dorn, "'I Had All Kinds of Kids in My Classes, and It Was Fine': Public Schooling in Richmond, California During World War I," *History of Education Quarterly* 45, no. 4 (Winter 2005).
11. Dorn.
12. Dorn.
13. Donna Graves, "Mapping Richmond's World War II Homefront," historical report prepared for National Park Service, 2004.
14. Interview with Selena Foster, "On the Waterfront."
15. Gerald D. Nash, *The American West Transformed*, 78.

25: Revolutionizing the Workplace

1. The story of Garfield joining Kaiser in Richmond, from Hospital Administration Oral History Collection, Lewis E. Weeks Series, "Sidney R. Garfield: In First Person, An Oral History, 1986"; Paul de Kruif, *Kaiser Wakes the Doctors.*
2. Tassava, 308.
3. Oregon Historical Society, Oral History Interview with Nona F. Pool, May 25, 1981.
4. Oregon Historical Society, Oral History Interview, Interview with Rosa N. Dickson, April 1980.
5. Historic American Buildings Survey (HABS No. CA-2718), Maritime Child Development Center, Alicia Barber, 2001.
6. *Fore 'n' Aft*, January 8, 1943.
7. Hospital Administration Oral History Collection, Lewis E. Weeks Series.
8. Hospital Administration Oral History Collection.
9. Hospital Administration Oral History Collection.
10. Hospital Administration Oral History Collection.
11. De Kruif, 95.
12. De Kruif, 97.
13. De Kruif, 107–10.
14. De Kruif.

26: The Map Speech

1. Heiner, 125.
2. Lane, 455–56.
3. "Reinhard Hardegen, Who Led U-Boats to America's Shore, Dies at 105," *New York Times*, June 17, 2018.
4. Heiner, 138.
5. Lane, 143.
6. Gannon, 303–5.
7. Herman, 183.
8. Goodwin, 319.
9. Goodwin.
10. "President's Plug Booms Map Trade," *New York Times*, February 22, 1942.
11. "On Progress of War," transcript of FDR speech, FDR Library, February 23, 1942.
12. Chart, Liberty EC-2 Cargo Ships Completed, from *Workhorse of the Fleet*, 112.
13. *Fore 'n' Aft*, June 4, 1942.

27: Strikes, Safety, and Sexism

1. "Todd Shipyard Men End Day's Walkout," *New York Times*, March 20, 1942.
2. Johnson, 36.
3. "Thousand Strike at Todd Shipyard," *Times and Daily News Leader*, San Mateo, CA, March 19, 1942.
4. Moore, 57.
5. Moore, 58.

6. Moore, 58–59.
7. "Gallup Vault: A Sea Change in Support for Working Women," July 20, 2017.
8. "October 12, 1942: Fireside Chat 23: On the Home Front," transcript, University of Virginia, Miller Center, Presidential Speeches.
9. Dorothy K. Newman, "Employing Women in Shipyards," U.S. Department of Labor, *Bulletin of the Women's Bureau* (1944): 192–96.
10. Lane, 300–301.
11. Lane.
12. Lane.
13. Herbert R. Northrup, "Negroes in a War Industry: The Case of Shipbuilding," *Journal of Business*, University of Chicago, July 1943.
14. Shirley Ann Wilson Moore, *To Place Our Deeds*, 47.
15. Moore, 53.
16. Moore, 50.
17. "Six Hurt as Ship Shoots from Ways," *Press Democrat*, March 29, 1942.
18. "65-Foot Fall Kills Worker," *Oakland Post Enquirer*, May 12, 1942.
19. Heiner, 134.

28: Building the Builders

1. "Submarine Sinkings," Draft Memorandum for Admiral King, June 19, 1942, George C. Marshall Foundation.
2. Klein, 319.
3. "First Class of 21 Apprentices Graduates at Bath Iron Works," *Bath Independent*, October 29, 1942.
4. "First Class of 21."
5. Moore, 43.
6. *Fore 'n' Aft*, March 12, 1943.
7. Heiner, 127.
8. Tassava, 251.
9. Lane, 264.
10. The history of Newport News Shipbuilding is drawn from William A. Fox, "The Apprentice School: Celebrating a Century."
11. "Adm. Land Paid 6 Cents for His Work on Ship," *Daily Press*, August 3, 1938.
12. G. Guy Via, "The Wartime Training of Shipbuilders," Society of Naval Architects and Marine Engineers, November 13, 1942.

29: Speed Kings

1. "Speed Kings," *San Francisco Chronicle*, May 3, 1942.
2. *Fore 'n' Aft*, May 14, 1942.
3. Lane, 454.
4. Lane, 455.
5. "The Wartime Training of Shipbuilders."
6. "The Wartime Training of Shipbuilders."

30: Wendy the Welder

1. Cillie Preston's story is from "On the Waterfront," interview conducted by Judith K. Dunning, 1985.
2. "Glamour Girls of '43," AP Archive, YouTube.
3. Sherna Berger Gluck, *Rosie the Riveter Revisited*, 12–13.
4. Archibald, xxxvii.
5. Karen Leona Beck, "Women Workers and Childcare During World War II: A Case Study of the Portland, Oregon Shipyards" (PhD diss., University of Oregon, 1981).
6. Sara Murphy, "Rosie, Wendy, and Government Girls: The Women Behind the War," National Museum of American History, March 16, 2022.
7. Archibald, xxxix.
8. Dunning interview, "On the Waterfront."
9. Tassava, 267.
10. Welding details from G. V. Slottman, "Production Welding and Cutting at West Coast Yards," *Marine Engineering and Shipping Review*, October 1942.

31: Gus

1. The story of Gus Clawson is from Augusta H. Clawson, "Shipyard Diary of a Woman Welder," 1944.
2. Ed Offley, "When War Erupted off Virginia Beach," U.S. Naval Institute, June 2022.

32: Lessons from Motor City

1. Heiner, 41.
2. Herman, 157.
3. Bourneuf, 112.
4. Lane, 225.
5. Lane, 224.
6. "Is the Mass Middle of the Market a Marketing Death Trap?" *Forbes*, March 26, 2019.
7. "Means of Production: Henry Ford Builds an Assembly Line," *Lapham's Quarterly*, 1922.
8. "Making Automobiles Last During World War II," National WW II Museum, January 6, 2022.
9. "More Women in Shipyards Foreseen by Union Leader," *Baltimore Sun*, September 8, 1942.
10. Lane, 238.
11. Lane.
12. Stein interview of Bedford.
13. Julian Street, "Abroad at Home: American Ramblings, Observations, and Adventures of Julian Street," 1914.
14. Daniel Gross, "Forbes Greatest Business Stories of All Time."
15. Lane, 238.

33: Darkness, Disgrace, Defeat

1. "The Times Electric News Sign Goes Dark Under Dimout, Probably for Duration," *New York Times*, May 19, 1942.

2. "In World War II, Blackouts Were Taken Seriously in Nearly All American Cities. Not Anchorage," *Anchorage Daily News*, January 31, 2021.
3. "In World War II."
4. "Nazi Saboteurs Captured! FDR Orders Secret Tribunal," *Washington Post*, January 12, 2002.
5. "8 Men, 6 Women Held as US Aides to Nazi Saboteurs," *New York Times*, July 14, 1942.
6. Goodwin, 347.
7. Goodwin.
8. Nathan Miller, *War at Sea: A Naval History of World War II*, 310–12.
9. David H. Lippman, "Convoy Is to Scatter: Arctic Convoy Disaster," *Warfare History Network*, Winter 2012.
10. David Irving, *The Destruction of Convoy PQ.17*, 130.
11. Irving, 136.
12. "SS Jeremiah O'Brien, Interpretative Training Packet," San Francisco National Maritime Historic Park, 1990.
13. Winston S. Churchill, *The Hinge of Fate*, 238–42.
14. Churchill.
15. "Out-Producing the Enemy: American Production During WWII," National WWII Museum.
16. William J. Vanden Heuvel, keynote address of the fifth annual Franklin and Eleanor Roosevelt Distinguished Lecture, October 17, 1996, Roosevelt University, Chicago.
17. "The Dark Legacy of Henry Ford's Anti-Semitism," *Washington Post*, October 10, 2014.
18. "Why Shipbuilding Is Our No. 1 Bottleneck," *Newsweek*, June 1, 1942.

34: Perfecting Prefab

1. "Richmond Shipyard Cranes Are Vastly More Powerful than Shipyard Cranes of World War I," *Fore 'n' Aft*, January 8, 1943.
2. Herman, 185.
3. Herman.
4. Edythe Esser interview, conducted for Rosie the Riveter World War II American Home Front Oral History Project by Sam Redman in 2011, Regional Oral History Project, Bancroft Library, University of California, Berkeley.
5. Bourneuf.
6. Bedford interview, Mimi Stein.

35: Pistol-Packin' Mamas

1. Jim Gates, "Commissioner Landis' Letter Sparked a Historic Response from FDR," National Baseball Hall of Fame.
2. Gates.
3. Stories about Cora Clonts, family photo album, courtesy of family of Cora Clonts.
4. "Anderson Symbolized Women in the Workplace in WW2," *Mississippi Enterprise-Journal*, September 22, 2013.
5. "Woman Welding Champ Meets Mrs. Roosevelt," *Salt Lake Tribune*, June 2, 1943.
6. Tassava, 220.
7. Heiner, 47, 121.
8. Heiner, 64.

36: Shipyard vs. Shipyard

1. "Subchasers Cut Losses, Says Vickery," *Oregon Journal*, July 20, 1942.
2. "Kaiser Visions U.S. Shipyards Building 500 Giants of Air," *Oregon Journal*, July 20, 1942.
3. "Kaiser Visions."
4. Leonard D. Heaton, *Medical Supply in World War II*, Office of the Surgeon General, Department of the Army, 1968.
5. Heiner, 127.
6. "Richmond Sets Pace in Shipbuilding," *Oakland Tribune*, July 23, 1942.
7. "Richmond Sets Pace in Shipbuilding."
8. "Sunnyvale Plants Gets Pennant," *Oakland Tribune*, July 24, 1942.
9. Heiner, 121.

37: A Liberty Carries a Legacy

1. "USS PT-109 on board SS Joseph Stanton," photograph from Bureau of Ships Collection in the U.S. National Archives, Wikimedia Commons.
2. "For JFK, Rhode Island Was a Second Home. Revisiting His Ties to the Ocean State," *Providence Journal*, November 17, 2023.

38: Stunt Ships

1. "Kaiser St. Johns Plant Launches Ship in Record-Breaking Time of 26 Days," *Oregonian*, August 28, 1942.
2. "Kaiser St. Johns Plant."
3. "Cheesebox on a Raft," *New York Times*, January 30, 2012.
4. Herman, 187.
5. Goodwin, 403–4.
6. "Fastest Ship Job in History," *Los Angeles Daily News*, August 29, 1942.
7. *Fore 'n' Aft*, September 3, 1942.
8. Amy Kesselman, *Fleeting Opportunities: Women Shipyard Workers in Portland and Vancouver During World War II and Reconversion*, 13.
9. Adams, 116.
10. Adams, 153.
11. "Fastest Ship Job in History," *Los Angeles Daily News*, August 29, 1942.
12. Transcript of interview with Clay Bedford, Mimi Stein, May 3, 1982.
13. Klein, 402.
14. Baime, 169.
15. Herman, 187.
16. "President Visits Kaiser Yard, See Vessel Launched," *Coos Bay Times*, October 1, 1942.
17. Herman, 188.
18. Herman, 187.
19. "10 Day Ship Launched at Kaiser Plant," *Salem Capital-Journal*, September 23, 1942.
20. "1,600 In Rush Here for Kaiser's Jobs," *New York Times*, September 23, 1942.
21. Herman, 188.
22. Mimi Stein interview with Bedford.

23. Stein interview.
24. Stein interview.

39: A Liberty's Victory

1. "The Gallantry of an Ugly Duckling," *American Heritage*, December 1969, https://www.americanheritage.com/gallantry-ugly-duckling.
2. Elphick, 18.
3. Elphick, 189.
4. Elphick, 197.
5. "The Gallantry of an Ugly Duckling."

40: Setting the Table

1. *Fore 'n' Aft*, November 12, 1942.
2. Fabry, 211.
3. Alyce Mano Kramer, *The Story of the Richmond Shipyards*, 48–50.
4. *Fore 'n' Aft*, November 12, 1942.
5. Franklin Roosevelt and Margaret Suckley, *Closest Companion*, 185.
6. Goodwin, 386.
7. Goodwin, 388.
8. *Fore 'n' Aft*, November 12, 1942.
9. My Day, November 18, 1942, Eleanor Roosevelt Papers, Digital Edition.
10. Goodwin, 339.

41: Hull No. 440

1. The story of Hull No. 440 comes from multiple sources: Henry J. Kaiser, "Building a Ship in 4 Days, 15 Hours, 25 Minutes"; "Hull 440," *Fore 'n' Aft*, November 12, 1942; Joseph K. Fabry, *Swing Shift*; Bernard Taper, "Life with Kaiser," *Nation*.
2. Taper.
3. *Fore 'n' Aft*, November 12, 1942.
4. *Fore 'n' Aft*, November 12, 1942.
5. *Fore 'n' Aft*, November 12, 1942.
6. Postal telegraph, Bedford to Kaiser, November 8, 1942, Henry J. Kaiser Collection, Bancroft Library, University of California, Berkeley.
7. Western Union Telegraph, Bedford to Kaiser, November, 9, 1942, Bancroft Library, University of California, Berkeley.
8. Heiner, 131.
9. "The Crash Heard Round the Yard," *Vancouver Columbian*, October 15, 1942.
10. Fabry, 216.
11. Fabry, 218.
12. Taper.
13. "Richmond Wondership to Test Pre-Fabrication Work," *Oakland Tribune*, November 11, 1942.

42: "Nuts to Seven Days"

1. Franklin D. Roosevelt Public Approval/Disapproval, Gallup Data, American Presidency Project.
2. Fabry, 220.
3. "New Kaiser Record," *San Francisco Chronicle*, November 13, 1942.
4. "New Kaiser Record."
5. Taper.
6. "On the Waterfront," interview of Tony Vinelli.
7. Mimi Stein interview with Clay Bedford.
8. Fabry, 225.
9. Fabry.

43: Aboard the *Peary*

1. The story of James Horton aboard the SS *Robert E. Peary* is drawn from the personal diary provided by his son John Horton.
2. *Fore 'n' Aft*, April 14, 1944.

Epilogue: From Liberty to Victory

1. Henry J. Kaiser, "Building a Ship in 4 Days, 15 Hours, 25 Minutes," 1943.
2. Kaiser, 147.
3. "They Hope to Find Cure for Schenectady's Ills," *Sunday Oregonian*, January 24, 1943.
4. Peter Thompson, "How Much Did the Liberty Shipbuilders Learn? New Evidence for an Old Case Study," *Journal of Political Economy* 109, no. 1 (2001).
5. Lane, 547.
6. Lane, 575.
7. Foster, 277.
8. American Presidency Project, Message on the Death of Henry J. Kaiser, August 25, 1967.
9. "Henry J. Kaiser, Industrialist, Dies in Honolulu at 85," *New York Times*, August 25, 1967.
10. Robert Feldman, "Sidney Garfield: A Personal Recollection," *Permanente Journal*, Summer 2006.
11. De Kruif, 120.
12. "On the Waterfront," interview of Lucille Preston conducted by Judith K. Dunning, 1985.
13. Obituary of Arthur J. Babineau, *Bangor Daily News*, August 30, 2024.
14. "William Francis Gibbs Dead," *New York Times*, September 7, 1967.
15. Heiner, 134.
16. "Churchill Praises Liberty Ship Speed," *New York Times*, September 27, 1942.
17. Heiner, 136.

BIBLIOGRAPHY

Adams, Stephen. *Mr. Kaiser Goes to Washington: Saga of a Government Entrepreneur.* Baltimore: Johns Hopkins University Press, 1993.

Archibald, Katherine. *Wartime Shipyard: A Study in Social Disunity.* Urbana: University of Illinois Press, 2006.

Asbury, Jonathan. *Secrets of Churchill's War Rooms:* Compact Edition. London: Unicorn, 2020.

Baime, Albert J. *The Arsenal of Democracy: FDR, Detroit, and an Epic Quest to Arm an America at War.* New York: Houghton Mifflin Harcourt, 2014.

Blair, Clay. *Hitler's U-boat War: The Hunters, 1939–1942.* New York: Modern Library, 2000.

Bonnett, Wayne. *Build Ships! Wartime Shipbuilding Photographs, San Francisco Bay, 1940–1945.* Windgate Press, 1999.

Borth, Christy. *Masters of Mass Production.* Indianapolis: Bobbs-Merrill, 1945.

Bourneuf, Gus, Jr. *Workhorse of the Fleet: A History of Liberty Ships.* American Bureau of Shipping, 1990.

Brokaw, Tom. *The Greatest Generation Speaks: Letters and Reflections.* New York: Random House, 2000.

Bunker, John. *Liberty Ships: The Ugly Ducklings of World War II.* Annapolis, MD: Naval Institute Press, 1972.

Churchill, Winston S., and Winston Churchill. *The Hinge of Fate.* London: Houghton Mifflin, 1986.

Clawson, Augusta. *Shipyard Diary of a Woman Welder.* Canton Street Press, 2013.

Cooke, Alistair. *The American Home Front, 1941–1942.* New York: Grove Press, 2007.

Davis, Kenneth S. *FDR: The War President.* New York: Random House, 2000.

Debley, Tom, and Jon Stewart. *The Story of Dr. Sidney R. Garfield: The Visionary Who Turned Sick Care into Health Care.* Permanente Press, 2009.

De Kruif, Paul. *Kaiser Wakes the Doctors.* London: Scientific Book Club, 1946.

Elphick, Peter. *Liberty: The Ships That Won the War.* Annapolis, MD: Naval Institute Press, 2001.

Fabry, Joseph B. *Swing Shift: Building the Liberty Ships.* Strawberry Hill Press, 1982.

Ferreiro, Larrie D. *Churchill's American Arsenal: The Partnership Behind the Innovations That Won World War Two.* Oxford: Oxford University Press, 2022.

Foster, Mark S. *Henry J. Kaiser: Builder in the Modern American West.* Austin: University of Texas Press, 2014.

Gannon, Michael. *Operation Drumbeat: The Dramatic True Story of Germany's First U-boat Attacks Along the American Coast in World War II.* Annapolis, MD: Naval Institute Press, 2009.

Geroux, William. *The Mathews Men: Seven Brothers and the War Against Hitler's U-boats.* New York: Penguin, 2017.

Gillen, Michael. *Merchant Marine Survivors of World War II: Oral Histories of Cargo Carrying Under Fire.* Jefferson, NC: McFarland, 2015.

Gluck, Sherna Berger. *Rosie the Riveter Revisited: Women, the War, and Social Change.* New York: Penguin Books, 1988.

Goodwin, Doris Kearns. *No Ordinary Time: Franklin & Eleanor Roosevelt: The Home Front in World War II.* New York: Simon & Schuster, 2013.

Harding, Stephen. *Dawn of Infamy: A Sunken Ship, a Vanished Crew, and the Final Mystery of Pearl Harbor.* New York: Hachette Books, 2016.

Heiner, Albert P. *Henry J. Kaiser, Western Colossus: An Insider's View.* Halo Books, 1991.

Henshaw, John. *Liberty's Provenance: The Evolution of the Liberty Ship from Its Sunderland Origins.* London: Pen & Sword Books, 2019.

Herman, Arthur. *Freedom's Forge: How American Business Produced Victory in World War II.* New York: Random House, 2012.

Hoehling, Adolph A. *The Fighting Liberty Ships: A Memoir.* Kent, OH: Kent State University Press, 1990.

Irving, David. *The Destruction of Convoy PQ-17.* New York: St. Martin's Press, 1989.

Jaffee, Walter W. *The Last Liberty: The Biography of the SS Jeremiah O'Brien.* Glencannon Press, 1993.

Johnman, Lewis, and Hugh Murphy. *British Shipbuilding and the State Since 1918: A Political Economy of Decline.* Exeter, UK: University of Exeter Press, 2002.

Johnson, Marilynn S. *The Second Gold Rush: Oakland and the East Bay in World War II.* Berkeley: University of California Press, 1996.

Jones, Herbert Granville. *Portland Ships Are Good Ships.* Machigonne Press, 1945.

Keegan, John. *The Price of Admiralty: The Evolution of Naval Warfare.* New York: Viking, 1989.

Kesselman, Amy. *Fleeting Opportunities: Women Shipyard Workers in Portland and Vancouver During World War II and Reconversion.* Albany: State University of New York Press, 2016.

La Du, Robert. *Her Finest Hour: Shipbuilding in the Portland Area During World War II.* Page, 2017.

Land, Emory Scott. *Winning the War with Ships: Land, Sea and Air.* Textbook Publishers, 2003.

Lane, Frederic Chapin. *Ships for Victory: A History of Shipbuilding Under the U.S. Maritime Commission in World War II.* Baltimore: Johns Hopkins University Press, 1951.

Levingston, Steven E. *Historic Ships of San Francisco: A Collective History and Guide to the Restored Historic Vessels of the National Maritime Museum.* San Francisco: Chronicle Books, 1984.

Meacham, Jon. *Franklin and Winston.* New York: Random House, 2003.

Melton, Herman E. *Liberty's War: An Engineer's Memoir of the Merchant Marine, 1942–1945.* Annapolis, MD: Naval Institute Press, 2017.

Milkman, Ruth. *Gender at Work: The Dynamics of Job Segregation by Sex During World War II.* Urbana: University of Illinois Press, 1987.

Miller, Nathan. *War at Sea: A Naval History of World War II.* Oxford: Oxford University Press, 1997.

Mitchell, C. Bradford, and Edwin K. Linen. *Every Kind of Shipwork: A History of Todd Shipyards Corporation, 1916–1981.* The Corporation, 1981.

Moe, Richard. *Roosevelt's Second Act: The Election of 1940 and the Politics of War.* Oxford: Oxford University Press, 2013.

Moore, Arthur R. *A Careless Word . . . a Needless Sinking: A History of the Staggering Losses Suffered by the U.S. Merchant Marine, Both in Ships and Personnel, During World War II.* American Merchant Marine Museum, 2006.

Moore, Shirley Ann Wilson. *To Place Our Deeds: The African American Community in Richmond, California, 1910–1963.* Berkeley: University of California Press, 2012.

Nash, Gerald D. *The American West Transformed: The Impact of the Second World War.* Lincoln: University of Nebraska Press, 1990.

Nelson, Craig. *V Is for Victory: Franklin Roosevelt's American Revolution and the Triumph of World War II.* New York: Scribner, 2023.

O'Brien, Phillips Payson. *How the War Was Won: Air-Sea Power and Allied Victory in World War II.* Cambridge: Cambridge University Press, 2015.

Overy, R. J. *Why the Allies Won.* New York: Norton, 1995.

Palmer, Michael D. *We Fight with Merchant Ships.* Indianapolis: Bobbs-Merrill, 1943.

Roosevelt, Franklin Delano, and Margaret Suckley. *Closest Companion.* Boston: Houghton Mifflin, 1995.

Sawyer, Leonard Arthur, and William Harry Mitchell. *The Liberty Ships: The History of the Emergency Type Cargoships Constructed in the United States During the Second World War.* London: Lloyd's of London, 1985.

Scott, Connie Porter. *South Portland and Cape Elizabeth.* Charleston, SC: Arcadia, 1995.

Snow, Ralph Linwood. *Bath Iron Works: The First Hundred Years.* Maine Maritime Museum, 1987.

Spector, Ronald H. *At War at Sea: Sailors and Naval Combat in the Twentieth Century.* New York: Penguin, 2002.

Strahan, Jerry E. *Andrew Jackson Higgins and the Boats that Won World War II.* Baton Rouge: Louisiana State University Press, 1994.

Tassava, Christopher James. *Launching a Thousand Ships: Entrepreneurs, War Workers, and the State in American Shipbuilding, 1940–1945.* Chicago: Northwestern University Press, 2003.

Ujifusa, Steven. *A Man and His Ship: America's Greatest Naval Architect and His Quest to Build the S.S. United States.* New York: Simon & Schuster, 2012.

Veronico, Nicholas A., and Nick Veronico. *World War II Shipyards by the Bay.* Charleston, SC: Arcadia, 2007.

Ward, Geoffrey C. *Closest Companion: The Unknown Story of the Intimate Friendship Between Franklin Roosevelt and Margaret Suckley.* New York: Simon & Schuster, 2012.

Wilson, Mark R. *Destructive Creation: American Business and the Winning of World War II.* Philadelphia: University of Pennsylvania Press, 2016.

Wolf, Donald E. *Big Dams and Other Dreams: The Six Companies Story.* Norman: University of Oklahoma Press, 1996.

Wollenberg, Charles. *Marinship at War: Shipbuilding and Social Change in Wartime Sausalito.* Western Heritage Press, 1990.

INDEX

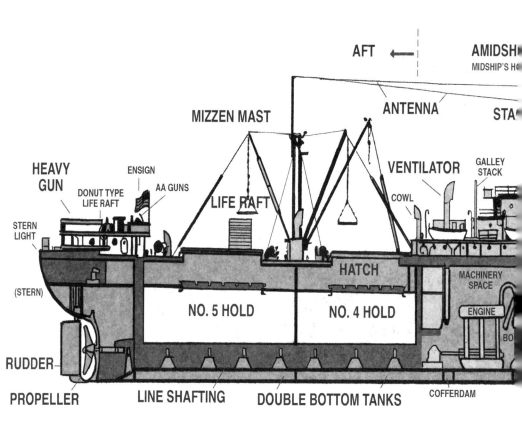

AFT ← AMIDSH
MIDSHIP'S H

ANTENNA STA

MIZZEN MAST

VENTILATOR GALLEY
STACK

HEAVY
GUN

ENSIGN

DONUT TYPE
LIFE RAFT

AA GUNS

LIFE RAFT

COWL

STERN
LIGHT

MACHINERY
SPACE

(STERN)

HATCH

NO. 5 HOLD NO. 4 HOLD

ENGINE

BO

RUDDER

PROPELLER LINE SHAFTING DOUBLE BOTTOM TANKS COFFERDAM